T0320221

Principles
of
Microeconomics

TITLES OF RELATED INTEREST

Principles
of
Microeconomics

PETER ELSE
PETER CURWEN

Routledge
Taylor & Francis Group

LONDON AND NEW YORK

First published in 1990
By Unwin Hyman Ltd
Reprinted 2003
By Routledge
11 New Fetter Lane, London EC4P 4EE

Transferred to Digital Printing 2003

British Library Cataloguing in Publication Data

Else, Peter
Principles of microeconomics.
1. Microeconomics
I. Title
II. Curwen, Peter J. (Peter Jeremy), 1945–
338.5

ISBN 0-04-338152-9 Pbk

Library of Congress Cataloging in Publication Data

Data applied for

Typeset in 10 on 12 point Times by Computape (Pickering) Ltd
North Yorkshire

CONTENTS

Contents

Contents

Contents

Contents

Contents

Contents

*Dedicated to the memory of Elsie M. Else
and to Adella Lithman*

PREFACE

This book is intended for use by students who have previously studied a course in economic principles, and who are now intent upon developing their knowledge of microeconomic theory. They are accordingly likely to be on the second year of either an economics or a business studies degree programme at a university or polytechnic. There are already a number of books in existence that claim to serve this market, but this is one of the very few to be directed specifically to meeting its needs.

In the first place, it is structured to take into account the standard teaching year's programme of 20–25 sequential lectures. The text is accordingly divided into 22 chapters, each of roughly equal length and difficulty, and each containing enough material, but no more, for one week of such a programme. Secondly, in order to achieve this objective, the content of each chapter has been rigorously adjusted so that it is pitched exclusively at the second-year student; repetition of matters covered in introductory texts (which students will probably still have in their possession) is kept to a minimum, and there is no attempt to push the student into the realms of final-year theory which he or she is not yet ready to comprehend. In these respects this text is different from most of those originating from the USA, which are designed for other purposes, nor, we hope, does it suffer from a tendency to be unnecessarily sophisticated for the intermediate market.

The compactness of the text should not, therefore, be mistaken for a failure to cover the necessary ground. It is our premise that the typical student will be more willing to read when he or she is presented with a reasonable, but also testing, weekly target. In the latter respect there is also the matter of mathematical sophistication to address. Numeracy has become an increasingly important criterion for success in understanding economic models, yet it can be overemphasized as well as underplayed. At the end of the day, the key issue is whether the average student can read through a text and follow the argument in comfort, irrespective of how it is presented. If he or she is bogged down with the mathematics, the student inevitably loses track of the economics. This book accordingly relies primarily upon the familiar diagrammatic exposition of introductory texts, although the diagrams are often more complex than those found at an introductory level and they require greater care in their interpretation. Where appropriate, however, other forms of mathematical representation such as calculus are used.

The final matter to address is balance. By concentrating exclusively on second-year material it has been possible to introduce topics treated only sketchily in much lengthier texts. In particular, recent developments in consumer theory and the theory of the firm are treated in some detail and in a manner compatible with the rest of the text. Microeconomic theory does not evolve in leaps and bounds, but it is still desirable to present an up-to-date version of models and to push into the background those that have shown little sign of evolution.

In conclusion, this book does not set out to be all things to all men. It succeeds or fails according to whether it has been differentiated from its competitors in a manner that evokes a sympathetic response from the students who must use it or something similar. We have set out to make the book user-friendly, and we look forward to the customers' verdict in this respect.

Peter Else
Peter Curwen
Sheffield
May 1989

CHAPTER ONE
THE BASIC THEMES OF MICROECONOMICS

The scope of microeconomics

Microeconomics is principally concerned with the behaviour of individual participants in the economy. Whilst the prefix 'micro' suggests a concern with small units, not all these participants – usually referred to as economic agents – are small in any absolute sense, since as well as individuals they include firms, governments, trade unions and many other organizations. They are nevertheless the basic decision-making units of an economic system and, despite their diversity and size, economists believe that their behaviour can usefully be analysed in the context of a common analytical framework. Traditionally, of these economic agents, individuals and firms have been the main focus of attention and that is reflected in this book. But in recent years particularly, the same analytical approach has been increasingly applied to other organizations, and some of the results of that work are also reflected in later chapters.

Microeconomics, however, goes beyond the analysis of the behaviour of individual agents in that it is also concerned with the way the decisions of economic agents interact in the determination of the allocation of resources between uses in an economy. In fact there are two aspects to economists' concern with the allocation of resources. The first is the positive aspect, in which the interest is basically in how resources are allocated under various conditions, although in this book, as in other similar books, the emphasis will be on situations in which resources are mainly allocated through markets, since that is an important common feature of western economies. The second aspect of concern, the normative aspect, stems from the first since, once an understanding of the factors determining the allocation of resources has been obtained, it is a natural consequence to enquire into the circumstances under which such an allocation might be improved. This is the particular concern of welfare economics, which is the subject of chapters 20–22, but particular normative issues are also raised in the preceding chapters.

Choice, rationality and utility

In studying the behaviour of economic agents, microeconomics is primarily concerned with the choices they make that have implications for the allocation of resources. It is thus basically concerned with the decisions agents make about how to use the resources at their disposal, particularly the extent to which they seek to use them for consumption, for production, or as a means of acquiring other resources through trade. The key assumption in the analysis of these decisions throughout microeconomics is that, in making choices, individuals behave *rationally*. That means no more than that, when faced with a number of possible choices, the agent will choose the one that appears to him to have *the most preferred outcome*. The agent's choice might seem odd to anyone else. It may even turn out to be a wrong choice from his own point of view, in that with hindsight he may have preferred to choose something else, but that is not the same thing as being irrational. An irrational choice is one in which an individual willingly and deliberately chooses something that in the light of all the information available to him is likely to yield a less preferred outcome to some of the other possibilities on offer. The possibility that people may behave irrationally from time to time, some perhaps more often than others, cannot be ruled out. But looking at the way in which man has applied his mind, over thousands of years, to the analysis of his environment with a view to controlling it and manipulating it to suit his own particular needs and convenience, an assumption that *in general* economic agents behave rationally does not seem an unreasonable one. However, since the idea of rational choice is so basic in microeconomics, it is desirable to consider a little more formally what it entails before moving on to a closer examination of how it applies to particular economic agents.

First and foremost, it requires individual agents to be capable of assessing a number of different states and ranking them in a definitive order of preference. More specifically, it implies an assumption that an individual agent, when faced with two states A and B, which may be two bundles of goods available for consumption, or alternatively production or trading possibilities, will be able to decide whether A is preferred to B, whether B is preferred to A or whether he is indifferent between them. That is the assumption of **comparability**.

A second assumption that is usually made is that, when the choice is extended to include one or more additional states, there will be consistency in the ordering of pairs of states, in the sense that if A is preferred to B, and B is preferred to C, then A will also be preferred to C. In more technical terms this means that *preferences are transitive*, and this is referred to as the assumption of **transitivity**. In some forms of social organization where decision-making relies on an aggregation of divergent individual preferences, as for example in voting procedures, it turns out that rational decision-making could be inconsistent with transitive preferences, but as far as individuals and more monolithic organizations are concerned it would seem reasonable to expect some degree of consistency. Transitivity will, therefore, be assumed in the following pages unless there are specific reasons to suggest the contrary.

The actual preference ordering that emerges under these conditions will, of course, reflect individual tastes and idiosyncracies. It will also depend on the nature and functions of the economic agent concerned. But the fact that an agent prefers a particular state to any others he could choose implies that it offers him more of something than any of the alternatives – the opportunity of more pleasure or satisfaction or possibly less dissatisfaction – and that ultimately lies behind the preference ordering. That vague 'something' is what economists refer to as **utility**. Another way of saying that a particular economic agent prefers state A to state B is, therefore, to say that state A yields more utility than B. Similarly, choosing the particular state that is highest of all those on offer in the individual agent's order of preference can be described as choosing the state offering the highest level of utility. In other words, rational behaviour can be identified with an attempt by economic agents to maximize their utility, and hence in subsequent chapters we will be very much concerned with an analysis of utility-maximizing behaviour.

What determines utility depends very much on the nature of the agent concerned. The relationship between utility and the variables on which it depends is referred to as a **utility function**, and one of our tasks in the following chapters will be to consider the nature of the variables in the utility functions of individual consumers, firms and other organizations, and any general properties that can be ascribed to them.

However, one further general assumption that is convenient to make for all agents is that of **continuity**. Continuity implies that there is a continuous relationship between the amount of utility and the variables on which it depends. Basically this means that, in any situation, changes can be defined yielding infinitessimally small changes in utility. If, for example, utility depends on only one variable, the utility function can be represented by a continuous curve on a graph. One obvious justification for this assumption is that in practice individual agents are typically faced with an infinite number of choices. Think, for example, of the number of ways in which Mr and Mrs Average can spend their weekly earnings, some of which will vary only very marginally from others. Rationality requires all these to be included within the preference function, and therefore necessarily implies something that at least closely approximates to continuity.[1] In practice, rationality may in fact be bounded, in that only a restricted range of possibilities may actually be considered when choices are made. This is largely because human beings have a limited capacity to assimilate and process information, but it doesn't materially affect the continuity assumption. The assumption of continuity has the further advantage that it facilitates the application of mathematical and diagrammatic techniques or analysis. Hence utility functions will be assumed to be continuous unless there appear to be good reasons to suppose otherwise.

It might be felt that there is some contradiction between the idea of a utility function to which specific mathematical properties can be assigned, and our original definition of utility as a vague 'something' reflecting relative satisfaction in some rather ill-defined way. It should be recognized at the outset, however, that the use of the utility function concept need not in itself imply that utility can be measured in precise quantitative terms. It is sufficient if different levels of utility can be reflected in an arbitrary index varying in the same direction as utility, which in turn simply requires that the levels of utility experienced in a number of different states can be compared to the extent of identifying whether one gives greater or less utility than the other. In other words, all it requires is that preferences are comparable and transitive.

A relevant distinction here is between **cardinal** and **ordinal** measurement. Cardinal measurement is possible when exact units of measurement can be defined, like metres or kilograms or degrees Celcius. Where this can be done, not only can different states be compared in the sense, for example, that it can be established that one object is heavier than another, but it is also possible to measure the difference and compare it with the difference between two other states. With ordinal measurement different states can be ranked in order, but nothing precise can be said about the magnitude of the difference between them. The question of whether and under what conditions it is possible to go beyond ordinal comparisons of utility levels is another issue to be considered more fully in a later chapter, but for the moment it is sufficient for the reader to be aware that the use of the concept of the utility function, and indeed the deduction of a number of important propositions about the behaviour of economic agents, requires no more than the ordinal measurement of utility.

Constraints on choice

Whilst rationality is one important element in the analysis of the behaviour of economic agents, another is the range of choices actually open to them. The ability of economic agents to maximize their utility tends in practice to be severely constrained by physical and environmental factors that restrict the availability of resources. Economic agents thus are typically faced with a *constrained* maximization problem, and one of our tasks in the following chapters will be to examine the constraints on the behaviour of the particular economic agents to be studied. In almost all cases, however, when man is faced with constraints on his activities, his natural reaction is to seek ways of evading the constraints, or at least of moving them in a way that widens the available choices.

As far as economics is concerned, four particular means of widening choices – production, research and development, trade, and cooperation with others in a variety of social organizations – are of such fundamental

4

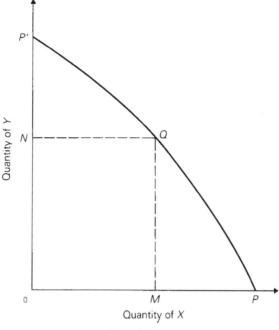

Figure 1.1

importance that their role in this context merits discussion before getting down to the more detailed analysis of the behaviour of particular agents.

Production

The first, and perhaps most fundamental, of these is production. In essence, production can be defined as the process of transforming resources or bundles of resources into something else.

The relationship between the output of any product and the quantities of resources, or inputs, used to produce it is reflected in a second important function, **the production function**. The properties of this function will be discussed in detail in Chapter 9, but, given scarce resources, in any state of technical knowledge there will still be a constraint on what can be produced and, therefore, ultimately on what can be consumed. This constraint is known as the **production possibility frontier**. In practice it will normally be multi-dimensional, but where the agent has the opportunity to produce two goods it can be shown on a diagram as a **production possibility curve**.

Such a curve is shown as PP' in Figure 1.1 and it can be interpreted as showing the maximum quantity of Y that can be produced with any quantity of X (or vice versa). Hence point Q on the curve indicates that N is the maximum of Y that can be produced with M of X, and that M is the maximum of X that can be produced with N of Y.

Whilst the precise shape and position of the production possibility curve will depend on the production functions for X and Y respectively and the total resources available, a downward-sloping curve can normally be expected since, if the available resources are fully utilized, more X can be produced only if resources are switched from the production of Y. In other words, the production of X has a cost in terms of the production of Y that has to be given up in order to release the resources required to produce X. Thus, at Q in the diagram the cost of the M of X that is produced is the potential $P'N$ of Y that is forgone.[2] At the margin, however, the number of units of Y that have to be given up to gain an extra unit of X in any given situation is reflected in the slope of the curve at the point representing that initial situation.

Alternatively, the slope of the curve can be interpreted as indicating the extra Y obtainable by giving up a unit of X, and this is defined as the *marginal rate of transformation of X into Y* (MRT_{XY}). However, it is often more useful to measure the cost of the two commodities in terms of some common numeraire such as money, rather than in terms of each other. In that case if, to take a particular example, the marginal rate of transformation of X into Y turns out to be n (i.e. n units of Y are gained if 1 unit of X is given up and the resources are switched to the production of Y) the implication is that in terms of that numeraire good, whatever it happens to be, the cost at the margin of 1 unit of X is the same as the cost of n units of Y, or

$$MC_X = nMC_Y$$

where MC_X and MC_Y are the marginal costs of X and Y respectively, and hence

$$MRT_{XY} = MC_X/MC_Y \quad (=n).$$

Since on this definition, with positive marginal costs, MRT_{XY} is the ratio of two positive numbers, it must itself be positive. Mathematically, however, the slope of the production possibility curve is the ratio of the change in Y to the change in X (or $\Delta Y/\Delta X$) for small movements along PP'. But since, given the curve's downward slope, X and Y change in opposite directions along the curve, ΔX and ΔY have opposite signs in that one is positive and the other negative and their ratio is accordingly negative. In strict mathematical terms, therefore,

$$\text{slope of } PP' = -MRT_{XY} = -MC_X/MC_Y.$$

Hence, if MC_X and MC_Y are invariant with respect to changes in output, their ratio (MC_X/MC_Y) is constant, and the production possibility curve is a negatively sloped straight line. If, however, MC_X increases relative to MC_Y

as the output of X increases, the curve is concave to the origin, as in the diagram, whilst in the opposite case it is convex.

Research and development

Research and development covers any activity designed to increase man's knowledge of his environment, and to apply that knowledge to the discovery of improved and more efficient methods of production and to the development of new goods and services. The wide and ever-increasing range of goods and services available for our enjoyment in advanced economies is the obvious result of this kind of activity, which can be characterized as widening choices by pushing the production possibility frontiers of economic agents outwards and increasing their dimensions. In fact, in much of microeconomics where the concern is the behaviour of agents and the resultant allocation of resources at a particular moment of time, the state of technical knowledge can be legitimately taken as given and constant. However, the actual allocation of resources to research and development, involving as it does the assessment of potential future gains from particular projects against current costs, is of itself an important issue within the scope of microeconomics.

Trade

Another way in which the choices open to economic agents can be expanded is through trade, which can be seen as a means of providing economic agents with an opportunity to move outside the constraints imposed by their production possibility frontiers.

As an example, let us take the case of individual A, who with the productive resources at his disposal can produce the output combinations along PP' in Figure 1.2. It can be seen that that particular production possibility curve has a constant slope of 0.5 so that

$$MRT_{XY}(= MC_X/MC_Y) = 0.5.$$

This means that, for every unit of X given up, A obtains 0.5 units of Y. If at the same time his neighbour B has the production possibility curve RR' with slope 1.0, he is giving up 1 unit of X for each unit of Y produced, although of course he is also giving up 1 unit of Y for each unit of X. In that situation, A's consumption choices will be expanded if he can obtain more than 0.5 units of Y for each unit of X given up, whilst B's will be expanded if he can give up less than 1 unit of Y for each unit of X consumed. Both can, therefore, gain from the opportunity to trade with each other at any exchange rate or price of between 0.5 and 1 unit of Y for each unit of X. At a trading price within that range, A is getting more Y for each unit of X than in the situation without trade, whilst B is giving up less Y for each unit of X.

With such a price, the greatest range of choices from A's point of view is

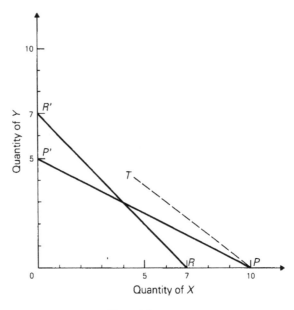

Figure 1.2

opened up if he is able to specialize completely in the production of X and to obtain all his requirements of Y through trade. In that case his consumption opportunities lie on a line through *P* steeper than *PP'* (but less steep than *RR'*) like the dashed line *PT*. But even if he is unable to obtain all his requirements of *Y* through trade, and has to produce some himself, the possibility of obtaining some Y at a lower cost through trade will still expand his choices.[3] B's position is similar except that he will obtain the greatest range of choices by specializing in the production of Y.

The attractions of trade are thus that it allows all parties access to a wider range of choices than if they had to rely on their own resources. These potential gains arise because trade enables individual agents to exploit what comparative advantages they may have in the production of any good by concentrating their productive efforts on that good, and by obtaining their requirements of other goods and services by trade.

This theory of comparative advantage should already be familiar to the reader, who may also recall that the operative phrase is *comparative* advantage. If individual B's production possibility curve was *SS'* in Figure 1.3, it would appear that A had some advantage in the production of both goods, perhaps because he had more or better productive resources at his disposal, or had more of the necessary skills. But A would still have the same comparative disadvantage in the production of Y that he had in the previous case, because he would still have to give up more X to produce 1 Y than B. The potential gains from trade are thus exactly the same as in Figure 1.3 despite the changed position of B's production possibility curve. Indeed,

8

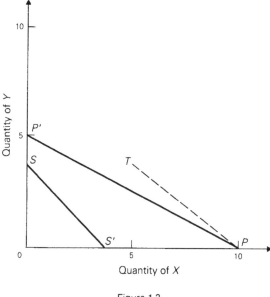

Figure 1.3

whatever the position of these production possibility curves, as long as their slopes (and thus their underlying relative costs) differ, choices can be expanded through trade.

In practice, the opportunities for individual agents to trade are considerably wider than suggested in this simple model, and the existence of a diversity of markets in which individual economic agents can buy and sell provides an obvious indication of the extent to which agents seek to widen their choices through trade.

Social organization

The final means of expanding choices we need to note is through social organizations. We define a social organization for present purposes as any grouping of two or more individuals in which decisions are made for the group as a whole. Examples thus include households, firms (from small craft cooperatives to giant multinational corporations), trades unions and also bodies such as football pool syndicates, golf clubs and the like.

The way these organizations go about their business is obviously likely to be as varied as their interests, but the details at this stage are not important, nor is the way they make their decisions, which may be dictatorial, democratic or some compromise between the two. The crucial point for the moment is that within social organizations there will be some capacity for centralized decision-making, in contrast to the decentralized decision-making involved with trade. Further, the production and consumption activities of the members of the organization are subject to coordination and

9

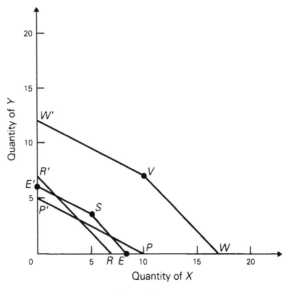

Figure 1.4

control by internal administrative procedures rather than by more impersonal market forces.

Despite the immense diversity of social organizations, a useful starting point to the discussion of their effects on choices is to consider their potential for providing an alternative to trade as a means of exploiting comparative advantages. Looked at from that point of view, if the individuals A and B with the production possibility curves in Figure 1.2 join together in a partnership, their combined production possibility curve, assuming their individual productive potential is not affected positively or negatively by the formation of the partnership, will be WVW' in Figure 1.4. In fact the aggregate consumption possibilities open to the partners along WVW' will be exactly the same as those opened up by trade.

The combination of X and Y at V will be that obtained if both individuals specialize in the production of the good in which they have the comparative advantage; points W and W' reflect the outputs produced if both individuals devote all their resources in the production of the same good, whilst the intermediate points on the curve indicate the possibilities with partial specialization by one of the individuals and complete specialization by the other. With this production possibility curve our partners decide together which of the available combinations of X and Y they prefer, and therefore which they should produce.

As well as deciding what to produce, however, the partners also need to decide how the output should be divided between them. One obvious possibility is for them to decide to divide whatever output is produced equally between them. In this case, the line ESE' in Figure 1.4 indicates the consumption possibilities open to each partner. Again, it should be clear from the diagram that consumption possibilities are opened up with the partnership arrangement that are not available to them if they have to rely solely on their own resources. Further, an unequal distribution of the goods produced need not preclude mutual gains, provided only that some part of each individual's consumption opportunities curve lies above his individual production possibility curve.

The fact that choices are expanded in this partnership in a similar way to our earlier simple trade model reflects the fact that specialization and trade are still effectively taking place. The difference is that they are taking place within the confines of an organization rather than across markets. In the case considered, the outcome of the two kinds of trading might be identical, but there are other relevant factors that might lead to advantages of one type of trading over the other. Detailed discussion of the factors relevant to particular types of organization is deferred to later chapters, but there are a number of more general considerations that are worth noting at this stage.

A crucial assumption underlying Figure 1.4 is that the productive potential of both A and B is unaffected by their coming together in a partnership. Within social organizations, however, it is often possible to exploit the benefits of *team production*, so that the production possibilities open to a group of individuals operating together are greater than the aggregate of the possibilities arising when they operate individually. If this is true in the case illustrated in Figure 1.4, the production possibility curve of the partnership will lie outside WVW', further expanding the choices open to individual partners.

A second potential advantage of social organization, for some at least, arises from the fact that with trade through markets an individual's consumption possibilities are still constrained by his initial endowment of resources. Thus in Figure 1.2, the curve showing A's consumption possibilities after trade (PT) is anchored at point P, which reflects the maximum X he can produce with the resources at his disposal. Within a social organization, an individual's share of what is produced is more open to discussion and negotiation. Hence particular individuals may prefer to 'trade' within social organizations if they feel that they are thereby likely to receive a greater share of the available output than if they traded through markets.

A third consideration is that trade through markets, since it involves the transfer of the right to use particular goods and services from one agent to another, essentially involves the exchange of what are called *property rights* over goods and services. It thus requires those property rights to be well defined, so that it is clear what is being exchanged. For example, it needs to be made clear whether the purchase of a piece of land entitles the buyer to exploit whatever resources lie beneath it or whether it just gives him rights to use the surface area for building, agriculture or whatever.

Further, the relevant property rights need to be enforceable to the extent that the enjoyment of anything offered for trade is conditional on an appropriate payment being made. For example, an individual in a particular neighbourhood may offer to provide, through the market, a security patrol that would have the effect of reducing the number of crimes against property in the area. If the patrol is effective it is likely that it will be of benefit to all living in the area, irrespective of whether they have contracted to 'buy' the services of the patrol. In these circumstances there is some incentive for people not to buy in the expectation that others will, so that they benefit in any case. In other words, there is an incentive for them to 'free-ride'. Furthermore, since this incentive is the same for all, the result may be insufficient market demand to make it worthwhile for anyone to provide the service. Nevertheless, provision might be possible if there is an appropriate social organization with powers to compel beneficiaries to contribute towards the cost of provision. In this case a government body with powers to levy taxes is an obvious possibility.

Fourthly, account must be taken of the fact that man is very much a social animal deriving utility from contact with others. He may, therefore, prefer to carry out productive and consumption activities in the company of others rather than in isolation. Hence, even when trade through markets and trade within social organizations have potentially the same effects on choices, the extra utility derived from the kind of social relationships that can be enjoyed within a social organization – whether it be a family, a club, a firm or whatever – may lead to some preference for the latter.

Other factors, however, are likely to work more in favour of trading through markets. In particular, when individuals trade through markets they make their own decisions about what to produce and what to consume in the light of their own preferences. In an organization, individual preferences may be brought to bear on particular decisions only indirectly and, in cases where decision-making within the organization is particularly dictatorial, not at all. Some individuals may, therefore, prefer to operate through markets for the freedom it gives them to choose according to their own preferences, rather than to be bound by collective choices even at some cost in terms of consumption opportunities.

In addition, it has to be borne in mind that both trading through markets and running organizations involve costs in the sense that they use resources that would otherwise be available to produce consumable goods and services. With any form of trading, transaction costs arise from the need to acquire information about the relevant market, to find buyers and to negotiate contracts. Within an organization these costs are reduced because the trading area is more circumscribed, uncertainty is reduced and contracts tend to be more standardized. However, resources are also needed to collect the information required by the centralized decision-makers, and to monitor individuals within the organization, to ensure that decisions are implemented. Relative transactions costs may therefore be an important factor in determining whether trade is across markets or within organizations.

Ultimately, therefore, whether individual economic agents seek to expand the choices open to them through market operations or through forming social organizations is likely to depend very much on the circumstances of any particular situation. Sometimes agents are not free to choose. People living and working in the UK cannot easily opt out of the obligations and benefits of the British state or their local jurisdiction. Similarly, the extent to which people are free to form organizations may be restricted if that organization were to pose a threat to others. It follows that the choice between market and non-market forms of operation is a recurring theme in microeconomics and therefore is one that we will be returning to at various stages in this book.

Concluding remarks

The main purpose of this chapter has been to introduce certain general ideas and concepts that underlie much of the remainder of the book, but since the discussion has of necessity been fairly wide-ranging it may be useful to conclude by summarizing the major points covered:

- Microeconomics is basically concerned with analysing the behaviour of economic agents and the implications of that behaviour for the allocation of resources.
- The theoretical analysis of the behaviour of economic agents normally proceeds on the assumption that they behave rationally in the sense of choosing the most preferred alternative when making choices.
- Rational behaviour can be expressed as utility maximization.
- Since resources are scarce, choices are normally constrained.
- These constraints are not fixed in any absolute sense, and such fundamental economic activities as production, research and development, trade, and the formation of social organizations have the effect of widening choices.

Notes

1   Nevertheless it has been argued that there may be important discontinuities in the utility function.
2   Alternatively PM can be regarded as the cost of producing N of Y in terms of X forgone.
3   The reader is invited to check this for him/herself by attempting Exercise 1.3 below.

Exercises

1.1 What do you understand by rational behaviour? Give examples of rational and irrational behaviour. Can the economist's assumption that economic agents behave rationally be justified?

1.2 'Utility is that property in any object, whereby it tends to produce benefit, advantage, pleasure, good or happiness . . . to that party whose interest is considered' (Bentham).
'Utility means the sum of pleasure and the pain prevented by the use of something' (Jevons).
'Utility is correlative to Desire or Want' (Marshall).
'What modern economists call "utility" reflects nothing more than rank ordering of preference' (Hirshleifer).
'Utility is a metaphysical concept of impregnable circularity' (Joan Robinson).

Evaluate the above in the light of what you understand by the concept of utility.

1.3 Consider the case of the individual with the production possibility curve PP' in Figure 1.2.

  (i) Draw in the curve showing what consumption possibilities would be available to him if he produced 6 units of X and 2 units of Y but could buy or sell 1 unit of X for 0.75 units of Y, and compare them with the possibilities open with complete specialization in the production of X.

  (ii) Assuming the same trading price, deduce how the amounts of X and Y that the individual would need to produce to give the greatest consumption opportunities after trade can be determined when the production possibility curve is concave to the origin rather than a straight line.

1.4 To what extent do you think that social organizations can be satisfactorily explained in terms of devices for overcoming constraints?

CHAPTER TWO
THE BASIC THEORY OF CONSUMER CHOICE

The analysis of individuals and households

In this and the next few chapters we will be concerned with the behaviour of individuals and households. This involves an investigation into the properties of their utility functions, the choices open to them and the implications of utility-maximizing behaviour.

Individuals and households are the economic agents principally concerned with the consumption of products of various kinds, so their behaviour has a particularly important influence on the demand for them. In addition, they are involved in the supply of certain products and services, especially of labour services. Our analysis therefore has to cover at some stage both buying and selling decisions. One potential source of difficulty is that some of the relevant decisions are made by individuals acting on their own behalf, whilst others are more collective decisions in the sense that they are made by, or on behalf of, multi-person households. Nevertheless, since households are generally made up of only a small number of individuals, it seems likely that household utility functions will have the same general properties as individual utility functions. Similarly, the constraints on household choice are essentially the same as those on individuals. Further, whilst the way household decisions are made may be an interesting subject for study, we are primarily concerned, as economists, with the end-product of the decision-making process. Hence for our present purposes there seems to be no strong case for distinguishing between individuals and households. In this section of the book, therefore, the basic decision-maker will be referred to as an individual on the understanding that the analysis also applies to individual households.

In the light of the above, this chapter will concentrate on the basic theory of individual choice whilst the following chapters will be concerned first with some further implications of that theory and will then examine some of the ways in which the analysis of choice has been further developed.

The properties of individual utility functions

Traditionally it has been thought that, whilst utility functions may vary considerably from individual to individual depending upon their different personalities and backgrounds, there are a number of common features within that diversity.[1] Three such features in particular can be identified.

The first follows from the idea that preferences might be expressed between different bundles of products. This implies that the utility obtainable from a particular bundle is related to the range of products it contains and the quantity of each involved. It would therefore seem reasonable to suppose that utility depends on, or is a function of, the quantities of all the products consumed. In other words, we can express the utility function as

$$U = U(q_1, q_2, \ldots, q_n), \qquad (2.1)$$

where U is the utility of an individual and q_1, q_2, ..., q_n represent the quantities of the various products consumed.

A second feature follows from the idea of scarcity. As long as the individual has only limited purchasing power, it is likely to be the case that consuming more of certain products, whilst the quantities of others consumed remain constant, increases utility. Since the extra utility obtainable from consuming an extra unit of one product when the quantity consumed of all others remains unchanged is the **marginal utility** of that product, our second common property simply suggests that the marginal utility of at least some products is positive.[2]

In this context a distinction can be made between 'goods' and 'bads'. Whilst a 'good' is something that gives positive utility, consumption of a 'bad' reduces utility (i.e. it produces disutility). In what follows, therefore, the term 'good' will be used in the precise sense implied by this distinction to indicate that the product involved yields positive rather than negative utility.[3] Obviously a utility-maximizing individual seeks to avoid 'bads' if he can, but sometimes either they are imposed on him by others (e.g. aircraft noise) or they may have to be endured before certain goods can be enjoyed. Thus, a tedious journey or a rough sea-crossing may be an unavoidable prerequisite to the enjoyment of the delights of Mediterranean beaches.

The third common feature ascribed to utility functions qualifies the second slightly in that it suggests that, whilst utility may increase as the quantity consumed of a particular product increases, successive units of consumption yield smaller increments of utility. This property of **diminishing marginal utility** simply implies that the effect on an individual's utility of increasing the consumption of one product, say apples, whilst keeping the quantity of all others constant, can be characterized by a diagram such as Figure 2.1a. In the diagram, U_o represents the utility obtainable from all other goods, which may of course be quite large in relation to any potential utility obtainable from apples (hence the broken vertical axis), and the curve U_oU is a total

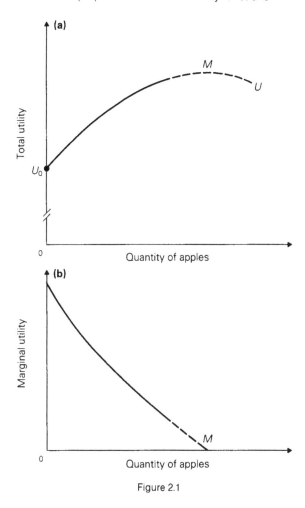

Figure 2.1

utility curve in that it traces out the effect on total utility of increasing the number of apples consumed. The postulated diminishing marginal utility is reflected in, and is indeed measured by, the declining slope of this total utility curve.[4] This means that plotting the value of the slope of U_0U against each quantity of apples, as in Figure 2.1b, provides a more direct expression of the relationship between marginal utility and quantity.

The idea of diminishing marginal utility has further implications for the distinction between 'goods' and 'bads' because it is apparent from Figure 2.1 that, if the consumption of apples is extended far enough along the dashed extensions of the curves, marginal utility might eventually become zero or even negative, in which case the total utility curve would turn downwards. At that stage, which is reached in the diagram when M apples are consumed, additional apples would be 'bads' rather than 'goods'. More generally, diminishing marginal utility implies that any 'good' consumed to excess may

17

become a 'bad'. Again, however, a utility-maximizing individual will seek to avoid increasing the consumption of any product to the point at which it starts to reduce his utility.

Whilst it is difficult to test empirically whether utility functions do have the general properties suggested above, these do not seem unreasonable if we look at them from the standpoint of our own experiences as consumers. Moreover, an exceedingly large range of mathematical functions can be specified having these properties, suggesting that they provide a framework within which a variety of individual tastes can be accommodated. Further, although we will need to give some further consideration to the form of the utility function below, certain useful initial insights into utility-maximizing behaviour can be obtained without specifying further details.

Utility-maximizing choices

Given that the consumer is likely to have limited income at his disposal, maximizing his utility simply involves allocating his expenditure between 'goods' (to the exclusion of 'bads') in such a way as to equalize the utility obtainable from the last unit of expenditure on each one consumed. Further, since the utility obtainable from the last unit of expenditure is its marginal utility divided by its price, the condition for maximum utility can be expressed as

$$\frac{MU_1}{p_1} = \frac{MU_2}{p_2} = , \ldots, = \frac{MU_n}{p_n} . \qquad (2.2)$$

The truth of this proposition can be demonstrated by considering a situation in which it doesn't hold or where, for example,

$$\frac{MU_i}{p_i} > \frac{MU_j}{p_j} \qquad i \neq j.$$

In this case it is possible for our consumer to increase his total utility by transferring units of expenditure from good j to good i, where they yield more utility. With diminishing marginal utility from each good, such a redistribution will reduce MU_j and increase MU_i, so that eventually a position will be reached at which the potential for further increases in utility will be exhausted. That will occur either when

$$\frac{MU_i}{p_i} = \frac{MU_j}{p_j} ,$$

or, if there is no level of consumption of j at which the above condition can be met, when the consumption of j has been reduced to zero. In the latter case, good j will strictly not feature in the utility-maximizing condition (2.2).

Indeed, in general, utility maximization involves confining expenditure not only to goods, but to goods with a sufficiently high marginal utility per unit of expenditure.

When condition (2.2) is met for all goods consumed, MU_i/p_i (any i) can be interpreted as the consumer's **marginal utility of expenditure** as it provides a measure of the utility obtained from the marginal unit of expenditure on any good, or, alternatively, the utility that will be lost if the individual is prevented from spending his last £1 or $1. Goods promising a lower marginal utility of expenditure, either because the utility obtainable is low or the price is high (or both), are initially excluded from the consumer's budget. However, given diminishing marginal utility for particular goods, a consumer might find it possible to derive more utility from consuming extra goods as his income increases than from buying more of goods already being consumed. This would, nevertheless, depend upon individual tastes.

In practice it may not be possible for condition (2.2) to be satisfied exactly because some products are available only in indivisible lumps. One cannot, for example, buy half a hammer. That problem may, however, be less serious than might appear at first sight because although, to take another example, things like houses come in large indivisible units, what actually gives the utility is, primarily, living space, which is much more variable in that individual houses can be extended or surplus rooms can be sub-let. Households can also vary the space they use by moving into larger or smaller premises. Similar considerations apply to a number of other products that may at first sight seem indivisible, but housing also provides an example of another situation where condition (2.2) may not hold exactly because adjusting the quantities consumed can take a considerable amount of time if buyers and sellers have to be found and lengthy legal procedures are involved. To avoid undue complications, problems of this nature will, for the most part, be ignored in our analysis. That means we are, in effect, assuming that all products are perfectly divisible and that expenditure decisions can be put into effect without significant delays. Whilst these are reasonable simplifying assumptions, they do mean that in some situations our analysis will not apply without some qualification.

Despite this, the picture that emerges from our discussion so far – of individuals spreading their purchases over a range of goods that expands as income increases – is one that seems to conform to everyday experience. As such it may be seen to provide some empirical support for our initial cautious assumptions about the form of individual preferences, particularly that of diminishing marginal utility. If we assume increasing marginal utility instead, then utility-maximizing behaviour involves the concentration of expenditure on a single product, which seems contrary to normal experience.

However, a further requirement of our theory is to provide some insight into the behaviour of consumers in the face of changes in the key parameters involved in their choice decisions such as income and prices. Unfortunately, condition (2.2) does not provide a very satisfactory basis for deducing the effects of such changes. It would help if it could be assumed that the marginal utility obtained from one good is completely independent of the quantities of other goods consumed, but that seems an unduly restrictive assumption to make since many instances can be quoted of goods for which it is unlikely to be the case. The marginal utility of petrol, for example, is likely to be very low for someone without any petrol-engined vehicles or appliances, but the greater the number of such appliances the individual acquires the more useful petrol becomes and therefore the greater the marginal utility (and indeed the total utility) associated with any level of consumption. On the other hand, if a cheap alternative to petrol becomes available which our vehicle-owner starts buying, he will have less use for petrol and its marginal utility will thereby be reduced.

Given this kind of interdependence, the marginal utility terms in condition (2.2) could be affected in a variety of ways when the pattern of purchases is changed in response to even relatively small price or income changes, thereby considerably complicating any analysis based solely on that expression. In taking the analysis further, therefore, we need the help of an analytical approach that can take on board interdependent utilities without introducing unnecessary complications. It should be noted further, recalling the discussion in Chapter 1 of the nature of utility, that condition (2.2), in the form in which it is written, is open to the objection that it implies that marginal utility is a concept capable of cardinal measurement. It is in order to overcome both of these problems that indifference curves are used.

Indifference curves and their properties

An indifference curve is simply a curve connecting points in a diagram representing bundles of products that give the consumer the same level of utility, or between which he is indifferent in the sense that each bundle yields equal satisfaction. Our first task is to consider what properties these curves might have.

In order to facilitate diagrammatic analysis, let us consider a situation in which a consumer is confined to the purchase of two products, apples and bananas, both of which are goods. In Figure 2.2, where quantities of apples and bananas are measured on the axes, each point represents a particular bundle of the two goods, with point P representing the bundle comprising 2 kg of apples and 4 kg of bananas. Assuming the comparability assumption (p. 2 above) holds, for any individual all other points in the diagram represent bundles of goods that are either preferred to P, regarded as inferior to P or ranked equally with P. The indifference curve through P therefore simply connects up this last category of points, and some idea of its shape can be obtained by referring back to the properties of utility functions considered in the previous section. As long as the marginal utility of both apples and

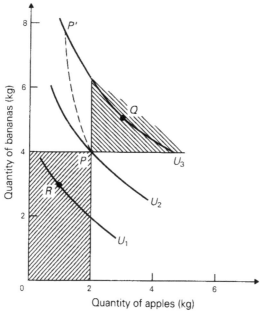

Figure 2.2

bananas is positive, any point in Figure 2.2, such as Q, lying in the shaded area above and to the right of P must represent a bundle of goods giving more utility than that at P since it involves more of at least one good and no less of the other. Conversely, but for corresponding reasons, any point in the shaded area below and to the left of P must represent a bundle of goods yielding less utility than that at P. Bundles of goods yielding the same utility as the bundle at P can, therefore, be located only to the 'north-west' or 'south-east' of P, suggesting that the indifference curve through P is downward sloping like the curve labelled U_2. Moreover, points such as Q representing bundles of the two goods yielding more utility than the bundle at P will be on an indifference curve representing a higher level of utility (U_3), which can thus be referred to as a higher indifference curve, whilst points such as R will be on the lower indifference curve U_1.

A further point to be noted is that, given our earlier assumption that preferences are transitive, these indifference curves cannot cross. The indifference curve through P cannot follow the path indicated by the dashed curve in the diagram, since if the bundle of goods at Q is preferred to that at P, and is ranked equally to that at P', which is the point where the dashed curve cuts U_3, transitivity requires that the bundle of goods at Q is also preferred to that at P' and therefore cannot lie on the same indifference curve.

Returning to the question of the shape of individual indifference curves, whilst scarcity suggests only that they are downward sloping, they are also

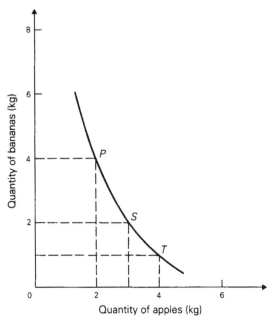

Figure 2.3

generally assumed to be convex to the origin. This is consistent with the idea of diminishing marginal utility in that the latter implies that the more of one good the individual has, the less of others he will be willing to give up to acquire more of the first. In the two-good case illustrated in Figure 2.2, the individual can give up only bananas in order to acquire more apples, so the suggestion is that the more apples the individual has the fewer bananas he will be willing to give up in order to obtain additional apples. This means that, whilst the individual with 4 kg of bananas and 2 kg of apples may be willing to give up 2 kg of bananas for a third kilogram of apples, he may be willing to give up only one further kilogram of bananas for a fourth kilogram of apples. In that situation, which is the one illustrated in Figure 2.3, the consumer's indifference curve through P, where P represents the original bundle of bananas and apples, would also pass through S and T, and it can be seen that the decreased willingness of the individual to sacrifice bananas as his use of apples increases gives the curve its characteristic convex shape when viewed from the origin.

In more technical terms, the rate at which the consumer is willing to give up bananas in order to obtain extra (or marginal) apples (that is, the number of bananas given up at the margin per extra apple) is termed the **marginal rate of substitution of apples for bananas** (MRS_{AB}). This is closely related to the slope of the indifference curve (relative to the horizontal axis) because the latter also reflects the change at the margin in the consumption of bananas (Δq_B) relative to the change in the consumption of apples (Δq_A) as it is the ratio of the two or $\Delta q_B/\Delta q_A$. However, since the indifference curve as drawn in Figure 2.3 is downward sloping, Δq_B and Δq_A are mathematically opposite in sign and its slope has a negative value, and is in fact the negative of the marginal rate of substitution of apples for bananas.[5]

But one further result should also be noted. When moving from P to S the change in utility associated with giving up the use of bananas can be expressed as the number of units given up multiplied by the marginal utility of bananas (MU_B)

$$\Delta q_B \cdot MU_B.$$

Similarly, the change in the utility from the extra apples can be expressed as

$$\Delta q_A \cdot MU_A.$$

Since P and S are on the same indifference curve, the losses and gains must exactly offset each other. Hence

$$\Delta q_A \cdot MU_A + \Delta q_B \cdot MU_B = 0,$$

or, rearranging,

$$MU_A/MU_B = -\Delta q_B/\Delta q_A,$$

and hence

$$MU_A/MU_B = MRS_{AB} \qquad (2.3)$$

and the slope of the indifference curve =

$$-MU_A/MU_B = -MRS_{AB}. \qquad (2.4)$$

An important implication of this result is that, whilst the assumption of convexity is closely associated with the idea of diminishing marginal utility, it is actually about *relative* marginal utilities rather than about marginal utility in any absolute sense. Hence, in making this assumption we avoid any need to concern ourselves with precisely how changes in the consumption of one product might or might not affect the marginal utility of the other. Further, since relative marginal utilities can be expressed as the marginal rate of substitution, which can in turn be defined in terms of quantities of products, any problems of measurement associated with the use of individual marginal utilities can be avoided. However, although the slope of an indifference curve reflects relative marginal utilities, it will be clear from (2.4) that as MU_A approaches zero the shape of the indifference curve also approaches zero, so the curve itself approximates to a horizontal line. Correspondingly, as MU_B

approaches zero the indifference curve approaches a vertical line. Further, if MU_A (or MU_B) becomes negative (i.e. A or B becomes a 'bad'), the indifference curve becomes positively sloped and then turns upwards (or inwards), reflecting the fact that in such cases more of the product with negative marginal utility reduces utility rather than increases it.[6]

Nevertheless, 'bads' apart, our analysis suggests that we can represent an individual's preferences by a set of indifference curves that are downward sloping and convex to the origin. Within that specification the precise form of the indifference curves will depend on individual tastes, but one further general factor should be noted which is that the closer a substitute one product is for another the less will the marginal rate of substitution decline. Indeed in the limiting case, if product A is regarded by the consumer as a perfect substitute for B, there will be no change in the marginal rate of substitution as the consumption of A increases and hence the indifference curves will be straight lines. With highly imperfect substitutes, however, a rapid decline in the marginal rate of substitution might be expected, resulting in more markedly convex indifference curves.

The budget constraint

Whatever the precise shape of his indifference curves, the rational consumer seeking to maximize utility will clearly seek to reach the highest possible indifference curve, but he will at the same time be constrained in his choices by the limited budget he is likely to have at his disposal.

In the two-product case, the choices open to him can be shown diagrammatically using what is termed a **budget line**. In the case of a choice between apples and bananas, the budget line can be interpreted as showing the maximum quantity of bananas that can be bought with a given income and with specified quantities of apples (and vice versa). Thus, to take the simplest kind of example, suppose our individual had £10 to spend when apples and bananas cost 50p and 40p a kilogram respectively: if he spent nothing on apples he would be able to buy a maximum of 25 kg of bananas; if he bought 10 kg of apples he could buy 12.5 kg of bananas; but if he were to buy 20 kg of apples he would not be able to buy any bananas at all as his total budget would have been exhausted. Plotting all the possible combinations of purchases on a diagram produces the budget line MN in Figure 2.4 and that line simply indicates the outer limit of the choices available to our consumer. With his £10 and the prices specified he will be in a position to buy any bundle of apples and bananas on MN, and also, if he feels so inclined, any bundle represented by a point in the positive quadrant below MN.

Mathematically, the budget line is simply the diagrammatic expression of the condition that, if all income is spent, total expenditure is equal to income. Hence, if the consumer's income is y and the prices of apples and bananas are

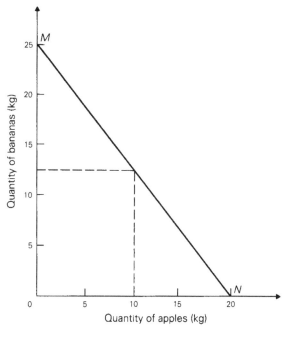

Figure 2.4

p_A and p_B respectively, the equation representing the budget line is

$$p_A q_A + p_B q_B = y. \tag{2.5}$$

Rearranging this expression, we can write

$$q_B = - \frac{p_A}{p_B} \cdot q_A + \frac{y}{p_B}. \tag{2.5a}$$

From this latter expression we can deduce that when $q_A = 0$, $q_B = y/p_B$, which simply tells us that the maximum possible quantity of B that can be purchased out of the given income represented by point M in the diagram is y/p_B. (Similarly the maximum purchase of A represented by N is y/p_A.) Expression (2.5a) also tells us that, starting from M, the purchases of B will have to be reduced by p_A/p_B for every unit of A purchased and thus that $- p_A/p_B$ is the slope of the budget line. The slope of the budget line therefore reflects the relative prices of the two goods (1.25 in our example) and is steeper the higher the price of apples relative to bananas. Moreover, its position relative to the origin reflects the consumer's income; the greater that income, the further from the origin the location of the budget line.

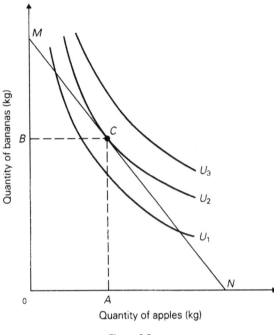

Figure 2.5

Utility-maximizing choices again

With the budget line setting a limit upon the choices available, the choice that the rational individual will make can be shown by superimposing that line on to his indifference curve diagram, as in Figure 2.5. Once this is done, it can be seen that he can obtain more utility than is obtainable from the bundles of apples and bananas on U_1 whilst those on U_3 are beyond his reach. Indeed, the highest indifference curve he can reach is U_2, and that is attainable only by buying the bundle of goods at C where U_2 is tangential to the budget line. Rational behaviour therefore requires the purchase of that particular bundle of goods (comprising A apples and B bananas).

Note that with downward-sloping indifference curves, the preferred point is on MN rather than below it, but the reader can easily test that the same will be true even if one of the products yields negative utility. Moreover, with convex indifference curves, one point on the budget line must be uniquely preferable to all the others. With C lying between M and N, as in Figure 2.5, at the preferred point characterized by the point of tangency between the indifference curve and the budget line, the slopes of both will be equal. If we recall what the slopes measure, we realize that at C

$$MRS_{AB} = p_A/p_B. \qquad (2.6)$$

This is formally identical to condition (2.2) above, which suggests that MU/p is the same for all goods consumed since

$$MU_A/p_A = MU_B/p_B$$

can be rearranged to give

$$MU_A/MU_B = p_A/p_B,$$

the left-hand side of which we have already seen (see expression (2.3) above) is the same as MRS_{AB}.

Nevertheless, the preferences of the individual could be such that the preferred point is M or N, which would involve what is called a corner solution. In that case, the optimal position need not involve tangency between the indifference curve and the budget line. In fact, if the preferred position is at M where no apples are consumed, then

$$MRS_{AB} \leqslant p_A/p_B$$

or

$$MU_A/p_A \leqslant MU_B/p_B,$$

which again is in line with our earlier conclusion that goods with an insufficiently high marginal utility of expenditure will not be consumed. Where both goods are consumed, however, condition (2.6) applies and, although diagrammatic analysis restricts us to two products only, reference to condition (2.2) above will confirm that condition (2.6) can easily be extended to take account of more products. In fact, where more than two goods are consumed, utility maximization simply requires that the marginal rate of substitution between any pair of goods consumed should be equal to their price ratio, or, more formally, that

$$MRS_{ij} = p_i/p_j \qquad i = 1, 2, \ldots n, \qquad i = j. \tag{2.7}$$

Alternatively, if in generalizing the analysis we are particularly interested in the demand for A in relation to other goods more generally, we can use the vertical axis to measure *expenditure* on all other products in terms of money or any other convenient numeraire product, provided that the prices of all these other products in terms of the numeraire remain unchanged, since a given level of expenditure will then represent a fixed bundle of those other products.

Concluding remarks

The preceding paragraphs suggest that, irrespective of whether the analysis covers two products or many, the conclusions must be the same. Essentially, they are that what the individual consumer seeks to buy of any good will depend on his tastes as reflected in his utility function, but will also depend upon its price, the prices of other goods and his income, which together set limits on his choices. When the consumer's tastes are fixed, therefore, we can define an individual's demand function in which the amount demanded of any good (q_i) is a function of the prices of all goods $(p_1 \ldots p_n)$ and his income (y) or

$$q_i = f(p_1, \ldots p_n, y) \qquad i = 1, 2, \ldots n. \tag{2.8}$$

Our next task is to investigate further the properties of this function by extending the analysis to consider what predictions can be made about the response of the consumer to changes in the income and price variables.

Notes

1   More recent developments in the theory have attempted to put less emphasis on the variability of tastes in determining the choices made by individuals. See Chapter 6 below.
2   In mathematical terms this implies that at least some of the first-order partial derivatives of the utility function (2.1), which represent the marginal utilities of each good, are positive.
3   This use of the term good also embraces 'services' like haircuts or medical treatment (provided they yield positive utility) which in other contexts (e.g. national income accounts) are sometimes distinguished from goods.
4   It is assumed that the reader is familiar with this aspect of the relationship between total and marginal curves. Diminishing marginal utility implies that the first-order partial derivatives of the utility function are declining functions of q_i (all i) or the direct second-order partial derivatives are negative.
5   Similarly, the slope of the indifference curve relative to the vertical axis is the negative of the marginal rate of substitution of bananas for apples.
6   Mathematically, with the utility function $U = f(q_A, q_B)$ for movements along an indifference curve (by total differentiation),

$$\frac{\partial U}{\partial q_A} \cdot dq_A + \frac{\partial U}{\partial q_B} \cdot dq_B = 0,$$

from which the slope of the indifference curve can be expressed as

$$\frac{dq_A}{dq_B} = -(\partial U/\partial q_A)/(\partial U/\partial q_B) = -\frac{MU_A}{MU_B}.$$

Exercises

2.1 The discussion of utility-maximizing choices normally assumes that the consumer's marginal utility of expenditure is still positive when all his income is spent. How would a utility-maximizing consumer allocate his expenditure if that wasn't the case? Express your answer:

    (a) in terms of condition (2.2) (p. 18 above), and
    (b) in terms of a two-product indifference curve diagram.

2.2 If utility maximization requires all income to be spent, how can (a) savings and (b) gifts to charities be explained in terms of rational behaviour?

2.3 How would the basic predictions of the theory of consumer choice be affected if indifference curves were *concave* to the origin?

CHAPTER THREE
THE COMPARATIVE STATICS OF CONSUMER BEHAVIOUR

In this chapter we analyse the effects of income and price changes on the individual's purchases of goods. Initially the changes are considered separately, but subsequently some composite changes are analysed and some further implications of the analysis discussed.

The effects of income changes

If income increases while prices remain constant, the slope of the consumer's budget line remains the same, but its position will change because the higher income allows more goods to be bought. Thus in Figure 3.1a, if M_1N_1 is the consumer's original budget line, an increase in income leads to the establishment of a new budget line such as M_2N_2 drawn parallel to M_1N_1 but farther away from the origin. The obvious effect of this change is to open up to the consumer the possibility of buying bundles of goods yielding more utility than was obtained in the original situation. Thus in the case illustrated in Figure 3.1a, where the consumer chooses the bundle of goods at C_1 on indifference curve U_1 when his budget line is M_1N_1, any point on the new budget line M_2N_2 between H and J, the points at which U_1 cuts M_2N_2, promise more utility than was obtained at C_1. Of all those points, the most preferred is that at which the new budget line is tangential to an indifference curve, namely C_2. The preferred bundle of goods for any other level of income such as M_3N_3 can similarly be identified, and a more general picture of how the consumer's purchases change as income changes can be obtained by drawing a curve through all the points corresponding to C_1 and C_2. This curve, labelled IEP in the diagram, is called the **income expansion path** (or the income consumption curve) as it traces the effects on the consumer's demand as income expands.

A more direct indication of the relationship between the consumer's demand for good A and his income is shown in Figure 3.1b. In this diagram,

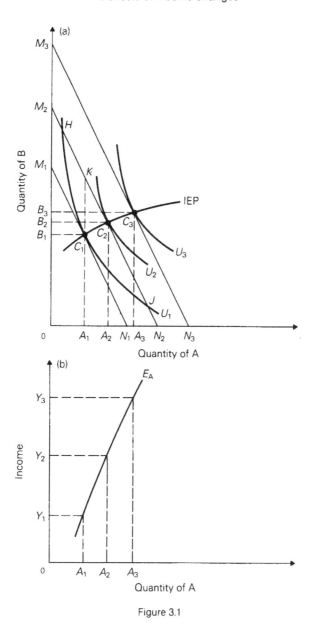

The effects of income changes

Figure 3.1

quantities of A are measured on the horizontal axis as in Figure 3.1(a), but income is measured directly on the vertical axis. If then the incomes associated with the budget lines M_1N_1, M_2N_2 and M_3N_3 are Y_1, Y_2 and Y_3 respectively, plotting the consumer's demand for A at each level of income produces the curve E_A, which is referred to as an **Engel curve**. A similar curve can also be derived for good B.

Returning, however, to Figure 3.1a, the income expansion path is an upward-sloping curve, suggesting that more of both goods will be purchased as the consumer's income increases. However, that is not the only possibility. It is also quite possible for a consumer with indifference curve U_1 to have an indifference curve tangential to M_2N_2 at a point between H and K, which is the point on M_2N_2 located vertically above C_1. In this case the consumer will wish to consume less A as his income increases, and his income expansion path (and the corresponding Engel curve in Figure 3.1b) will be backward sloping. Similarly it is also quite possible for the consumer's new preferred position to involve less B than at C_1. We cannot, therefore, make any definite prediction about the effect of an increase in income on a consumer's demand.

Nevertheless, even though we cannot make unambiguous predictions, we can place goods into particular categories. It should be clear from Figure 3.1 that there must be an increase in demand for at least one of the goods when income increases. Further, the notion of scarcity suggests that a normal sort of reaction to increased income is for people to want to buy more. Hence goods for which the consumer's demand increases as his income rises are referred to as **normal goods**. In contrast, goods for which the consumer's demand falls as his income increases are referred to as **inferior goods**, because of the implication, again given scarcity, that the consumer is reducing his purchases of that good because with his higher income he can now afford to buy what he regards as a superior alternative instead. Nevertheless, it cannot be assumed that some goods are always normal goods and that some goods are always inferior. A good may exhibit normal characteristics at some levels of income and inferior characteristics at others. Indeed, all inferior goods must be normal up to some level of income if they are to attain a level from which demand can decline. Moreover, since whether a good is normal or not depends on the precise form of the consumer's indifference map, it would seem to depend very much on individual tastes – what is an inferior good for some need not be so for others.

The effects of own price changes

Turning now to the effects of price changes, we will concentrate for the moment on the effects on the demand for a good of a change in its own price, deferring until later the analysis of the effects of other price changes.

In the case illustrated in Figure 3.2a, MN_1 is the consumer's original budget line. Given that the slope of the budget line is $-p_A/p_B$, an increase in the price of a good A (p_A) will leave the consumer facing a steeper budget line such as MN_2. This must pass through M (since the amount of B that can be bought with the given income is unaffected) and intersect the horizontal axis to the left of N_1, reflecting the reduction in the amount of A that can be bought. The preferred bundle of goods in this new situation can be identified

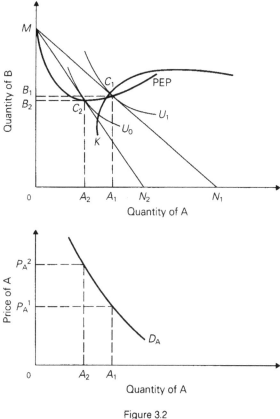

Figure 3.2

in the usual way, and in the case illustrated is that at C_2. Also, as in the case of income changes, the way the choice bundle varies as the price of A changes further can be traced through all such points as C_1 and C_2. The curve joining all these points is referred to as the **price expansion path** (or price consumption curve) and is labelled PEP in the diagram. It will be noted that the curve is shown as passing through M. This is because it seem reasonable to suppose in the light of the previous discussion that, given a sufficiently high price for A, the demand for it will be reduced to zero, and all the consumer's income will be spent on other goods.

In the case illustrated, the demand for A falls as its price increases, suggesting a traditional downward-sloping demand curve (showing the relationship between the price of A and the consumer's demand for it) of the form illustrated in Figure 3.2b, but again it should be clear from the diagram that that is not the only possible result. U_0 could be tangential to MN_2 at a point to the right of C_1 (i.e. between K and N_2) without violating any of our assumptions about the form of the preference function. It appears, therefore, that as in the case of income changes we cannot make any definite prediction about the effects upon the demand for a good of a change in its price but, again, we can look at the various possibilities. In doing that, however, it is helpful to consider the effects of price changes in more detail.

In moving from C_1 to C_2 the consumer is being forced to move to an inferior position just as he would be if his income were to fall, but he is also responding to a change in the relative prices of the two goods. This suggests that we can break down the total effect of the price change into two components, one reflecting the consumer's reaction to being worse off, which for obvious reasons is called **the income effect**, whilst the other reflects the consumer's reaction to the change in relative prices, which for reasons that will shortly become apparent is known as **the substitution effect**.

We can isolate the substitution effect by considering what will happen to the consumer's demand if, when the price of A is increased, he is given an offsetting increase in income, known as **the compensating variation**, which will allow him to be no worse off than at C_1, in terms of the utility he is obtaining. This means that he will need to be given sufficient extra income to enable him to reach a point on the indifference curve passing through C_1. In the case illustrated in Figure 3.3, this requires him to be given extra income equivalent to MJ in terms of B, which will move his budget line to JK. This will allow him to obtain the same level of utility that he enjoyed before the price change by purchasing the bundle of goods at T. The change from C_1 to T is then the **substitution effect** of the price change in that it reflects the extent to which the individual substitutes other goods for the one whose price has risen when he is responding solely to a change in relative prices. As far as the demand for A is concerned, it can be seen from the diagram that the substitution effect (labelled SE_A in the diagram) is *negative* in the sense that it reduces the demand for A from A_1 to S, but it is also negative in the more general mathematical sense that the change in demand is in the opposite direction to the price change. Moreover, our assumption that indifference curves are convex to the origin implies that the substitution effect will *always* be negative whatever the individual's preferences and however great or small the price increase, because any point of tangency between the indifference curve U_1 and a budget line steeper than MN_1 must, given the shape of the indifference curve, be to the left of C_1.

However, continuing with our analysis, if the movement from C_1 to T in Figure 3.3 reflects the substitution effect, the remainder of the overall response to the price change, which is reflected in the movement from T to C_2, must be the income effect. This is simply the effect on the consumer's demand that occurs if the consumer is initially at T with budget line JK and his income is reduced by MJ (the compensating variation of the price change). Since this is a straightforward income change we can, as before, make no general prediction about its outcome. However, recalling the distinction between normal and inferior goods from the previous section, if A is a *normal* good, a reduction in income reduces the consumer's demand for it. Hence in this case, which is the one illustrated in Figure 3.3, the income effect of the price

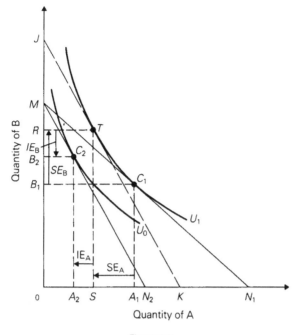

Figure 3.3

increase (IE_A) also reduces demand for A. In general, therefore, so far as normal goods are concerned, the income effect of the price increase reinforces the substitution effect, so that overall there can only be a reduction in the quantity demanded. If A is an inferior good, however, the income effect of a price increase increases the demand for A rather than reduces it, so that income and substitution effects operate in opposite directions.

Whilst with normal goods we can accordingly make definite predictions about the effects of a price change, with inferior goods some ambiguity necessarily arises, but again the possibilities can be classified. One such is where the negative substitution effect outweighs the positive income effect so that the net effect of a price increase is still to reduce demand. The other is the opposite case where the income effect is greater than the substitution effect so that demand increases as price falls. Goods in this second category are referred to as **Giffen goods** after Sir Robert Giffen, a nineteenth-century economist. They were given this name following Marshall's suggestion (1938 p. 132) that Giffen originally pointed to the possibility of this kind of result. Whether Giffen was really aware of this possibility has recently been doubted (see, for example, Stigler (1947) and O'Brien (1985)), but the label is well established and will no doubt stick. More pertinent to our present discussion, however, is whether Giffen goods are anything more than a theoretical curiosity.

For an inferior good to be a Giffen good it must have a large income effect relative to its substitution effect. The size of the substitution effect depends for any given price change on the curvature of the indifference curve, and is greater the closer the indifference curve is to a straight line, which in turn reflects how good a substitute B is for A. The size of the income effect, however, depends not only on the effects of income changes on the consumer's demand but also on the proportion of income spent on the good. A change in the price of a good accounting for only a small proportion of a consumer's budget cannot make him much better or worse off, but a change in the price of a good accounting for a significant proportion of the consumer's total expenditure (for example housing) might have an appreciable effect on his purchasing power and thus have relatively significant income levels.

If Giffen goods occur at all it can therefore only be in the case of goods with no close substitutes (and thus small substitution effects) and that account for a fairly large proportion of the consumer's budget. In addition, for the same reason that a good is unlikely to be inferior at all levels of income, it is unlikely to exhibit Giffen characteristics at all prices. All this indicates that the Giffen good might be a rather rare occurrence. Whilst this is a conclusion that will need to be qualified in the light of some of our later discussions, it suggests that, unless we have strong reasons for thinking otherwise, we can conclude that consumers will in general tend to reduce their purchases of any goods whose price rises, and vice versa.

The effects of a change in the price of another good

To complete our analysis of the effects on a consumer's demand for good A of changes in specific variables, we need to consider the effect of a change in the price of another good such as good B. However, we can equally well proceed by using Figure 3.3 to examine the effects of the increase in the price of good A in relation to the demand for good B. In the situation shown, the demand for B rises from B_1 at the initial price of A, when the budget line is MN_1, to B_2 when it is MN_2 reflecting the higher price for A.

Again, it is helpful to consider the income and substitution effects of the total change but this time with particular reference to their effect on the demand for B. In fact, it should be clear from the diagram that in this two-good case the substitution effect on B is the mirror image of that on A since, in the move from C_1 to T, B is substituted for A. In other words, the substitution effect on B is always positive. As usual, however, the income effect can go either way. If B is an inferior good, the income effect reinforces the substitution effect and adds further to the demand for B, but if it is a normal good, as in the case illustrated, the income effect is negative. We therefore have another of those cases where income and substitution effects operate in opposite directions, but here it arises in the normal case as opposed to the, by implication, more unusual inferior case. Again, in the absence of predictability, we resort to classification and distinguish between **gross substitutes** and **gross complements**. Gross substitutes for A are those goods for which the overall effect of an increase in the price of A is to increase demand. Thus, in Figure 3.3, B is a gross substitute for A. Conversely, a gross complement to A has a small substitution effect relative to its income effect so that overall the demand for it falls as the price of A rises.

One important limitation of Figure 3.3 is, however, that it suggests that the substitution effect of an increase in the price of A on the demand for B must be positive. Whilst that is true in the strict two-good case in which there is only good B that can be substituted for A, it need not be the case when purchases are spread over more than two goods. If expenditure on all other goods is substituted on the vertical axis of Figure 3.3, then, whilst the substitution effect of an increase in the price of A will be to increase that expenditure in total, the possibility within that higher total of less being bought of goods that are strongly complementary to A cannot be excluded. For example, if there is an increase in the price of electric storage heaters, it seems reasonable to suppose that the equivalent to the bundle of goods at T will include less electricity as well as fewer storage heaters and correspondingly more of other goods. This suggests that a more detailed classification of goods in terms of the effect on them of a change in the price of any given good might be made according to whether the relevant substitution effects were positive or negative, but for most purposes the simple classification into gross substitutes and complements is adequate.

Composite changes

So far we have considered the effect of changes in one variable on the consumer's demand for a good when all other relevant variables remain unchanged. For completeness some consideration of more composite changes is desirable.

One particular case, which is of some theoretical importance in this context, is that in which all relevant prices and the consumer's income increase (or decrease) in the same proportion, such as, for example, 10 per cent. In that situation, returning to the two-good case illustrated in our previous diagrams, the consumer's budget line is unaffected since the ratio of the prices of the two goods, reflected in the slope of the budget line, remains unchanged as does the ratio of income to prices reflected in the intercepts. With an unchanged budget line, however, our rational consumer has no need or incentive to change his purchase plans. We thus conclude that there is no effect on demand. On the face of it that seems a rather trivial and indeed self-evident result, but it does, nevertheless, impose an important restriction

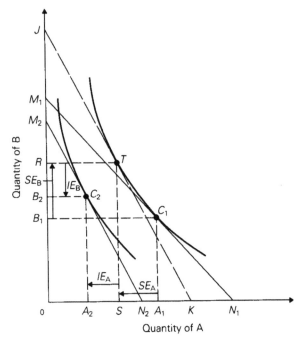

Figure 3.4

on the form of the demand function. In mathematical terms it requires the function to be homogeneous of degree zero,[1] and whilst there are a large number of mathematical forms that are broadly consistent with our previous analysis of the effects of changes in individual variables, only a relatively small sub-set of them have this particular property.[2]

This property also implies a lack of **money illusion**. Money illusion arises when individuals react to rising prices at a time of inflation but neglect to take account of the fact that their income is increasing at a similar rate. Sometimes people talk as though they suffer from money illusion, particularly when they start reminiscing about the 'good old days' when one could take the family for a day trip to Blackpool, treat them to fish and chips and a ride on the big-dipper and still come home with change out of a £5 note, but neglect to mention that in that golden age £5 represented a large proportion of most people's weekly earnings. Whether money illusion is reflected in their actual behaviour as opposed to their conversation is, however, more open to doubt.

Nevertheless, perhaps of more practical interest than the case where all prices and income change in the same proportion is the one where they change in differing proportions. In this case, income and substitution effects can again be used. Take, for example, the case illustrated in Figure 3.4 where the budget line shifts from $M_1 N_1$ to $M_2 N_2$. Such a movement might reflect an increase in the price of good A relative to B coupled with a reduction in income, but its effects can be analysed in just the same way as a simple price change. Thus a substitution effect can be identified in the usual way by considering what will happen if the consumer is given a compensating variation in income that will allow him to reach his original indifference curve. This will put him on the dashed budget line JK and allow him to buy the bundle of goods at T involving less A and more B than in the initial situation but the same utility. The income effect will then, as usual, be represented by the consumer's response to a movement of the budget line from JK back to M_1N_1, which will depend on whether either of the goods is inferior or not. In fact, the only departure from the previous analysis is in the size of the income effect, which in this case reflects a combination of money income and price changes rather than just a single price change in isolation.

Some additional results

The emphasis of the analysis so far has been on the absolute effect of particular changes in the demand for a specific good. However, when relating changes in one variable to changes in another, economists often prefer to use the concept of **elasticity**, which, by comparing changes in proportional terms, eliminates any dependence on arbitrarily defined units and provides for more meaningful comparisons between goods.

Three specific elasticities can be defined that are of particular relevance to our present analysis. The first is the **income elasticity of demand**, which for any good i can be defined as

$$\eta_i = \frac{\text{proportionate change in the demand for good } i}{\text{proportionate change in income}} = \frac{\Delta q_i/q_i}{\Delta y/y}, \quad (3.1)$$

where Δq_i and Δy refer to small changes in the quantity of i demanded and income respectively. The second is the ordinary or **own price elasticity of demand** (since it relates changes in demand to changes in the good's own price), which is defined as

$$\epsilon_{ii} = \frac{\text{proportionate change in demand for good } i}{\text{proportionate change in the price of } i} = \frac{\Delta q_i/q_i}{\Delta p_i/p_i}, \quad (3.2)$$

The third is the **cross-price elasticity of demand**, which relates the change in the demand for one good to changes in the price of another. The cross-price elasticity of demand for good i with respect to changes in the price of good j can be defined as

$$\epsilon_{ij} = \frac{\text{proportionate change in demand for good } i}{\text{proportionate change in the price of good } j} = \frac{\Delta q_i/q_i}{\Delta p_j/p_j}. \quad (3.3)$$

The reader should note that in the symbolic notation used for the above expressions, as in 3.1 to 3.3 above, the Greek letter η is used to denote income elasticities, with the subscript relating to the particular good concerned, whilst ϵ is used to denote a price elasticity. With the latter, the first subscript relates to the good whose demand is being considered whilst the second refers to the good whose price is changing. In practice, these elasticity concepts[3] tend to be estimated and used more commonly at the level of the aggregate (market) demand for a particular good. However, at the level of the individual consumer there are some important relationships between the various elasticities that are worth noting, and it is also useful to show how these measures relate to our previous analysis of income and price changes.

Taking income elasticity first, in the cases illustrated in our previous diagrams the income elasticities of the two goods are reflected primarily in the slope of the income expansion path. In the case illustrated in Figure 3.5, if the income expansion path between C_1 and C_2 were to follow the dashed straight line drawn from the origin through point C_1, the demand for both A and B would increase proportionately with income. The value of the income elasticity of demand for both goods would, therefore, be unity. However, in the diagram, the actual income expansion path is shown as being steeper than OC_1, indicating that the increase in the demand for A is less than it would be if the income expansion path followed the dashed line and thus that the demand for A increases by a smaller proportion than the increase in income, whilst the converse is true for B. Hence $\eta_A < 1$ and $\eta_B > 1$. The demand for A can therefore be described as *inelastic* with respect to changes in income whilst the demand for B is *elastic*. In general, therefore, at any point on the income expansion path, its steepness relative to the slope of the straight line drawn from that point back to the origin reflects the relative income elasticities of demand for the two goods.[3]

It should also be apparent that the smaller the income elasticity of demand for A the greater must be that for B. This is simply a reflection of the fact that the increases in the consumer's demands for the goods are ultimately constrained by the increase in his income, since the total additional expenditure cannot exceed the additional income. A more than proportionate increase in the demand for one good must, therefore, be offset by a less than proportionate increase in the other.

Turning now to the price elasticities, when the demand curve for a good is conventionally downward sloping, the quantity demanded and its price change in opposite directions, so that if Δq_i in expression (3.2) is positive, Δp_i is negative, and vice versa. In strict mathematical terms, therefore, ϵ_{ii} must be a negative quantity. Sometimes economists ignore the minus sign and express the price elasticity of demand as a positive number. Whilst that might be excusable when the ordinary price elasticity of demand is the only elasticity measure considered, if there are a number of elasticity measures involved in the discussion, as here, consistency demands that each should be given its

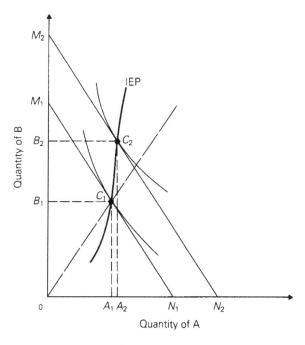

Figure 3.5

correct mathematical sign, and that will be the practice adopted throughout this book. Except in the case of Giffen goods, therefore, the own price elasticity of demand will always be taken to be a negative quantity. In general, negative elasticities will arise whenever the relevant variables change in opposite directions, while positive elasticities will reflect situations in which the variables change in the same direction.

Some indication of the size of the own price elasticity of demand can also be obtained from the individual's indifference curve diagram. The reader may recall that, when the demand for a good is elastic with respect to its own price (i.e. $\epsilon_{ii} < -1$), total expenditure increases when price falls, whilst the converse is true when demand is inelastic (or $-1 < \epsilon_{ii} < 0$).[4] Now, in terms of Figure 3.6, when the consumer is at C_1 on budget line MN_1, he buys B_1 of B and A_1 of A. From that we may infer that, since his income in terms of B is M, he effectively gives up MB_1 of B to obtain A_1 of A. In other words, his expenditure on A in terms of B (which, as explained above, could be a numeraire good such as money) is represented by MB_1 in the diagram. Similarly, if following a fall in the price of A the consumer moves to C_2, his expenditure on A will be MB_2 in terms of B, which, in the case illustrated where the price expansion path is downward sloping over the relevant range of prices, is greater than MB_1. The fall in the price of A, therefore, is in Figure 3.6 associated with a rise in expenditure on it, suggesting that the consumer's demand for A is elastic with respect to its own price. Similarly an upward-

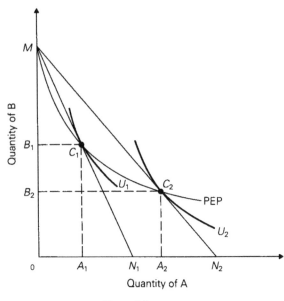

Figure 3.6

sloping price expansion path would indicate falling expenditure on A with a falling price suggesting inelastic demand, whilst a horizontal price expansion path would suggest an own price elasticity of -1.

Moreover, the slope of the price expansion path also reflects the cross-price elasticity of demand for B with respect to the price of A, which is negative in the case illustrated because a fall in the price of A is associated with a rise in the demand for B, whereas it would be positive if the price expansion path was upward sloping. Again, clearly, there is a relationship between the two because all the changes have to be accommodated within a budget that is fixed in money terms. An elastic demand for one good with respect to its own price has thus to be offset by negative cross-price elasticity for the other.

Concluding remarks

Returning to the main theme of this chapter, a basic conclusion must be that it is not always possible to make unambiguous predictions about the effects of price and income changes because of the potential diversity of consumers' tastes. However, whenever price changes are involved we have seen that a useful approach is to decompose the price changes into income and substitution effects. This is helpful because the direction of the substitution effect can often be predicted from the general properties ascribed to consumers' utility functions, and it was suggested that for most goods purchased by consumers the substitution effect is likely to be the dominant one.

More formal support for that assertion is found in what is called the **Slutsky equation** after the Russian economist who first derived it. Expressed in terms of elasticities, the Slutsky equation can be expressed in general terms as follows;

$$\epsilon_{ij} = \epsilon_{ij}{}^* - k_j \eta_i. \tag{3.4}$$

In this equation (and some indication of its derivation can be found in the Appendix to Chapter 4), ϵ_{ij} is the elasticity of demand for any good i with respect to a change in the price of any good j, which might be good i (in which case the elasticity is an own price elasticity as defined in (3.2)) or some other good (in which case it would be a cross-price elasticity as defined in (3.3)). $\epsilon_{ij}{}^*$ is defined similarly except that it is the price elasticity when income effects have been removed. Of the other terms, η_i is the income elasticity of demand for good i as in (3.1), whilst k_j is the fraction of the consumer's income accounted for by good j. Of the two terms on the right-hand side of expression (3.4), therefore, the first reflects the substitution effect and the second the income effect. Moreover, it can be seen that the latter is weighted by k_j, which, given the wide range of goods purchased by a typical consumer in a normal market economy, is likely to be, for most goods, well under 0.1, thereby diminishing the potential size of the income effect. The equation therefore appears to confirm the view that when income and substitution effects operate in opposite directions, as when the price of an inferior good increases, the likelihood of the income effect being sufficient to outweigh the substitution effect seems to be small.

Notes

1 A function such as $y = f(x_1, x_2), \ldots, x_n)$ is defined as being homogeneous of degree λ if multiplying the independent variables (i.e. all the x terms) by a constant, k, multiplies the dependent variable, y, by λ^k. When $\lambda^k = 1$, as with the demand function of an individual, $k = 0$.

2 The function form

$$q_A = p_A{}^{-\alpha} \cdot p_B{}^\beta \cdot y^\gamma + c,$$

where c, α, β and γ are constants, is one in which q_A falls as p_A increases and rises as p_B and y increase whatever the value of c, but only in the case where $\alpha = \beta + \gamma$ and $c = 0$ would the function be homogeneous of degree zero.

3 These elasticities can also be defined using the partial derivatives of the demand function. Thus if the demand function for good i is $q_i = f(p_1, \ldots, p_n, y)$

$$\eta_i = \frac{\partial q_i}{\partial y} \cdot \frac{y}{q_i},$$

and similarly for the other elasticities.

4 Remember that with negative numbers, $-2 < -1 < 0$, or conversely, $0 > -1 > -2$. These numbers representing elastic demand (all > 1) are represented as larger negative numbers and hence must be < -1. This problem recurs on pp. 174–5.

Exercises

3.1 Using indifference curves, analyse the effects of the introduction of student railcards on an individual student's demand for rail journeys. What does your analysis suggest will be the effect of the student railcard scheme on:

(i) the total demand for rail journeys,

(ii) the total revenue earned by British Rail on its passenger services?

3.2 The government of Academia discovered that on average students spent £120 per year on meals in their university refectories. Consequently, it offered either to increase student grants by £40 a year, or to pay a subsidy to the refectories to enable them to cut all prices by one-third. If you were asked to advise the Students' Union, which alternative would you recommend that they accept?

3.3 Mr Bloggs buys 40 bags of coal per year, on which he has to pay a tax of 25 pence per bag. Would he be better or worse off if tax on coal were removed and he was required to pay income tax amounting to the same total sum per annum instead? Can any general conclusions be drawn from your analysis about the relative desirability of different forms of taxes?

3.4 In a period of national emergency, the government introduces a points rationing system by which each consumer is given an equal number of points per week, and each commodity the consumer buys has a points 'price' as well as a money price. Using a two-good model, show how the introduction of such a rationing system affects the consumers' choices. Analyse also the effects of a change in the money price of a good.

CHAPTER FOUR
THE INDIVIDUAL AS A SELLER

So far we have considered the individual as a buyer and consumer of goods with a given source of money at his disposal, but we have not discussed in any detail how that money can be acquired. One obvious possibility is for it to be obtained by selling something, and most people obtain the means to buy goods by selling labour services. Since there is no reason to suppose that individuals are any less rational in their selling decisions than in their buying decisions, it seems reasonable to analyse them in a similar way and that is the task of this chapter. Selling decisions, of course, determine what the consumer supplies to the market rather than what he demands from it, but apart from that the underlying considerations are basically similar. To emphasize these similarities we will start by considering the case of an individual with a stock of goods that he can either use himself or sell to the market, and then go on to show how the analysis can be applied to the supply of labour services and to the supply of savings.

The supply of goods

To relate the discussion as closely as possible to that of the previous chapters, let us consider a situation in which an individual owns an orchard that, one autumn, yields him a crop of apples that he can either keep for his own use or take to the market and sell. If he sells apples he can buy other goods with the proceeds, so essentially he is faced with a set of choices that can be expressed in the form of a standard budget line as in Figure 4.1. In this case, however, assuming the consumer has no other sourse of income, the position of the budget line is determined by the size of the initial apple crop since if, in terms of the diagram, that crop amounts to S, that is also the maximum quantity of apples he can consume, and S is the point where the budget line meets the horizontal axis. The opposite extreme would be for the individual to sell all his apples and spend the proceeds on other things. If the price of apples is denoted by p_A per kilogram, the revenue obtainable from selling S kilograms

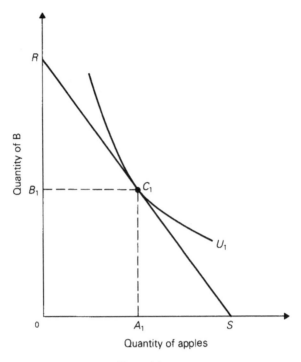

Figure 4.1

would be $S \times p_A$. The point R in Figure 4.1, where the budget line cuts the vertical axis, then indicates the quantity of some other good B that could be bought with the revenue, or, as in previous cases, the revenue itself in terms of money or some other numeraire good. If the quantity of B is measured on the vertical axis,

$$R = S \times p_A/p_B.$$

More generally, points on the budget line have to satisfy the condition that the consumer's expenditure on B is equal to the revenue obtained from the sale of A. In algebraic terms they thus reflect the condition

$$p_B q_B = p_A(S - q_A), \qquad (4.1)$$

where S is the initial stock of A at the consumer's disposal, and q_A and q_B are the quantities of A and B *consumed* as before. Condition (4.1) is therefore the budget line equation in this case, and it can be rearranged to give

$$q_B = -p_A/p_B \cdot q_A + S \cdot \frac{p_A}{p_B}. \qquad (4.1a)$$

46

From this expression we can confirm that, when $q_A = 0$, $q_B = S \cdot p_A/p_B$ and deduce that the slope of the budget line is $-p_A/p_B$, exactly as in the case where the consumer is a buyer of both goods. This should not be unexpected because, although the individual does not have to pay a cash price for his apples, the real cost to him of consuming them is still p_A per unit as that is the potential income he forgoes by consuming a unit of A rather than selling it.

With this budget line, the optimum choice can be determined in the usual way where the budget line is tangential to an indifference curve, and is thus again where

$$MRS_{AB} = p_A/p_B.$$

Note that, once again, point C_1 represents the bundle of goods that the individual represented in the diagram would like to consume and thus reflects the consumer's demand for the goods. But point C_1 also determines what the individual is willing to supply to the market, since with S kilograms of apples available and A_1 required for his own use, the quantity available to the market is

$$S - A_1 = A_1 S.$$

We can now proceed to examine the effects on the optimal choice position C_1 of possible movements of the budget line, just as in the previous chapter. The equivalent to the income change considered there is an increase (or decrease) in the original stock of apples. The effects of such a change can be analysed in the same way as income changes on pages 30–2 above, but unless our individual is in a position to benefit from a (literal) windfall gain from neighbouring orchards, that kind of change may not be all that likely. We will therefore concentrate on the effects of a change in the price of apples.

If the price of apples were to increase, the budget line would become steeper but with one important change from the case considered on pages 32–6 above. In that case, where the individual was just a buyer, the change in the price of A caused the budget line to rotate about its point of interception with the vertical axis, which itself remained unaffected by the change. In the present case, where the individual is a seller, the fixed point is the budget line's point of intersection with the horizontal axis, S, reflecting his initial stock of apples. Therefore, when the price of apples changes, the budget line rotates about S. Hence in Figure 4.2 an increase in their price changes the budget line from SR_1 to SR_2, giving a new preferred bundle of goods on the latter. However, the analysis of the change in terms of income and substitution effects can proceed exactly as before.

As in previous cases, we can isolate the substitution effect by considering what will happen if we adjust the individual's income to restore his original level of utility by, for example, confiscating some of his original stock of apples. In Figure 4.2 that will push the budget line back to the dashed line

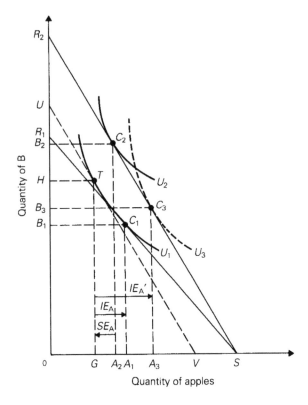

Figure 4.2

UV, and in that situation the individual's optimum choice is at T, involving fewer apples and more B than at C_1. As far as the individual's use of apples is concerned, *the substitution effect is again negative* and reduces the consumption of the good whose price has risen. But in this case it is not so much the price the consumer has to pay that has risen but the potential revenue from the sale of apples that he forgoes by consuming them himself.

Whilst the substitution effect is exactly as before, the income effect is different basically because our individual is better off rather than worse off, following the rise in the price of apples, and the income effect thus reflects the consumer's response to an outward shift in his budget line (from UV to SR_2 in Figure 4.2) rather than to an inward shift. If, therefore, an apple is a normal good, the income effect will be positive and tend to increase the consumption of apples, whilst if apples are inferior the opposite is true. Only when the good sold is an inferior good, therefore, does the income effect reinforce the substitution effect and produce a definite reduction in the quantity of the good consumed. In the more normal case, the income effect operates in the *opposite* direction to the substitution effect, producing another situation in which we cannot make any definite prediction about the effect of the price change. We can only say that, if the income effect outweighs the substitution effect, the individual's use of apples increases whilst in the opposite case it decreases. Moreover, we cannot in this case argue that the first of these results is unlikely because the income effect can be expected to be small. When that argument was used in Chapter 3 it was justified on the grounds that the proportion of a consumer's income spent on most individual goods is in fact small. In the present case, however, where the sale of apples could be a major source of income for our individual, any income effects could be quite large, and we have to accept that the effect of a change in price of a good on the seller's consumption of it is basically unpredictable.

This is reflected in Figure 4.2, where both possible outcomes are shown. If the consumer's preferences are such that the indifference curve tangential to SR_2 is the continuous curve U_2, the new preferred position at C_2 involves a smaller quantity of apples than at C_1, and it thus reflects a situation in which the substitution effect of the price change on the consumer's demand for apples exceeds the income effect. The opposite case arises when the indifference curve tangential to SR_2 is the dashed curve U_3.

In this analysis of price changes we have so far focused on the bundles of goods that our individual wishes to consume, but as already suggested, we can also deduce from the same diagram what the individual is willing to supply at any price. In Figure 4.2 we have confined ourselves to the analysis of the effects of a single price change, but clearly, by considering further variations of prices, we could get a more general indication of how the desired consumption bundle varies with price by drawing in the relevant price expansion path. In Figure 4.3a, the curve PEP reflects the case where the substitution effect dominates, whilst the curve PEP' reflects the opposite case where the income effect dominates, at least within the region of the initial price reflected in the budget line SR.

In that initial situation, as has already been indicated, the individual is willing to supply to the market that part of his original stock that he does not wish to consume. In the case illustrated this is SA_1 and it can be seen that, in the case where the individual's price expansion path is PEP, more apples will be released to the market as the price of apples rises, suggesting a normal upward-sloping supply curve like S in Figure 4.3b (where OQ_A is equal to SA_1). The price expansion path PEP' is, however, reflected in a backward-bending supply curve like S'. This does not necessarily imply that there will also be a backward-bending market supply curve, since one individual's backward-bending curve might be more than counterbalanced through other individuals being willing to supply more as price increases, but it does point to that as a possible eventuality. Moreover, our analysis indicates that it is likely to be less of a theoretical curiosity than the Giffen good and to have more empirical relevance.

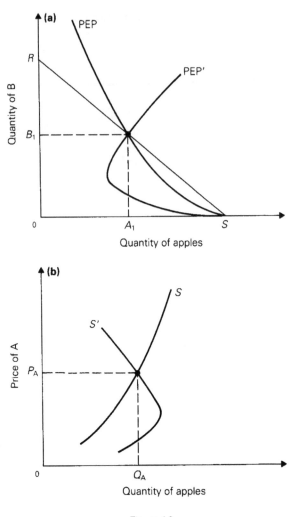

Figure 4.3

Labour supplies

Whilst the number of people selling commodities may not be all that great in relation to the total population, the relevance of the analysis is much wider because it can be applied without significant amendment (other than relabelling the axes in the diagrams) to the analysis of the supply of labour services. In this case the relevant initial stock is time. Individuals have a fixed number of hours available, which they can use for either work or leisure. But if they use it for work they earn income and, generally speaking, the longer they work the more income they earn. The choice, then, is essentially between income, yielding purchasing power over goods, and leisure, but in other

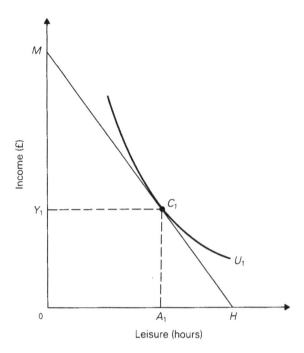

Figure 4.4

respects the choice is exactly the same as in the previous case, as should be apparent from Figure 4.4.

In the diagram, leisure is measured on the horizontal axis, and H represents the maximum hours available in the relevant period, which may be a week or a month. Income, representing purchasing power, is measured on the vertical axis, and M is the income that the individual can enjoy if he works all the available hours. Then, if w is the wage rate per hour, which to simplify we assume to be constant irrespective of the number of hours worked, and if the individual has no income other than from work,

$$M = w \times H,$$

suggesting that the income–leisure choices open to the individual are those on the budget line HM. In fact, points on HM satisfy the condition that

$$y = wh_w$$

where y is income and h_w the number of hours worked. But if h_s is the number of hours of leisure the consumer enjoys, then by definition

$$h_w + h_s = H,$$

and hence

$$y = w(H - h_s). \qquad (4.2)$$

This, therefore, is the equation of the budget line and it has a slope of $-w$, which is the opportunity cost of a unit of leisure in terms of the earnings forgone. Given the choices on HM and the preferences of the individual reflected in a set of indifference curves, of which U_1 in the diagram is one, the individual's optimum position involves him dividing up the available time between A_1 hours of leisure and HA_1 hours of work, giving him an income of Y_1.

In practice, the choice between income and leisure is affected by overtime payments, tax liabilities and the like. Moreover, the freedom of individuals to choose their hours of work in a particular job may also be limited by institutional arrangements, but in the longer run, at least in a reasonably fully employed economy, they may be able to move towards the income–leisure combination most suited to their tastes, either by negotiation or, if necessary, by changing jobs. The reader is invited to explore the effects of such factors by working through Exercise 4.2 at the end of this chapter.

Returning to the case illustrated in Figure 4.4, once the individual's preferred position has been reached, an increase in the wage rate has exactly the same effect on the budget line as an increase in the price of apples discussed in the previous section. The analysis of its effects is identical and therefore need not be repeated in detail except to note that we are again in a situation in which, as long as leisure is a normal good (and the extent to which communities have in the past tended to take more leisure with increased prosperity suggests that it is reasonable to assume that leisure *is* a normal good), income and substitution effects on the demand for leisure operate in opposite directions with an unpredictable outcome.

However, it is perhaps worth considering in a little more detail what might determine the ultimate direction of change. Essentially, of course, it is a matter for individual preferences, but it should be evident that the income effect on the demand for leisure is more likely to dominate the substitution effect when the individual concerned has a strong preference at the margin for leisure as opposed to income. Such a preference may be due to the attractiveness of leisure-time occupations, but a more important influence might well be the disutility associated with work. It might be the case, therefore, that the individuals in jobs that are particularly arduous or tedious, where their working conditions are unpleasant, or where they are required to work unsocial hours are those who would show a strong preference for leisure, at least once earnings had reached a reasonable sort of level, to the extent that they would have a backward-sloping supply curve.

All this is relevant to the question of whether high taxes discourage effort and whether a reduction in tax rates would encourage people to work longer hours. In the simple case of a proportional income tax, a reduction in the tax rate has the same effect on the individual's budget line as an increase in the wage rate. Our analysis therefore suggests a substitution effect reducing the

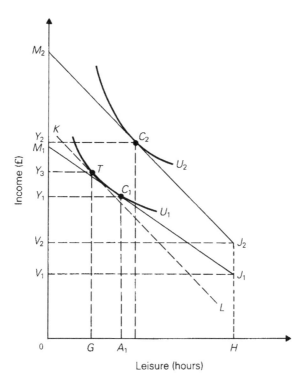

Labour supplies

Figure 4.5

demand for leisure, and an income effect working in the opposite direction. Moreover, this income effect is greater, the more non-labour income the individual receives. The effect of non-labour income on the situation depicted in Figure 4.4 is simply to displace the budget line vertically, and Figure 4.5 illustrates the case where an individual has a net-of-tax non-labour income of V_1, so that his budget line effectively starts at J_1 rather than at H (since no leisure has to be given up to obtain the initial block of income). This gives him the choice of income–leisure combinations along J_1M_1, the slope of which reflects the initial net-of-tax wage rate. If the tax rate applying to all sources of income is now reduced, his budget line becomes steeper, but it is also pushed upwards because the tax reduction gives him more non-labour income than before (V_2 in the diagram), suggesting a new budget line of J_2M_2. The substitution effect can be isolated in the usual way and can be seen to reduce the leisure required from A_1 to G, but the compensating variation in income required to isolate the substitution effect is increased by the need to compensate for the increase in non-labour income of V_1V_2 as well as for the benefits from the change in the tax rate on labour income. The real income change underlying the income effect is thus also greater, and there is accordingly an extra income effect on the demand for leisure; and the greater

53

the individual's non-labour income, the greater this effect might be. In fact, the analysis appears to suggest that tax rate reductions would be more likely to lead to increased willingness to work, the more the income effect can be suppressed.[1]

The supply of savings and intertemporal choice

Apart from labour, the other main 'good' that ordinary individuals and households may be in a position to sell is the use of financial resources. When individuals put money in bank or building society accounts, or invest in shares or other securities, they are making funds available for use by financial institutions in return for which they receive interest or dividend payments. Individuals can only do this if they save some of their current income rather than spend it all, as was assumed in the previous analysis. However, by saving they are able to build up a stock of assets that can be used to finance future purchases. Decisions to save rather than to spend on goods for immediate consumption therefore involve some assessment of the expected utility from the use of goods in the future as compared to the present. Similar consider-ations underlie the decisions of other individuals to spend more than their current income in the present, and to borrow money in order to finance the deficit. The analysis of savings decisions therefore opens up the whole question of intertemporal choice and introduces an extra dimension into our discussion, although in terms of its basic essentials the analysis of inter-temporal choice is no different from the analysis of the other choice situations considered in this chapter.

If we limit ourselves initially to two periods, namely this year and next year, we can think of an individual receiving income payments in each year and deciding how to allocate his expenditure on consumption goods between the two years. Figure 4.6 thus depicts a situation in which an individual expects an income of Y_0 this year and Y_1 next year, a combination represented by point M. Since the individual can, if he wishes, match his expenditure in each year exactly to his income, M must be one point on his budget line. However, if he can borrow or lend at some rate of interest r, his choices are considerably expanded. At one extreme he can spend nothing at all this year, giving him a sum to spend next year, including interest on his savings, of

$$Y_0 + rY_0 + Y_1 = Y_0(1 + r) + Y_1,$$

and this is represented by point N_1 in the diagram.[2] At the other extreme he might plan to spend as much as he can this year and nothing next year. His expenditure this year can then be expressed as

$$Y_0 + x,$$

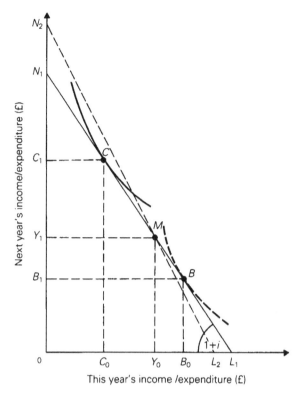

Figure 4.6

where x is the maximum amount he can borrow on the strength of his expected future earnings. That represents the maximum sum that he could repay, with interest charges added, out of his next year's income. Hence, assuming he can also borrow at the rate of interest r,[3]

$$x(1 + r) = Y_1 \text{ and } x = Y_1/(1 + r)$$

and his total expenditure this year cannot exceed

$$Y_0 + Y_1/(1 + r),$$

which is represented by point L_1 in the diagram.

The budget line thus joins N_1ML_1. Moreover the slope of the budget line is $-(1 + r)$, because $(1 + r)$ is the cost of present consumption in terms of forgone future consumption.[4] Thus, if the rate of interest is 5 per cent, every £1 spent this year reduces potential expenditure on consumption next year by £1.05, either because current savings are reduced or because borrowings have to be repaid.

Given the budget line N_1L_1, an individual's preferred position can be indicated in the usual way by a point of tangency between the budget line and an indifference curve, and typically there will be some people like the individual at C who will want to spend less than his current earnings, and some like the individual at B who prefers to spend more. It should be recognized, however, that this is not solely a question of tastes, as borrowing and saving are the ways in which most individuals match their pattern of lifetime spending to their pattern of lifetime earnings.

Once the initial position has been established, the effects of changes in incomes or in the interest rate can be analysed exactly as in the previous sections, except that, if the interest rate changes, the budget line rotates about point M in the diagram, because with no saving or borrowing the combination of present and future consumption at M must still be available. The dashed line N_2L_2 thus indicates the budget line arising with a higher rate of interest than in the initial situation. From the position of that line it should be clear that any one starting off from a position between M and L_1 on the old budget line, and thus borrowing this year, is faced with the same sort of change as the buyers of good A above, and so the analysis of that case applies here without modification. However, individuals initially between M and N_1, spending less than their income this year, are in a similar position to the sellers of apples and suppliers of labour considered in the preceding sections of this chapter, and are therefore subject to the same conflicting income and substitution effects on their current level of consumption.

Nevertheless, one additional insight does emerge from the above discussion, which is that it is not so much income that constrains the individual's choice but wealth. An individual's wealth is the value of the assets that he has at his disposal, which may include physical assets, such as buildings and machinery, financial assets including holdings of securities, bank balances and the like, as well as the value of the labour services he can offer, sometimes called his **human capital**. But the value of all of these assets is determined by the consumption opportunities they confer upon their owner. Thus so far as the individual in Figure 4.6 is concerned, he has assets yielding income of Y_0 this year and Y_1 next year, which give him the possibility of consuming L_1 ($= Y_0 + Y_1/1 + r$) this year. L_1 is therefore a measure of his current wealth. If this is denoted by W,

$$W = Y_0 + \frac{Y_1}{1 + r}.$$

This expression is also referred to as the present value of the individual's income stream, since it represents the sum of money that the individual needs to have in the present to give him the same consumption opportunities as his two income payments. Moreover, this concept generalizes to any number of periods. This can be seen by considering the potential effect on the individual's current expenditure of income of Y_2 in year 2. This would allow him

56

to borrow more in year 0 subject to being able to repay the sum involved with two years' interest added in year 2. The maximum additional sum he could borrow on that basis would be Z, such that

$$Z(1 + r) + Z(1 + r)r = Y_2,$$

since $Z(1 + r)$ would be the debt outstanding after 1 year and $Z(1 + r)r$ would be the interest accruing on that debt in the second year. But since, by simple algebra,

$$Z(1 + r) + Z(1 + r)r = Z(1 + r)^2$$

$$Z = \frac{Y_2}{(1 + r)^2},$$

and overall

$$W = Y_0 + \frac{Y_1}{(1 + r)} + \frac{Y_2}{(1 + r)^2}.$$

Correspondingly, with incomes in years 0 to n of $Y_0, Y_1, \ldots, Y_n$,

$$W = Y_0 + \frac{Y_1}{(1 + r)} + \frac{Y_2}{(1 + r)^2} + \ldots + \ldots \frac{Y_n}{(1 + r)^n}.$$

In this context the consumer's choice problem is to plan his consumption over time in order to maximize his utility subject to the constraint that the present value of his consumption does not exceed his wealth. One problem here is, of course, that there may be some uncertainty attached to future income, but that is one of the problems that will be looked at in Chapter 7 below.

Concluding remarks

In this chapter we have seen how the basic approach to the analysis of consumer choices, and the effects on those choices of income and price changes, developed in Chapters 2 and 3, can be applied to situations in which the individual is a seller. That has taken us into an analysis of labour supply and savings decisions and we have seen how income and substitution effects operate in these situations.

For the purposes of exposition, choices between goods, income–leisure choices and present–future spending choices have been treated separately, but it will be readily appreciated that they are, in practice, all interconnected.

For example, how much income is available to allocate between present and future consumption and between goods depends on how much time is spent working. A change in the wage rate therefore can affect choices in all these areas. This interdependence can be dealt with theoretically in the context of a multi-period model in which the consumer is characterized as maximizing his utility, specified as a function of the amount he consumes of each individual product in each period of his life, subject to the value of his lifetime expenditure being constrained by his wealth. Although doubts may be raised about the realism of such a model of the consumer's decision-making process, the more partial approach we have used in this text is, as we have seen, capable of producing quite useful insights into the market behaviour of individuals. Moreover there are further implications of the analysis that have yet to be explored.

Appendix: The Slutsky equation

If the price of good j changes by Δp_j, the overall effect on the quantity demanded of good i (Δq_i) can be expressed as follows

$$\Delta q_i = \Delta q_i^s + \Delta q_i^y \tag{4.A1}$$

where Δq_i^s and Δq_i^y are the components of the total change arising from the income and substitution effects respectively. Dividing both side by Δp_j (and we are here including the case where $i = j$ as well as those where $i \neq j$), we get a corresponding expression for the rate of change of q_i with respect to p_j which is

$$\frac{\Delta q_i}{\Delta p_j} = \frac{\Delta q_i^s}{\Delta p_j} + \frac{\Delta q_i^y}{\Delta p_j} . \tag{4.A2}$$

However, when the price of goods rises by Δp_j, the extra cost to the consumer of maintaining his original purchases is approximately $q_j \Delta p_j$.

The effect of this on good i can be expressed as

$$- q_j \Delta p_j \cdot \frac{\Delta q_i}{\Delta y} ,$$

where $\Delta q_i / \Delta y$ is the rate at which the consumer increases his use of good i per unit increase in income.

Substituting in equation (4.A2) we get

$$\frac{\Delta q_i}{\Delta p_j} = \frac{\Delta q_i^s}{\Delta p_j} - q_j \cdot \frac{\Delta q_i}{\Delta y} . \tag{4.A3}$$

This expression can be converted to elasticity form by multiplying both sides by p_j / q_i to give

$$\frac{p_j}{q_i} \cdot \frac{\Delta q_i}{\Delta p_j} = \frac{p_j}{q_i} \cdot \frac{\Delta q_i^s}{\Delta p_j} - \frac{p_j}{q_i} \cdot q_j \frac{\Delta q_i}{\Delta y} .$$

But since

$$\eta_i = \frac{\Delta q_i}{\Delta y} \cdot \frac{y}{q_i},$$

$$\frac{\Delta q_i}{\Delta y} = \eta_i \cdot \frac{q_i}{y},$$

and

$$\in_{ij} = \in_{ij}{}^* - \frac{p_i q_i}{y} \cdot \eta_i = \in_{ij}{}^* - k_i \cdot \eta_i.$$

Notes

1   In practice, of course, income taxes are often levied at different rates for different levels of income. Some of the implications of that can be explored by working through Exercise 4.2 at the end of this chapter.

2   Note that in this formulation r must be expressed in fractional terms. Hence with a 5% rate of interest $r = 0.05$ because the interest received on Y_0 after 1 year at that rate of interest is $0.05 Y$.

3   This assumes borrowing and lending rates are the same. In practice, borrowers are charged higher rates of interest than lenders receive, although the two rates are related. It is left to the reader to work out how that affects the analysis. See Exercise 4.4.

4   This can be derived algebraically from the condition that expenditure in year 1 cannot exceed income in year 1 plus savings plus interest from year 0 (or minus borrowing plus interest). Hence, if Y_0 and Y_1 are the relevant incomes and X_0 and X_1 the relevant expenditure, the equation of the budget line is

$$X_1 \leq Y_1 + (Y_0 - X_0)(1 - r)$$

where $Y_0 - X_0 > 0$ if the individual saves in year 0 and < 0 if he borrows, which with given Y_0 and Y_1 can be represented by a straight line of slope $-(1 + r)$ with an intercept on the vertical axis of Y_1, as in Figure 4.6.

Exercises

4.1   A nomadic tribe in North Lapland spends its time hunting reindeer. Some of the reindeer meat is kept for consumption by the tribe, but the rest is traded in local markets for other goods. It is observed that when the price of reindeer meat rises the amount the tribe is willing to supply to the market declines. Does this mean that reindeer meat is an inferior good?

4.2   An individual who can freely vary his hours of work can earn £5 an hour but has no other sources of income. The first £50 he earns each week is tax free. On the next £100 he pays a 25% income tax and on any earnings over £150 per week he pays 40% tax. In this situation he chooses to work for 40 hours. Examine the effects on the individual's choice of the replacement of this tax structure by a simple proportional tax applying to all income set at a rate to yield the same revenue if the individual continued to work for 40 hours. Does your answer shed any light on the advantages or disadvantages of a progressive income tax?

4.3 The standard analysis of income–leisure choices assumes that individuals can vary their hours of work. What modifications to it are required to deal with a situation in which individuals are unable to vary their hours of work?

What conclusions can be drawn about the value of leisure-time:

(a)   to an individual who would prefer to work less than he has to, and
(b)   to an individual who would prefer to work more?

4.4 An individual expects to receive £1000 in income this year and £1200 next. He can borrow or lend this year at a rate of interest of 10%, but it can be assumed that all debts will be paid off next year. Analyse the effects of an increase in the rate of interest if he was:

(a)   a borrower this year, and
(b)   a lender.

CHAPTER FIVE
THE MEASUREMENT OF INDIVIDUAL WELFARE CHANGES

Introduction

The emphasis of the analysis of the previous chapter was primarily on the individual's response to changes in price and income variables. In this chapter we will be more concerned with the effects of such changes on the individual's utility. Whilst the discussion is fairly technical in places, it does have practical implications, because from a policy viewpoint it is often desirable to know whether an individual is better or worse off as a result of any changes that might be contemplated and, when comparing different changes, by how much. If utility was something that could be measured in well-defined cardinal units, all this would create no serious problems. In the absence of such units, however, we are driven to seek indirect measures of utility changes. In this chapter we consider some that have been suggested on the basis of the standard analysis of consumer's choice developed in previous chapters.

All those measures to be considered attempt to measure utility changes in monetary terms. Again, this is useful from a policy viewpoint because if the expected utility gains from a policy decision, such as whether or not to build a Channel tunnel or to leave the Common Market, can be expressed as monetary benefits they can more easily be compared with the costs, which are also typically expressed in monetary terms. Nevertheless, the main interest of policy-makers is, in practice, likely to be in aggregate gains and losses, whilst in this chapter the main concern is with measuring the gains and losses accruing to individuals. The problems involved in aggregating individual gains are among the concerns of welfare economics, which constitutes the final section of this book. However, it is necessary to establish how individual gains and losses can be measured before contemplating the problems of aggregation.

Compensating and equivalent variations

One obvious measure of the extent to which an individual is better or worse off as a result of some change, which is suggested by the discussion on page 34 above, is the **compensating variation**. It will be recalled from that discussion that the compensating variation is the change in income required, following a price change or set of price changes, to leave the individual with the same level of utility as he had before the change. Thus, in the case illustrated in Figure 5.1, where M_1N_1 is the budget line and C_1 represents the preferred bundle of goods in some initial situation, while M_2N_2 is the budget line and C_2 the chosen bundle in some subsequent situation, the compensating variation is the change in the individual's income necessary to move his budget line to the position indicated by the dashed line JK, which would just enable him to buy the bundle of goods at D_1 yielding the same utility as the initial chosen bundle. It will be noted that this compensating variation can be measured in terms of the quantities of either good in the diagram (i.e. as N_2K of good A or M_2J of good B), or in terms of a numeraire good, or in money terms, in which case it would be $N_2K/p_A = M_2J/p_B$ where p_A and p_B are the prices of A and B respectively. However, if the vertical axis of the diagram is used to measure expenditure on goods other than A in money terms, the monetary value of the compensating variation is denoted simply by M_2J. Given that our primary interest at present is in monetary measures of utility change, the latter will be the approach adopted in the remainder of this chapter.

It should also be recognized that the compensating variation concept can be applied to more than simple price adjustments. If, from the situation in which the budget line is M_1N_1, good A is suddenly withdrawn from the market, the only choice open to consumers is to spend OM_1 on other goods. This would involve less utility than before, but in the situation depicted in the diagram the individual can regain his previous level of utility if he is given extra income of M_1H. M_1H is, therefore, the compensating variation associated with the loss of the opportunity to buy A at the price reflected in the initial budget line, and thus provides a measure of the benefits to the individual of being able to buy A at that price. This suggests that the compensating variation may have some role to play in assessing the benefits to consumers of particular facilities. For example, if A is the number of railway or bus journeys between two centres, then M_1H, being the sum the consumer needs to compensate him for not being able to use the service, can be used as a measure of the loss he suffers if the service is withdrawn. Estimates of users' compensating variations can, therefore, be of potential usefulness to government agencies in deciding whether to allow the service to be withdrawn, or whether to pay a subsidy to allow it to continue (an issue that will be discussed more fully in Chapter 22).

However, one problem with this whole approach is that it does not provide the only possible measure of the individual's utility change. Instead of

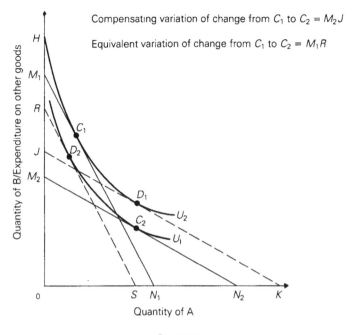

Figure 5.1

considering what sum of money would compensate for some change or the loss of some facility, we can estimate the adjustment to the consumer's income that is equivalent, in terms of its effect on the consumer's utility, to the change. Thus, in Figure 5.1, the consumer suffers the same loss of utility as in the move from C_1 to C_2 if relative prices remain unchanged and his income is reduced by M_1R, leaving him on the dashed budget line RS, touching the indifference curve U_1 at D_2. M_1R is then termed the **equivalent variation** in income, as it is the income change yielding the same utility change as the original price changes.

In general, the equivalent variation need not be the same as the compensating variation. The relationship between them is explored more fully below, but one point that should be apparent from Figure 5.1 is that the equivalent variation of the change that moves the consumer from C_1 to C_2 is the compensating variation of the opposite change. If the consumer is originally at C_2, with budget line M_2N_2, and his budget line is subsequently moved to M_1N_1 with C_1 his preferred bundle of goods, the compensating variation of that change representing the reduction in his income necessary to reduce his utility to the level enjoyed at C_2 is M_1R and the corresponding equivalent variation is M_2J.

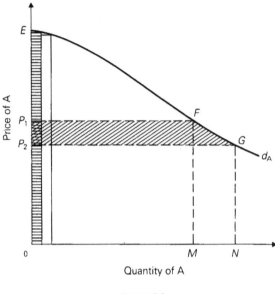

Individual welfare changes

Figure 5.2

Consumer's surplus

An alternative approach to the measurement of welfare change is through what may be the more familiar concept of consumer's surplus. In the form popularized by Alfred Marshall (1920, pp. 124–33) this can be measured on a diagram such as Figure 5.2 as the area between the demand curve and the horizontal line drawn at the prevailing price level. Thus when the price is P_1, it is measured by the area P_1EF, which represents the difference between what the consumer is willing to pay for M units of A, represented by the area $OEFM$, and the amount that he actually has to pay, represented by OP_1FM. Similarly, at the lower price of P_2 the consumer's surplus is P_2EG, and from that we can deduce that the change in consumer's surplus that is a measure of the extent to which the individual is better off as a result of the price change is P_2P_1FG.

Consumer's surplus and compensating variations

One obvious problem arising when discussing the relationship between the change in consumer's surplus and the measures considered earlier is that the measure of consumer's surplus has been defined in terms of an area under a demand curve, whilst compensating and equivalent variations were defined as distances in an indifference curve diagram.

Fortunately, however, the latter can also be expressed as areas under a

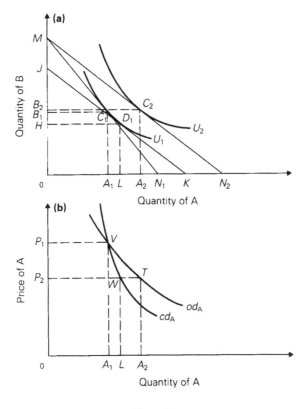

Figure 5.3

demand curve where the relevant demand curves are **compensated demand curves** rather than the conventional or, as they are usually referred to in this context, **ordinary demand curves**. The distinction between the two can be explained with the help of Figure 5.3.

Figure 5.3a is the standard indifference curve diagram showing the effect of a fall in the price of good A, with MN_1 the initial budget line and MN_2 that prevailing after the price change as a result of which the consumer moves from point C_1 to C_2, thereby increasing his purchases of A from A_1 to A_2. The actual relationship between price and the amount of A demanded is traced in Figure 5.3b by the curve od_A, which is the ordinary demand curve on which points V and T correspond to points C_1 and C_2 in the upper diagram. The compensated demand curve cd_A also traces out a relationship between the price of A and the amount demanded, but subject to the condition that the consumer is compensated, by adjustments to his income, for any changes in his utility. In the case illustrated, this requires his income to be reduced by MJ (the compensating variation for the price change), which pushes the consumer's budget line back to JK such that he can only just attain his original level of utility. In these circumstances his consumption of A at the lower price is L, rather than A_1, suggesting that the compensated demand curve is cd_A in Figure 5.3b. How the compensating variation relates to the compensated demand curve can also be investigated with the help of this diagram.

In the same sense that the ordinary demand curve can be interpreted as showing the price an individual is prepared to pay for specific units of a commodity, the compensating variation can be interpreted as showing the maximum amount he can pay without reducing his utility. Moreover, just as the total amount the individual is willing to pay for a specific increase in his use of a commodity can be represented by the area under the relevant part of the demand curve, the maximum amount he can pay without reducing his utility can be represented by the area under the relevant part of his *compensated* demand curve. Hence the total sum of money that the individual could give up without affecting his utility level, in the situation represented in Figure 5.3b as his use of A increases from A_1 to L, is indicated by the area under his compensated demand curve over that quantity range, which is A_1VWL. In Figure 5.3a, however, the sum of money given up in the movement down indifference curve U_1 from C_1 to D_1, which is the equivalent to moving down cd_A in Figure 5.3b from V to W, is B_1H. Hence B_1H in Figure 5.3a represents the same sum of money as the area A_1VWL in Figure 5.3b.

However, B_1H is not the compensating variation; that, in Figure 5.3a is MJ, but the connection between B_1H and MJ can be traced from the fact that in Figure 5.3a along the vertical axis

$$MJ + JB_1 + B_1H \equiv MH \equiv MB_1 + B_1H.$$

Hence

$$MJ \equiv MH - JB_1 - B_1H$$
$$\equiv (MB_1 + B_1H) - (JB_1 + B_1H)$$
$$\equiv MB_1 + B_1H - JH. \tag{5.1}$$

Now MB_1 is the consumer's expenditure on A when he is at C_1 since it is his total income, OM, less his expenditure on other goods, OB_1. The equivalent area in Figure 5.3b is the rectangle OP_1VA_1. Similarly, JH is the consumer's expenditure on A (out of an income of OJ) if he is at D_1, which corresponds to the rectangle OP_2WL in Figure 5.3b. Substituting in expression (5.1) for these suggests that, in terms of Figure 5.3b, the compensating variation of the price change is

$$OP_1VA_1 + A_1VWL - OP_2WL = P_2P_1VW,$$

which compares with the change in consumer's surplus of P_2P_1VT in the same diagram. The key relationships in this argument are summarized in Table 5.1.

Table 5.1 The components of the compensating variation

		Diagrammatic representation	
		Fig. 5.3(a)	Fig. 5.4(b)
(i)	Expenditure on A with price P_1 and income OM	MB_1	OP_1VA_1
(ii)	Expenditure on A with price P_2 and income OJ	JH	OP_2WL
(iii)	Sum of money given up in move from C_1 to D_1 along U_1 which is compensated for by A, L of A	B, H	A_1VWL
(v)	Compensating variation $[= (i) + (iii) - (ii)]$	MJ	P_2P_1VW

In Figure 5.3a, commodity A is a normal good, and to avoid undue complications we have concentrated on that case in our present discussion. (Exercise 5.1 below invites the reader to work out for him/herself how the analysis is affected if A is an inferior good.) However, there is one further problem to be noted, which arises because the compensated demand curve cd_A is not unique. In fact, there is a compensated demand curve associated with each possible level of utility. One such demand curve can, therefore, be drawn if the consumer is kept on indifference curve U_2. This is shown as the curve cd_B in Figure 5.4, which is essentially a reproduction of Figure 5.3b with certain additions.

This second compensated demand curve passes through T because when the price of A is P_2, A_2 of A needs to be purchased to put the consumer at C_2 in Figure 5.3a on indifference curve U_2, but again it is steeper than the ordinary demand curve because, in the case illustrated, a compensated price increase has a smaller effect on demand than an uncompensated price increase. Moreover, using cd_B, we may conclude that the compensating variation for an increase in the price of A from P_2 to P_1 is P_2P_1ST. Further, since it will be recalled that the compensating variation of a price increase is equal to the equivalent variation of a price fall, and vice versa, we may conclude that P_2P_1ST is the equivalent variation of our original reduction in price, representing the sum of money the consumer would accept in compensation for forgoing the price reduction. Moreover, it should be clear from the diagram that the equivalent variation is greater than the change in consumer's surplus, which in turn is greater than the compensating variation, although in the cases of price increases these relationships are reversed.

One further comment can be made on the relationship between these measures of utility change. The observant reader may already have recognized that the movement down the compensated demand curve cd_A in Figure 5.4 (and Figure 5.3b) resulting from the fall in price of A from P_1 to P_2 is the substitution effect of the price change. This means that the horizontal

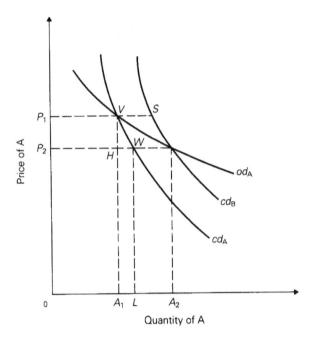

Figure 5.4

distance between the compensated demand curve cd_A at W and the ordinary demand curve must be the income effect of the price change. Similarly, the horizontal gap between the ordinary demand curve at V and the compensated demand curve cd_B is the income effect of the opposite price change. If, therefore, income effects are small, for example because purchases of commodity A account for a small proportion of the consumer's budget (which is likely to be the case with most goods), the divergence between the ordinary demand curve and the compensated demand curves is small and hence so are the differences between the compensating and equivalent variations and consumer's surplus. Indeed, if the income effects are zero, both compensated demand curves in Figure 5.4 coincide with the ordinary demand curve and all three measures of utility change are the same. In most circumstances, therefore, the change in consumer's surplus can be regarded as an acceptable approximation to its corresponding compensating or equivalent variation,[1] and this is a conclusion we can make use of in some of our later discussions.

Cost differences

One problem with all of the measures of utility that we have discussed so far is that they require information about the demand functions of *individuals*,

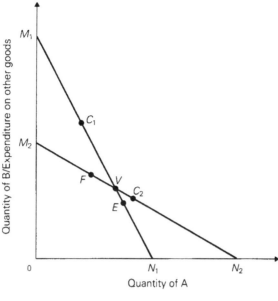

Figure 5.5

which may be difficult to obtain.[2] However, it may be possible to obtain some alternative indication of the effects of changes on the individual on the basis of more limited information. This can be seen with the help of Figure 5.5, in which M_1N_1 and M_2N_2 are the budget lines faced by a consumer in two different situations, exactly as in Figure 5.1 above, and C_1 and C_2 indicate the consumer's preferred bundle of goods in each situation. Given the information in Figure 5.1, it is not at all clear whether the individual is in a better position at C_2 than at C_1, because although it is possible to draw a downward-sloping convex indifference curve through C_1 to pass below C_2 it is also possible to draw one like the curve U_2 in Figure 5.1, which passes above it.

In some cases, however, the choices actually made allow us to deduce whether the consumer moves to a better or worse position, even when the budget lines cross. Suppose, for example, that with the budget line M_2N_2 the bundle of goods at F rather than that at C_2 is chosen as the preferred bundle. Since F lies below M_1N_1, it represents a bundle of goods that could have been chosen when the budget line was M_1N_1. The fact that it was rejected in favour of C_1 when the latter was available must imply, assuming rational behaviour on the part of the consumer, that the bundle of goods at C_1 is preferred to that at F and thus yields more utility. Similar considerations would apply to any other point on the M_2V segment of M_2N_2 (including V) because all the bundles of goods on that segment could have been chosen, but were rejected, by the consumer in the initial situation. Moreover, the fact that they could have been chosen with the consumer's initial level of income must imply that at the initial set of prices they would have cost in total no more than the bundle of goods at C_1.[3] We may therefore conclude that if, in the second situation, the consumer chooses a bundle of goods that would have cost, at the initial prices, the same or less than the bundle of goods actually purchased in the initial situation, the consumer would definitely have moved to a lower indifference curve and would therefore be worse off.

In more formal terms we can state that a sufficient condition for a reduction in the consumer's utility is

$$p^1_A q^2_A + p^1_B q^2_B \leq p^1_A q^1_A + p^1_B q^1_B,$$

where the superscripts attached to the variables indicate the relevant prices and quantities of the two goods in the first and second situations respectively. Since the same reasoning can be applied when the consumer buys more than two goods, we can write, as a general condition for a reduction in the consumer's utility, using 'sigma' notation as a shorthand for summation.[4]

$$\Sigma p^1 q^2 \leq \Sigma p^1 q^1. \tag{5.2}$$

We can derive a similar condition for an improvement in the consumer's position. If, in the initial situation with the budget line $M_1 N_1$, the consumer had chosen the bundle of goods at E rather than that at C_1, and moved to C_2 when the budget line changed to $M_2 N_2$, we could deduce that this would have improved his position because the bundle of goods at E was still available in the new situation but was rejected in favour of that at C_2. Similar considerations also apply to the choice of any point along VN_1 (again including V). All these points were available in the second situation because the bundles of goods they represent cost no more to buy, at the prices then prevailing, than the bundle actually chosen. Hence we may deduce that if the cost of the initial bundle of goods at the new prices does not exceed the cost of the bundle of goods actually purchased at the new prices, the consumer must have moved to a better position. In more formal terms, a sufficient condition for an improvement to the consumer's position in the two-good case can be written as

$$p^2_A q^1_A + p^2_B q^1_B \leq p^2_A q^2_A + p^2_B q^2_B,$$

and to cover the more general case we may write, again using sigma notation,

$$\Sigma p^2 q^1 \leq \Sigma p^2 q^2. \tag{5.3}$$

In general, therefore, if either of conditions (5.2) and (5.3) is satisfied, we can deduce whether the consumer is better or worse off, in the absence of any precise information about the form of his preferences. It is only when neither condition is satisfied that we cannot be sure whether the individual is better or worse off.

All this is of relevance to the ways in which changes in standards of living tend to be discussed in the course of topical discussion in the press or on television. The main source of reference for this kind of discussion tends to be the estimates in the national income accounts of the Gross National Product of an economy valued at some constant base year prices. These are taken to provide a measure of aggregate output and, by implication, income in real terms, and the estimates of aggregate output per head derived from these figures are taken to provide an indication of movements in the average standard of living in the economy. In this approach, so far as the individual is concerned, interest is centred on his change in real income as measured by (using the same notation as in expressions (5.2) and (5.3))

$$\Sigma p^1 q^2 - \Sigma p^1 q^1. \tag{5.4}$$

What this expression measures is the difference between the cost of the bundle of goods purchased in the initial situation and in the new situation, both at the initial prices. This **cost difference** is then often taken to indicate the extent to which the average individual has become either better or worse off in period 2 compared with period 1. However, whilst condition (5.2) above suggests that it is legitimate to conclude that the average person is indeed worse off if expression (5.4) is negative, it need not be the case that he is better off if (5.4) is positive, because condition (5.3) might not, in that case, be satisfied. Moreover, even if the cost difference indicates correctly whether the individual is better or worse off, as a measure of the magnitude of the change in the individual's utility it might differ substantially from the compensating and equivalent variations discussed in the preceding section.

Index numbers

In practice, however, discussion of changes in living standards is perhaps more often conducted in terms of percentage changes rather than absolute changes, and also frequently involves the use of index numbers. Two particular types of index number used in this context are the Laspeyre and Paasche quantity indexes. The Laspeyre quantity index, which we will denote as Q_L, expresses current quantities consumed valued at some base year prices as a percentage of base year quantities also valued at base year prices, whilst the Paasche quantity index (Q_P) expresses current quantities at current prices as a percentage of the initial year's quantities at current prices.[5] Using previous notation we can write

$$Q_L = \frac{\Sigma p^1 q^2}{\Sigma p^1 q^1} \times 100$$

and

$$Q_P = \frac{\Sigma p^2 q^2}{\Sigma p^2 q^1} \times 100.$$

Reference back to conditions (5.2) and (5.3) respectively then suggests that, if in period 2

$$Q_L \leqslant 100,$$

the average individual would definitely be worse off in that period, whilst if

$$Q_P \geqslant 100$$

he would be better off; if neither condition holds, no definite conclusions can be drawn one way or the other.

Alternatively, discussions about living standards are sometimes conducted in terms of price index numbers. With these, however, the same sort of ambiguities arise as with previous measures. Again, a distinction can be made between the Laspeyre price index, denoted here as P_L, which conceptually compares the cost of a bundle of goods consumed in some base year at current prices with its cost in the base year, and the Paasche price index (P_P), which compares the cost of the bundle of goods actually consumed at current prices with its cost in the base year. In more formal terms, the Laspeyre price index can be expressed as

$$P_L = \frac{\Sigma p^2 q^1}{\Sigma p^1 q^1} \times 100;$$

the UK index of retail prices is essentially of this form. The Paasche price index can similarly be expressed as

$$P_P = \frac{\Sigma p^2 q^2}{\Sigma p^1 q^2} \times 100.$$

Inferences about the standard of living are then often made on the basis of comparisons between changes in money income and changes in the price level, as measured by one of these index numbers, on the grounds that individuals are better off if incomes increase by more than prices. The extent to which such inferences are valid can again be tested using conditions (5.2) and (5.3).

Condition (5.3) suggests that a consumer is unambiguously better off if

$$\Sigma p^2 q^1 \leqslant \Sigma p^2 q^2,$$

but if we divide both sides of this expression by $\Sigma p^1 q^1$ we get

$$\frac{\Sigma p^2 q^1}{\Sigma p^1 q^1} \leq \frac{\Sigma p^2 q^2}{\Sigma p^1 q^1} . \tag{5.5}$$

Multiplying both sides by 100 gives us the Laspeyre price index on the left-hand side and an index of money income, compared with the initial period, on the right-hand side. Condition (5.5) then tells us that if in any year the Laspeyre price index is less than the income index the average consumer is indeed better off compared with the base year. Hence, in the UK context it is perfectly correct to argue that if incomes increase by more than the retail price index average standards of living have improved, but it can be shown that the reverse is not necessarily the case. Dividing condition (5.2) by $p^2 q^2$ gives

$$\frac{\Sigma p^1 q^2}{\Sigma p^2 q^2} \leq \frac{\Sigma p^1 q^1}{\Sigma p^2 q^2} . \tag{5.6}$$

as a condition for reduced utility. However, we can make more sense of this condition by looking at the reciprocals of each side, bearing in mind that, when both sides are equal, their reciprocals are equal, but when they are unequal the direction of the inequality is reversed.[6] Hence, if (5.6) holds,

$$\frac{\Sigma p^2 q^2}{\Sigma p^1 q^2} \geq \frac{\Sigma p^2 q^2}{\Sigma p^1 q^1} , \tag{5.7}$$

or, in other words, the consumer is definitely worse off if the Paasche price index is greater than the index of money income. But if neither condition (5.5) nor condition (5.7) is satisfied, as might be the case if the Laspeyre price index is greater than the index of money income, it is impossible to tell whether the average consumer is worse off or better off without further information.

Nevertheless, it is important not to exaggerate the importance of these ambiguities. If the Laspeyre price index is considerably in excess of the income index, then the Paasche price index is likely to be as well and there can be little doubt that the consumer is worse off. Caution, however, is required when the differences between the various indices are small.[7]

Notes

1 Willig (1976) argues that in most cases the margin of error involved in measuring compensating variations by consumer's surplus is likely to be less than 2 per cent. He also suggests a procedure for estimating the former from the latter in cases that would produce larger errors.

2 It might be thought that the estimation of compensating or equivalent variations also requires some knowledge of individual consumer's preferences. However, when the relevant demand functions have been derived it is in principle possible to derive mathematically the underlying utility functions (e.g. see Varian, 1984).

3 Actually of course, the bundle of goods at V would have cost the same at the initial prices as that at C_1, since it lies on $M_1 N_1$, but all the other bundles on M_2 would have cost less.
4 Using this notation $\Sigma x \cdot y$ is defined as $x_1 \cdot y_1 + x_2 \cdot y_2 \ldots + x_n \cdot y_n$, where n can be any number.
5 These index numbers are named after their initial developers.
6 If $x = y = 2$, $1/x = 1/y = 1/2$,
   but if $x = 2$ and $y = 3$, $x < y$ but $1/x > 1/y$ since $1/2 > 1/3$.
7 This is quite apart from any caution that may be required because of any deficiencies in the data from which such index numbers are derived.

Exercises

5.1 A consumer buys Q_0 of good X when its price is P_0. Deduce the relationship between the consumer's ordinary and compensated demand curves by considering the effects of changes in the price of X:

(a) in the case where X is an inferior good but not a Giffen good,
(b) in the case where X is a Giffen good.

5.2 Under what circumstances is the equivalent variation of a price change less than the compensating variation?
5.3 In your view, is the concept of consumer's surplus 'an analytical tool of great power' (Hicks) or 'a totally useless theoretical toy' (Little)?
5.4 A household spends its entire income on food and clothing. Suppose the price of food rises and the price of clothing falls. Show, using diagrams and index numbers, the conditions under which the household is (a) better off and (b) worse off.
5.5 Another household spends its entire income on three goods, X, Y and Z. Using the following data, consider whether the individual is better or worse off in year 2 than in year 1.

	Year 1		Year 2	
	Q	P	Q	P
Good X	20	5	18	6
Good Y	15	6	18	5
Good Z	10	8	11	7

CHAPTER SIX
THE CHARACTERISTICS APPROACH TO CONSUMER BEHAVIOUR

Introduction

In the previous chapters we have been concerned with what has come to be regarded as the standard or traditional theory of consumer behaviour built on the work of Hicks and Allen, which dates back to the 1930s, and the earlier work of the Russian economist Slutsky. In this and the next chapter we turn to some more recent developments that attempt to extend the scope of the traditional theory.

The first two developments to be considered, both of which were initiated in the mid-1960s, arose from a concern that the traditional theory left many aspects of consumers' choices explicable only in terms of tastes. Whether a good was inferior or not, or whether pairs of goods turned out to be gross complements or gross substitutes, appeared to be little more than an accident of random individual preferences. Moreover, all changes in demand that could not be explained in terms of price or income changes could only be attributed to changes in those preferences. The developments pioneered by Lancaster and Becker, which are discussed respectively in this and the following chapter, are both concerned to investigate whether there are other, more objective, factors that influence choices but that cannot be taken account of within the framework of the traditional theory. Both developments start from a recognition that consumption can be viewed in the same sort of way as production, that is, as a process requiring inputs and yielding an output, but, as we shall see, they do it in rather different ways.

A second limitation of the traditional theory is that it assumes that consumers are adequately informed about the goods available to them, and about their qualities and prices, and can thus make their optimal selections without too much difficulty. In practice, consumers are typically less than perfectly informed about the choices open to them. It is possible in most cases for them to obtain more information, at some cost in terms of time and money, but deciding whether to spend the necessary resources in pursuit of more information is also complicated by uncertainty about the outcome. Chapter 7 below gives some indication of how economists have attempted to deal with these problems.

The characteristics approach and the utility function

The starting point to the first development in the theory of consumer choice to be discussed, which, in its early stages, was almost entirely the work of Kelvin Lancaster,[1] is that goods are consumed not so much for their own sake as for their distinctive attributes or, as he termed them, **characteristics**. Thus apples are consumed not for their 'appleness' but for their distinctive taste, the nutrients they contain and also perhaps because of the more sensual pleasures associated with biting into a crisp, juicy apple. Any individual good can, therefore, be regarded primarily as an input into a consumption process capable of yielding more than one output. That consumption process thus corresponds directly to a production process yielding joint products, as, for example, when harvesting a field yields a joint output of grain and straw. All this suggests that the consumer's utility can more accurately be described as a function of the quantities of the characteristics that constitute the outputs of the consumption process, rather than of the quantities of the goods consumed, which are simply the inputs. Hence, instead of writing our utility function in the form of expression (2.1) on p. 16 above, we can write it as

$$U = g(c_1, c_2, \ldots, c_n), \tag{6.1}$$

where $c_1, c_2, \ldots, c_n$ are the quantities of the various characteristics enjoyed. Similarly, in our diagrammatic analysis, the implication is that our indifference curves should indicate equi-preferable bundles of characteristics, as in Figure 6.2 below, rather than equi-preferable bundles of goods.

One immediate advantage of this approach is that it provides a basis for examining the relationship between goods, because a distinction can be made between goods that share common characteristics, but either have them in differing proportions or mix them with differing selections of other characteristics, and goods that have no characteristics in common. Thus Golden Delicious apples have characteristics in common with other sorts of apples and also with pears and peaches, but hardly anything in common with paper handkerchiefs. This suggests that the choice of one good in preference to another may be a reflection as much of its objective physical properties as of the more subjective preferences of the consumer. The more traditional theory of the preceding chapters effectively ignores these physical properties.

Indeed, it has to treat a choice between Golden Delicious and Granny Smith apples in exactly the same way as the choice between apples and paper handkerchiefs, and in both cases it can explain the choice decisions only in terms of individual tastes. The characteristics approach as developed by Lancaster provides, as we shall see, a basis for taking these more physical attributes of goods into account.

The choice set and optimal choices

One important feature of developed western economies is that consumers are typically able to choose between a number of varieties of the products they buy, be they apples, soap powders, washing machines or cars. Indeed, Lancaster takes as a working hypothesis that the number of goods probably exceeds the number of characteristics. However, in order to draw out the similarities and differences in comparison with the traditional theory of the preceding chapters, we will start by considering a situation in which the number of goods is equal to the number of characteristics and also, to keep within the scope of diagrammatic analysis, where the number of both is two. (Again, for the most part this involves little loss of generality.)

Thus in Figure 6.1 we consider the choice between two types of breakfast cereal, A and B, each containing the same two characteristics E, which might be derived from some special energy-giving ingredient, and F, which might be fibre content. Each gram of cereal A is assumed to contain 0.3 units of E and 0.2 units of F. In terms of the diagram, therefore, consumption of this particular product allows the consumer to have the bundles of characteristics on the ray OA, whose slope reflects the proportions in which it provides the two characteristics. A similar ray, OB, can be constructed for product B, and the one drawn in the diagram reflects an assumption that B is more F-intensive than A, giving 0.4 units of F per gram but only 0.1 units of E. If the consumer buys one of the two products his position on the relevant ray depends on how much of the product he consumes. Thus if he consumes 50 grams of A, yielding 15 units of E and 10 units of F, he will be at H in Figure 6.1, whilst if he consumes 100 grams of A he will be at J. It may also be noted that, for each additional gram of A (or B) consumed, the consumer will move the same distance up OA (or OB). The distance from any point on the ray back to the origin is thus proportional to the amount of A consumed at that point (hence $OJ = 2OH$), which means that, whilst quantities of character-istics are measured on the axes of the diagram, quantities of goods can be measured along the product rays.

Now let us suppose that our consumer decides to spend £1 on breakfast cereals, and cereal A can be obtained at a cost of 1p per gram, whilst cereal B costs 1.25p per gram. If he buys only A he is able to buy 100 grams, giving him the bundle of characteristics at J in the diagram, whilst if he buys only B

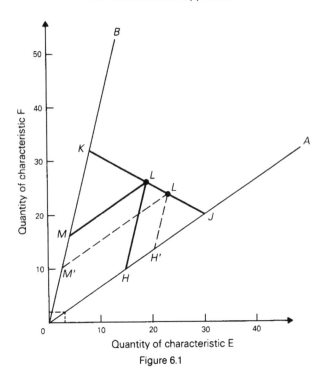

Figure 6.1

he gets 80 grams, giving him 8 units of E and 32 units of F, represented by point *K. J* and *K* thus represent two alternative bundles of characteristics he can buy with £1, but there are others as well. For example, by spending 50p on each product he can buy 50 grams of A and 40 of B, giving him a total of 19 units of E and 26 units of F, which is represented by the point *L* in the diagram, lying mid-way between *K* and *J*. Moreover, it can easily be checked that other allocations of his total budget yield other combinations of characteristics lying on the straight line drawn between *K* and *J*, suggesting that in the present context *JK* can be viewed as the consumer's budget line. Unlike the budget lines of Chapter 3, however, it does not extend to the axes because there is no way the consumer can obtain from these two products more than 4 units of F per unit of E or more than 1.5 units of E with each unit of F; his choices are, therefore, confined to the area bounded by O*A* and O*B*. It may also be objected that even within that area choice may be constrained by indivisibilities in the availability of the two goods. Breakfast cereals, after all, are typically sold in packets containing more than 100 grams. However, it is important not to exaggerate the difficulties. The unit of consumption of breakfast cereals tends to be much smaller than the unit of purchase and individuals are freely able to indulge their tastes by consuming one variety one day and another the next, or even by mixing them together.

Whilst *JK* in Figure 6.1 is a budget line, it differs from the budget lines we have used previously in that it joins the bundles of characteristics that can be bought with a given sum of money rather than bundles of goods themselves. It also differs from them in that its slope indicates the relative prices of the two characteristics (or the price of characteristic E in terms of characteristic F) rather than the relative prices of the two goods involved. The goods' prices are reflected in the slope of *JK*, because if the price of good A is more than the 1p per gram assumed in the case illustrated, less of both characteristics will be obtainable when £1 is spent on A. *J* will then be located nearer the origin, which will thus make *JK* steeper. But the slope of *JK* also reflects the proportions in which the characteristics are contained in the two goods. This can easily be shown in the case of our numerical example.

One way of interpreting the slope of *JK* is that it indicates the extra F that can be obtained per unit of E given up when a unit of expenditure is transferred from product A to product B. In the case illustrated, given that the price of A is 1p per gram, 1p less spent on A reduces the amount of E and F obtained from the consumption of A by 0.3 and 0.2 units respectively. If that unit of expenditure is then transferred to the purchase of B at ·1.25p per gram, 0.8 units of B can be obtained, giving 0.08 additional units of E and 0.32 additional units of F. Overall, therefore, 0.12 units of F will be gained in exchange for 0.22 units of E, or 12/22 units of F will be gained per unit of E given up. The reader can easily confirm for himself, by drawing his own diagram, that the slope of *JK* in our example does have this value, but the important point to remember is that in calculating it we needed to know both the commodity prices and the quantity of E and F per unit of each product.

In more general terms, the slope of the budget line can be expressed as

$$-\frac{f_B \cdot p_A/p_B - f_A}{e_A - e_B \cdot p_A/p_B}, \qquad (6.2)$$

where e_A and f_A are the quantities of E and F respectively per unit of good A, and e_B and f_B are defined similarly for good B.[2] This expression provides further confirmation that the slope of the budget line depends both on the proportions in which characteristics are combined in the two products as well as their prices. It may also be apparent from expression (6.2) that if p_A were to rise sufficiently relative to p_B (bearing in mind that in the case illustrated $f_B > f_A$ and $e_A > e_B$) the denominator may change sign. If that happened, *J* in the diagram would have moved so far down O*A* towards the origin that it would lie to the left of *K*. Conversely, with a sufficiently low price of A relative to B, *J* could lie above *K*. Whilst, therefore, in the case illustrated in Figure 6.1 the budget line is downward sloping, this need not always be the case.

One other point that we need to be aware of in our later discussion is that, although points in the diagram represent bundles of characteristics, the quantities of goods involved at any point can, in fact, be observed quite easily. It has already been noted that the quantity of A or B required to produce a particular bundle of characteristics measured by some point on

OA or OB can be measured by the distance between that point and the origin. Thus OH in Figure 6.1 represents 50 grams of A and OJ ($= 2OH$) represents 100 grams, whilst along OB, OK represents 80 grams of B. We have also seen that point L in the diagram can be reached by someone consuming 50 grams of A combined with 40 grams of B.

Now if starting from L we were to deprive the consumer of his 40 grams of B, in terms of the diagram he would have moved back to H. Moreover, since removing product B from the consumption bundle is to remove characteristics in the proportions represented by the slope of OB, it must follow that the line drawn between L and H, which is the path followed by our consumer, must have the same slope as OB. This suggests that if we had not known where H was to start with (and thus how much A was consumed at L), we could have found it by drawing a line back from L, parallel to OB, to the point at which it cuts OA. Similarly, the equivalent point on OB can be found by drawing a line back from L to M, parallel to OA. OM then represents the quantity of B consumed at L, and the reader can confirm from his own diagram that $OM = 0.5OK$ and therefore represents 40 grams of B. Similar considerations apply to any other bundle of characteristics within the area bounded by OA and OB. Thus the bundle at L' requires purchases of OH' ($> OH$) of A and OM' ($< OM$) of B, and it can be readily seen that the closer L' is to J the more A and the less B is involved. Hence, whilst the choice set in the diagram comprises all the bundles of characteristics in the area bounded by the budget line JK and the rays OA and OB, each point within it can be identified with a specific bundle of goods.

Having identified the choices available, we can now move on to consider the implications of rational choice, which as usual simply involves choosing the most preferred bundle of characteristics of those available or that promising the most utility. But since the utility function represented by expression (6.1) is assumed to have the same general properties as the utility functions of previous chapters, it can be represented by a conventional set of downward-sloping indifference curves drawn convex to the origin as in Figure 6.2. In that diagram, therefore, with the budget line JK, the bundle of characteristics at T, where JK touches the indifference curve U_2, is the preferred one, requiring purchases of OR of A and OS of B. This preferred position need not necessarily involve the purchase of both goods, and indeed would only involve both goods with a downward-sloping budget line.

With a budget line such as KN there is a *corner* solution in that all the available budget is spent on B, producing the bundle of characteristics at K, whatever the precise form of the consumer's preferences. In that case, the choice of K is on efficiency grounds rather than a reflection of individual tastes, because any other point in the choice set involves less of one or both characteristics than can be obtained at K. We will come across other examples of how the characteristics approach introduces efficiency considerations into the theory of consumer choice later, but our next task is to consider the effect of income and price changes.

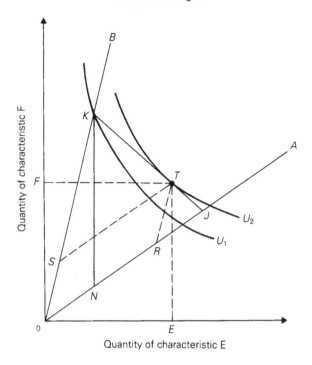

Income changes

Figure 6.2

Income changes

Given the similarities between the way the optimum choice with a given budget is depicted in Figure 6.2 and the corresponding analysis of Chapter 2, it must be clear that the analysis of the effects of income and price changes on the demand for characteristics can also proceed on similar lines to that of earlier chapters. Thus, in Figure 6.2, an income change will shift the budget line JK parallel to itself, while relative price changes will be reflected, as already indicated, in changes in its slope. Moreover, the effects of price changes can be decomposed into income and substitution effects exactly as in Chapter 3. Indeed, there would be no need to discuss the effects of these changes further were it not for the fact that the characteristics approach provides some additional insights into the nature of inferior goods and, by implication, Giffen goods. Strictly speaking, all that the traditional theory can say about inferior goods is that the preferences of some consumers might be such that less of some goods are consumed as their income increases; it has nothing to say about the circumstances under which that situation might arise. Lipsey and Rosenbluth (1971), building on the foundations laid by Lancaster, argue that the characteristics approach is able to say rather more.

Within the characteristics framework, the conditions under which a good is an inferior good for an individual consumer can be examined with the help

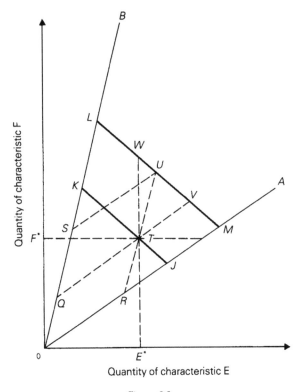

Figure 6.3

of Figure 6.3. In that diagram, an initial solution is depicted with the budget line *JK*. In the interests of clarity, the relevant indifference curves are not shown on the diagram, but it can be supposed that *T* is the initial preferred position requiring O*R* of good A and O*Q* of good B, which together provide *E** of characteristic E and *F** of F.

Now suppose that as a result of an increase in income the consumer's budget line is moved to *ML*. With downward-sloping, convex to the origin, indifference curves, the new preferred position could lie anywhere on *ML*, so we can proceed by considering the implications of the choices represented by particular points on that line. Consider, first, what happens if point *U* is the new preferred position. *U* has particular significance because it is located where the line *RT* (drawn parallel to O*B*), when extended beyond *T*, cuts *ML*. This means that the line drawn back from *U* parallel to O*B* is *UTR* and thus the quantity of A consumed at *U* is O*R*, exactly the same as the quantity consumed at *T*. At *U* the consumer enjoys more of both characteristics than he did at *T*, but all these extra characteristics are obtained from increased purchases of good B (from O*Q* to O*S*) rather than good A. Once it is appreciated that point *U* involves the same quantity of A as point *T*, it should also be clear that if any point on *LM* to the left of *U* is chosen (such as *W*) it must involve a *smaller* demand for good A than at T. In other words, the choice of a point anywhere on that section of the new budget line above U signifies that A is an inferior good. Note that inferiority of a good is not dependent on the inferiority of any characteristic. We have not ruled out the possibility of inferior characteristics. Indeed, since in the diagram W is actually located vertically above T, the choice of any point above W means that characteristic E is inferior. Between W and U, however, whilst good A is inferior, both characteristics are 'normal' in the sense that the demand for both increases with income.

So far we have concentrated on the demand for good A, but the effects of the income change on the demand for good B can be examined in the same way. Thus, in the situation represented in Figure 6.3, it should be evident that the choice of any point on ML to the right of V signifies that B is an inferior good. In fact, both goods are normal only if the preferred point on ML lies between U and V. On the face of it, therefore, in the case illustrated, where UV is less than half the length of ML, the chances of one or other of the two goods being inferior seem quite high.[3]

To get a better idea of the circumstances under which inferior goods might arise, consider again the implications of point U being the preferred point on ML. Since TU is drawn parallel to OB, the choice of U implies that the consumer wishes to increase his use of the characteristics in exactly the same proportions in which they are combined in good B (f_B/e_B in terms of the notation used in expression (6.2) above) and he can do this by spending all of his additional income on good B. However, the choice of a point to the left of U arises if the proportion in which he wishes to increase his use of F relative to E (i.e. the ratio of his desired increase in F to his desired increase in E, which can be denoted as f^d/e^d) is greater than f_B/e_B. In this case, the increase in characteristics can only be obtained by the consumer both spending all his extra income on good B, and in addition substituting some B for A in his purchases from his original income. The condition required for A to be inferior can therefore be stated as

$$f^d/e^d > f_B/e_B. \tag{6.3}$$

Similarly, of course, we can expect B to be inferior if

$$f^d/e^d < f_A/e_A. \tag{6.4}$$

Now the observant reader may have realized that f^d/e^d can be interpreted as the slope of the income expansion path, and that (6.3) implies that that slope is greater than the slope of OB.[4] Moreover, since the slope of the income expansion path is related to the ratio of the relevant income elasticities of demand,[5] good A is more likely to be inferior the higher the consumer's income elasticity of demand for characteristic F relative to the income elasticity of demand for E, which is its comparatively abundant characteristic.

In more general terms, therefore, it would appear that goods are likely to be inferior if they share some basic characteristics with other goods that also offer more in the way of characteristics with high income elasticities. Thus public transport may be able to meet a demand for basic journeys to work or shopping journeys, but since, in general, it has less to offer than travel by private car in terms of comfort and convenience (the demand for which is highly income elastic), it should come as no surprise to learn that the demand for public transport tends to fall as income rises. In this and similar cases therefore, the analysis of consumers' demand for products in terms of their characteristics provides some understanding of how the attributes of a good can affect demand in a way that is impossible within the traditional theory discussed in the preceding chapters.

Price changes

Turning now briefly to price changes, Figure 6.4 illustrates the case where a fall in the price of good A has changed the budget line from *JK* to *LK*. With *T* the preferred point on *JK*, involving the purchase of O*R* of A and O*S* of B as before, the possible effects of the price change on the demand for A can be traced as in the previous diagram. Thus *U* is located on *LK* where *RT*, when produced beyond *T*, cuts *LK*, and hence as before the selection of any point to the right of *U* would imply an increase in the demand for A whilst points to the left would involve a decrease. In the latter case, A would be a Giffen good, but again that need not imply any 'Giffenness' attaching to characteristic E. An increase in the demand for E will, if the preferred point on *LK* lies between *W* (which is again located vertically above *T*) and *U*, be accompanied by a reduction in the demand for A.

In fact we could go further and, by decomposing the effects of the price change into its constituent income and substitution effects along the lines established in Chapter 3, show that it is not necessary for characteristic E to be inferior for A to be a Giffen good. Moreover, that exercise (which is left to the reader to perform for him/herself) can be used to confirm that, even when the complications of characteristics are added, good A can only be a Giffen good if it is also inferior. It should also be clear that Giffen goods again constitute a rather special case, since inferior goods need not necessarily be Giffen goods. Nevertheless, Lipsey and Rosenbluth argue that the likelihood of Giffen goods cannot be dismissed as readily as it tends to have been on the basis of the more traditional analysis, as it is no longer purely a question of the relative sizes of income and substitution effects but is also a question of the availability of goods sharing particular characteristics. It also follows that the proportion of a consumer's income spent on a good is of less

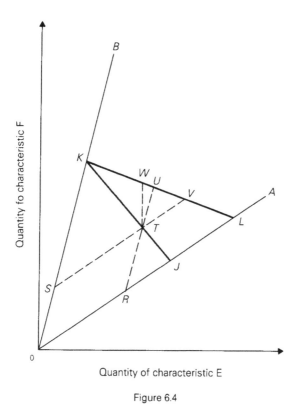

Figure 6.4

importance than is suggested by the traditional theory as set out in Chapter 3 above. The potential range of goods with Giffen properties might, therefore, be quite high.

The multi-product case

Turning to the case that Lancaster thought likely to be more typical, in which there are more products than characteristics, the most straightforward approach is to continue with the analysis of a situation with two characteristics but to add a third product. Thus in Figure 6.5, OA and OB indicate the characteristics available with various quantities of goods A and B, whilst OC is the corresponding ray for a third good C. The obvious consequence of the addition of the third good is that any bundles of characteristics along OC, such as that at L, can be obtained by consuming C alone as well as by consuming OL_A of A and OL_B of B in combination as previously. But in addition, any bundle of characteristics between OA and OC can be obtained from an appropriate combination of either A and C or A and B, whilst

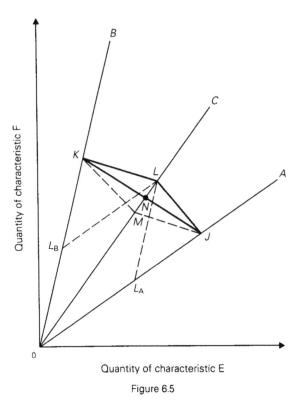

Figure 6.5

bundles of characteristics between O*B* and O*C* can be obtained by combining in appropriate amounts either A and B or B and C. In other words, the one-to-one relationship between bundles of characteristics and the bundle of goods required to obtain them, which was a feature of the previous analysis, no longer applies and consumers can choose between different ways of making up their required bundle. In this situation, other things being equal, the rational consumer will choose the bundle of goods that gives him the required characteristics at least cost. Efficiency considerations thus become a central feature of the choice process.

This can be seen more clearly if we consider the choices available when the consumer has a fixed budget to spend on the three goods. If *J* in Figure 6.5 is the point reached when all the budget is spent on A, and *K* is the corresponding point when all the budget is spent on B, then, as before, points on *JK* can be reached by spending the money available on various combinations of A and B. Similarly, if *L* can be reached by spending all the total budget on C, points on *JL* can be reached by dividing the expenditure between A and C, whilst points on *KL* can be reached by buying combinations of B and C. However, it should be clear from the diagram that all consumers, whatever their preferences, will want to avoid buying combinations of A and B in the case illustrated, because that would restrict them to points on *JK* when they could reach points along *JLK*, offering more of one or both characteristics for the same outlay, by purchasing appropriate bundles of A and C or C and B. But if the price of C is at a higher level, so that when the entire budget is spent on C only the smaller bundle of characteristics at *M* can be reached, all possible combinations of goods involving C will be rejected as they yield fewer characteristics (those represented by points on the dashed curve *JMK*) than can be obtained by combining A and B.

In fact, the analysis suggests that the consumer's choice process is really a two-stage one. First of all, the *efficient* choice set has to be identified – and at that stage certain goods or combinations of goods will be rejected by all rational consumers independently of their preferences. Then, secondly, a choice has to be made between efficient points, and that is the stage at which individual preferences are brought to bear. Hence, with a reasonable distribution of individual preferences, and the efficient choices indicated by *JLK*, all three goods will be sold but no single consumer will buy more than two goods. In fact, the latter result applies if there are more than two goods because again efficiency is served by concentrating purchases on two goods as in Figure 6.5.[6]

Returning to the case illustrated in Figure 6.5, we have already observed that if the price of C is too high, so that O*M* is the maximum that can be bought with the consumer's given budget, the demand for C will be zero. But with respect to the circumstances under which demand is reduced to zero, it is useful to consider what might happen to the demand for C if its price was initially at the level allowing O*L* to be bought, but was then increased gradually. In effect this would result in point *L* moving inwards along O*C* with the slopes of *KL* and *JL* being changed correspondingly. Nevertheless as long as *L* remains above *N*, where O*C* intersects *JK*, the consumer's demand for C will fall continuously (unless C is a Giffen good, in which case it would rise). But once the price had risen sufficiently to push *L* below *N*, the demand for C drops to zero immediately because buying C is no longer an efficient way of obtaining any desired bundle of characteristics. Consumers will therefore substitute other goods for the good whose price has risen, but this substitution effect, unlike the substitution effect of standard theory, is unrelated to consumers' preferences. To make the distinction clear, Lancaster called it an **efficiency substitution effect**. Moreover, this effect implies that the demand curve for C takes the form illustrated in Figure 6.6, with a discontinuity at the price of P_N above which there is no demand. In contrast, although the traditional theory allows for the possibility of zero demand at sufficiently high prices, the reduction in demand as price rises is predicted to be a continuous one.

One final property of the characteristics approach that should be noted is the ease with which it can accommodate the introduction of a new product. Under the traditional theory it has to be assumed either that preferences are defined over the initial range of products, in which case the consumer's

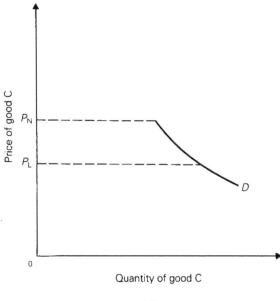

Figure 6.6

response to a new product can be explained only in terms of a change in preferences, or, alternatively, that consumers' preferences are defined over all possible present and future goods. With the latter approach the introduction of a new product involves the reduction in its price from some infinitely high level to one sufficiently low to induce positive demand. The first alternative is unsatisfactory as it implies that consumers' preferences have changed when they are simply responding to a change in their environment, whilst the second requires consumers to be almost omniscient. With the characteristics approach, by contrast, a new good can be viewed simply as something providing a set of characteristics in differing proportions to any existing good. In terms of our diagrammatic approach, therefore, it involves no more than the addition of the third product C in Figure 6.5 to the earlier two-good analysis, and from what we have already seen it should be clear that the effect on the consumer's pattern of purchases simply depends upon whether the new product enables the consumer's underlying preferences to be met more efficiently.

Nevertheless, although the characteristics approach does provide some new insights into consumer behaviour, it is not without its own limitations. While it provides a useful framework for theoretical analysis, it would be difficult in practice to identify all the characteristics that might be associated with any .given product, and more difficult still to measure all of them quantitatively. Moreover, it has been suggested that the assumption of linear relationships between the quantities of characteristics and the quantity of goods is unduly restrictive. Finally, if consumption is to be viewed as something akin to production, some allowance needs to be made for the possibility of inputs other than goods. What has come to be called the **household production function** approach does allow for other types of input, so we must now give that due consideration.

Notes

1 The approach was introduced in Lancaster (1966a) and Lancaster (1966b) and developed in more detail in Lancaster (1971).
2 This expression for the slope of the budget line can be denoted by the ratio $\Delta f/\Delta e$, where Δf is the net increase in the consumption of characteristic F involved in any movement along the budget line and Δe is the net reduction in characteristic E. Then, if Δq_A and Δq_B are the changes in the respective quantities of goods A and B purchased,

$$\Delta e = e_A \cdot \Delta q_A + e_B \cdot \Delta q_B$$

and

$$\Delta f = f_A \cdot \Delta q_A + f_B \cdot \Delta q_B.$$

Hence

$$\frac{\Delta f}{\Delta e} = \frac{f_B \cdot q_B + f_A \cdot q_A}{e_A \cdot q_A + e_B \cdot q_B} = \frac{f_B \cdot q_B/q_A + f_A}{e_A + e_B \cdot q_B/q_A}.$$

But since along the budget line

$$p_A \cdot \Delta q_A + p_B \cdot \Delta q_B = 0$$

$$\Delta q_B/\Delta q_A = -p_A/p_B,$$

so substituting into the above expression for $\Delta f/\Delta e$ gives expression (6.2) as in the text.
3 Lipsey and Rosenbluth also argue that the more identical the two products, in the sense that the closer OB is to OA, the more likely it is that one of them will be inferior, but that is partly a consequence of the restriction they impose on their utility function that all characteristics have positive income elasticities.
4 Again we have refrained from drawing possible income expansion paths in Figure 6.3 to avoid overloading the diagram, but clearly they can be derived exactly as in Chapter 3 above.
5 The slope of the income expansion path can be expressed as

$$\frac{f^d}{e^d} = \frac{f^d/y}{e^d/y} = \frac{\eta_b \cdot q_f}{\eta_e \cdot q_e},$$

where η_e and η_f are the income elasticities of demand for characteristics E and F respectively and q_e and q_f are the initial quantities consumed.
6 See Exercise 6.2, but it should also be noted that, where there are more than two characteristics, efficiency need not preclude the purchase of more than two goods.

Exercises

6.1 What are the characteristics consumers might look for in:

(a) a take-away pizza
(b) a meal in an expensive restaurant
(c) a copy of *The Sun*
(d) a pop concert?

6.2 Consumers have a choice of four brands of toothpaste, A, B, C and D, which contain, as active ingredients, a substance that helps to prevent tooth decay (*DP*) and one that makes the teeth sparkling and white (*WH*) in the quantities specified in the following table:

	Milligrams per tube	
	DP	*WH*
A	48	48
B	40	56
C	30	75
D	20	80

A tube of each brand costs 80p. Individual choices will obviously depend on their preferences, but which of the four brands would consumers with access to the above information *not* consider buying? What action could its producer take to make it more acceptable to consumers?

6.3 Suppose that only brands A and B of those in the previous question were on the market. Under what circumstances would the demand for A be reduced to zero?

6.4 'If goods X and Y have characteristics E and F in differing proportions, with each unit of X having more of characteristic E than good Y, good X is likely to be inferior for a given consumer if his income elasticity of demand for characteristic E is low relative to his income elasticity of demand for characteristic A.' Explain and discuss.

6.5 Show that in the above case it is not necessary for characteristic E to be inferior for X to be a Giffen good.

CHAPTER SEVEN
TIME, INFORMATION AND UNCERTAINTY

Time as a scarce resource

The distinguishing feature of the development in the theory of consumer choice that is to be examined first in this chapter – the household production function approach – lies in its explicit recognition, following the work of Becker (particularly Becker, 1965), that time is an important input into the consumption process and is also, for many people, a scarce resource. In this development, consumption is viewed as an activity requiring the input of one or a number of goods coupled with the time of the consuming agent. It thus presents, it is claimed, a more realistic model of what happens when 'goods' are consumed because, clearly, even a simple activity like drinking a cup of tea requires inputs of tea leaves, hot water, milk and maybe sugar as well, together with the use of assorted containers – teapot, milk jug, cup, etc. – and 10 minutes or so drinking time. Other activities can involve the use of a wider range of goods and considerably more time. Utility is then assumed to be derived from the activity rather than directly from the goods consumed, and to be related to the amount of the various activities undertaken rather than to the quantities of goods. The utility function can thus be written as

$$U = h(z_1, z_2, \ldots, z_n), \qquad (7.1)$$

where the z terms refer to the quantities of the various activities, such as the number of cups of tea drunk or rounds of golf played. Then, because goods are inputs into the consumption process, an individual's demand for goods is ultimately determined by the amounts of the various activities he undertakes. Hence, bearing in mind that a good may be used as an input into a variety of activities, we may write the individual's demand function for any good A as

$$q_A = \phi(z_1, z_2, \ldots, z_n),$$

where q_A is the quantity of A demanded.

The theory as developed by Becker and his colleagues does not necessarily require any particular restrictions to be imposed upon the form of this relationship, but it will simplify our exploration of the theory if we assume that this relationship is linear,[1] so that the total quantity of good A required for the ith activity can be expressed as

$$q_A{}^i = a_i z_i \qquad (i = 1, 2, \ldots, n), \qquad (7.2)$$

where a_i is the quantity of good A required for each unit of that activity. Time as another input into the production process can be treated similarly, so we can write

$$t_i = s_i z_i, \qquad (7.3)$$

where s_i is the amount of time required for each unit of the ith activity.

Constraints on choice

The consumer is still, of course, subject to a budget constraint in that his total expenditure cannot exceed his income (denoted as in previous chapters by y). Hence, assuming the consumer's activities involve the use of goods $1, 2, \ldots, m$,

$$\Sigma p_j q_j \leq y \qquad (j = 1, 2, \ldots, m), \qquad (7.4)$$

where the p terms are the prices of the goods. But, with time also a scarce commodity, the consumer is additionally subject to a time constraint in that the sum of the time spent on consumption activities plus any time spent working cannot exceed the total time available, hence

$$t_1 + t_2 + , \ldots, + t_n + t_w \leq T, \qquad (7.5)$$

where T is the total time available in a day or week or whatever period of time is considered appropriate for the analysis, and t_w is the time the individual spends working rather than consuming.

To aid our usual diagrammatic approach we limit ourselves to a situation in which there are only two activities and, for the moment at least, consider the case in which only one good is required for each activity. Thus if good A is the good required for activity 1, and good B is used in activity 2, then the product/activity relationships reduce to

$$q_A = a_1 z_1 \qquad (7.2a)$$

and

$$q_B = b_2 z_2 \tag{7.2b}$$

and the budget constraint becomes

$$p_A q_A + p_A q_B \leqslant y$$

or, using (7.2a) and (7.2b),

$$p_A a_1 z_1 + p_A b_2 z_2 \leqslant y, \tag{7.6}$$

suggesting that the choices of z_1 and z_2 available when income is equal to expenditure can be expressed in terms of a conventional budget line like MN in Figure 7.1. The slope of this line ($- p_A . a_1 / p_B . b_2$), as usual, reflects relative prices, but this time it is the relative cost of the two activities taking into account the quantity of goods required for each unit of activity. Similarly the time constraint, which in the two-good case is

$$t_1 + t_2 + t_w \leqslant T,$$

can, using (7.3), be written

$$s_1 z_1 + s_2 z_2 \leqslant T - t_w, \tag{7.7}$$

which, when all the available time is used, and assuming for the moment that working time is fixed, can be represented by another line on the diagram, shown as TU in Figure 7.1. This is also a budget line in that it indicates various possible allocations of the time budget, and its slope reflects the relative costs of the two activities in terms of time ($- s_1 / s_2$). The case illustrated thus implies that activity 1 is more time-intensive than activity 2.

Utility-maximizing choices

As the diagram is drawn, TU lies outside MN, and so if these are the relevant budget lines the main constraint on the choices of the individual is a shortage of money. No matter how he allocates his limited funds he has time to spare, and if his preferences are represented by the indifference curves in the diagram he can do no better than to choose the combination of activities at C_P. For anyone in that position time is not really a scarce commodity and, therefore, does not influence his choices, and the only modification to the standard analysis is that the marginal rate of substitution and price ratio at the utility-maximizing position relate to activities rather than to goods. There are, no doubt, many people in the world in this sort of situation, including the unemployed, many pensioners and those with low fixed incomes generally.

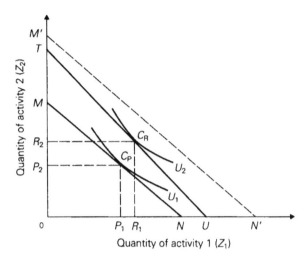

Figure 7.1

However, there may also be some considerably more affluent people who find themselves in the opposite situation, with more money than they can spend. Their money budget line will lie wholly outside the time constraint and will thus be like the dashed line $M'N'$ in the diagram. Their choices are then constrained by time rather than money, leaving C_R, where TU is tangential to one of their indifference curves, as their best attainable position. The results of the the standard analysis thus need more modification in this case, because at C_R the individual's marginal rate of substitution is equal to the time–cost ratio of the two activities rather than to the price ratio, since utility maximization requires, in this case, marginal utilities per unit of time rather than of money to be equalized. Moreover, this optimum position is not affected by changes in the individual's income or in prices, unless they are sufficient to move $M'N'$ inside TU, because clearly such changes cannot affect the position or the slope of TU.

The other possibility is the more intermediate one, illustrated in Figure 7.2, where the money budget constraint MN and the time budget constraint TU intersect at L. In this case the choices open to the consumer are those in the shaded area bounded by the kinked line MLU. Thus whether he ends up with surplus cash or spare time will depend on his preferences. However, both budgets will be exhausted if point L is the preferred position.

In the case illustrated, where the time budget line is steeper than the money budget line, utility maximization requires in general terms

$$s_1/s_2 \geqslant MRS_{12} \geqslant p_A a_1/p_B b_2,$$

with the first two terms being equal if the preferred point is on LU and the second two terms being equal if it is on ML.

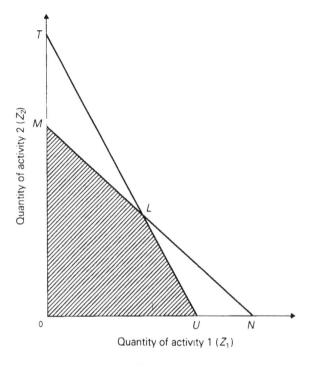

Figure 7.2

However, there is one important element in the theory of the allocation of time as developed by Becker *et al.* that we have not yet introduced, and that is its assumption that the time available for consumption activities can be traded off against income. Income can be increased by spending more time at work (and vice versa), but that necessarily reduces the time available for consumption activities. As has already been observed, not everyone is in a position to vary their income in this way, but many people may have some opportunities to do so, even if it involves a spot of moonlighting on a second job, and any individual short of money but with time to spare would, no doubt, be more than happy to exploit them.[2]

Assuming therefore, as does Becker, that working hours are freely variable so that time can be traded off against money without restriction, working time (t_w) and income (y) in our earlier budget equations become variables, and, allowing for the possibility that individuals may have some non-labour income, the relationship between them can be expressed as

$$y = w \cdot t_w + v, \tag{7.8}$$

where w is the individual's hourly wage rate and v is his non-labour income ($v > 0$). Since any spare money (or time) can now be freely traded for time (or money), all resources can be used up. Expression (7.7) will therefore be satisfied as an equality and we can use it to rewrite (7.8) as

$$y = w(T - s_1 z_1 - s_2 z_2) + v,$$

and, substituting this expression into (7.6), we get

$$(p_A a_1 + w s_1) z_1 + (p_B b_2 + w s_2) z_2 = wT + v. \tag{7.9}$$

We are thus able to collapse our original money and time constraints into a single total resource constraint, which simply says that the value of all the resources used in consumption activities must be equal to (or at least cannot exceed) the value of all the original time and monetary resources available to the consumer. Given that it is of the same mathematical form as all the other budget lines we have met, it can be shown in the same way on a diagram, but its slope is now

$$- \frac{(p_A \alpha_1 + w s_1)}{(p_B b_2 + w s_2)},$$

which is the ratio of the full resource costs of each activity.

The consumer's utility-maximizing position is found in the usual way (as at C_L in Figure 7.3, where RS is the relevant resource constraint) and is thus where the marginal rate of substitution between the two activities is equal to the above resource cost ratio or, perhaps more meaningfully, where

$$\frac{MU_1}{(p_A a_1 + w s_1)} = \frac{MU_2}{(p_B b_2 + w s_2)}, \tag{7.10}$$

where MU_1 and MU_2 are the marginal utilities associated with their respective activities. Naturally, this expression can be extended to any number of activities. Furthermore, an extension in the number of goods involved in each activity can be accommodated simply by adding terms reflecting their costs to the denominators. Moreover, whilst (7.10) is the usual condition that the marginal utilities per unit of expenditure should be equalized across all activities, it involves a rather broader view of expenditure than in the form of the expression that originally appeared in Chapter 2. As such it has a number of important implications.

First of all, it suggests that whilst the analysis of the effects of commodity price changes can be carried out in the standard way, since an increase in p_A or p_B will change the slope of the budget line and give rise to the normal income and substitution effects, more care has to be taken with the analysis of income changes. Only a change in non-labour income would leave the slope of the budget line unaffected. An increase in income derived from an increase in the individual's wage rate raises the full resource cost of the more

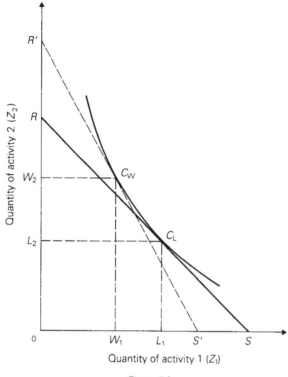

Figure 7.3

time-intensive commodity, and thus in the case illustrated above (where s_1 is assumed to be greater than s_2) increases the slope of the budget line. This kind of income change will therefore have substitution effects on the demand for goods as well as income effects.

Secondly, it suggests that two individuals facing different wage rates will face budget lines with different slopes, so that, even if the total value of resources available to them is the same and their preferences are identical, the individual with the higher wage rate will tend to choose less time-intensive activities.

Thirdly, as with the characteristics approach, there may be different input combinations that can be used to produce the same 'output', and the choice between them may be made purely on efficiency grounds. For example, consider a meal that can be made from the basic ingredients for £1 with a preparation time of 1 hour, but that is also available in convenience form at a cost of £3 with a preparation time of a quarter of an hour. To an individual with a wage rate of £4 per hour, the full cost (including time) of making the dish from the basic ingredients is £5, but in its convenience form it is only £4. To an individual with a wage rate of only £2 per hour, however, the convenience form costs £3.50 whereas preparing it from the basic ingredients costs only £3. From an efficiency point of view, therefore, they would make different choices.

Thus, in general, this approach provides an explanation for the way in which people in western economies have increasingly moved towards more time-saving methods of satisfying their wants with the use of convenience foods; an expanding array of electric gadgets in their homes; and their own cars for personal transport as their incomes have increased. It also provides an explanation for changes in an individual's pattern of consumption over time. For example, students, who are always short of money but (except when assignment deadlines or examinations dictate otherwise) less short of time, are often happy to spend hours putting the world to rights over a cup of coffee and are frequently found using cheap but slow, and sometimes uncertain, means of travel like long-distance coaches or hitchhiking. But once in employment the former student puts a higher value on time and his choices move towards less time-intensive activities like the working lunch and travel by high-speed train. In later life, however, following retirement, time once again becomes a cheap resource and time-intensive activities like gardening or, in the case of public figures, writing memoirs become more prominent.

Throughout the above, the changing patterns of consumption are responding to changes in price variables, but the other parameters in the budget equation may also be subject to change. For any activity involving manual or mental dexterity, whether it be do-it-yourself home improvement, solving crossword puzzles or even perhaps reading economics textbooks, the time taken to complete a 'unit' of activity will tend to fall as the individual becomes more proficient and, as mistakes decline, the quantities of goods used up in that activity may decline as well. Thus over time the individual becomes more efficient at converting inputs into useful outputs and the overall cost of the activities concerned will accordingly be reduced. Alternatively, if the activity is something like playing the guitar or even listening to records, where the scope for saving resources is more limited, the activity becomes more pleasurable as skill or knowledge increase. In either case, the effect is to increase the marginal utility per unit of expenditure, which in turn can be expected to lead to some adjustment to the individual's pattern of activity.

A clear benefit from the amendments to the conventional theory of consumer behaviour incorporated in this chapter is, therefore, that they permit the analysis of the kind of changes discussed in the preceding paragraphs, which might otherwise only be attributed to changes in tastes. Whilst an individual's tastes may change over time, it is important to try and identify as far as possible the influence that other, possibly more objective, factors might have on an individual's behaviour. One advantage of the household production function approach is that it allows us to go further in this respect than any other.[3]

Moreover, it can be observed that, although the variables that have been at the centre of the discussion in this chapter are rather different from those that feature in the discussion of the characteristics approach, the two approaches are by no means incompatible. Both conceive of consumption as a process of transforming inputs into outputs but, whilst the characteristics approach is concerned with a decomposition of the output bundle into its various attributes, the concern of Becker and his colleagues has been to bring a wider range of inputs within the scope of the analysis. This suggests that there may be scope for combining the two approaches into a model that views consumption as a process in which many inputs are combined to produce a number of joint outputs. However, that is not a line that we pursue here because the pay-off from such a model in terms of additional insights into consumer behaviour is not all that great.

Imperfect knowledge and uncertainty

As already observed, the traditional theory of consumer behaviour assumes that consumers are well informed about what goods and services are available and the prices at which they can be obtained. The developments of the basic theory discussed so far, by adding to the analysis other factors influencing consumption decisions, take this further by assuming that the consumer is also well informed about product characteristics and the ways in which products and time need to be combined in a variety of activities. If consumers, and indeed economic agents generally, are less than fully informed (as is usually the case) about many of the variables relevant to the particular decision they are making, this can clearly influence their decisions. Similarly, uncertainty about the outcome of any decision they make may also have some effect. A further task of this chapter is, therefore, to consider the problems of information and uncertainty and some of their effects on the behaviour of consumers.

The problem of information

In recent years, developments in what has come to be called the *economics of information* have led to important insights both in micro- and macro-economics, but, as with the developments discussed in Chapter 6 and in the first part of this chapter much of this work dates no further back than the 1960s. Indeed, in 1961 Stigler was moved to write that information 'occupies a slum dwelling in the town of economics' (p. 213) and was largely ignored. Stigler himself is one of a number of economists who have attempted to make this particular dwelling a more respectable one, and nowadays it is one of the more fashionable residences in the town. However, whilst much of the work involved in this process of 'gentrification' has been of a highly technical nature, some indication of what is involved can be obtained by looking at the problem of information in fairly basic terms.

When the information available to an economic agent is less than complete, information is a scarce commodity but, like any other scarce commodity, it is usually obtainable at some cost. Consumers can readily buy a variety of publications containing information about goods and services they might be considering buying. They can also spend time making personal enquiries to potential sellers about what they have on offer and their trading prices. Sellers also have an interest in ensuring that potential buyers are informed about their products and accordingly provide information through advertising and sales promotion activities.[4] Such information may be provided at little or no money cost to consumers, but to make use of it consumers need to spend time analysing and assimilating it. Moreover, since the interests of sellers, which are in promoting the sales of their particular product, diverge from the interests of consumers, which are to find the most efficient ways of satisfying their various needs, the consumer is usually in a position in which he can derive positive benefits from more information.

Looking at the issue from the consumer's point of view, we can simplify without losing the essence of the problem by considering the case of a consumer wishing to buy 1 unit of a particular standardized product, which might, for example, be a particular type of car, or a 'family'-sized packet of a particular brand of cornflakes. He may be aware that there are a number of possible suppliers and that their prices vary, but we assume that he doesn't know initially which supplier is offering the desired good at the lowest price. The benefits from acquiring more information are, therefore, the potential savings in cost from locating the cheapest source of supply. In general terms these benefits can be expected to increase as the search for information covers more suppliers, and that they reach a maximum when all suppliers have been investigated. However, it would also seem reasonable to suppose that these benefits will increase at a decreasing rate. Probability theory suggests that quite a good approximation to the overall distribution of prices can be obtained from an appropriate sample. Without going into the details of what might constitute an optimal sampling strategy, intuitively it should be clear that the more sellers are investigated the less likely it is that lower-cost sources of supply will remain to be discovered. This suggests a relationship between the number of suppliers investigated and the expected search benefits of the form illustrated by the curve OB_1 in Figure 7.4, where B_1^{max} are the expected benefits obtainable from investigating all possible suppliers (N^{max} in the diagram) and are thus the maximum potential benefits.

The costs of searching for information will also increase as the number of suppliers investigated increases, but probably in this case at an increasing rate, because the last ones investigated are likely to be the less accessible ones requiring more search effort. This is reflected in the curve OC in Figure 7.4. Faced with potential costs and benefits of this nature, the rational consumer will be happy to continue expanding his search effort as long as the expected

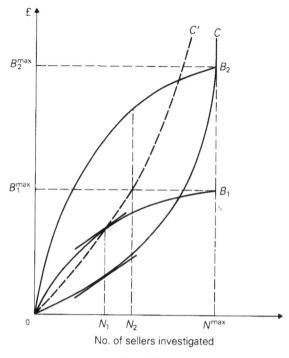

Figure 7.4

benefits from any additional search (i.e. the marginal benefits) are greater than the additional, or marginal, costs, but will not continue searching beyond the point at which they are equal. In terms of the diagram, marginal costs and marginal benefits are measured by the slopes of OB_1 and OC respectively and so the optimal amount of search is determined where the two curves are parallel to each other, which, in Figure 7.4, is when N_1 sellers are investigated.

In the case illustrated, the consumer stops well short of being perfectly informed, and it should be clear from the diagram that this must always be the case. When all possible sellers are investigated, the curve OC approaches the vertical and is therefore much steeper than OB_1, which at that stage is approaching the horizontal. The cost of obtaining the last bit of information would, therefore, considerably exceed the likely benefit.

However, a number of other deductions can also be made from this analysis. First, if the individual is wanting to buy 2 units of the commodity rather than 1, then the potential benefits from searching are doubled, and can thus be represented by the curve OB_2 in the diagram, while his costs, since they are related to the number of sellers investigated rather than to the quantity of goods bought, remain unaffected. With the doubling of the expected benefits involved, the slope of OB_2 when N_1 sellers are investigated is greater than that of OC and hence it is worthwhile for the consumer to search further. In fact the new optimum level of search in the diagram is N_2. For similar reasons, comparing two goods with a similar lack of information about prices, it would be worthwhile for the consumer to put more search effort into the one with the higher price.

The optimal search time may also vary between individuals, particularly since searching is an activity that takes time. Individuals with high wage rates, and therefore high values placed upon time, will face steeper search cost curves, like the dashed curve OC' in the diagram, and will therefore want to spend less time searching. If we recall the discussion in the first part of this chapter, they will also, obviously, have an incentive to use less time-intensive methods of search.

However, one important feature of the search problem introduces considerations that have not featured in our analysis so far, and that is the uncertainty attached to the benefits from searching. If an individual increases his search efforts there is a possibility that he will locate a cheaper source of supply, but it is not certain. This raises the question of how potential benefits to which a degree of uncertainty attaches might be valued by the consumer. Since there are a number of areas in which there is also some uncertainty about the outcome of a consumer's decisions, it is useful to consider the issues raised in a more general context, which is the task of the next section.

Risk and uncertainty

When there is some uncertainty attached to the gain from any action or event we need to consider the **expected benefits**. This term has a precise meaning in situations involving uncertainty and is defined as the potential gain multiplied by the probability of that gain being realized. The probability of an event (or group of events) occurring is the ratio of the number of outcomes in which it (or they) occurs to the total number of possible outcomes. Thus, if an unbiased dice is tossed, the probability of a 6 being thrown is 1/6, and the probability of a number less than 6 being thrown is 5/6. It will be noted that these two probabilities add up to 1 because one or other of the two outcomes is certain to arise, and the probability of an event that is certain to occur is always unity. Thus if an individual were to receive £100 if a 6 was thrown, his expected gain from the toss of the dice would be £16.67 ($= 100 \times 1/6$). If, however, the individual had to pay £10 for taking part in the dice-tossing game, his expected gains from a 6 would be reduced to £15 ($= 90 \times 1/6$). He would also have to take into account his expected losses when a number other than 6 was thrown. Since the probability of that happening is 5/6, these expected losses would be £8.33 ($= 10 \times 5/6$), leaving him with total expected gains of

$$£15 - £8.33 = £6.67.$$

In more general terms, therefore, we can define the expected gain from any activity with n possible outcomes with probabilities $\pi_1, \pi_2, \ldots, \pi_n$ as

$$E(y) = y_1\pi_1 + y_2\pi_2 + \ldots + y_n\pi_n, \qquad (7.11)$$

where $y_1, y_2, \ldots, y_n$ are the net gains from each outcome (which may be positive, negative or zero) and in which

$$\pi_1 + \pi_2 + \ldots + \pi_n = 1,$$

since all possible outcomes are covered.

Another way of looking at these expected gains is as the average gain per toss of the dice (going back to our original example) if the dice is tossed a sufficiently large number of times, because then a 6 would turn up on roughly one-sixth of the occasions. Thus, if the game is played a sufficient number of times, the outcome is fairly certain, and the consumer would be indifferent between playing the game and receiving a certain sum equal to the expected outcome. However, in many choice situations involving uncertainty, the decision the consumer has to make is whether to 'play the game' once. Thus in the search example of the previous section our consumer was deciding whether to undertake one particular unit of search activity. This distinction is important because, although the expected gain may be calculated as a particular sum of money, the actual outcome may be a loss if the consumer's search is unsuccessful; so the consumer may take a rather different view of the benefits of the search than the prospect of receiving the expected value of those benefits with certainty.

Precisely how he would compare the two would depend on his attitude to risk. An individual is said to be **risk-averse** if in a choice between a certain sum of money and taking part in an activity with uncertain outcomes but the same expected gains he chooses the former. If he chooses the latter he is said to be **risk-loving**, and in the intermediate case where he is indifferent between the two he is said to be **risk-neutral**. In general, it is assumed that people are typically risk-averse, and some empirical justification for this assumption can be found in the existence of a sizeable and generally profitable insurance industry, which provides people with an opportunity, on payment of an appropriate premium, to avoid the losses arising from a variety of potential disasters that might possibly befall them. In taking out insurance policies, individuals are expressing a preference for the certain loss of a relatively small sum of money over the possibility of incurring much greater costs if their house were to burn down or their car was to be stolen, even though the probability of such events may be quite low. Further, the fact that the insurance industry has costs that have to be covered and also hopes to make a profit means in practice that what consumers pay out in insurance premiums has to be greater than the expected value of the losses being insured against.[5]

However, risk aversion also suggests that people will not be willing to accept a fair bet, that is, to pay £5 for a 50:50 chance of winning £10, or, in terms of our earlier example, to pay £16.67 for the chance of gaining £100 when a 6 is thrown on a dice. But again, the fact that a thriving gambling industry exists suggests that many people are willing to accept not only fair bets but also the unfair bets that are necessary to allow bookmakers, football pool companies and bingo promoters to cover their costs. In this type of activity consumers appear to be choosing to take part in a gamble with expected returns less than the (certain) sum of money that they have to pay to participate, which suggests risk-loving behaviour. Since many gamblers are also likely to have insurance policies of one sort or another, it begins to look as if there might be some inconsistency in human behaviour. This may be due in part to a tendency for some people to overestimate their chances of success, either because they are unaware of the actual probability of success, or because they think they have some special information or skill that they can exploit to increase their personal chance of success. Nevertheless, the apparent contradictions may perhaps be more satisfactorily explained by recognizing that people play bingo or fill in football pool coupons not just because of the expected winnings, but because they regard them as pleasurable activities (although their potential utility is obviously enhanced by the prospect of winning something). If that is the case, expenditure on gambling needs to be treated in exactly the same way as expenditure on other activities and need not be inconsistent with risk aversion.

Choice under uncertainty

For economists, the assumption of risk aversion has a further attraction in that it implies a utility function of the traditional form. This can be seen in Figure 7.5. On the axes are measured the incomes that the individual receives in two different states of the world – and as such they are referred to as **state-contingent** commodities. Now let us suppose that an individual with £100 at his disposal has the opportunity to take part in the simple type of dice game we have referred to earlier, but this time we will assume that he wins £75 if a 5 or a 6 is thrown but has to pay £25 for the privilege of playing the game. It is thus again a fair game, and in this situation the consumer can be viewed as having the choice between two activities – playing the game (activity A) or not playing the game (activity B). If he plays, there are two possible outcomes, namely a net gain of £50 if he wins, which can be regarded as state of the world 1, or a net loss of £25 if he loses (state of the world 2). If he did not take part we could also identify what he would get in each state of the world, but it would be the same in each. In tabular form we can express the outcome of these activities in terms of the sum of money the consumer has afterwards as follows:

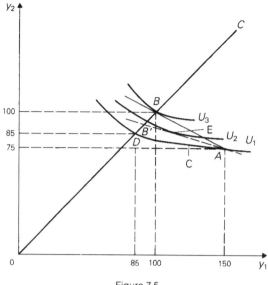

Figure 7.5

	Activity A	Activity B
Outcome in state 1 (y_1)	150	100
Outcome in state 2 (y_2)	75	100

The outcome of action A can thus be plotted as point A in Figure 7.5 and the outcome of action B as point B. Because the latter involves the same outcome in both states, it is on the 45° line drawn from the origin, which in this context can be referred to as the **certainty** line, since any point on it represents a certain outcome, whatever the state of the world. Moreover, since risk aversion implies that a certain situation will be preferred to any risky situation with the same expected returns, risk-averse consumers will prefer point B, involving a certain outcome of £100, to point A, suggesting that their indifference curve passing through A cuts the certainty line somewhere below B. Moreover, we can also observe in the case illustrated, where the indifference curve cuts the certainty line at D, with a certain outcome of £85, that the individual is willing to pay up to £15 to avoid the uncertainties involved in the situation at A.

We can take the analysis a little further if we make the assumption, which underlies much of the economic analysis of uncertainty, that the individual ranks choices in terms of their expected utility. The definition of expected utility is similar to that of expected monetary gains in expression (7.11) above, in that it involves the relevant utilities multiplied by the probability of their occurrence. Thus the expected utility from taking action A in our example can be expressed as

$$E(U^A) = U(150)1/3 + U(75)2/3,$$

where $U(150)$ and $U(75)$ denote the **utilities** derived from incomes of 150 and 75 respectively, or, in more general terms, we can write, using similar notation,

$$E(U^A) = U(y_1{}^A)\pi_1 + U(y_2{}^A)\pi_2, \qquad (7.12)$$

where $y_1{}^A$ and $y_2{}^A$ are the outcomes of action A in states 1 and 2 respectively. If expression (7.12) holds for small movements along an indifference curve, the expected gain in utility from the expected increase in y_2 is equal to the expected loss from the reduction in y_1. Hence

$$\Delta y_1 \pi_1 MU(y_1) + \Delta y_2 \pi_2 MU(y_2) = 0$$

and

$$\frac{\Delta y_2}{\Delta y_1} = - \frac{\pi_1 \cdot MU(y_1)}{\pi_2 \cdot MU(y_2)}, \qquad (7.13)$$

which is an expression for the slope of the indifference curve. From this it follows that along the certainty line, where $y_1 = y_2$, the associated marginal utilities must also be equal, and so the slope of the indifference curve will be $-\pi_1/\pi_2$, which is the negative of the ratio of the probabilities ($1/2$ in our example). However, at A, where $y_1 > y_2$, the normal assumption of diminishing marginal utility implies that $MU(y_1) < MU(y_2)$, which in turn suggests that the indifference curve at A is, in the case illustrated, flatter than at points on the certainty line. In other words, the indifference curves representing the individual's preference in Figure 7.5 should have the normal convex shape.[6]

Now in choosing B in preference to A, the individual gains £25 in state 2 for the loss of £50 in state 1. The slope of the straight line drawn between A and B also has a slope equal to the negative of the ratio of probabilities $-\pi_1/\pi_2$. If, therefore, the individual has the opportunity to buy 'certainty' at a 'fair' price through the market, the relevant budget line is the straight line drawn through AB, and his preferred position is at B where the slope of his indifference curve is also equal to $-\pi_1/\pi_2$. In other words, he will seek to insure against all potential uncertainties in his income. If, however, the terms offered by the insurance companies are not fair, as is likely to be the case because of their need to cover their costs, the relevant budget line through A is like the dashed line AB' in Figure 7.5, which is less steep than AB. In that situation the individual's optimal position must be at a point such as E, which involves the individual moving nearer to the certainty line than his starting point but still experiencing some uncertainty.

The problem of information again

Having analysed the basic choice problem we could go on to consider the effects on the consumer's position of changes in the price of certainty, but clearly the analysis would proceed along the familiar lines first set out in Chapter 3. Instead, therefore, we will return briefly to the problem of information.

The preceding analysis can be applied directly when a consumer is imperfectly informed and the outcome of searching for more information is subject to uncertainty in the following situation. Suppose you have been given £500 by a rich aunt to buy a computer and you have discovered a dealer offering the model you want to buy for £400. You have also heard an unconfirmed rumour that there is a dealer in a town some distance away selling the same model for £325. If you estimate the cost of travelling to this other town and searching for the rumoured cut-price dealer at £25 and the probability of finding a computer for sale at £325 as 1/3, you are faced with exactly the choice situation in Figure 7.5 above. If you don't search (activity B), you have certain savings of £100 out of your gift, which can be spent on software, throwing a party for your friends, or whatever. But if you search (activity A), you have the chance of extra net savings of £50, but you may also end up £25 worse off. If you are risk-averse, as in the case illustrated, you will prefer the certain outcome, but if the search costs were lower, or the probability of finding a cheaper computer was higher, you might be tempted to search.

However, a situation like this – where there are, in effect, only two sources of supply – is clearly a rather special case. We must therefore consider how the analysis can be generalized. One simple approach is to adapt Figure 7.4, which allows for any number of sources of supply, to include uncertainty. In the case of the risk-neutral individual, this can be done simply by redefining the benefit curve to measure the *expected* rather than the actual benefits from investigating particular numbers of suppliers and then proceed as before. Thus in Figure 7.6, EB_N is such an expected benefits curve, so that if the curve C represents, as before, the costs of searching particular numbers of suppliers, the best strategy for the individual would be to investigate N_N suppliers. For the risk-averse individual, however, we would need to adjust the expected benefits curve to allow for the disutility involved with uncertainty. This could be done by subtracting from the expected benefits at each point the amount the individual would be willing to give up to avoid the uncertainties involved. This sum corresponds to the £15 that the individual in Figure 7.5 was willing to give up to avoid the uncertainties involved at point A. This then produces a benefit-from-search curve like EB_A lying below EB_N, predicting less search activity (N_A) than in the risk-neutral case. With a risk-loving individual (not shown in the diagram), the adjustment would be in the opposite direction because of the extra utility obtained by the individual from the risks involved in searching.

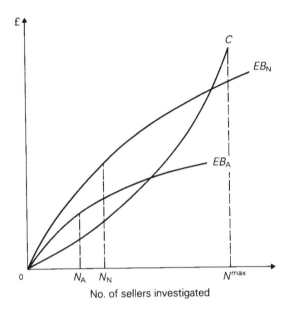

Figure 7.6

In this way we can obtain some insight into the way consumers may react to less than perfect information. But we must also recognize that there are other complications that need to be taken into account in a more complete analysis. Strictly speaking, Figure 7.6 implies a situation where the individual, having decided how many sellers to investigate, investigates them all simultaneously. This might be the case if, for example, the individual is making enquiries by post. But often the search process involves investigating potential suppliers in sequence. In that case, the consumer can decide, after any given seller has been investigated, whether to search further, and that can have an important influence on the amount of search undertaken.

To express the problem in more specific terms, the individual might know initially that the good he is seeking to buy is available at prices ranging between p_L and p_H ($p_L < p_H$), but does not know the identity of the lowest-price seller. When he starts searching, suppose the first seller he encounters quotes a price of p_1, where $p_L < p_1 < p_H$. Whether he accepts that price straight away or continues searching will then depend on his estimate of the expected benefits of *continuing* to search, which depends on the potential savings from finding a lower price and the estimated probability of finding one. Clearly both are likely to be less if p_1 is close to p_L than if it is close to p_H. The total amount of search undertaken, therefore, will depend on how successful the searcher is at discovering low-cost suppliers fairly quickly. The individuals in Figure 7.6, therefore, might in some cases investigate fewer sellers than indicated and in others more, although in a large number of searches the average number of sellers investigated could be expected to approximate to N_N and N_A respectively.

These, however, are matters that are looked at in more detail in more advanced courses and to pursue them further would take us beyond our immediate purpose, which is simply to show how the basic theory of consumer choice can be extended to deal with the problem of choice when information is incomplete and where there is uncertainty. Nevertheless, it needs to be borne in mind that imperfect information and uncertainty arise in some degree in all situations in which economic agents operate, and can be a significant factor affecting their behaviour, as will become apparent at various stages in the following chapters.

Notes

1   Becker himself makes this assumption in Becker (1965), but more general formulations can be found in later works such as Michael and Becker (1973) and Stigler and Becker (1977).
2   In terms of the diagram this pushes the money budget line outwards and the time budget line inwards.
3   The aim in Stigler and Becker (1977), where these matters are extensively discussed, is to go further and establish the proposition that tastes are 'stable over time and similar among people'.
4   The effect of advertising on firms is considered at a later stage.
5   This oversimplifies a little, since insurance companies would also claim that their expert knowledge and access to financial markets enables them to obtain a better financial return on the money paid to them as premiums than their clients could get for themselves, and the benefits of this are also reflected in the terms on which they sell insurance.
6   Strictly speaking, in this case the convexity of the indifference curves is due to the diminishing marginal utility of income rather than to risk aversion as such, but any additional dislike of risk would simply accentuate the convexity of the curves.

Exercises

7.1   Compare and contrast the effects on a consumer's choices of an increase in his non-labour income and an increase in his wage rate.
7.2   A car owner wishing to polish his car has a choice between two brands of polish, *Quickwax* and *Permabrite*. Both brands cost the same price per tin, and with each brand a tin contains just enough polish to polish his car once. *Permabrite*, however, takes longer to apply but gives better protection against rust. How would the consumer decide which polish to buy? How, and under what conditions, would his choice be affected by an increase in his wage rate?
7.3   'The household production function approach to the analysis of consumers' choices permits the analysis of changes in consumers' behaviour that can only be attributed to changes in tastes with the more traditional approach.' Explain this statement and give examples.
7.4   'If the income elasticity of demand for a particular good is positive, consumers will always

increase the time spent searching for cheaper sources of supply when their income rises.' Is this statement true or false?

7.5 It has been estimated that the utility that Sally, an impecunious student, would receive from money gifts of various amounts is as follows:

Gift (£)	100	200	400	600	800
Utility	250	400	650	850	1000

If she was given a lottery ticket for a prize of £800, what price would she be willing to accept for the ticket if the probability of winning the lottery was:

(a) 0.25
(b) 0.4?

What do your answers suggest about the individual's attitude to risk?

CHAPTER EIGHT
FROM INDIVIDUALS TO FIRMS

Introducing the firm

Having looked in some detail at the behaviour of the individual, we turn now to the analysis of a second important economic agent – the firm. A firm, like the proverbial elephant, is difficult to define but is nevertheless a reasonably recognizable entity, and the indications are that there are currently of the order of half a million firms of one sort or another operating in the United Kingdom concerned with the production and trading of a great variety of goods and services. They range from small one-man businesses to giant multinational undertakings whose annual turnover is comparable to the gross national product of some European countries. Amongst them can be found immense diversity not only in size and in what they produce, but in the way they are organized, how they are financed, the conditions under which they operate, and so forth. Despite all this diversity, they share, like elephants, certain common features.

Perhaps the most common feature of firms is that they are all involved in production of one form or another, that is, in transforming inputs into an output of goods and services. Indeed, the firm has been defined as 'the fundamental unit of organisation of production in a market economy' (Greenwood, 1982). Whilst this may be the case, it will be recalled that households can also be viewed as being involved in production. In recognition of this it might be argued that, whereas household production is largely geared to generating utility for members of a household, production in firms is carried out with a view to the potential financial gains attainable by selling their products on the market. Again, although this may also be true, it still doesn't provide an entirely satisfactory distinction between the two because many households also produce labour services for the market (requiring inputs of food, rest and relaxation, etc.) if nothing else.

However, the fact that it is difficult to draw a line between households and firms is not important for our purposes. In general terms, economic agents produce for the market rather than for their own direct use in order to exploit whatever comparative advantages they may have, and to benefit from the gains from trade.[1] If this production for the market involves no more resources than the household can itself provide, then the analysis of the behaviour of the agent concerned involves little more than the analysis covered in Chapter 4. From the point of view of economic analysis, the interest in the firm as a distinct economic agent arises when it starts reaching out beyond the individual household and mobilizes the labour and capital resources of other households for its own productive purposes, particularly since firms produce all but a tiny proportion of total marketable output. By way of introduction to the subsequent chapters of this book, therefore, this chapter will be concerned initially with a discussion of the factors underlying the development of firms, defined, as suggested above, as organizations concerned with production for the market employing the resources of more than one household. It will then go on to consider some of the consequent implications for the organization of firms and for their objectives.

Firms as employers

We can learn something of the circumstances under which an economic agent producing for the market will employ labour by considering the effects of such employment on the choices open to that agent. For example, take the case of an individual with a given plot of land at his disposal producing garden produce for the market. The output produced will obviously depend on the hours of work put in, but in these circumstances (variable labour applied to fixed land and other inputs) we might expect diminishing returns to the labour input (see p. 131 below). Hence the additional output produced by an extra hour's labour will fall as the total hours worked increase. With given market prices for the output, this will also mean that the revenue arising from the sale of the output from an extra hour's labour will also decline as the total hours worked increase.

The relationship between the number of hours worked and the revenue yielded can, therefore, be represented by an upward-sloping curve of diminishing slope. However, since working involves the sacrifice of leisure, it implies the kind of relationship between sales revenue and leisure depicted by the curve MB in Figure 8.1, where M represents the total hours available and B the revenue obtainable by working all the available hours. In other words, the individual is faced with a trade-off between leisure and income similar to that considered previously, except that the constraint on choices is concave to the origin. If the choices on (or inside) MB are the only ones available to our producer, the optimal utility-maximizing choice will be at D, where one of the producer's indifference curves is tangential to MB. At this point the producer will enjoy L hours leisure and spend LM hours working, from which he will derive an income of R.

Now suppose our producer has access to a labour market in which he can

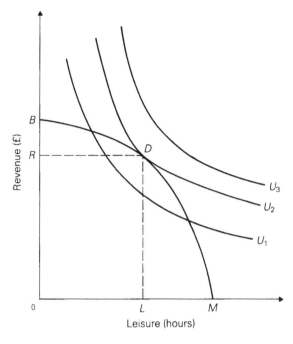

Figure 8.1

buy and sell labour services at a market determined rate of £w per hour. The possibility of selling his own labour to others is important because it means that the opportunity costs of working on his own are the earnings forgone by not working for someone else (assuming that this doesn't involve any additional disutility), and it may be the case that these opportunity costs are so high that it is not worthwhile carrying on his own production.

In terms of the diagram, the income–leisure choices obtainable by working for others can be represented (as in Chapter 4) by a straight line drawn through M with slope equal to the wage rate. If this happens to lie wholly above MB in Figure 8.1, then, clearly, the individual can ultimately reach a higher level of utility by working for others rather than for himself. However, if the income–leisure choices from working for others are represented by a line such as MN in Figure 8.2, which lies below MB (or by one that is partly below MB and partly above), the situation is not quite so straightforward.

The complications arise because the optimal situation will involve the individual spending some of his time working for himself and some working for some other employer. For example, if in the case illustrated in Figure 8.2 the individual decides initially to spend MT hours working for himself, this will yield an income of W, and if subsequent hours are spent working for someone else the income–leisure choices available to him will lie on the dashed line RF drawn parallel to MN. Clearly, the choices on RF are superior to those on MN and, in the case illustrated, some of the opportunities open

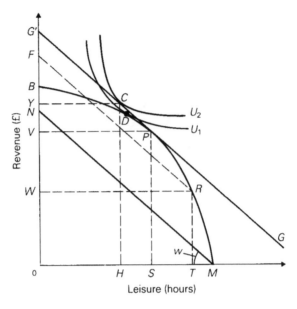

Figure 8.2

are superior to those on *MB*. However, it should be equally clear from Figure 8.2 that even better choices will be opened up if our individual moves further up *MB* by spending more time working for himself. In fact, the optimal range of choices will be available if he moves up *MB* to point *P* where the line drawn parallel to *MN*, labelled *GG'*, is tangential to *MB*. This will involve spending *MS* hours working for himself in order to obtain an income of *V*, but if additional income is still desired more can then be earned by selling his labour to someone else than by working for himself. Hence, if the individual's preferences are as illustrated by the indifference curves *U₁* and *U₂*, utility will be maximized at *C*, where the individual will receive *Y* income and have *H* hours leisure, while his total working time of *MH* hours will be split between work on his own plot (*MS* hours) and work for someone else (*SH* hours).

All this, of course, indicates why a person may become an employee as well as a producer, whereas our more immediate concern is with the circumstances under which a producer might wish to become an employer, buying labour rather than selling it. This, however, is also explicable in terms of our current analysis. Indeed, it will happen if our producer's preferences are such that he prefers more leisure than can be obtained at *P* rather than less. Such is the case illustrated in Figure 8.3. If a producer with the preferences indicated there finds himself at *P*, he will be able to improve his position by taking more leisure and working less. But if, instead of simply reducing the amount of labour used on his land, he was to hire workers at the market rate of *w* per hour to work in his place he will, in terms of the diagram, be able to move down *PG* rather than *PM* and thus again have access to a superior range of

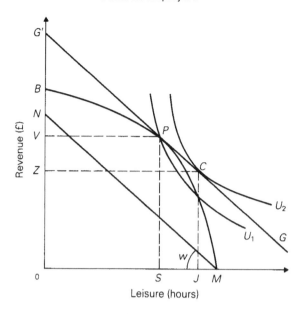

Figure 8.3

income–leisure choices. He will effectively be buying back leisure through the market at a cost (in terms of a reduction in income) less than the cost of reducing production; in the case illustrated, his utility will be maximized by employing SJ labour, which will then allow him to enjoy an income of Z and leisure of J.

However, a producer's desire to employ labour will in most cases go beyond a desire to get someone to work in his place while he goes off for a round of golf; it will arise from a desire to overcome the constraints on the amount of labour that an individual can supply. In Figures 8.1–8.3 the maximum labour-time the individual can supply is M, but it might well be the case that the slope of the curve MB is still greater than the slope of MN at the point where it cuts the vertical axis. In other words, the revenue from the use of extra labour will still exceed its cost. It will not now be possible for any extra labour to be supplied by the producer, however workaholic he might happen to be, but it will be obtainable through the market. Thus, in the case illustrated in Figure 8.4, the point P, where GG', defined as in Figure 8.2, is tangential to MB, is to the left of the vertical axis and requires a total labour input of MQ, which in this case is rather more than can be supplied by one individual. However, it again provides the potential employer with superior income–leisure choices to any other level of employment and, as in the previous case, his utility-maximizing position C can be reached by buying in an appropriate quantity of labour, which in this case is JQ. Again, the amount of labour employed reflects the employer's preferences for income and leisure, but on this occasion the influence of those preferences is

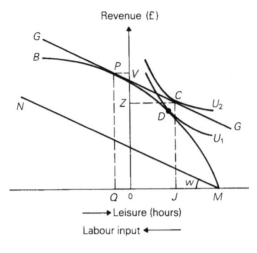

Figure 8.4

proportionately smaller and becomes more marginal the further P is to the left of the vertical axis. As P moves to the left, therefore, the more fundamental reason for the employment of labour becomes the desire to exploit technical possibilities of production that require more labour than can be supplied by one individual (or household if that is considered the appropriate unit).

Underlying all the preceding analysis is the assumption that the basic units of labour input, labour hours, are homogeneous in the sense that one additional hour's labour has the same effect on output whoever supplies it and wherever it is supplied. Quite apart from the differing skills and capabilities of individuals, however, the effects of an extra unit of labour may vary according to when it is supplied. In particular, several units of labour may be more productive when supplied simultaneously rather than in succession. This is, for example, the case when there are heavy or bulky objects to be handled. Certain tasks that are unmanageable by one person working alone can often easily be handled by two or more people working together. In other words, there may be advantages in team production and that, as Alchian and Demsetz (1972) have argued, provides a further important reason for the creation of firms employing labour. Thus again the need to employ labour arises from the technical conditions of production, but in this case it is more the capacity constraints on individuals that need to be overcome rather than the time constraints.

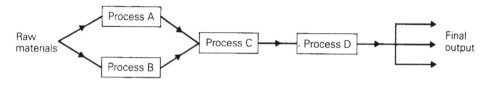

Figure 8.5

Firms versus markets

Whilst the analysis of the previous section provides some insight into why economic agents employ labour, it by no means explains all facets of the typical modern firm. In particular, it does not explain why many people are employed to do specific self-contained tasks that they could easily perform either as individual producers or within a separate firm specializing in that type of work. For example, typing services, cleaning services and the like could easily be bought in from specialist agencies. Indeed, they often are, but many firms prefer to have the services provided by their own employees. Similarly, many firms carry out a series of processes on a particular product when it would be technically feasible for them to concentrate on one or at least a smaller number of processes. Obviously, transport costs can be reduced if successive production processes are carried out on the same site, but that in itself need not require one single firm to be responsible for all stages of production. It would be perfectly possible for a number of firms to rent space within a larger factory building with each responsible for part of the productive process, and again, no doubt, it does sometimes happen.

Thus, in the case illustrated in Figure 8.5, where the transformation from raw materials to finished products involves four distinct processes, separate firms could be involved at each stage, with those responsible for process A and process B buying raw materials and selling their output to the firm responsible for C, and so on down the line. Furthermore, technical conditions might allow for more than one producer at each stage. Thus there might, for example, be two firms engaged in process A and three in B, all selling to one firm engaged in process C, which in turn might sell to five firms producing the final output. But with this arrangement each firm has to negotiate contracts with at least two other parties, depending on the number of firms it is buying from and selling to. Such negotiations involve the use of resources, particularly labour time, and therefore impose transactions costs. If, however, one firm is responsible for everything from the purchase of raw materials to the sale of final output, the need for each individual or group to negotiate with a number of others will be eliminated. Instead they will have to negotiate only one contract with the firm relating to their own activities within the firm. Total transactions costs will, therefore, be reduced.

Hence firms may be seen, as Coase (1937) originally suggested, as institutions serving to reduce the transactions costs that independent market agents might otherwise incur. In addition, they reduce the degree of uncertainty in the sense that those involved in individual processes no longer have to worry about whether the market will be able to supply materials and absorb output or about possible adverse movements of market prices. In a unified firm, such matters are someone else's responsibility. But in any case the dependence on market transactions will be much reduced and the resources devoted to the various processes will be coordinated through the administrative and planning procedures of the firm rather than by market forces. Or as Coase saw it, quoting one of the more picturesque phrases of Sir Dennis Robertson, firms may be seen as 'islands of conscious power in this ocean of unconscious co-operation like lumps of butter coagulating in a pail of buttermilk' (Coase, 1937, p. 388).

The classical model of the firm

The previous analysis presupposes that some individuals – usually referred to in this context as entrepreneurs – have property rights in productive assets, giving them the power to decide how they are used and entitling them to any residual earnings from the use of those assets after contractual obligations have been met, whilst others don't and are thus willing to accept the role of employees. This is essentially what is implied in what can be referred to as the 'classical' model of the firm developed by Marshall and his successors, but it is instructive to ask what grounds there might be for accepting this model of the organization of firms rather than others. To some extent the classical model rests on an assumption that access to property rights in productive assets is restricted. If this were not the case, an organizational model allowing some sharing of residual earnings would be more appropriate. Such co-operative organizations do exist and have been analysed by economists, but they remain comparatively rare in western economies.

One possible explanation of the restriction in the access to property rights in productive assets lies in the distribution of wealth. The ownership of wealth confers an ability to acquire productive assets, and in societies with an uneven distribution of wealth some individuals are in a better position to acquire productive assets than others. Further, if, as is usually the case, the distribution of wealth is skewed, the number of people with the wealth to acquire productive assets might be quite small, particularly in comparison to the number of people whose main asset is their capacity to provide labour services – hence the dichotomy between labour and capital in the writings of classical economists such as Smith, Ricardo and Marx. However, this does not provide a complete explanation, because, with reasonably efficient capital markets providing individuals with the opportunity to borrow funds, the ownership of wealth need not be a prerequisite to the acquisition of

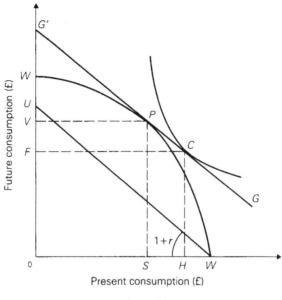

Figure 8.6

productive assets. Indeed, the analysis of the conditions under which the individual would make use of such markets in the pursuit of productive opportunities is formally identical to the analysis of the use of labour markets discussed above, except that the choice is between present and future consumption opportunities rather than between income and leisure.

Thus an individual with an initial endowment of wealth may use it either to finance current consumption or to invest in productive assets yielding a return in the form of opportunities for future consumption. In the two-period situation illustrated in Figure 8.6 (corresponding to the two-period analysis in Chapter 4), where the initial holding of wealth is W, the relevant choices can be represented by the investment opportunities curve WW, which is similar to the curve MB in Figure 8.1 above. With no access to capital markets, the consumer's optimal choice is simply where an indifference curve is tangential to WW, corresponding to point D in Figure 8.1; but access to a capital market, in which an individual can borrow or lend at a market determined rate of interest r, will also allow the individual to trade off present for future consumption along WU in Figure 8.6, which has a slope of $(1 + r)$.[2] In that case, just as in Figure 8.2, the optimal range of choices is opened up at point P on WW where the line GG' drawn parallel to WU is tangential to WW. To reach P the individual will need to invest WS in productive assets, but having done that he will have access to all the opportunities for present and future consumption arising along GPG'.

Whether the individual enters the market as a borrower or a lender then depends on his preferences. If his preferences are such that his optimal consumption point on GPG' is to the left of P, the funds required to finance his current consumption will be less than the S he will still have available, so he will have surplus funds to lend. If, on the other hand, his preferences are such that his optimal consumption point is to the right of P, as in the case illustrated, he will need to borrow. In fact, with a utility-maximizing position at C, his total current expenditure requirements will be H for consumption plus WS for investment. With W available from his own resources, therefore, he will need to borrow SH. Out of his future income of V he will then have an obligation to repay VF, which is simply SH plus interest or $SH(1 + r)$, leaving OF to spend on future consumption.

As in the employment case there is no necessity for the optimum production point to be to the right of the vertical axis. Indeed, the investment opportunities curve could lie wholly to the left of that axis. Whereas all individuals have an initial stock of time that they can allocate to work or leisure activities, not all individuals have an initial stock of wealth. Nevertheless, access to investment opportunities promising future income may still be obtained by borrowing, and the optimal choice can be identified in the same way as in Figure 8.6. Such a case is illustrated in Figure 8.7, where it will be considered in more detail.

It would seem to be the case, therefore, that the distribution of wealth should not limit access to productive opportunities. Whilst this is a conclusion that we will want to qualify somewhat in the next section, it suggests we should look for other reasons why access to property rights in productive assets may be restricted.

One possibility is that, even though everyone may be in a position to acquire productive assets, not everyone may have the entrepreneurial skills needed to exploit the opportunities available. These entrepreneurial skills include an ability to assess where there might be some scope for profitable productive activities, and a capacity for taking appropriate managerial decisions on what to produce, how to produce it and how to negotiate beneficial contracts with buyers and sellers. Furthermore, all this has to be allied to a temperamental inclination for this kind of activity. If the relevant entrepreneurial skills are scarce, then the numbers of people willing and able to set up firms may not be all that great, since most people will prefer to exploit what comparative advantages they may have as employees or in other respects. In other words, it is not so much the access to productive opportunities that may be restricted as the ability to exploit them.

A further argument for the classical firm arises from the problems involved with team production, which have been stressed by Alchian and Demsetz (1972). The problem arises because with team activity there is no obvious way of measuring the contributions that individuals make to the team effort, and thus no easy way of relating the rewards individuals get to their efforts. In this kind of situation the rewards tend to be distributed according to some arbitrary rule acceptable to the members of the team, such as, for example, equal shares. With that kind of arrangement, only a proportion of the reduction in earnings that would arise if one member of the team reduced his effort would be borne by the person concerned. In a team with few members any unilateral slackening of effort may be detectable by other members, who can then take remedial action, which might take the form of a renegotiation of the way the team's earnings are distributed or, in extreme cases, expulsion from the team. With a large group, however, malingering may be less easily detected and, moreover, the disincentives to individuals in terms of reduced earnings will be much reduced. In these circumstances it becomes useful to have someone acting in a supervisory or managerial capacity monitoring performance and relating rewards to effort. But we may then ask what incentive the manager has to perform his job effectively? One possibility might be to make him accountable to the team as a whole; alternatively, if (as in the classical firm) the manager is the person entitled to the residual earnings, the necessary incentives will automatically be there since the more effectively he does his job the better off he will be. Of course, once a firm gets above a certain size, effective supervision may require a team of supervisors rather than just one, and with even larger firms there might need to be several layers of supervisors forming a hierarchical structure. Nevertheless, provided the top managers are entitled to the residual earnings, there will be every incentive to them to ensure effective supervision.

In a competitive environment, therefore, it may be argued that firms organized along 'classical' lines will stand the best chances of survival, and thus should ultimately emerge as the dominant form of industrial organization. Unfortunately, whilst many such firms do exist in the real world, in terms of their contribution to output and the resources they employ they are by no means the dominant form. Although some form of hierarchical structure is almost universal, at least within larger firms, it is much less common for the property rights in their productive assets to be concentrated in the hands of one person or a small group. A more usual situation is one in which the property rights are shared amongst a large number of people and institutions who effectively have no managerial role to play. We need to consider, therefore, what hitherto neglected influences could account for the development of such organizations.

The modern business corporation or managerial firm

A particularly important omission from the preceding discussion has been a proper recognition of the uncertainty attached to the operation of any business enterprise. It has been noted above that one advantage of firms as organizations responsible for coordinating operations that could otherwise be coordinated through markets is the reduction in the level of uncertainty faced by the individual components of the enterprise. However, the uncertainty facing the enterprise as a whole is also an important factor in determining its structure. This uncertainty arises because the returns associated with any productive activity can be forecast only with some degree of error, and are subject to variation over time in a manner that can rarely be accurately foreseen.

Such uncertainty can create considerable difficulties for a large firm organized on classical lines and financing its activities by borrowing at fixed interest rates, since relatively small changes in revenue can lead to disproportionately large changes in the earnings of the entrepreneur, which are the residual when all other costs have been met. If Mr Micawber could be plunged from bliss to despair by a reduction in his income from £1.01 to 99p, how would he have viewed a change from a profit of £2 million to a corresponding loss? Normal risk-averse individuals will naturally seek some way of avoiding such large fluctuations in their income by inducing others to accept at least some of the risks involved. In the modern business firm, this is done by raising funds to finance its operations by the sale of securities, which entitle the holders to a share in the residual earnings of the firm, rather than by borrowing. The buyers of these securities become 'shareholders' with certain property rights in the residual earnings of the firm depending on the size of their holdings. They also share the risks, as fluctuations in profits are reflected in fluctuations in the return that they get from their shares, although the institution of limited liability, which absolves shareholders from responsibility for the debts of the firm, puts a lower limit on the losses that they can suffer.[3]

Since shareholders are affected by the success or otherwise of any firm in which they hold shares, they naturally have some interest in the way it is run. Institutionally, this interest is reflected in the voting rights that they acquire with their shares. However, since individual shareholders cannot be assumed to have the skills, the information or indeed the inclination to participate in detailed managerial decision-making, in practice their interests are served by the delegation of managerial responsibility to specialist managers who report to annual (and sometimes other) general meetings of their companies at which shareholders can exercise their voting power.

This arrangement provides a potentially more active role for those with wealth at their disposal than was suggested in the discussion of the classical firm, since wealth provides the power to buy large numbers of shares and the more shares an individual has the greater his voting power and thus the more influence he can have on the affairs of the firm. However, many holders of wealth prefer to spread the risks of holding shares by investing in a number of firms. Moreover, so far as the largest companies are concerned, few individuals have the wealth to enable them to buy a controlling interest. With many firms, therefore, ownership of shares is divided up amongst a large number of individuals and institutions, and thus the power that any one of them can exercise over the appointment of managers and the decisions they make is somewhat limited. This situation means that there is likely to be a separation of ownership from the control of a company in the sense that, whilst technically the managers are making decisions on behalf of the owners and should have their interests in mind, in practice they may well have considerable discretion to pursue their own objectives with potentially significant effects on the behaviour of the firm, as will be seen below.

The objectives of the firm

Having considered the factors that lead to the establishment of firms as distinct from households, our final concern in this chapter is with the objectives of firms because they obviously have an important bearing on how firms behave. It seems reasonable to suppose, as in previous chapters, that individual decision-makers will be concerned to maximize their own utility, but it is necessary to consider whether that has any general implications for the behaviour of firms.

So far as the classical firm is concerned, one particular conclusion of the above analysis was that the optimal production position – the position that allowed the entrepreneur to maximize his utility – was actually independent of his preferences. It will, therefore, clearly be instructive to examine the properties of this optimum production point a little more closely. It might be suspected that something is being maximized at that point, but the question is what? Concentrating for the moment on the optimal employent of labour as illustrated in Figures 8.2, 8.3 and 8.4 above, it can be seen that, in geometrical terms, it is determined at the point where the vertical difference between the curve MB and the line MN is at its maximum, which is at P in every case. But since the height of the curve MB above the horizontal axis indicates the total revenue obtainable from the employment of different quantities of labour, and MN indicates the total market value of the labour inputs (i.e. the wage rate × man-hours), what is being maximized at P is

total revenue – total labour cost.

Moreover, since Figures 8.2–8.4 are constructed on the assumption that any other inputs involved in the production process are fixed in quantity, their costs are also fixed. Hence, maximizing the difference between total revenue and labour costs also maximizes profits, which constitute the difference between total revenue and total costs. It would appear, therefore, that a necessary condition for the entrepreneur to maximize his utility is that he employs the quantity of labour, and by implication produces the quantity of output, that yields maximum profits.[4]

However, Figures 8.2–8.4 present what is essentially a short-run view of the situation in which some inputs are fixed in quantity. In the longer run, it might be expected that utility maximization by the entrepreneur will again

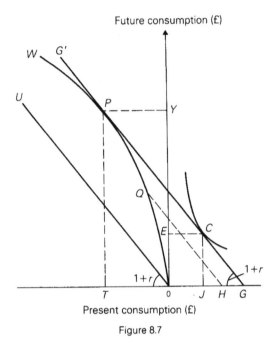

Figure 8.7

require maximum profits, but a more precise view of what would be involved can be obtained by considering the problem in the context of the kind of optimal investment decision outlined above. Thus in Figure 8.7, which is basically similar to Figure 8.6 except that it illustrates the case where the individual has no initial endowment of wealth, the curve OW indicates the potential future income obtainable from various levels of (investment) expenditure on productive assets in the present financed entirely by borrowing.

This future income is, of course, the profit obtainable from the use of the productive assets, and the implication of the analysis is that whatever quantity of assets is purchased they will be used in such a way as to maximize the profits from their operation, because the greater the profits earned the higher will OW be relative to OU, the slope of which reflects the cost of borrowing, and the better the opportunities for present and future consumption opened up for the entrepreneur. As before, the optimal point on OW is at P, where the vertical distance between OW and OU is a maximum, but for present purposes more insight is obtainable by recognizing that P is also the point where the horizontal distance between OW and OU is maximized. This maximum horizontal distance is measured by OG in Figure 8.7, where G is the point at which the line drawn through P parallel to OU cuts the horizontal axis.

From the diagram it can be seen that

$$OG = TG - OT,$$

124

but given that the slope of PG ($= TP/TG$) is $(1 + r)$

$$TG(1 + r) = TP \ (= OY).$$

TG is thus the amount of money that would need to be lent now at the going rate of interest r to produce a sum of TP in the future. This implies that the promise of TP in the future is equivalent to having TG now, or, in the more conventional terminology, TG is the present value of the future return of TP. Since OT is simply the sum of money that needs to be spent now on productive assets in order to produce a future income of TP, OG is the difference between the present value of the future returns from these assets and their current cost, which is usually referred to as their **net present value**.

Whilst OG represents the net present value of the future returns at P, the net present value of the returns yielded at any other point on OW, such as Q, can similarly be shown as the distance between the origin and the point where a line of slope $(1 + r)$ drawn from that point cuts the horizontal axis. Thus the net present value of the returns at Q on OW in Figure 8.7 is OH. This, of course, is less than OT, and it should also be clear from the diagram that the net present value of the returns at any point on OW other than P will be less than OT. P, therefore, is the point involving the level of investment in productive assets with the greatest net present value. Hence utility maximization by the entrepreneur can be seen as requiring the level of investment in productive assets that maximizes the net present value of the firm's future profit stream.

One limitation of the diagrammatic approach used so far is that it relates strictly to a two-period situation, whereas in practice productive assets may yield returns over a number of periods. However, the present value concept can easily be generalized. If an asset yields returns of R_1, R_2 up to R_n in n successive future years, then the sum of money that would need to be lent at a rate of interest r to yield R_1 in year 1 is $R_1/(1 + r)$. Similarly, the sum needed to yield R_2 in year 2 would be $R_2/(1 + r)^2$ and the sum needed to yield R_n in year n would be $R_n/(1 + r)^n$. The present value of the whole stream of returns is then simply the aggregate of all these amounts and is thus

$$\frac{R_1}{(1 + r)} + \frac{R_2}{(1 + r)^2} + \ldots + \frac{R_n}{(1 + r)^n}.$$

Further, if access to these returns requires an expenditure on productive assets of C_0 in the present (i.e. in year 0), the *net* present value of the returns is

$$\frac{R_1}{(1 + r)} + \frac{R_2}{(1 + r)^2} + \ldots + \frac{R_n}{(1 + r)^n} - C_0,$$

and the entrepreneur's choices between present and future consumption are optimized when C_0 is chosen to produce the stream of returns with the greatest net present value.

Again it might appear that maximizing net present values should involve short-run profit-maximizing behaviour, which will ensure that the returns in each period are as great as possible. However, that will only strictly be true if the returns in each period are independent of the returns in all other periods. In some situations it might be the case that attempts to maximize short-run profits in one period might, by raising prices, lead either to the attraction of more competition in the longer run or to a loss of consumer goodwill, which will reduce profitability in subsequent periods and which, if sufficiently large (that is, if the discounted future losses exceeded the short-run gains), reduce the firm's net present value and hence the utility of the entrepreneur. Nevertheless, subject to that qualification, utility maximization by the entrepreneur can be seen as involving the maximization of profits in the short run, and in the longer term the acquisition of the quantity of productive assets that maximizes the net present value of the firm's income stream.

Turning now to the managerial firm, the separation between ownership and control that it involves means that key decision-makers will gain little or no direct benefit from increases in profits and therefore will have less incentive to maximize profits. Profitability may be one of the arguments in the manager's utility function in the sense that it may be taken as an indication of how successful he is at his job, but there are likely to be other variables involved as well. Amongst the latter could be the environment in which the manager works, his financial remuneration and other perks of the job. It has also been argued by Williamson (1964) and others that an important variable might also be the size of the business, as managerial posts in large businesses are likely to confer more status and command higher salaries than comparable posts in smaller concerns. But whatever the precise details of the managerial utility function (and these issues are discussed further in Chapter 16 below), it is clear that there is likely to be a trade-off between profits and certain other managerial objectives, which in turn may lead, depending on the actual form of the managerial preferences, to decisions being taken that result in less than maximum profits being earned.

Nevertheless, the ability of managers to pursue their own objectives at the expense of profits may be constrained in a number of ways. First of all, the directors of a company are technically accountable to shareholders for their stewardship of the firm's assets. If shareholders are not satisfied by the performance of the company, they can give vent to their dissatisfaction at the company's annual general meeting and can as a last resort remove the directors from their posts. In practice, however, they do not have easy access to the information required to monitor directors' performance closely. To acquire that information is costly in terms of time and effort, and for an individual shareholder to make good use of it he needs to persuade a sufficient number of fellow shareholders to support him, which requires further expenditures. Shareholders may not, therefore, be in a position to impose effective direct constraints on managerial discretion. Nevertheless, if they are dissatisfied with the performance of a company in which they hold shares, they can always sell those shares and that may in practice have a more potent influence on managerial behaviour. If a sufficiently large number of a firm's shareholders are trying to dispose of shares, the market value of the company will fall and make it vulnerable to takeover by individuals or groups who see the opportunity of making a more profitable use of the firm's assets. Since such a takeover often involves the replacement of the firm's existing management, it is an outcome that the incumbent managers may prefer to avoid by self-restraint in their pursuit of objectives that have an adverse effect on profits.

In effect, therefore, the managers' ability to maximize their own utility will be constrained by the need to satisfy the expectations of shareholders, but how stringent a constraint that is in practice will depend on how well informed and efficient the market for shares happens to be. With a perfect market, the equilibrium price of a firm's shares will be such that the total value of those shares will be just equal to the net present value of its expected future profits. Any deviation from that level will immediately attract a queue of eager buyers or sellers, with the result that the share price will be pushed back to its equilibrium level. But, perhaps more significantly, any depression in the value of the shares because of departures from profit-maximizing policies will immediately be apparent in a fully informed market, and attract takeover bids. It will thus be difficult for the firm to do anything other than attempt to maximize its profits. In the real world, of course, markets are less than perfectly informed and may well have other imperfections, so there is likely to be some scope at least for the exercise of managerial discretion.

However, the competitive environment in which firms find themselves may impose additional constraints in that the more competitive the markets in which they operate, the more difficult it is for them to earn profits over and above the amounts required to keep their shareholders happy. Indeed, in limiting cases, it would be impossible for firms to earn more profits than those required to satisfy shareholders, so to meet shareholders' expectations they will effectively be forced back to profit-maximizing behaviour whatever the preferences of their managers.

The conclusion seems to be, therefore, that as a working hypothesis it can reasonably be assumed that entrepreneurial firms conforming more or less to the classical model will seek to maximize their profits. However, given that securities markets are likely to be less than perfect, it would seem that similar assumptions can be used for firms in which ownership is divorced from control only if they are operating in sufficiently competitive markets. The same conclusion also applies to other types of firms, e.g. labour-managed firms, because competition will again limit the extent to which they can pursue non-profit objectives and survive. With restricted competition, however, such firms can be expected to take the opportunity to pursue objectives other than profit maximization.

The implications of these conclusions will be explored in more detail in subsequent chapters, but one other factor that is likely to impinge on the behaviour of all types of firm should be noted before proceeding further. In this chapter the profits under discussion have strictly related to the difference between total revenue and the opportunity costs of all the inputs used to produce that revenue, where opportunity costs are defined in their conventional sense as the value of the inputs in their best alternative uses. This definition of profits – sometimes referred to as economic profits – need not be exactly the same as the firm's accounting or reported profits because the opportunity costs of some inputs, particularly those that are owned rather than hired, are not always reflected very accurately in accounting conventions, and indeed are not always known very precisely. But more importantly, if firms' own estimates of these costs are inaccurate, they will find it difficult to maximize their profits in the strict sense even if they want to.

However, this is only a reflection of the more general problem, already discussed in Chapter 7 above, that economic agents are rarely, in practice, fully informed about the choices open to them. As we have seen, it may be possible for the agents to acquire more information, but that invariably involves additional costs. Moreover, as Simon (1985) has pointed out, human capacity to absorb and process information is also limited. Hence, whilst individual agents may be rational in the sense of seeking to choose the most preferred situation, their rationality may be 'bounded' by a lack of appreciation of the full range of opportunities open to them. This can lead to what has been referred to as 'satisficing' behaviour, rather than the optimizing behaviour implied by much of the preceding discussion. The implications of this for firms' behaviour will also be considered in more detail in Chapter 16.

Notes

1 It is assumed that the reader is familiar with these ideas.
2 It will be recalled from Chapter 4 above that $(1 + r)$ is the cost of present consumption in terms of future consumption forgone, because an additional £1 spent now means that there will be £$(1 + r)$ less to spend in the future.
3 The worst that can happen is for the return on shares to fall to zero. The shares would then be worthless, but the individual shareholder's losses would be limited to the original cost of his shares plus the interest forgone on alternative forms of investment.
4 This analysis does, of course, assume that the entrepreneur's labour has a market value. Ng (1974) has argued, contrary to views expressed earlier, that, even in the absence of a market for managerial labour, utility maximization by the entrepreneur would still require profit maximization, although the derivation of the profit-maximizing position would not be the same as in Figures 8.2–8.4.

Exercises

8.1 A self-employed painter and decorator finds that he can work for a larger contractor for as many or as few hours as he wants for a fixed rate of £4 per hour. Assuming he gets no additional disutility from working for someone else, under what conditions would he:

(i) give up his own business and work only for the contractor,
(ii) work both for his own business and the contractor,
(iii) work only for his own business,
(iv) work only for his own business and employ another person at the market rate of £4 per hour?

8.2 Why is most productive activity carried on by firms rather than individuals who trade with each other?

8.3 Why do firms tend to be organized on hierarchical lines rather than as partnerships between equals?

8.4 'As far as owner–managers are concerned, utility maximization and profit maximization amount to the same thing.' Explain and discuss this statement.

8.5 What alternatives to the profit-maximizing assumption do you think might be appropriate for:

(a) a firm in which ownership is divorced from control,
(b) a labour-managed firm,
(c) a nationalized industry?

CHAPTER NINE
THE PRODUCTION FUNCTION
AND
ITS PROPERTIES

Introduction

If, as suggested in Chapter 8, the most obvious common feature of firms is that they are all involved in production (defined as the process of transforming inputs into outputs), the relationship between quantities of inputs and the resultant quantity of output is of fundamental importance to them. Indeed, although this relationship, known as the **production function**, is essentially an engineering or technological relationship, it ranks alongside the utility function as one of the more basic determinants of the allocation of resources in a market economy. In general terms it can be expressed as

$$q = f(y_1, y_2, \ldots, y_n), \tag{9.1}$$

where $y_1, y_2, \ldots, y_n$ are the quantities of the different inputs employed and q is the *maximum* output per period that can be produced with those inputs. It thus essentially indicates what is technically feasible with given quantities of inputs.

Moreover, if the maximum output obtainable from a given bundle of inputs is produced, production is said to be **technically efficient**, because it is technically impossible to produce more without using more inputs. This concept of technical efficiency is highly relevant to the discussion of the behaviour of firms, because profit-maximizing firms at least (and for the moment we can concentrate our attention on them) must strive to be technically efficient. Firms with objectives other than profit maximization may, under certain circumstances, choose to be technically inefficient, but that would be incompatible with profit maximization because it would imply the existence of an opportunity to increase profits by reducing the quantity of inputs used, and therefore costs, without reducing output.

130

However, we also need to be aware that technical efficiency is only one aspect of efficiency relevant to the profit-maximizing firm. As we shall see below, the production function is in many cases likely to be such that a given level of output can be produced with more than one combination of inputs. In these circumstances the firm also needs to be efficient in the sense of choosing the input combination involving the smallest aggregate cost. This type of efficiency is referred to as **economic efficiency**, as it depends on economic variables in the form of input prices as well as the technical factors underlying the production function.

In later chapters we shall see that there are other aspects of economic efficiency in addition to cost minimization, but our more immediate concern in this chapter is to examine the nature of the relationships implied by the production function between the quantities of inputs used by a firm and its output when it is technically efficient, and then to consider the implications of economic efficiency for input choices.

In all this discussion we obviously need to recognize that the nature of the production function varies considerably from product to product. There is clearly a world of difference between the harvesting of the raw material for bird's nest soup and the production of the modern marvels of advanced technology. Nevertheless, as with utility functions, economists have sought to identify those properties of production functions that characterize all productive activity in order to gain insights into the nature of the more general influences on firms' behaviour. The first major task in this chapter will, therefore, be to examine these common characteristics.

The 'law' of diminishing returns

Probably the most well-known property attributed to production functions is enshrined in the so-called 'law' of diminishing returns, which has already been alluded to in Chapter 8 above (p. 112), and which postulates that, if the quantity of one input alone is increased, output will, sooner or later, increase at a diminishing rate, producing a relationship between output and the quantity of a variable input, Y, of the form indicated by the curve *TP* in Figure 9.1a. This curve, which rises steeply at low values of Y but then starts to flatten out as diminishing returns set in, is termed the **total product curve** for Y, as it indicates the relationship between the total output or product and the quantity of Y used in its production.

The law of diminishing returns can also be expressed in terms of the **marginal product** of Y (the addition to output arising from the employment of the last unit of the variable input), because it implies that this marginal product, which is measured by the slope of the total product curve in Figure 9.1a, at some stage starts to decline as the quantity of Y is increased.[1] The marginal product curve in Figure 9.1b, *MP*, which illustrates this relation-

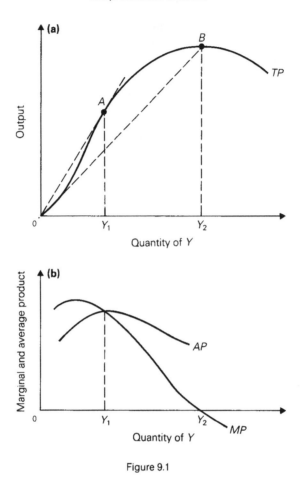

Figure 9.1

ship, thus provides a more direct illustration of the general 'law'. Note that the marginal product may, as in the case illustrated (where more than Y_2 of the variable input is employed), decline to a negative value (which is reflected in the downward-sloping section of the total product curve in Figure 9.1a), but this involves an inefficient use of inputs in the sense that fewer inputs could be employed without reducing output and is therefore a situation that a profit-maximizing firm would seek to avoid.

Also shown in Figure 9.1b is the average product curve (AP) showing how output per unit of the variable input changes as the quantity of that input employed increases. At any point on the total product curve in Figure 9.1a, the magnitude of the average product is measured by the slope of the straight line drawn back to the origin. Thus, the average product of Y at B is measured by the slope of the dashed line OB. More generally it should be clear from the diagram that the average product of Y increases until point A on TP is reached, where Y_1 is employed (and where OA is also tangential to the total product curve, reflecting the fact that at this point average product equals marginal product), and declines thereafter. It should also be apparent that the normal average–marginal relationships apply in that, when the marginal product exceeds the average product (e.g. when less than Y_1 of Y is used and the slope of TP at any point is greater than the slope of the line drawn back from that point to the origin), the average product is rising, and in the opposite case, where the marginal product is less than average product, it is falling. However it is assumed that the reader is sufficiently familiar with these relationships, which are dealt with at length in most introductory texts, to require no further elaboration.

Substitution between inputs

The law of diminishing returns, as depicted in Figure 9.1, imposes a constraint on the extent to which output can be increased, basically because the quantity of all the other inputs used in the productive process remains unchanged. The next step, therefore, is to consider the effect of changing the quantities of other inputs, but, to keep the situation within the scope of diagrammatic analysis, we will consider a situation in which only two inputs, Y and Z, are employed.

In Figure 9.2a, therefore, TP_1 is the relationship between output and the quantity of input Y when some fixed initial quantity of Z (OZ_1 in Figure 9.2b) is employed. If the quantity of Z employed is now increased (to Z_2 in Figure 9.2b), as long as the marginal product of Z is positive, for any quantity of Y employed, output will increase. In other words, a new relationship between output and the quantity of input Y, lying above the old one, will be formed, like TP_2 in Figure 9.2a.

An important implication of this is that, if we wish to produce a given quantity of output such as Q_1 in Figure 9.2a, amongst the options open to us would be to use the initial quantity of Z (Z_1) with Y_3 of Y, or to use more Z ($Z_2 > Z_1$) and less Y ($Y_2 < Y_3$). Further increases in Z would make possible further reductions in Y without reducing output. If we now plot in Figure 9.2b all the combinations of Y and Z that produce an output of Q_1 and draw a curve through all the plotted points, we obtain the curve labelled Q_1. Similarly, another curve, Q_2, can be drawn to show the combinations of Y and Z required to produce the higher output of Q_2, and corresponding curves can be drawn for any other level of output.

These curves are called **isoquants** for the obvious reason (since 'iso' means equal) that they join up points in the diagram yielding equal quantities of output and they provide a graphical representation of the production function corresponding to the graphical representation of consumers' utility functions in indifference curve diagrams. As with indifference curves, they are downward sloping to the extent that one input can be substituted for

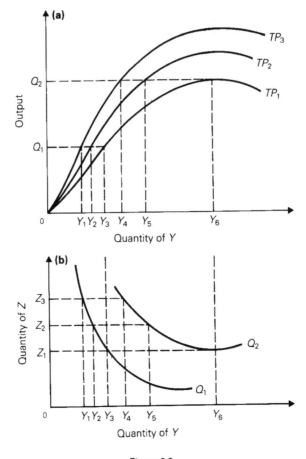

The production function

Figure 9.2

some quantity of the other without affecting output. It also seems reasonable to assume that, as in the utility case, it will become increasingly difficult to substitute one input for another as the use of one increases and the use of the other declines. In diagrammatic terms this means that isoquants, like indifference curves, will generally be convex to the origin, as in Figure 9.2b, getting flatter as Y increases relative to Z. In more technical terms, we can say again that the marginal rate of substitution of Z for Y – the quantity of Z that needs to be substituted for a marginal unit of Y to keep output unchanged, which in this production context is referred to as the **marginal technical rate of substitution** ($MTRS_{ZY}$) – declines as Y increases, and this is reflected in the slope of the isoquant ($= -MTRS_{ZY}$). Moreover, just as in the indifference curve case the marginal rate of substitution is equal to the ratios of the marginal utilities, in this case it is equal to the ratio of the marginal products, MP_Y/MP_Z.[2]

In addition, Figure 9.2a suggests that there are likely to be limits to the

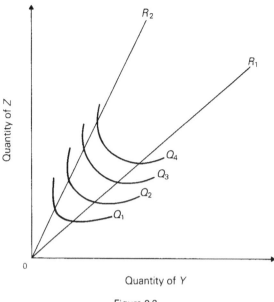

Figure 9.3

extent to which substitution can take place. Indeed, in the case illustrated, if an output of Q_2 is produced, that limit is reached when Y_6 of Y is employed with Z_1 of Z. In that situation, additional units of Y could no longer be used as a substitute for units of Z. In fact, because with more Y than Y_6 the marginal product of Y is negative, more Z rather than less would be needed to maintain output at its original level of Q_2. This means that, in Figure 9.2b, the Q_2 isoquant becomes upward sloping for quantities of Y greater than Y_6. Similar considerations apply at the opposite extreme, where the limits to which Z can be substituted for Y are reached. At that point (not shown in Figure 9.2), the marginal product of input Y becomes negative, and so the isoquant again becomes positively sloped.[3]

These limits to substitution are often made explicit, on the isoquant diagram, by the insertion of additional curves drawn through all the points at which the isoquants become horizontal and vertical, as in Figure 9.3. These additional curves, which are labelled R_1 and R_2 in that diagram, are called **ridge lines**. Points in the areas outside the ridge lines then again represent technically inefficient uses of resources because they involve the use of inputs with negative marginal products, which means that it would be technically possible to produce the same output with fewer inputs. Efficient producers would, therefore, try to avoid these zones and choose between input combinations within the ridge lines. From that point of view, the efficient producer is no different from the rational consumer avoiding 'bads', but the use of ridge lines provides us with a reminder that the producer's choices may, in practice, be severely constrained by the technical conditions of production to such an extent that the area between the ridge lines is quite small. Indeed, in extreme cases, of which the provision of taxi services provides an example (as the provision of a taxi service for 1 hour requires 1 hour's input of driver's time and 1 hour's input of vehicle time), there would be minimal scope for substitution between inputs, and the ridge lines would coincide.

Returns to scale

Where producers do have a choice of input combinations we obviously need to consider what choices they are likely to make, but before going on to that there is one further aspect of the technical relationship between inputs and outputs to consider and that relates to the scale of production.

The scale of production is increased if all inputs are increased in the same proportions, and the effect of this on output is expressed in terms of **returns to scale**. Constant returns to scale occur when the increase in output is proportional to the increase in the use of inputs. Doubling the inputs used will then double output. This is the case illustrated in Figure 9.4a. In terms of an isoquant diagram, increasing inputs in the same proportion simply means moving along a straight line ray from the origin. Two such rays are shown in Figure 9.4a, and along both it can be seen that doubling output from 1 to 2 units requires the quantity of both inputs to be doubled, but a more general property is also reflected in the diagram in that successive isoquants are equidistant from each other along the rays.

The other possibilities are increasing and decreasing returns to scale. With increasing returns to scale, illustrated in Figure 9.4b, output increases more than proportionately to the quantities of inputs employed, so that along any straight line ray from the origin the isoquants get closer together. With decreasing returns to scale, however, illustrated in Figure 9.4c, where the increase in output is proportionately less than the increase in the use of inputs, the converse is true.

In economic theory much attention has been paid to the constant returns to scale case, partly because in that case the production function has convenient mathematical properties and partly because of its potential empirical significance. The convenient mathematical properties arise because, with constant returns to scale, in mathematical terms the production function is what is called a **linearly homogeneous function** or, alternatively, a **homogeneous function of degree 1**.[4] In terms of its economic implications, one consequence of this is that the average and marginal products of the inputs depend only on the proportions in which the inputs are employed and not on the scale of output.[5] At all points along any straight line ray, drawn through the origin in Figure 9.4a, therefore, the average and marginal products of inputs Y and Z remain unchanged. This means that a

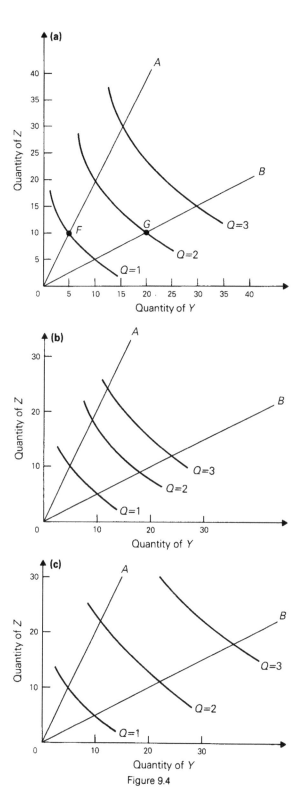

Figure 9.4

movement from any point on OA, in the diagram, to any point on OB must have the same effects on the average and marginal products of Y and Z as a movement from F to G, in which the use of Y is increased from 5 to 20 units, whilst the use of Z is unchanged at 10 units. Since, with diminishing returns to the variable input, the latter change can be expected to reduce the marginal product of Y, the same must be true for a movement from any point on OA to any point on OB. Moreover, if along any straight line rays through the origin the marginal products of Y and Z are the same, the slopes of the isoquants that are determined by the ratios of the marginal products must also be the same. In other words, the isoquants are parallel to each other along the rays as well as being equidistant. This, of course, applies when the ratio of the marginal products is zero and infinite as well as at more intermediate values. Hence, with this kind of production function, the ridge lines defined in the previous section are also straight lines through the origin and the area containing all the technically efficient input combinations is a triangular wedge.

One much-quoted production function that exhibits constant returns to scale and its associated properties is the **Cobb-Douglas** production function when expressed in the form

$$q = Ay^{\alpha}z^{1-\alpha}, \tag{9.2}$$

where α is a constant between 0 and 1 and A is another constant, which represents the output produced by a combination of 1 unit of each input. This function, named after the two men who pioneered its use, was originally applied to empirical data for the USA (see Douglas, 1934). It is also often expressed in a more general form as

$$q = Ay^{\alpha}z^{\beta}, \tag{9.3}$$

where β is also a constant between 0 and 1. In this form it is still a homogeneous function and has parallel isoquants, but it has constant returns to scale only in the special case where $\beta = 1 - \alpha$, as in expression (9.2). In the more general form of (9.3), the function is homogeneous of degree $\alpha + \beta$, which means that in its economic context it exhibits increasing returns to scale when $\alpha + \beta > 1$, and decreasing returns to scale when $\alpha + \beta < 1$.

However, whilst these functions have been fitted to empirical data, it has usually been at an aggregated economy-wide or industry-wide level rather than at the level of an individual firm, which is our concern here. But at the level of the individual firm, the idea of constant returns to scale is of practical significance because in principle they should always be available. If a given factory, with 5 machines and 10 workers, produces 100 units of output per week, it should always be possible to double weekly output by building an identical factory alongside the first, equipping it with 5 machines identical to those in the first factory and employing 10 similar workers. The real question then becomes one of identifying the particular circumstances that prevent the realization of constant returns to scale. One possibility is clearly where increasing the scale of production allows individual workers to concentrate more on specific tasks and thus increases their productivity and produces a more than proportionate increase in output. By contrast, however, doubling managerial inputs might not always double managerial 'output' because of the need for members of the managerial team to devote more time to exchanging information with colleagues.

Another important reason for non-constant returns to scale arises from limitations on the ability of producers to adjust all the relevant inputs. This is seen most obviously in the case of extractive industries. Whilst a mining or quarrying concern can double its labour force and equipment, it cannot double the inputs supplied by nature, the material it is trying to extract from the earth. Once all the reserves of a particular material are being exploited, an increase in the inputs controlled by the mining or quarrying organization must then ultimately lead to a less than proportionate increase in output. Firms in such industries, therefore, at least as far as the inputs they control are concerned, effectively face a situation in which there are decreasing returns to scale.

Other instances of non-constant returns arise because the supply of some inputs is 'lumpy', in that only a restricted range of quantities is available. Hence, whilst it might always be possible to double the quantity of most inputs employed in any existing situation, it may not be possible to halve those quantities. In other words, there are **indivisibilities** in the supply of inputs. An example is provided by a railway company operating a service over a single-track branch line: it could reduce the actual train service over the line, but would find it difficult to make a proportionate reduction in 'track' inputs. Because of such indivisibilities, increases in output might require a less than proportionate increase in some inputs over some ranges of output, and a more than proportionate increase over others.

Another concept of scale

So far, we have discussed the concept of scale in terms of the quantity of inputs, but there is another aspect of scale that is equally important, and that is the size of inputs. Much capital equipment comes in a variety of sizes, but we cannot very easily think in terms of returns to that kind of scale because not all inputs can be scaled up in size. An operator of transatlantic air services may be able to buy larger aircraft, but there is a limit to the extent to which he can hire larger pilots and stewardesses. Nevertheless, the availability of different-sized aircraft can be handled in our production function analysis by treating the use of different aircraft as different technologies involving different types of input. Thus if there are two types of aircraft, A and B, the operator of a given air service can be characterized as being faced with a choice between using type A aircraft, with a production function that can be expressed as

$$q = f(y_A, z),$$

and using type B with a production function

$$q = g(y_B, z),$$

where, in each case, q is the output expressed in terms of passenger journeys, z is the relevant labour input, and y_A and y_B are the inputs of aircraft service hours in each case.

With three input variables, the choices available cannot easily be shown diagrammatically, but the decision on which of the two methods of operating the service to use will actually depend on their relative costs. In this context, if the cost of carrying a given volume of traffic is lower with the larger aircraft, there are **economies of scale**. It should be clear, however, that whether such economies exist depends more on relative prices than the technical factors embodied in the individual production functions. In other words, it is a question of economic efficiency rather than purely technical efficiency.[6] We should note, however, that this concept of economies of scale is a rather broader one than that of returns to scale as defined in this section. With constant input prices, increasing returns to scale must necessarily imply economies of scale, but economies of scale can arise in other situations. Indeed, in our aircraft example (if the lumpiness of aircraft inputs is ignored), the production function for each aircraft type is likely to involve roughly constant returns to scale, because doubling the traffic will require double the aircraft-hours, crew-hours and the like, but economies of scale would exist as long as the cost per seat mile was lower in larger aircraft than smaller ones.

The linear programming variant

We have already noted that the inability of producers to make adjustments to the quantities of some of the inputs they use may give rise to non-constant returns to scale over some ranges of output, but it may also have more significant implications for the whole form of the production function. Consider, for example, the case of a firm manufacturing some product with a production line requiring labour inputs (man-hours) and machine inputs (machine-hours).[7] In this kind of situation, substitution between man-hours and machine-hours might be possible if the speed of the production line can be varied. Increasing the speed of the production line then reduces the number of machine-hours required to produce a given output, but may

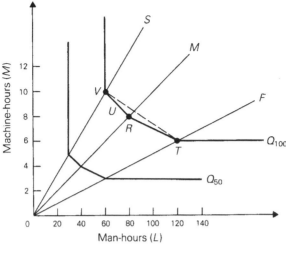

Figure 9.5

require more workers to be employed to complete all the tasks involved in the production of the final output. It would thus involve the substitution of man-hours for machine-hours and thus the use of more labour-intensive methods of production.

To illustrate what is involved, suppose there are three possible speeds at which our firm's production line can operate – slow, medium and fast – and that at the slow speed 6 workers are required to operate the line, at the medium speed 10 are required, and at the fast speed, 20. More specifically, this means that 6 man-hours per machine-hour are required at the slow speed and similarly for the other speeds. The input combinations satisfying these requirements can be represented in Figure 9.5 by the rays OS, OM and OF respectively.

Now suppose it is also the case that 100 units of output can be produced by the input combinations in the following table:

	Slow	Medium	Fast
Man-hours (L)	60	80	120
Machine-hours (M)	10	8	6

These input combinations are represented by the points V, R and T in Figure 9.5. However, the same output can also be produced using different input combinations using a mixture of speeds. For example, if 50 units of output could be produced at each speed with exactly half the inputs specified in the above table (i.e. at each speed there are constant returns to scale and no restrictions on the availability of each input), then the 100 units of output could be made up of 50 units produced at the slow speed (requiring $30L$ and $5M$) and 50 produced at the medium speed (requiring $40L$ and $4M$). The total input requirements would then be $70L$ and $9M$, represented by point U, the mid-point of the straight line joining V and R in the diagram, and it can easily be confirmed that producing 100 units of output with other combinations of these two speeds would require input combinations represented by other points on VR. Similarly, producing the same output combinations of the medium and fast speeds can be shown to involve the input combinations on RT, and combining the fast and slow speeds would require the input combinations on the dashed line VT.

It should, however, be apparent from a comparison of the points on VT with those on VR and RT in the diagram that the input combinations along VT are technically inefficient in the sense that 100 units of output can be produced using fewer inputs by combining the medium speed with either the fast or slow ones. The kinked line VRT, therefore, shows all the *efficient* input combinations that the firm can use to produce 100 units of output. As such it constitutes the downward-sloping section of the firm's 100 unit isoquant (Q_{100}) corresponding directly to the downward-sloping sections of the isoquants featured in earlier diagrams. Like them, it suggests that, as the number of man-hours employed increases, the marginal rate of substitution of man-hours for machine-hours falls, but in discrete steps rather than continuously. There is also a limit to the extent to which man-hours can be substituted for machine-hours. This is reached at T, where the entire output is produced using the most labour-intensive method. To the right of T, the isoquant will be (at best) parallel to the horizontal axis, since adding further man-hours can add nothing to output. There is also a corresponding limit, at V, to the extent to which machine-hours can be substituted for man-hours, beyond which the isoquant is drawn parallel to the vertical axis.

Isoquants for other levels of output can similarly be derived, and that showing the input combinations required to produce 50 units of output is also shown in Figure 9.5 (as Q_{50}). With constant returns to scale at each machine speed setting, this cuts OS, OM and OF halfway between the origin and points V, R and T respectively, and the corresponding segments of the isoquants between the rays will be parallel to each other.

This particular type of production function is referred to as the **linear programming** production function, as the linearity of all its components enables linear programming techniques to be used to determine optimal input combinations. That indeed is its main strength, because if, as the developers of the approach have suggested (see, for example, Dorfman, 1953) it presents a better approximation to the conditions found in manufacturing-type industries than the more traditional type of production function (sometimes referred to as the **neoclassical** production function) outlined in the previous sections, the problems of choosing optimal input combinations in the highly technical multivariate situations faced in modern industries is a more tractable one for management if linear programming techniques can be used. However, for analytical purposes, the differences between the two approaches are more in matters of detail than substance. Indeed, the greater the range of speeds the producer in our example has at his disposal, the closer his isoquant diagram would approximate to those in earlier diagrams with their smooth curves convex to the origin.

Cost-minimizing input combinations

Whilst a firm's production function may indicate a number of different combinations of inputs that can be used to produce a given level of output, the actual combination of inputs used will depend on input prices and the firm's utility function as reflected in its operational objectives. However, if the firm is seeking to maximize its profits (and for the moment we will ignore other possible objectives), it will need as a first step to ensure that whatever quantity of output it decides to produce is produced at minimum cost. The next step in our analysis, therefore, is to examine the consequences of cost minimization for the choice of inputs, and that is a step that takes us beyond the realm of technical relationships into questions of economic efficiency.

If, to simplify, we assume that firms, like consumers, are price takers in the markets in which they buy their inputs, and are thus faced with prices that they cannot influence directly,[8] the quantities of inputs that can be obtained for a given sum of money can be represented, on the firm's isoquant diagram, by a straight line with a slope reflecting the price ratio of the inputs, just like the consumer's budget line. In this particular context, this line is referred to as a **constant cost curve** for the obvious reason that it joins up bundles of inputs that can be bought for the same total cost, but its properties are exactly the same as those of the consumer's budget line. Hence its slope is the negative of the input price ratio and its intercepts indicate the maximum quantities that can be bought of each input with the given sum. In contrast to the individual consumer, however, firms are likely to be less constrained in their purchases of inputs by a fixed budget and can be expected to be in a position to vary their expenditure if it is profitable for them to do so. Other constant cost curves, parallel to the first, can therefore be added to the diagram reflecting higher or lower levels of expenditure, and the firm can be characterized as seeking the constant cost curve representing the lowest total outlay consistent with the production of the desired level of output. Thus in Figure 9.6, M_1N_1 is one constant cost curve, while M_2N_2 and M_0N_0 are others indicating input combinations that can be bought at the same prices for a higher and lower sum respectively.

If then, in the same diagram, the curve Q_0 is the isoquant showing the combinations of inputs required to produce an output of Q_0, it can be seen that the costs of producing that output are minimized when the input combination at T_0, involving Y_0 of Y and Z is used. Moreover, it should also be clear that, as in the case of an individual consumer, the optimal choice is again at a point of tangency, but this time between an isoquant and a

The production function

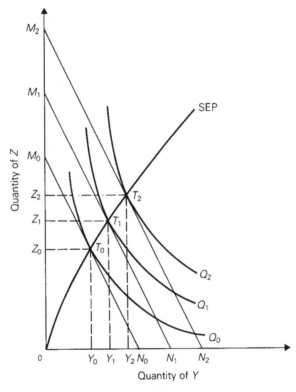

Figure 9.6

constant cost curve. Hence, the condition for a cost-minimizing choice of inputs in the case illustrated is that the slopes of the two curves are equal, or

$$MTRS_{XY} = p_Y/p_Z, \qquad (9.4)$$

where p_Y and p_Z are the prices of inputs Y and Z respectively. The optimal input combinations for other levels of output can be found in the same way, and in the diagram the cost-minimizing input combinations for outputs of Q_1 and Q_2 are those at T_1 and T_2 respectively.

Moreover, this condition, like the corresponding condition for the maximization of a consumer's utility can easily be generalized. Indeed, whatever the number of inputs employed, costs are minimized when the marginal technical rate of substitution between any pair of them is equal to the ratio of their respective prices. Alternatively, since the marginal technical rate of substitution between any pair of inputs is equal to the ratio of their marginal products, we can express this condition as

$$\frac{MP_1}{p_1} = \frac{MP_2}{p_2} = \ldots = \frac{MP_n}{p_n}, \qquad (9.5)$$

144

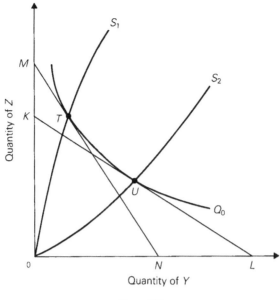

Figure 9.7

which simply means that the marginal product per unit of expenditure on each input must be the same.

Returning to the two-input case, drawing a curve through all points satisfying condition (9.4) produces a curve known as the **scale expansion path**, which is labelled SEP in the diagram. Like the corresponding consumer's income expansion path discussed in Chapter 3 above, this curve can take a variety of forms, depending on the underlying production functions. Moreover, the possibility of *inferior inputs* producing a backward- or downward-sloping expansion path need not be ruled out. However, if the production function exhibits constant returns to scale, so that the slopes of all isoquants are equal along any ray drawn from the origin, the scale expansion path along which condition (9.2) is satisfied is a straight line, with a slope depending on the prevailing input price ratio. With other than constant returns to scale, the scale expansion path can also be a straight line, but only when the production function is mathematically homogeneous.

If the input price ratio changes, the slope of all the constant cost curves must also change. This in turn will affect the optimal input combinations associated with any level of output and thus change the whole scale expansion path. Thus in Figure 9.7, if from some initial situation represented by the constant cost curve MN, the price of Y falls relatively to Z (or the price of Z rises relative to Y), so that the constant cost curve tangential to the Q_0 isoquant becomes KL, the optimal input combination is changed from that at T to that at U, involving more of Y and less of Z. Similar considerations obviously apply to the optimal ways of producing other levels of output and

145

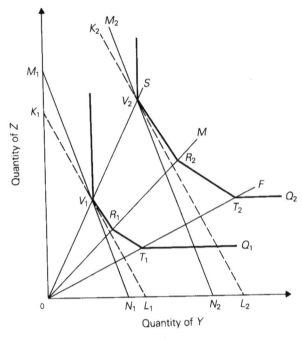

Figure 9.8

so a new scale expansion path is generated (OS_2 in the diagram) passing through rather more Y-intensive input combinations than the original scale expansion path OS_1.

Some slight qualification to these conclusions becomes necessary, however, when we consider the linear programming variant of the production function. In that case, as should be apparent from Figure 9.8, except in the rather special case where the constant cost curves have the same slope as one of the straight line segments of the isoquant, the least-cost input combination will be at one of the kinks in the isoquant, suggesting that one particular process will always be less costly than all others and that the scale expansion path will coincide with that particular process ray. Hence, in the case illustrated, with constant cost curves M_1N_1 and M_2N_2, process S is the optimal process. In this situation, however, changes in input prices need not always lead to changes in optimal input proportions. In the case illustrated, with the constant cost curves K_1L_1 and K_2L_2, the optimal input combinations still lie along OS. Nevertheless, with a sufficiently large fall in the price of Z relative to Y to produce a constant expenditure curve flatter than V_1R_1, the optimal input proportions would change, requiring the use of a more labour-intensive method of production. A more discontinuous adjustment to changing input prices can therefore be expected with a linear programming production function than in the previous 'neoclassical' case.

With given input prices, however, whatever the precise form of the production function, firms will seek to adjust their use of inputs along a particular expansion path and the diagrams can be used to provide some indication of the relationship between total costs and output. Thus from Figure 9.6 above we can deduce that an output of Q_0 can be produced for a total cost of $N_0 \times p_Y$ ($= M_0 \times p_Z$), while Q_1 can be produced for a total cost of $N_1 \times p_Y$. Nevertheless, in going on to examine how the profit-maximizing firm's desired level of output can be determined, it is useful to be able to express the relationship between a firm's costs and output, known as its **cost function**, more directly. The properties of that function are the concern of the next chapter.

Notes

1 Mathematically, the marginal product of the ith input is the partial derivative of the production function with respect to the quantity of that input, which in the case of the production function (9.1) is $\partial q/\partial y_i$. Diminishing returns imply that the second-order direct partial derivative $2^1q/\partial y_i^2$ is negative.
2 The proof of this is the same as the proof that, in the indifference curve case, $MRS_{XY} = MU_X MU_Y$ on p. 22 (Chapter 2) above.
3 Since the slope of the isoquant is $- MP_Y/MP_Z$, whenever either MP_Y or MP_Z has a negative value the isoquant becomes positively sloped, and it is horizontal and vertical at the points where MP_Y and MP_Z are zero respectively.
4 The function $q = f(y, z)$ is defined to be homogeneous of order m, if multiplying the independent variables, y and z, by any constant, n, multiplies the value of the dependent variable, q, by n^m. Hence, if $m = 1$, q increases proportionately with y and z.
5 A proof of this proposition can be found in Chiang (1974).
6 The situation here is basically the same as that faced by the consumer in the situations discussed in Chapters 6 and 7 above where he was faced with either different ways of obtaining a given bundle of characteristics or different ways of performing some activity. In all these cases the final choice depends on the relative costs of the various alternatives.
7 To be realistic we should also include inputs of raw materials in the analysis, but if they are always strictly proportional to output they can be ignored for present purposes.
8 Situations in which firms can influence input prices by their behaviour are considered in Chapters 17 and 18 below.

Exercises

9.1 Explain carefully what you understand by:
    (i) the law of diminishing returns,
    (ii) decreasing returns to scale,
    (iii) diseconomies of scale.

9.2 The constant returns to scale production function has properties of great importance. What are they?

9.3 A production function is of the form represented by the equation

$$q = 10yz - 4y^2 - 3z^2,$$

where q is the output produced per period, whilst y and z are the quantities of two inputs employed. Show that with this function there are increasing returns to scale and derive expressions for the average and marginal product curves, commenting on their shape.

9.4 In the case of a manufacturer producing a single product with two inputs:

(i) show how the least-cost input combination can be determined,

(ii) deduce the effect of an increase in output on the use of inputs when there are

    (a) constant returns to scale, and

    (b) increasing returns to scale.

9.5 A firm can choose between three processes in the production of its product. Process I requires the use of 40 machine-hours and 60 man-hours to produce 100 units of output; process II requires 30 machine-hours and 75 man-hours to produce the same output; whilst process III requires 20 machine-hours and 100 man-hours. Which is the cheapest process when the cost per machine-hour is £8 and the hourly wage rate is £4. What changes in the cost of the inputs would be necessary to induce the firm to choose one of the other processes?

CHAPTER TEN
COSTS AND COST FUNCTIONS

Introduction

In the last chapter the costs incurred by a firm were introduced as the sum of the costs of all the inputs employed, or in symbolic terms as

$$C = p_1 y_1 + p_2 y_2 + , \ldots, p_n y_n, \qquad (10.1)$$

where C represents total costs, $y_1, y_2, \ldots y_n$ the quantities of the various inputs employed and $p_1, p_2, \ldots p_n$ their respective prices. Further, it was also pointed out that a profit-maximizing firm must seek to use the specific bundle of inputs that minimizes its costs, and to adjust its use of inputs, as it adjusts its output, along a particular expansion path, which is determined by the underlying production function and relative input prices. Points along that expansion path then determine the specific relationship between costs and output, constituting the firm's cost function, which can, therefore, be expressed as

$$C = F(q), \qquad (10.2)$$

where, adapting the basic production function expression (9.1),

$$q = f(y_1{}^*, y_2{}^*, \ldots, y_n{}^*),$$

in which $y_1{}^*, y_2{}^*, \ldots y_n{}^*$ define the cost-minimizing input quantities used in the production of output, q.

As the cost function is essentially the relationship between costs and outputs along an expansion path, it is strictly defined for given input prices. This means that any change in input prices leads to a shift in the cost function, reflecting the associated change in the position of the expansion path. In practice, of course, the input prices faced by a firm may be subject to frequent change, but our main concern in this chapter is to examine the basic relationship between costs and output with *given* input prices. So far, however, it has been implied that each input, whether it is a labour, capital or material input, has its readily identifiable price, which constitutes the cost to the firm of using it. In fact this is not always the case, so before discussing the form of the cost function we must consider what the cost of using an input might be. But, even more fundamentally, we must start by attempting to clarify the meaning of cost that is relevant to our analysis.

The nature of costs

It is perhaps most natural to think of the cost of an input in terms of the money outlay associated with its use but, as already indicated in Chapter 8 above, what is particularly relevant is what economists call the **opportunity cost** of employing the input. This is conceptually the value of the opportunities forgone by devoting an input to one activity rather than another; it thus represents what the firm could obtain by transferring the input to some alternative use. In some cases this may simply be the sum of money that has to be paid for the use of the input, but in others it may be different. Thus the opportunity cost of a bag of cement used in a building project can in most cases be taken to be the price paid for it in the market, because that price represents the reduction in the outlays required for some alternative project if the bag of cement was used for that instead, or the return that could be obtained by selling it to someone else. By contrast, a firm owning its own premises may only incur monetary expenditure on heating, lighting, cleaning and maintenance, but the opportunity cost of its use of the premises includes the rent that it forgoes by occupying them rather than letting them out to another user. Similarly, a firm buying capital equipment out of retained profits avoids having to pay interest charges on the loans required to finance the purchase, but nevertheless incurs an opportunity cost of the interest or return forgone on alternative uses of the funds.

Since a profit-maximizing firm always seeks to use its inputs where they produce the greatest return, another way of looking at the cost of using an input is as the sum that would need to be received by a profit-maximizing firm to keep it in its present use. Suppose, for example, a person running a one-man, one-vehicle road haulage business used his vehicle to carry miscellaneous loads for a variety of customers, but was offered a contract by another firm that would yield him a surplus of £400 a week after all operating costs had been met for using the vehicle exclusively to carry goods for that firm. In those circumstances the £400 would constitute an opportunity cost of using the vehicle for miscellaneous duties, and the returns from that work would have to be at least that amount to keep the vehicle in its present use. This means that our definition of cost includes what, in accounting terms, might be regarded as profits. This has led some writers to refer to the 'profits' that have to be earned to keep the resources of the firm in their present use as

normal profits, but as long as it is understood that costs are defined in their proper opportunity cost sense, which automatically includes these normal profits, there is no need to distinguish them from any other element of cost.

So far we have highlighted cases where the opportunity cost of using an input exceeds the monetary outlays associated with its use, but it is important to recognize that there are also situations where the opposite is true. For example, once a firm has bought some expensive equipment that can't be hired out to someone else, as might be the case if it was highly immobile and specific to the firm's own activities, then the opportunity cost of using it is little more than its running cost plus any depreciation attributed directly to its use, while the large initial outlay required to purchase and install the machine is of no relevance. Similar considerations apply if the equipment is hired for, say, £100 per month on a contract specifying some minimum hire period, such as a year. With no possibility under the terms of the contract, short of bankruptcy, of avoiding the monthly hire charge until the contract expires, the monthly payment of £100 cannot be part of the opportunity cost of using the machine during the contract period – again only the basic running costs are relevant.

This suggests that another approach to the identification of the relevant economic cost is through the idea of the **avoidable costs** of producing some good or service, which are the costs that can be avoided by *not* producing it. With the hired machine considered above, during the hire period the machine's hire costs are not avoided by not using it. Only the running costs are avoided. However, returning to our first example of a bag of cement used in a building project, the costs of that cement can, in most cases at least, be avoided by not proceeding with the project.

Short- and long-run costs

The concept of avoidable cost is also useful in drawing our attention to the time element, since costs that are not avoidable in the immediate future may be avoidable at some later stage. Thus, in the example of the hired machine above, once the contract period has expired the hire costs can be avoided by not renewing the contract. Similarly, for equipment purchased outright, the capital cost cannot be avoided in the immediate future by not using it, but can be avoided in the longer term by not replacing the equipment when it becomes worn out. Indeed, with most inputs there may be at least a short period over which their costs are not avoidable. For example, workers may be on a contract entitling them to one month's notice of dismissal. The costs of employing them for the next month are not, therefore, avoidable although the costs of employing them for longer are.

One consequence of all this is that the costs of employing many inputs are lower in the immediate short run than in the longer term. However, for most firms there is the added complication that the period of time over which costs are avoidable may differ considerably between inputs. As a result, the avoidable costs currently associated with the production of 10 units of output may differ from the avoidable costs of producing 10 units of output next week, and even more from the avoidable costs of producing it in a month's time or next year. However, it can be argued that the most significant distinction is between situations in which there are some costs that cannot be avoided and situations in which all costs can be avoided. Hence, in economic analysis, it is customary to simplify by considering only two situations, the **short run**, in which there are some costs that cannot be avoided, and the **long run**, in which all costs can be avoided. We adhere to this convention in this book, but the reader should always be aware that this is a simplification and that in practice firms may also be faced with any number of 'medium'-run situations.[1]

An alternative approach to this distinction between the short and long run is to define the former as a situation in which the availability of some inputs is fixed, and the latter as a situation in which all inputs can be freely varied. In this context, buildings, plant and machinery are often cited as examples of inputs that can only be varied in the long run because of the time involved in the design and structure of new plant and indeed in the reorganization of existing plant. However, this approach ignores the fact that the relevant input variable of the production function is not the quantity of plant and machinery the firm may have at its disposal (sometimes loosely referred to as the quantity of capital), but the extent to which that plant and machinery is used, which can be measured in terms of the number of machine-hours of various sorts supplied. Hence, whilst the firms may be faced with a fixed quantity of machines in the short run, it is likely to have considerable discretion over how, and to what extent, to operate them. It may decide to operate them round the clock for 24 hours a day, or just for the normal 7 or 8 hour working day. Alternatively, if sales decline unexpectedly, the machines could be operated for only a few hours a day or, if need be, not at all. The total quantity of machinery will impose an upper limit on the quantity of machine-hours that can be supplied in the short run, but below that limit there is likely to be considerable flexibility, and where such flexibility exists the main distinction between the short run and the long run is that the opportunity costs of using the plant are likely to be lower in the short run than in the long run.

The implications of this will be explored in more detail below, but we will start our discussion of the form of the firm's cost function by considering the long run, in which all costs are avoidable and there are no constraints on the extent to which any input can be varied.

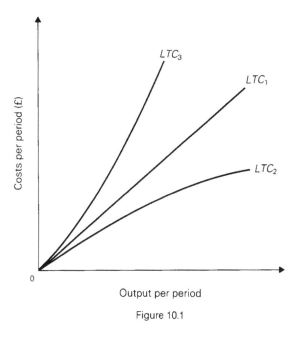

Figure 10.1

Long-run cost functions

In terms of the two-input analysis of Chapter 9 above, the firm can expand its use of inputs in the long run, as it increases its output, along its scale expansion path, which is determined by the points of tangency between constant cost curves, whose slopes reflect the relative long-run opportunity costs of the two inputs, and the isoquants of the firm's production function. Where the firm employs more than two inputs, we can imagine a similar expansion path in n-dimensional space defining the least-cost input combinations. Hence, if input prices are given and fixed, the relationship between the firm's costs and output is determined entirely by the underlying production function.

In this context, whether there are constant, increasing or decreasing returns to scale is especially relevant. If, for example, there are constant returns to scale, with output increasing in the same proportion as the use of inputs, costs must also increase proportionately to the quantity of inputs and output. This, in turn, means that the firm's total cost curve, relating total costs to output, must be a straight line through the origin, like LTC_1 in Figure 10.1. Similarly, with increasing returns to scale, output increases more than proportionately to the inputs employed, and so total costs increase less than proportionately to output, resulting in a total cost curve like LTC_2 in the diagram, whilst decreasing returns to scale result in a curve like LTC_3.

It was, however, suggested in the discussion of the production function

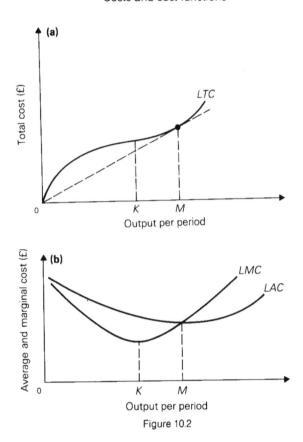

Figure 10.2

that, in principle, access to constant returns to scale should always be available because it should always be possible, as long as inputs of an appropriate quality can be obtained, to double output by duplicating an existing productive situation. Nevertheless, it was also noted that, when the scale of an activity is increased, there might be some productivity gains from specialization. Moreover, that was all on the basis of a given technology in which output is expanded by using more of the same inputs in the same way that they had been used before. But in that context it was also noted that producers might have access to economies of scale by switching to alternative technologies involving some different inputs (as in the example of different-sized aircraft). These two possibilities suggest that it may not be unusual for firms to be faced with declining long-run average costs over some range of outputs at least. In addition, it was also suggested that, once production reaches a critical level, the opposite tendency might be experienced because of managerial diseconomies and, particularly in the case of extractive-type industries, the fixity of natural inputs. These possibilities have led economists to suggest that, as a firm's output increases from low levels, costs increase initially less than proportionately to output, but that eventually they will begin to increase more than proportionately. This implies that the long-run total cost curve is typically of the form illustrated in Figure 10.2a, in which costs increase less rapidly than output initially, but then start to increase more rapidly when the effects of managerial (or other) diseconomies begin to show themselves.

For the purpose of analysing the firm's behaviour, however, these relationships are more usually expressed in terms of average and marginal cost curves. These can be derived from the total cost curve in exactly the same way that average and marginal product curves were derived from a total product curve in the previous chapter. Thus, at any level of output, marginal cost is indicated by the slope of the total cost curve while average cost is determined by the slope of the line drawn from the total cost at that output back to the origin. Hence the marginal cost curve associated with the total cost in Figure 10.2a is *LMC* in Figure 10.2b, which declines until an output of *K* is reached and then starts rising, while the corresponding average cost curve, *LAC*, has a similar shape, but reaches its lowest point at an output of *M*.

Nevertheless, although long-run average cost curves of this vaguely saucer-shaped form are widely assumed to be typical of firms, it needs to be recognized that the theoretical arguments supporting that assumption are fairly speculative. Indeed, whilst empirical studies have confirmed that many firms are able to enjoy reduced average costs as output increases over some range of output, the generality of eventually increasing average costs is less firmly established. In many cases it seems that, when long-run average costs reach their lowest level, the curve flattens out rather than starts rising immediately.[2]

Short-run cost functions

The case with one variable input

Turning to the short run, the case that can most easily be related to the properties of the production function is that in which the quantity of only one of the inputs used by the firm can be varied. In that case, if y_v is the quantity of the variable input and p_v its price, expression (10.1) for the cost of all the inputs reduces to

$$C = p_v y_v + k, \tag{10.3}$$

where k is the cost of the fixed inputs, which, of course, are not avoidable in the short run. In a sense, this case is relatively straightforward because, with only one variable input, output (q) is uniquely related to the quantity of the variable input, so that, so long as p_v remains constant, we can rewrite the cost function as

$$C = f(q) + k. \tag{10.4}$$

Table 10.1

Output/day	MC	TVC	AVC	AFC	ATC
1	10	10	10	40	50
2	9	19	9.5	20	29.5
3	8	27	9	13.33	22.33
4	10	37	9.25	10	19.25
5	14	51	10.2	8	18.2
6	21	72	12	6.67	18.7
7	33	105	15	5.7	20.7
8	55	160	20	5	25

In addition, with only one variable input, the conditions for the operation of the law of diminishing returns are met, so the marginal product of the variable input must at some stage decline. This can easily be shown to have a direct effect on the behaviour of marginal cost.

If the marginal product of the variable input is MP_v, the cost per unit of that input, p_v, represents the avoidable cost of producing MP_v extra units of output. That means that marginal cost, which is the cost of producing 1 extra unit of output, can be expressed as p_v/MP_v. This expression indicates that, with constant p_v, the marginal cost of output is inversely proportional to the marginal product of the variable input, so that, if the latter rises, marginal cost falls and vice versa. If, therefore, the marginal product curve is of the form illustrated in Figure 9.1b, rising initially until the use of the variable input reaches a particular level and then falling as the effect of diminishing returns is experienced, marginal costs change in the opposite direction, falling when the marginal product is rising and rising when the marginal product is falling.

This kind of situation is reflected in the figures set out in Table 10.1. In the second column of the table it can be seen that marginal cost (MC) declines until an output of 3 units a day is produced and increases thereafter, and the curve MC in Figure 10.3 has been obtained by plotting the relevant values. Taking the analysis a stage further, the third column in the table, which is obtained by adding the marginal costs cumulatively, shows the total costs that can be avoided by not producing particular levels of output, or what is usually referred to as **total variable cost** (TVC), and which, of course, is the part of total cost covered by the term $f(q)$ in expression (10.4). The resultant **average variable costs** (AVC) are shown in the fourth column of the table and plotted to obtain the curve AVC in Figure 10.3.

Since the firm can profitably produce any unit of output for which the revenue obtained exceeds its avoidable cost, these two curves provide all the cost information the firm needs to decide how much to produce in the short run. Nevertheless, it is also useful to have some information about the longer-run viability of a particular situation, and this can be done by adding information about the cost of fixed inputs (i.e. fixed costs = k in expression

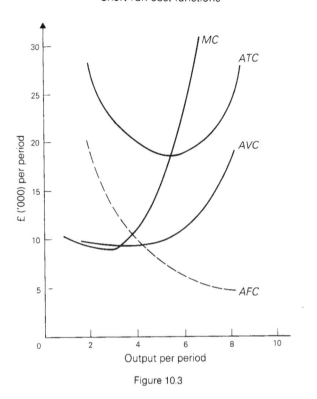

Figure 10.3

(10.4)), which are only avoidable in the long run, to the table and diagram. Thus with fixed costs of £40 per day, the figures of average fixed cost (AFC) in the fifth column of Table 10.1 can be obtained and these are plotted to obtain the average fixed cost curve, labelled *AFC* in Figure 10.3, which is a downward-sloping rectangular hyperbola, reflecting the decline in the cost of the fixed inputs per unit of output as they are spread over a larger quantity of output. Aggregating average fixed and variable cost then produces the figures in the final column of the table and the traditional U-shaped average total cost curve (*ATC*) in the diagram, the downward-sloping section of which reflects the influence of declining average fixed costs, while on the upward-sloping section the effects of diminishing returns to the variable input dominate. It will also be noted that the diagram illustrates the standard average/marginal relationship in that average cost declines when marginal cost is less than average cost and increases in the opposite case.

Differing short- and long-run opportunity cost

We suggested earlier in the chapter that, although the quantity of plant and machinery that a firm has available may be fixed in the short run, the inputs to the production process supplied by that plant and machinery may still be varied, at least up to some maximum level, and that as a result the difference between the short and long run is likely to be characterized not so much by differences in the fixity of particular quantities of certain inputs, but more by differences in the opportunity cost of using those inputs. In this situation we can still express costs as in (10.4) by the expression

$$C = f(q) + k,$$

but $f(q)$ now includes the short-run opportunity costs of all the inputs, whilst k represents the long-run opportunity costs, which are not avoidable in the short run. We must, nevertheless, consider the implications of these changes for the form of short-run cost curves.

Figure 10.4 illustrates the production function of a firm with two inputs using an isoquant diagram as developed in the last chapter. $E_L F_L$ is a constant cost curve reflecting the long-run costs of using the two inputs. In the short run, the fixed quantity of plant and machine available imposes an upper limit of M^* on the number of machine-hours available, but if the short-run opportunity cost of using the available plant and machinery up to that level, consisting mainly of its operating costs, is less than the long-run cost, which also includes capital costs, the constant cost curves reflecting the short-run relative input prices must be steeper (with machine-hours measured on the vertical axis) than $E_L F_L$. Hence in the diagram $E_S F_S$ is a constant cost curve reflecting short-run costs. Whilst, therefore, if the firm wanted to produce an output of Q_0, in the long run it would seek to use the combination of inputs at T_L, the combination at T_S would be the one minimizing avoidable input costs in the short run, and that involves more machine-hours and fewer man-hours than T_L. Moreover, point T_S must involve a lower outlay than T_L, reflecting the fact that fewer costs are avoidable in the short run than in the long run. More importantly, it can be seen that the scale expansion path in the short run lies along OS_2 rather than OS_1 and generally involves a more intensive use of the machine inputs. However, with an upper limit of M^* on the number of machine-hours available, once point H is reached, where OS_2 cuts the horizontal line M^*R and where an output of Q_1 is produced, the firm can expand no further along OS_2, but must instead use input combinations along HR if it wants to produce more output. The firm's short-run cost-minimizing expansion path must, therefore, follow the thick black line OHR in the diagram characterized by a kink at H.

In this situation, assuming (in the short run) a given constant returns to scale technology, total costs increase proportionately to output as the firm moves along OHR, until point H is reached, but will then start rising faster than output. This can be seen from the diagram by considering the cost of increasing output from Q_1 to Q_2. If more machine-hours were available, the firm would choose (in the short run as well as the long run) the input combination at J to produce Q_2, and marginal cost would be as before. Now the constant cost curve at J parallel to $E_S F_S$ lies along JK. This means that, with the available machine-hours restricted to M^*, the man-hours that could

158

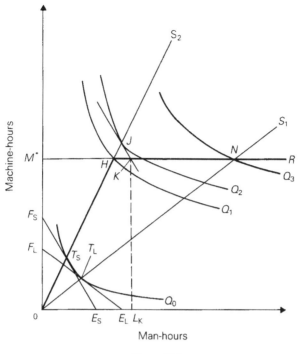

Figure 10.4

be combined with M^* machine-hours for the *same total outlay* as at J would be L_K, but it can be seen from the diagram that more man-hours than that would be needed if output was to be raised to Q_2. All this implies that short-run average variable and marginal costs are constant until the output at which the fixed plant and machinery are fully utilized is reached, and then start rising, producing curves like those in Figure 10.5. It will be noted that there is a discontinuity in the marginal cost curve at the output Q_1, which arises because the rate at which costs increase as output increases changes discontinuously at that point. However, such discontinuities may not be very large, so the important characteristics of the short-run marginal and average variable costs curves is that they are constant up to a certain point and then start rising.

We have drawn these conclusions on the basis of an analysis of a situation involving only two inputs, but it can readily be shown that increasing the number of inputs makes little difference to our conclusions. However many variable inputs there might be, if output can be expanded along the multi-dimensional equivalent of S_2 in Figure 10.4 with constant returns to scale, then again there will be a range of output over which marginal and average variable costs are constant, but once capacity constraints are approached costs will start rising as in the two-input case. One complicating factor with a number of fixed inputs is that maximum utilization of some inputs may be reached before that of others. This may introduce further

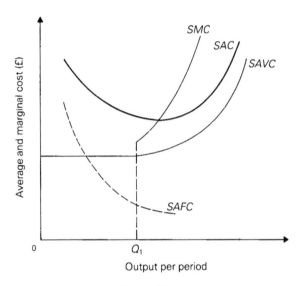

Figure 10.5

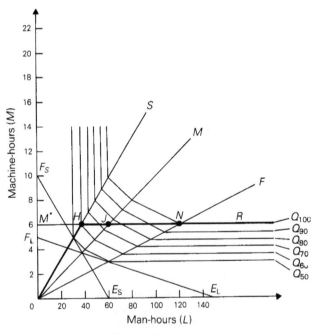

Figure 10.6

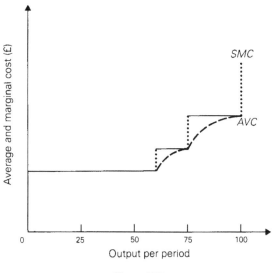

Figure 10.7

discontinuities or irregularities in the upward-sloping section of the marginal cost curve, but would not affect its more general properties.

Similar considerations apply if the production function is of the linear programming type considered in the previous chapter. This can be seen from Figure 10.6, which illustrates the same situation as Figure 9.5 but includes more isoquants. If, once more, the maximum machine-hours available are M^*, and short-run relative opportunity costs are reflected in the slope of E_SF_S, the firm's short-run expansion path is again OHR. For the same reasons, as in previous cases, marginal cost is constant until the output at point H is reached and then increases. But in this case, at higher outputs it follows the step pattern illustrated in Figure 10.7. The explanation for this is the nature of the isoquants and the way their slopes change along HR. From Figure 10.6 it can be seen that the additional man-hours required to produce 10 additional units of output are constant between H and J and between J and N, but are greater along JN than HJ. In other words, the marginal product of labour is lower between J and N than between H and J and so marginal costs are correspondingly higher. Once point N is reached, however, output can be increased no further and so the marginal cost of output becomes effectively infinite.

In all these cases, when fixed costs are added, the overall effect is to produce a broadly U-shaped short-run average (total) cost curve similar to that of the previous section, although in the linear programming case in particular there may be some irregularities reflecting those in the AVC curves (as in in Figure 10.7). Nevertheless, as suggested earlier, the important curves for the firm's short-run output decisions are the marginal and average variable cost curves, which our analysis suggests tend to be horizontal until capacity constraints begin to be met. This is significant because empirical studies have suggested that firms often think average variable costs behave in this way. Whether this is a convenient simplification or an accurate reflection of the actual conditions they face is not clear, but if firms believe that the relevant functions are of that form, then that belief is likely to shape their decisions and needs to be incorporated in our analysis.

The relationship between long- and short-run cost functions

Having discussed the form of long- and short-run cost functions, it remains to consider the relationship between them. For that it is useful to start by returning again to the short- and long-run expansion paths depicted in Figures 10.4 and 10.6 above. If we concentrate our attention on Figure 10.4 (although the same arguments could equally be applied to Figure 10.6), it will be recalled that in the short run, with a fixed plant sufficiently large to allow a maximum input of M^* machine-hours, the short-run avoidable costs of producing an output of Q_0 are minimized, with the relative prices in the diagram, when the inputs at T_S are used rather than those at T_L, the preferred input combination when longer-run adjustments to plant size can be made. This implies that, with the given plant size, the short-run avoidable or variable costs incurred in the production of an output of Q_0, which are reflected in the constant cost curve $E_S F_S$, are lower than the total costs reflected in $E_L F_L$. Moreover, it should be apparent that similar considerations must apply to any output less than Q_3, which is the output produced at point N in Figure 10.4, where the short- and long-run expansion paths OHR and OS_1 intersect. For outputs a little greater than Q_3, the avoidable costs in the short run may also be less than long-run costs, but, if the short-run cost of expanding output rises sharply as output increases, this relationship may eventually be reversed. In other words, if the curve LTC in Figure 10.8a shows the relationship between total cost and output in the long run, as the firm moves along its long-run expansion path, the curve showing the relationship between short-run variable costs and output ($STVC_1$ in the diagram) lies below LTC as shown, at least up to some output greater than Q_3 (which is equivalent to Q_3 in Figure 10.4)[3].

At the same time it must be apparent that the *longer-run* avoidable cost of producing Q_0 in Figure 10.4 with the inputs at T_S, which includes the costs that are fixed in the short run as well as those included in $STVC_1$, must be greater than the long-run costs of the inputs at T_L, otherwise the particular bundle of inputs at the latter point would not be preferred in the long run. Further, the same must also apply at all other points along OHR, with the sole exception of N where the same input combination is used in the long and short run. Hence in terms of Figure 10.8, adding fixed costs to $STVC_1$ simply

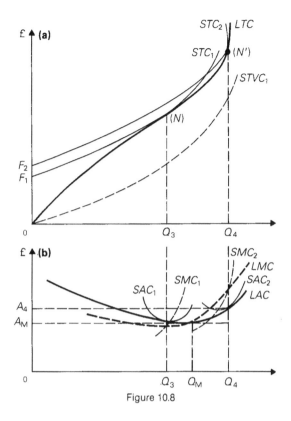

Figure 10.8

displaces it vertically by the amount of the fixed costs to produce the short-run total cost curve STC_1, which lies above LTC at all points other than the one labelled N (to indicate that it corresponds to N in Figure 10.4), where an output of Q_3 is produced. At this point, short- and long-run costs are momentarily the same, so the curves touch.

The curve STC_2 is defined similarly to represent a situation where there is more plant available capable of providing more machine-hours. In this case, fixed costs would be higher in the short run but the output at which short- and long-run costs are the same (Q_4 in the diagram) is also higher than Q_3 and that is reflected in the way STC_2 is drawn. Other curves could also be constructed for other possible sizes of plant, and when that is done the long-run total cost curve, LTC, which by definition reflects the lowest possible cost of producing each level of output, appears as an **envelope** curve, round the lower boundary of the area covered by all the short-run total cost curves. If plant size is sufficiently variable, the maximum input of machine-hours can be varied continuously and the long-run total cost curve will be a smooth curve as in the diagram. If, however, as may well happen in practice, the way in which plant size can be adjusted produces discrete rather than continuous changes in capacity, there could be some kinks in LTC.

We can link this diagrammatic representation to expression (10.4) by including in the latter a variable s, which is fixed in the short run and variable in the long run. Since the value of s is likely to have some influence on variable costs and will ultimately determine (short-run) fixed costs, the appropriate amended form of (10.4) is

$$C = f(q, s) + k(s). \tag{10.5}$$

This expression defines the family of relationships between C and q, including one for each possible value of s, which are represented by the short-run curves in Figure 10.8a. The long-run cost curve then shows the relationship between C and q, when, at each and every value of q, s is set at the level that minimizes total costs. Thus in Figure 10.8a, with an output of Q_4, the cost-minimizing value of s is that required to produce the short-run total cost curve STC_2, whilst with an output of Q_3 it is that underlying STC_1. But we must also conclude, since k is an increasing function of s, that total costs can only be reduced by increasing s if it produces a more than offsetting reduction in variable cost represented by $f(q, s)$. If s is at less than its optimal value, this must be the case. Hence, a characteristic of the optimal values of s must be that the opportunities for reducing costs are exhausted, and that the marginal reduction in variable cost is just equal to the marginal increase in fixed cost.[4]

Returning to Figure 10.8, the relationship between the short- and long-run average cost curves is basically similar to that between the total cost curves. In Figure 10.8b, LAC is the long-run average cost curve derived from LTC in Figure 10.8a. Since the short-run costs of producing an output of Q_3 with the original plant are the same as the long-run costs, the short- and long-run average costs ($= TC/Q_3$) must also be equal. Also, since with the same plant the short-run total costs of outputs both greater and smaller than Q_3 are higher than the long-run total costs, the same must apply to their corresponding average costs. Hence the short-run average cost curve in this case is shown as SAC_1 in Figure 10.8b; it touches LAC at the output of Q_3 but at all other outputs lies above it. Similar considerations apply to SAC_2, which is the short-run average cost curve derived from STC_2. Hence, it can be shown that, if all possible short-run average cost curves were added to Figure 10.8b, the long-run average cost curve, LAC, would be the *envelope* curve of all the short-run average cost curves.

With the marginal curves, however, the situation is a little different, but again we can deduce the nature of the relationship between the short- and long-run curves by considering the relationship between STC_1 and LTC in the vicinity of point (N) in Figure 10.8a. As has already been suggested, STC_1 touches LTC at (N), which means they are tangential to each other and their slopes are the same. From this we can obviously conclude that at that point short- and long-run marginal costs are equal. However, by inspecting the diagram we can see that, for outputs less than Q_3, the slope of STC_1 is less than the slope of LTC, implying that $SMC_1 < LMC$, whilst for outputs greater than Q_3 the opposite is true. This means that the short-run marginal cost curve SMC_1 must *intersect* LMC from below, as in Figure 10.8b, rather than be tangential to it. The same must also apply to SMC_2, the short-run marginal cost curve associated with SAC_2, which intersects LMC at an output of Q_4. The difference between the two cases is that in the latter, since Q_4 is on the rising part of LAC, marginal costs are greater than average costs and hence the point of intersection between LMC and SMC_2 must lie above the average cost curves rather than below them.

Minimum average cost and economic efficiency

One consequence of a cost function like that illustrated in Figure 10.8 above is that average cost is lower at some outputs than others. This seems to raise questions of efficiency since, superficially at least, a firm producing at or near the minimum point of its average cost curve has the appearance of being more 'efficient' than firms at other points on their cost function. However, discussion of this issue has tended to become confused because of a failure to distinguish between efficiency from the point of view of the firm and efficiency from a wider point of view.

When the individual firm is considered, it needs to be remembered that the cost curves were defined to reflect the minimum costs of producing any output in the relevant (short- or long-run) situation facing the firm when the output obtained from any bundle of inputs employed is as great as it technically can be. In other words, if the firm can keep the cost of producing any output to the level indicated by the relevant cost curve it is operating efficiently in both the technical and economic senses defined in the intro- duction to Chapter 9. However, it can be argued that, in the long run, the efficiency with which resources are allocated in the economy as a whole can be improved if the number of firms producing a particular product is adjusted so that all can produce at the minimum point of their long-run average cost curves. Thus, in the case illustrated in Figure 10.8b, if there were a number of firms, with the average cost curve illustrated, all producing Q_3 of the product in question, whilst individually they would all be producing efficiently, the long-run overall costs of supplying the same total output could be reduced if the number of producers were to be reduced sufficiently to allow the firms remaining in the industry to increase their output to Q_M, at which their long-run average costs are minimized. Similarly, in situations where long-run average cost curves turn upwards as in Figure 10.8b, if individual firms are producing an output greater than that at which average costs are minimized, the overall cost of producing the same output can be reduced by increasing the number of producers.

However, the same argument cannot so easily be applied in the short run, because the movement of firms into and out of an industry is essentially a longer-run adjustment process, involving as it does the adjustment of fixed inputs. Indeed, it can be argued that the minimum point of a firm's short-run average cost curve is of no particular significance. It might be thought that if a firm was producing at such a point its plant would be optimally adjusted, but that would not be the case if the firm was operating where its long-run average cost curve was sloping downwards or upwards, because, in both cases, the curve would pass below the minimum point of the short-run average cost curve, indicating that costs could be reduced in the long run by adjusting plant size. In fact, the relationship between a firm's short- and long-run marginal cost curves is of more operational significance because, if short-run marginal cost is greater than long-run marginal cost, it is more efficient in the long run to accommodate extra output by expanding plant rather than by using the existing plant more intensively. But if short-run marginal cost is lower than long-run marginal cost, the existing plant is not being used optimally, so the opposite is true. Indeed, in such cases, unless output can be increased, some reduction in plant size is called for.

The multi-plant firm

We conclude this chapter with two extensions to our basic cost analysis. The first is concerned with a firm operating more than one plant. Short- and long-run cost functions can, of course, be identified for each plant, but the additional issues we need to consider are the allocation of output between plants and the derivation of an aggregate relationship between costs and output for the firm as a whole.

As far as the first of these issues is concerned, profit-maximizing firms will seek to minimize the cost of producing any output, which normally involves allocating output between its plants to equalize the marginal cost in each.[5] This can be seen with the help of Figure 10.9 relating to a firm with two plants, which we can label X and Y. Initially we can consider a situation in which the firm is producing a total output of Q_1. If we measure the output produced in plant X conventionally along the horizontal axis from left to right, then the output required from plant Y can be measured from Q_1 in the opposite direction. Thus, if the output of plant X is OA, as long as the total output remains at Q_1, the output of plant Y is measured by AQ_1. The short-run marginal cost curve for X (SMC_X) is, therefore, drawn in the normal way but the corresponding curve for Y (SMC_Y) is drawn from right to left starting from the vertical line drawn from Q_1. The optimal allocation of the total output between the two plants is then where the two marginal cost curves intersect, because at that allocation $SMC_X = SMC_Y$, and it involves an output of OB from X and BQ_1 from Y. Any other distribution of output, such as that at A, involves higher costs, because the savings in costs in plant X arising from the reduction in its output from OB to OA, which are measured

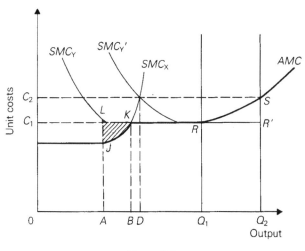

Figure 10.9

by the area under its marginal cost curve between the two outputs, $BKJA$, are less than the increase in costs in Y (measured by $BKLA$) arising from the additional output it has to produce. In fact, in the diagram, the net increase in costs arising from the change in the distribution of output from that at B to that at A is represented by the shaded area JKL, and it can be shown that similar additional costs arise whenever the firm moves away from the allocation of output between the plants at which their marginal costs are equal.

We can also use the diagram to see the effect of increasing total output and to derive an aggregate short-run marginal cost curve. If aggregate output is increased to Q_2, SMC_Y now starts from the vertical line drawn from Q_2 at R' and is thus displaced to the right. If its new position is that indicated by the curve SMC_Y',the cost-minimizing allocation of output is at D, involving a higher level of marginal cost than the original position, with OD being produced in X and DQ_2 in Y. Now since in the initial situation the firm was producing an output of Q_1 at a marginal cost of C_1, a combination represented by point R in the diagram, and since in the new situation it is producing Q_2 at a marginal cost of C_2, a combination represented by point S, R and S are points on the aggregate marginal cost curve. Other points can be found in a similar way and together they generate the aggregate marginal cost curve shown as AMC in the diagram. When the total output is less than B, this curve coincides with SMC_X, because output can only be produced in Y at a higher cost. Then, in the case illustrated, as total output is increased above B, initially all the extra output is produced in Y but, when SMC_Y starts rising, both plants contribute to further increases in total output.

Alternatively, the aggregate marginal cost curve can be derived by adding the individual marginal cost curves horizontally, but whatever approach is used, once the aggregate curve has been produced, the associated average variable and average total cost curves can also be derived and together they can be used as the basis for the further analysis of the firm's behaviour. Moreover, these aggregate curves share the underlying properties of the functions relating to individual plants. In our subsequent analysis, therefore, we do not distinguish between single- and multi-plant firms on the grounds that broadly similar cost functions apply in both cases.

The multi-product firm and joint costs

So far our analysis has concentrated on the case of a firm producing a single product, but since in practice most firms produce a range of products we need to give some consideration, in this second extension of our basic analysis, to the cost function of the multi-product firm. In formal terms, the multi-product case poses no severe problems as we can simply specify the cost function as

$$C = F(q_1, q_2, \ldots, q_n), \tag{10.6}$$

where $q_1, q_2, \ldots, q_n$ denote the quantities of the various products produced. The identification of the marginal cost of any one product is also straightforward: it is simply a question of observing the effect on total cost of a marginal increase in the output of that product.[6]

However, the marginal cost of one product need not be independent of the quantities produced of the other products. For example, where products are complementary in production, increasing the output of one may make it easier to produce others and reduce their marginal cost. Similarly, where products are substitutes in production, in the sense that they make competing claims on the same productive resources, increasing the production of one may hinder the production of others and increase their marginal cost.

Another complication is that average cost, in this context, is a more slippery concept because the production of more than one product often involves a situation in which certain inputs contribute to the activities of the firm as a whole rather than to the output of a particular product. This may be the case, for example, with the managerial and administrative services provided by the firm's head office, but it might equally be the case with certain types of plant and capital equipment. The problem that arises centres round the question of whether, and to what extent, the costs of the inputs involved can be allocated to individual products. Here again, the concept of avoidable cost is helpful, and the way the problem can be dealt with can be explained with the help of a simple example.

Suppose that a firm produces two products, A and B, the production of which is carried out in two separate establishments so that there is no difficulty in identifying the production cost of each product. Suppose also, however, that the firm's central management carries out managerial functions for both products at a cost of £5m per annum. Now clearly, if the firm is to continue in operation, the aggregate surplus over production costs for the two goods must be sufficient to cover these central management costs, or

$$S_A + S_B > 5, \tag{10.7}$$

where S_A and S_B are the individual surpluses in £ million. But even if this condition is satisfied, the firm may be interested to know whether it could improve its profitability by abandoning the production of one of its two products. In considering this it needs to ask itself what its management costs might be if it concentrated on one product, and it might come up with the following estimates;

Management costs if A alone is produced, £3.5m
Management costs if B alone is produced, £3.0m

From the first of these statements we can conclude that adding the production of B to the production of A adds £1.5m (= £5.0m – £3.5m) to management costs. £1.5m expenditure can, therefore, be avoided by *not* producing B and thus can be counted as part of the cost to the firm of producing B. Similarly, we can conclude that the management costs that can be attributed to the production of A are £2.0m (= £5.0 – £3.0m). From this information the firm will be able to conclude that it is worthwhile continuing the production of A if $S_A > £2.0$m, and worthwhile continuing the production of B if $S_B > £1.5$m, provided, of course, that total management costs are also covered (i.e. that $S_A + S_B > £5$m).

It will be noted that the management costs attributed to the production of A and B do not account for the total £5m; there is still £1.5m unallocated to either product. These costs are truly joint costs, and where they exist no determinate estimate of the total cost of producing the individual products can be made, and there can be no corresponding estimate of average cost. Nevertheless, these joint costs have to be covered, if the firm is to survive, from the surpluses earned from the sales of the individual products as indicated by condition (10.7) above, but whether they are covered entirely by the surplus from A or by the surplus from B or by a combination of both does not matter.

Notes

1   d'Alessi (1967) analyses the implications of this in more detail.
2   See, for example, the discussion in Hay and Morris (1979) and the more detailed survey in Walters (1963).
3   In the interests of generality the long-run cost curves in Figure 10.8 have been given the more

traditional form of Figure 10.2 rather than the linear form (like LTC_1 in Figure 10.1) that would arise with the constant returns to scale production function depicted in Figure 10.4.

4 Since, for any given value of q, C is minimized when

$$\partial C / \partial s = f_s + k'(s) = 0,$$

where f_s is the change in the cost of producing an output of q and $k'(s)$ is the marginal cost of increasing s. Obviously, if $k'(s) > 0, f_s < 0$.

5 Exceptions arise when the firm is operating along a downward-sloping marginal cost curve.

6 The marginal cost of product i is also indicated by the partial derivative $\partial C / \partial q_i$.

Exercises

10.1 Under what conditions does the cost of using an input in production differ from the money outlay arising from its use?

10.2 Why are short-run marginal cost curves assumed to be U-shaped?

10.3 Can any general conclusions be drawn about the shape of long-run average cost curves?

10.4 Explain the relationship between:

(i) a firm's short- and long-run *average* cost curves

(ii) a firm's short- and long-run *marginal* cost curves.

10.5 It is normally suggested that production of a good should continue as long as the revenue from its sale is sufficient to cover avoidable costs. What qualifications to this principle need to be made when more than one product is produced and there are joint costs?

10.6 You are the manager of a self-drive van hire firm that currently owns five vans. There is sufficient demand to keep four of them fully occupied throughout the year. The fifth van, however, is hired out for only half of the 300 days in the year that you are open for business. (Maintenance and repairs are carried out by an outside contractor on days when your business is closed.)

(i) Given the following information, would you sell the fifth van now or keep it in operation?

> Rental charge: £25 per day plus 35p per mile.
> Average daily mileage when hired: 50.
> Fuel costs: 12p per mile.
> Maintenance and repair costs: £150 per year plus 15p per mile.
> Licence and insurance: £650 per year.
> Current sale price of van: £5,000.
> Expected depreciation of sale price over the year: £1,200.
> Current rate of interest: 10%.

(ii) If you were given the chance to bid for an annual fixed-price contract requiring the van to be available at short notice for 30 days' use scattered randomly throughout the year, each involving 100 miles a day, what is the minimum price you would bid?

CHAPTER 11
DEMAND, REVENUE AND PROFIT MAXIMIZATION

Introduction

Having discussed the relationship between a firm's output and its costs, we can begin to turn our attention towards the firm's output decision. In this chapter we will concentrate exclusively on the decisions of a profit-maximizing firm, but, since the firm's profits are the difference between its revenue and costs, we must first of all consider the determinants of the revenue arising from the firm's activities and thus the determinants of its revenue function.

Revenue functions, like cost functions, can be expressed in total, average and marginal terms. Where, however, a product is sold for a single uniform price, average revenue is necessarily equal to price and the firm's average revenue function is, to all intents and purposes, its demand function, although strictly speaking we should refer to it as the firm's *inverse* demand function to emphasize that price (= average revenue) is the independent variable rather than the quantity demanded. We can, nevertheless, start our examination of the firm's revenue function by reviewing the variables affecting demand.

The demand for the firm's product

In practice, firms sell their products either to final consumers or to other firms and organizations who use them as inputs into their own productive activities, or to some combination of both. We do, in fact, examine firms' demand for goods and services for use as inputs in some detail in later chapters, but since the basic properties of the demand functions facing firms are similar whatever type of economic agent buys their output, we can, without too much loss of generality, start our discussion of firms' demand functions by considering the case of a firm producing a good for final consumption by individuals. The total demand for the good is then simply the sum of the demands of all the individuals who buy it, and thus depends on the variables that featured in our discussion of consumer behaviour in earlier chapters.

From that discussion (in Chapters 2 and 3) it will be recalled that an individual's demand for any good depends upon its price, the prices of other goods that may be substitutes or complements, his spending power, determined by income and wealth, and his preferences. Subsequent chapters, covering developments and extensions of the basic theory, emphasized the attributes or characteristics of the product (Chapter 6), the extent to which it needs to be combined with other inputs (particularly time) in the consumption process, and the information about the good and its availability (which were all discussed in Chapter 7). Moreover, the corresponding properties of other goods may also have some effect on the demand for the good, just as their prices do. This suggests that the demand for any individual product produced by a firm depends upon a large number of variables. Only a relatively small number of these, however, are likely to be under the firm's *direct* control. Those that are may include the price of the product, its quality, and the amount of information about the product available to consumers. Nevertheless, in making decisions about these variables the firm will need to take into account the influence of other variables, and of those the most important are likely to be the prices and qualities of products produced by other firms, particularly where they are competing firms producing close substitutes. However, the effect they have depends on the type of competition the firm faces, and we will be considering different types of competition in following chapters.

For the moment, therefore, we will consider a situation in which the value of all the variables controlled by other economic agents is given, so that we can concentrate on the relationship between the demand for the firm's product (for the most part we will be dealing with a firm producing a single product) and the variables that it can influence directly. In short, we are considering a situation in which the demand function for firm i can be expressed as

$$q_i = f(p_i, b_i, a_i), \tag{11.1}$$

where q_i is the demand for the product per period, p_i is its price, b_i is a variable reflecting the quality of the product and a_i is the information available to consumers. Our task in this chapter, therefore, is to examine the nature of the relationship between q_i and each of the other variables and to draw out the implications of these relationships for profit-maximizing behaviour. The approach will be to consider first the basic price/quantity relationship and the associated requirements for profit maximization, when the other two variables are constant, and then to show how the analysis can be extended to take account of changes in b_i and a_i. In the final section of the chapter we have a brief look at the additional complications arising in a multi-product firm.

The price variable

Our analysis of consumer behaviour suggested that, other things being equal, a consumer's demand for a good in most cases increases as its price falls. We noted that in the case of Giffen goods, where negative income effects are sufficient to outweigh positive substitution effects, demand for inferior goods could increase as price falls, but concluded that they are likely to be rather exceptional cases. Moreover, when we aggregate across all the consumers of a firm's product to obtain the demand curve facing the firm, it can be argued that the Giffen-type case is likely to be even more exceptional, because a Giffen good to one person is not necessarily a Giffen good to everyone else. Further, the effect of a few people reducing their purchases may be more than offset by the effect of new buyers attracted to the good as its price falls. Overall, therefore, it can be argued that the general tendency for demand to increase as price falls is likely to be sufficiently strong to swamp the more idiosyncratic behaviour of particular individuals.

Contrary to this, it is sometimes suggested that, where consumers are less than perfectly informed about the quality of a product, they may take price as an indicator of quality. Hence, if the price of a product increases, some people may be attracted to buy it because of the higher quality they attribute to it, and this effect could, potentially, offset any reduction in sales to more knowledgeable buyers. Again, however, since with many, if not most products, the bulk of the demand comes from regular buyers who are likely to be reasonably aware of product quality, it can be argued that this sort of perverse behaviour on the part of individuals is not likely to upset the general tendency for demand to fall as price rises and vice versa.

Nevertheless, we also need to recognize at this stage that an individual firm is typically one of a number of firms supplying a particular product. This means that there are close substitutes and, in some cases, perfect substitutes available to consumers, which in turn means that the demand for an individual firm's product may be highly elastic with respect to price. Indeed, in some cases, even a small increase in price may be sufficient to reduce the demand for a firm's product to zero as buyers switch to the lower-priced products of rival producers. Equally, in such situations a small reduction in price may increase demand more or less infinitely. The limiting case is where demand is perfectly elastic so that firms are faced with a demand or average revenue curve that is horizontal at the current price level, like that in Figure 11.1a. Effectively this means that the firm has no real control over the price at which it sells its product; it can only accept or *take* the given price. Firms with this kind of demand curve are, therefore, referred to as **price takers**.

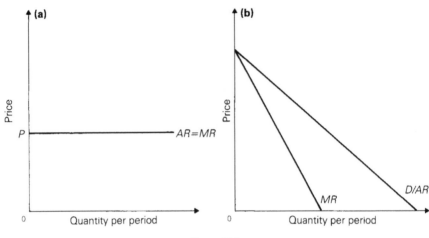

Figure 11.1

However, whilst such firms cannot vary their price, the horizontal demand curve implies that they can sell as much as they like at the going price. With each additional unit selling at the same price, marginal revenue (MR) is also constant and equal to price, whilst total revenue is proportional to output.

In contrast, firms facing less than perfectly elastic downward-sloping demand curves, of the kind illustrated in Figure 11.1b, can vary their price, and are thus referred to as **price makers**. They have to accept, however, that what they can sell (when other relevant variables are constant) is determined by the price they choose or, alternatively, that the price or average revenue they can obtain for their product depends on the quantity they wish to sell. With a downward-sloping average revenue curve, the marginal revenue curve lies below the average revenue curve (as illustrated in Figure 11.1b), because the revenue from the sale of the marginal unit is offset by reduced revenue from intra-marginal units. Indeed, the reduction in the revenue from these intra-marginal units may be greater than the revenue from the marginal unit itself, so that overall total revenue falls and marginal revenue is negative.

The diagram actually illustrates the case of a straight line demand curve and, in this particular case, the marginal revenue curve bisects any horizontal line drawn from the vertical axis to the average revenue curve.[1] Hence, the output at which marginal revenue is zero is exactly half the output at which price is zero. Unfortunately, this convenient property does not apply to non-linear demand curves. With demand curves that get steeper as price falls, the marginal revenue curve cuts horizontal lines drawn from the vertical axis more than half way to the demand curve,[2] whilst if the demand curve becomes less steep as price falls the opposite is true.

The reader may also recall from his earlier studies that whether total revenue increases or decreases as price falls depends on the price elasticity of demand (e_P), since when demand is inelastic (that is when $-1 < e_P < 0$) a reduction in price yields a proportionately smaller increase in demand and thus reduces total revenue, but when demand is elastic ($e_P < -1$) the opposite is true. The precise relationship between marginal revenue and the elasticity of demand is

$$MR = P(1 + 1/e_P), \tag{11.2}$$

where P is the product price.[3] From this we can confirm that when demand is inelastic marginal revenue is negative, since $1/e_P < -1$, and that when demand is elastic (and $-1 < 1/e_P < 0$) marginal revenue is positive. Alternatively, we can rearrange (11.2) to get

$$P - MR = -P/e_P, \tag{11.3}$$

which tells us that the difference between price and marginal revenue is inversely related to the negative of the elasticity of demand and is thus smaller, for a given price, the more elastic the demand. Moreover, we can confirm from this that as the demand for the firm's product becomes infinitely elastic, as in the price-taker case, the difference between price and marginal revenue reduces to zero.

Profit maximization in the short run

At this point we can relate our conclusions about the basic form of the firm's revenue function to the cost functions in the previous chapter, so that we can examine the conditions for profit maximization. Since profits are simply the difference between total revenue and total cost, we can start our analysis from the firm's total revenue and total cost curves. Also, because the same basic principles apply whether the firm is a price taker or a price maker, we will concentrate our attention on the latter case and indicate what our results imply for the special case of the price taker where appropriate. Thus in Figure 11.2a, the curve TR is the total revenue curve of a price maker with a downward-sloping demand curve.[4] Also, since we are concerned with decisions in the current period, the short-run relationship between costs and output is the relevant one, so TC represents a possible short-run cost curve for the firm.[5] The profit curve, π, is then derived by plotting points representing the vertical distance between TR and TC at each level of output, and it shows that profits are negative at low levels of output, rise to a maximum at an output of Q_3, and decline thereafter.

Now the fact that at an output of Q_3 the vertical distance between TR and TC is greater than at any other output means that TR and TC are, at that output, parallel to each other since, wherever TR is steeper than TC, profits can be increased by expanding output, and where TR is less steep than TC the

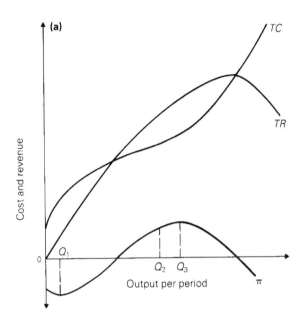

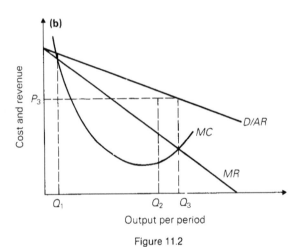

Figure 11.2

opposite is true. But since the slopes of these curves are equal to marginal revenue (*MR*) and marginal cost (*MC*), respectively, we may conclude that a necessary condition for profit maximization is that

$$MR = MC. \tag{11.4}$$

This is, of course, the standard **first-order** condition for profit maximization,[6] with which the reader will no doubt already be familiar, and it can be confirmed by referring to Figure 11.2b in which the marginal revenue and marginal cost curves derived from their respective total curves in Figure 11.2a are shown as *MR* and *MC*. In Figure 11.2b it can be seen that with outputs a little below Q_3, such as Q_2, marginal revenue is greater than marginal cost, or

$$MR - MC > 0.$$

In other words, marginal profit (the profit to be obtained from an extra unit of output) is positive. Hence, increasing output adds to profits and is a desirable step for the firm to take. Once, however, output has reached Q_3, this is no longer the case, since

$$MR - MC = 0$$

and, if output exceeds Q_3,

$$MR - MC < 0,$$

and profits can be increased by reducing output. All this suggests that another feature of the profit-maximizing output is that marginal profit ($= MR - MC$) must be declining. This is the case at output Q_3 in the diagram because there marginal cost is rising and marginal revenue is falling, but more generally it is true as long as marginal costs are declining less rapidly than marginal revenue, or, in diagrammatic terms, where the marginal cost curve cuts the marginal revenue curve from below.

This is the **second-order** condition for profit maximization,[7] and is an important additional condition because, although (11.4) is always satisfied where profits are maximized, it can also be satisfied where they are not. One such point is at output Q_1 in Figure 11.2. But a glance at Figure 11.2b should be sufficient to confirm that Q_1 is not a maximum profits output, because producing an extra unit of output adds to profits since, for outputs just in excess of Q_1, $MR - MC > 0$. In fact, with output Q_1, profits are minimized rather than maximized, so it is always important to remember that an equality of marginal cost and marginal revenue indicates a maximum profits position only if marginal costs are declining less rapidly (or increasing more rapidly) than marginal revenue as output increases. In our subsequent discussion we do not always make specific reference to this condition. It is, however, reflected in the way all the diagrams are drawn and the reader should always be aware of its importance.

Having identified the profit-maximizing output, we can read off the price at which that output can be sold from the demand curve in Figure 11.2b (which is P_3), but we can also use the relationships derived in the previous section to examine the properties of the profit-maximizing price in more detail. Using expression (11.2) we can conclude that, when $MR = MC$,

$$MC = P(1 + 1/e_P)$$

or

$$P = MC/(1 + 1/e_P) > MC, \qquad \text{since } (1 + 1/e_P) < 1,$$

or alternatively, dividing both sides of (11.3) by P, we get

$$\frac{P - MC}{P} = -\frac{1}{e_P} \qquad\qquad (11.5)$$

or, with a little more manipulation,[8] we can deduce that

$$\frac{P - MC}{MC} = -\frac{1}{e_P + 1}. \qquad\qquad (11.6)$$

We can thus see that the firm can arrive at a profit-maximizing price by adding a margin to marginal cost dependent on the elasticity of demand, and that the more inelastic the demand, the higher the margin, in relation to marginal cost, to be added. Thus, with an elasticity of demand of -10, the margin is 1/9th ($= 11.11\%$) of marginal cost, whilst with an elasticity of -3 it is 1/2 (or 50%). The profit-maximizing condition (11.4), however, imposes a limit on the extent to which demand can be inelastic, since, with $MC = MR$, as long as MC is non-negative (> 0), which is certain to be the case, marginal revenue must also be non-negative. This means that $e_P < -1$ and thus that demand must be elastic rather than inelastic.

At the other extreme, we can also see from (11.5) that if the firm is a price taker, where demand is infinitely inelastic, when profits are maximized $(P - MC)/P$ is zero, and hence price must be equal to marginal cost. This can be confirmed by drawing the diagram corresponding to Figure 11.2 for a firm that is a price taker, but that is an exercise that is left to the reader.

One final point to note in connection with Figure 11.2 is that although, in that diagram, profits are more than sufficient to keep the firm in business, it needs to be recognized that the maximum profits output could involve losses (or negative profits). In those circumstances the firm would have to decide whether to continue in production. Obviously, if in the longer run there was no change in the situation, the firm would have to close down, but in the short run, as indicated in the previous chapter, it would be worthwhile continuing in production as long as the price is sufficiently high to cover the costs avoidable in the short run, or, in other words, as long as it exceeds average variable cost.

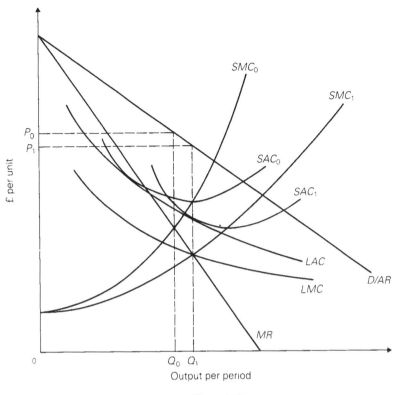

Figure 11.3

The long-run situation

Moreover, even in the absence of losses, the firm would keep its longer-run prospects continually under review because some decisions, particularly those involving the reorganization of plant and capacity, take time to implement. In this respect the simplest case to consider is where the firm's cost and revenue functions are expected to remain unchanged for the foreseeable future. In that case the important question is whether costs can be reduced, and profits thereby increased, by adjusting plant size or, to use the notation of expression (10.5) above, by adjusting the variable s. As indicated in the last chapter, that depends on the relationship between short- and long-run marginal cost at the current profit-maximizing output. If, as in the case illustrated in Figure 11.3 when the short-run marginal cost curve is SMC_0 and the firm is producing an output of Q_0 (where $SMC = MR$) and selling at P_0, it can reduce the cost of producing Q_0 in the longer run by increasing its plant size, thereby shifting its short-run marginal cost curve to the right. But then it would be able to increase profits further by increasing output and lowering price. In fact, in the diagram, the long-run optimum position is

179

where the short-run marginal cost curve is SMC_1, output is Q_1 and price is P_1, such that

$$MR = SMC = LMC, \tag{11.7}$$

which is also, of course, a position in which

$$SAC = LAC.$$

In the real world, however, the position may be constantly changing because of changes in consumers' incomes, changes in tastes and changes in the conditions of supply of related products. Further, cost functions are also subject to change because of changing input prices and improved technical knowledge, in response to which it might be necessary to obtain new equipment and change production techniques. But again, the long-run aim would be to make the adjustments necessary for the firm to be in a position in which condition (11.7) can be satisfied when all the adjustments have been made.

The information variable

We turn now to the non-price variables in the firm's demand function as summarized by expression (11.1), and consider first the variable a_i representing the information available to consumers, since the analysis of that variable relates most straightforwardly to the preceding discussion.

In practice, consumers obtain information about the products they consider buying from a variety of sources, but firms can add to that information through advertising and other sales promotional activities. The information firms provide may not be precisely the information the consumer requires, but since the main advertising media – such as television, newspapers and magazines – are relatively low-cost sources of information, at least for people who watch television or read the publications for the information and entertainment they provide, advertising (and from here we use the term to cover sales promotion activities generally) has the effect of reducing the cost of acquiring information for many potential customers, and thus has a similar effect on their demand as a reduction in price. In addition, it is also sometimes argued that, since advertising is often overtly persuasive, if successful it changes people's preferences in favour of the advertised products. However, whether it actually does that, or whether it simply confirms that the advertised products have the characteristics individuals are seeking from them (consciously or unconsciously), doesn't really matter from our point of view because in either case the effect is to increase demand.

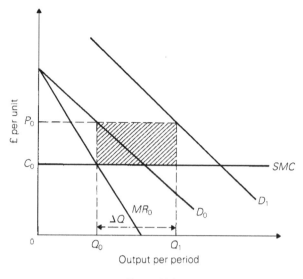

Figure 11.4

So far as the firm is concerned, therefore, the effect of advertising is to increase the amount it can sell at any price. It thus pushes the demand curve for the advertised product out to the right. Hence in Figure 11.4, if the demand for the firm's product without advertising is D_0, the effect of a given advertising campaign might be to push the demand curve out to D_1 and to increase the sale of the product, when the price is P_0, from Q_0 to Q_1. Whether such an advertising campaign is worthwhile then depends on whether the extra net revenue generated by the advertising is greater than the cost of the campaign.

In the case illustrated in Figure 11.4, in which, to simplify, marginal costs (denoted by the curve SMC) are constant, the extra net revenue generated by the advertising, which is the revenue from the extra sales less the additional production costs involved, is represented by the shaded area. It can also be expressed as

$$(P_0 - C_0)\Delta Q,$$

where ΔQ is $Q_1 - Q_0$. In slightly more general terms we can, therefore, say that any increment in advertising (ΔA) is worthwhile as long as

$$(P - MC)\Delta Q > \Delta A.$$

But it also seems reasonable to suppose that, as advertising increases, its effectiveness at the margin declines as the uninformed (or unpersuaded) customers become increasingly those that are difficult to reach (or persuade). Hence the profit-maximizing firm will seek to expand its advertising expenditure up to the point where the marginal revenue from advertising is equal to its marginal cost, or where

$$(P - MC)\Delta Q = \Delta A. \tag{11.8}$$

The conventional rule for the equality of marginal revenue and marginal costs, subject to the relevant second-order conditions, thus emerges again but with respect to advertising rather than output.

Whether the position reached when condition (11.8) is met is the ultimate profit-maximizing condition depends on how the advertising affects the price elasticity of demand for the firm's product. If it leaves that elasticity unchanged (and initially $MC = MR$ as in Figure 11.4), no adjustments to price are required. But it is sometimes suggested that advertising, by increasing brand loyalty, tends to make demand less elastic with respect to price and thus increases the profit-maximizing price–cost margin. In that case, therefore, an increase in price would enable profits to be further increased.

We can, however, explore the implications of profit maximization with advertising in a little more detail. In the first place, we can define an elasticity of demand with respect to advertising, following the pattern of other elasticities, as

$$e_A = \frac{\text{proportionate change in the amount demanded}}{\text{proportionate change in advertising expenditure}}.$$

Using the notation of expression (11.8) we can then write

$$e_A = \frac{\Delta Q/Q}{\Delta A/A} = \frac{\Delta Q \cdot A}{\Delta A \cdot Q}. \tag{11.9}$$

Rearranging, we get

$$\Delta Q/\Delta A = e_A \cdot Q/A,$$

and since from (11.8)

$$\Delta Q/\Delta A = 1(P - MC),$$
$$e_A \cdot Q/A = 1/(P - MC),$$

or

$$A/Q = (P - MC) \cdot e_A$$

and dividing both sides by P we get (since $R = P \cdot Q$)

$$A/R = (P - MC)\cdot e_A/P.$$

From our previous analysis and expression (11.5) above we know that, at the profit-maximizing output and price,

$$(P - MC)/P = -1/e_P.$$

Hence we may deduce that, with profit-maximizing values of both advertising and price (or output),

$$A/R = -e_A/e_P. \tag{11.10}$$

This is the Dorfman–Steiner condition, after the two economists who first deduced it (Dorfman and Steiner, 1954), and it tells us that a condition of profit maximization is that advertising expenditure expressed as a proportion of total revenue, which is more usually referred to as the **advertising–sales ratio**, should be equal to the negative of the ratio of the advertising and price elasticities of demand. Thus, if the latter is -3.0 and the advertising elasticity is 0.6, this condition tells us that when maximizing its profits the firm spends 1/5th or 20 per cent of its revenue on advertising and that this proportion increases the more elastic demand is with respect to advertising and the less elastic it is with respect to price.

Product quality

Moving on to the remaining variable in the firm's demand function, b_i, representing product quality , we come to an aspect of the firm's decision-making process that has not, hitherto, received much attention in textbooks, despite the work of such writers as Hotelling (1929) and Chamberlin (1933) who incorporated aspects of the problem into their analysis more than fifty years ago. However, in recent years, particularly since Lancaster developed his characteristics approach to consumer demand, which we discussed in Chapter 6, interest by economists in the problems involved has grown and has generated a substantial body of literature.[9] In fact, the idea that products contain bundles of characteristics that give utility to consumers provides a useful starting point to our discussion because varying product quality can be seen as changing the component characteristics of the product in some way.

In the literature an important distinction is made between **vertical** and **horizontal** product differentiation. Two products are said to be vertically differentiated if one contains more of at least one of their characteristics without having any less of any other. By contrast, two products are horizontally differentiated when one contains more of some characteristics but fewer of others.

A firm may, therefore, vary its product vertically by adding to (or reducing) the quantity of one or more characteristics in each unit. In this respect it might, for example, increase the alcoholic content of some drink it produces or improve its keeping qualities, or simply increase the quantity sold in its standard bottles or cans. If the product price is kept constant, as long as the enhanced characteristic is one that consumers desire then the demand for the product should increase, but so also will the cost of the product. However, the product improvement is worthwhile as long as the extra revenue produced is greater than the increase in costs, or where, in the case where costs per unit do not vary with output,

$$P \cdot \Delta Q > (C + \Delta C) \Delta Q + \Delta C \cdot Q, \qquad (11.11)$$

in which ΔQ is the extra output sold and ΔC is the increment in unit costs. The first term on the right-hand side of (11.11) then reflects the cost of the extra output, while the second term reflects the increase in the cost of producing the original output. But, in addition, if this condition is satisfied, the implication must be that further improvements to the product would also be profitable. This would continue to be the case until a position was reached at which

$$P \cdot \Delta Q = (C + \Delta C) \Delta Q + \Delta C \cdot Q, \qquad (11.12)$$

which is yet again the familiar equality between marginal cost and marginal revenue.

With horizontal variation of the product, costs might not necessarily increase; they could stay the same or even decrease. Also, although the change in the proportions in which characteristics are combined is likely to make the product more attractive to some groups of consumers, it might make it less attractive to others, so ΔQ might also be positive or negative. Nevertheless, the general principles remain unaffected. The product variation is again worthwhile if condition (11.11) is satisfied and the product should continue to be varied up to the point at which condition (11.12) is met.

It need not always be the case, however, that the product price is kept constant after a quality change, particularly if the level of marginal cost changes. Generally price will need to be adjusted to bring marginal revenue into equality with marginal cost again but, once price is changed, further product changes may be worthwhile. Theoretically these adjustments should continue until the firm finds the variety of product for which the profits, when $MC = MR$, are greater than for any other. In practice, the firm is likely to be uncertain of the reaction of consumers to product changes, and the need to devote resources to market research to determine what product changes are likely to be worthwhile and what are not is likely to be an inhibiting influence on product change.

The multi-product firm

So far we have concentrated exclusively on firms producing a single product, but since in practice many firms actually produce a range of products we need to take some account of what that implies for profit-maximizing behaviour. The firm has to take advertising and quality decisions for each product as well as price/output decisions, but here we will ignore the former and concentrate our attention on the basic price and output variables. In one sense, the extension to more than one product is straightforward because profit maximization simply requires (subject to the usual second-order conditions) that the firm produces where the marginal revenue for each product is equal to its marginal cost. However, interdependencies between the firm's products can have a significant effect on what is involved when these seemingly simple profit-maximizing conditions are met.

In the last section of Chapter 10 we noted that there may be some interdependence on the cost side in that the marginal cost of one product may be affected positively or negatively by the quantities of others produced. Similar interdependence can also arise on the demand side. Thus, if a car manufacturer lowers the price of one of his models to boost its sales, it may reduce the sales of other models in his range, particularly those with fairly similar characteristics. Conversely, if a firm in the computing business reduces the price of its computers, it may experience an increase in the demand for software that can be used with that computer, as well as for the computer itself.

The implications of the latter kind of case can be explored further with the help of Figure 11.5 in which D_X is a firm's demand curve for product X and MR_X is the marginal revenue curve defined in the normal way to show, for any level of output, the effect on the total revenue from the sale of X of a marginal increase in the output of X. However, if increasing the sales of X also increases demand for another product that the firm produces, which we can call Y, the *actual* extra (net) revenue received by the firm from the sale of an extra unit of X is

$$MR_X + \Delta Q_Y(P_Y - MC_Y),$$

where ΔQ_Y is the change in the sales of Y, P_Y its price and MC_Y its marginal cost (which again, to simplify, we can assume is constant over the relevant range of output), and this is the extra revenue that needs to be compared with marginal cost for profit-maximization purposes.

In diagrammatic terms this additional revenue can be represented by an 'augmented' marginal revenue curve somewhere to the right of MR_X, depending on the magnitude of the knock-on effect. If, in the case illustrated, the relevant augmented marginal revenue curve is AMR_X, the profit-maximizing output of X, given the price of Y, is Q_0. But, with the demand curve D_X, that output can only be sold at a price of P_0, which is less than the

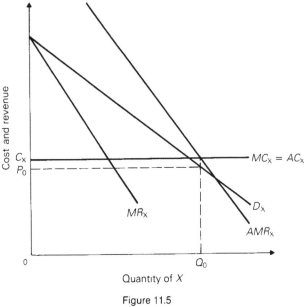

Figure 11.5

marginal and average cost of producing it (C_x). Profit maximization thus requires, in this case, X to be sold at a loss, because the losses on X are more than made up by the beneficial effects of the relatively low price of X on the profitability of Y. In these circumstances X is referred to as a **loss leader**, because the low price of the loss-making product leads consumers to increase their purchases of the firm's other products to such an extent that profits are increased overall. Of course, the favourable effect of a reduced price for X may not be sufficient to justify selling at a loss. The augmented marginal revenue curve may cut the marginal cost curve to the left of its point of intersection with the demand curve. Nevertheless, this kind of inter-dependence is clearly what lies behind the attempts by supermarkets and other retailers to attract customers into their shops with 'special offers' and the like, in the expectation that this will increase the sales of their other products.

For products that are competitive, in the sense that increasing the sales of one reduces the sales of the other, the analysis is similar except that the augmented marginal revenue curve lies to the left of the original marginal revenue curve. In both cases, however, the interdependence creates further complications in the movement to a profit-maximizing position. In the case illustrated in Figure 11.5, for example, when the firm adjusts the output and price of X to what appear to be the profit-maximizing levels, one effect will be to change the position of the demand curve for Y. If, therefore, before the adjustment to the output of X the marginal revenue for Y had been equal to its marginal cost, after the adjustment that would no longer be the case. But if adjustments are then made to the output of Y, further adjustments will be required to the output of X before the ultimate profit-maximizing position is reached. Movement towards a profit-maximizing position may, therefore, be a rather tortuous and involved process.

We have already hinted that similar considerations apply when the firm is varying its product, and indeed they apply in any situation in which the number of decision variables exceeds one. They therefore apply to the cases discussed in previous sections of this chapter and also, as we shall see in Chapter 17, to the situation where the firm is trying to determine the optimal employment of a number of inputs. In that chapter we develop a diagrammatic approach that takes these interdependencies between two decision variables into account. A similar approach can equally be applied to the problems discussed in this and the previous two sections of this chapter, and at a later stage the reader might like to experiment to see how it works for him/herself. Meanwhile, without going into such detail, this chapter should have given some insight into the range and complexity of the decisions firms have to make even without taking account of the effects of competitive conditions, which is our next major concern. These complexities, as indicated in Chapter 8, amongst other things have led to the suggestion that firms are likely to be satisficers rather than maximizers, but that is also an issue to be considered further below.

Notes

1 A straight line demand curve can be represented by an equation of the form

$$P = a - bQ,$$

where a and b are constants. The equation of the total revenue function is then (since $R = PQ$)

$$R = aQ - bQ^2,$$

which can be differentiated to derive the equation of the marginal revenue function, which is

$$dR/dQ = a - 2bQ.$$

From this we can see that when $P = 0$, $Q = a/b$, but when $MR = 0$, $Q = a/2b$.

2 A simple example of this is when the demand curve is

$$P = a - bQ^2$$

because then

$$R = aQ - bQ^3$$

and

$$MR = a - 3bQ^2.$$

Hence, when $P = 0$, $Q = (a/b)^{\frac{1}{3}}$, and when $MR = 0$,

$$Q = (a/3b)^{\frac{1}{3}} = 0.58(a/b)^{\frac{1}{3}} > 0.5(a/b)^{\frac{1}{3}}.$$

3 With $R = PQ$,

$$MR = \mathrm{d}R/\mathrm{d}Q = P + Q\mathrm{d}P/\mathrm{d}Q$$
$$= P(1 + Q/P\mathrm{d}P\mathrm{d}Q) = P(1 + 1/e_P).$$

4 It should be recalled that average revenue at any point is denoted by the slope of a straight line drawn back to the origin.

5 Since the exact form of the curve does not affect the basic analysis, the total cost curve has been drawn with a view to illustrating particular points relating to profit maximization rather than to reflect precisely our previous discussion about the shape of such curves.

6 The profit function can be expressed as

$$\pi = R - C,$$

where R and C are both functions of output Q, and is thus at a maximum where

$$\mathrm{d}\pi/\mathrm{d}Q = \mathrm{d}R/\mathrm{d}Q - \mathrm{d}C/\mathrm{d}Q = 0$$

or where $\qquad \mathrm{d}R/\mathrm{d}Q\ (= MR) = \mathrm{d}C/\mathrm{d}Q\ (= MC)$.

7 The second-order condition for a maximum requires

$$\mathrm{d}^2\pi/\mathrm{d}Q^2 = \mathrm{d}^2R/\mathrm{d}Q^2 - \mathrm{d}^2C/\mathrm{d}Q^2 < 0$$

or $\mathrm{d}^2R/\mathrm{d}Q^2 < \mathrm{d}^2C/\mathrm{d}Q^2$

where $\mathrm{d}^2R/\mathrm{d}Q^2$ is the rate at which MR is increasing and $\mathrm{d}^2C/\mathrm{d}Q^2$ is the rate at which MC is increasing.

8 From (11.5)

$$\frac{P - MC}{MC} = -\frac{P}{MC \cdot e_P}$$

$$= \frac{-P}{P(1 + 1/e_P)e_P} = \frac{-1}{e_P + 1}.$$

9 For a recent survey see Waterson (1989).

Exercises

11.1 What, if anything, is different about profit maximization in the long run compared to profit maximization in the short run?

11.2 A firm's inverse demand function can be represented by the equation

$$P = 100 - 2Q,$$

where P is price and Q is the quantity demanded, and its total cost function is expressed by the equation

$$C = 1000 + 8Q.$$

Calculate, by equating marginal cost and marginal revenue, the firm's profit-maximizing output, price and the resultant profits. Confirm that in this case, when profits are maximized,

$$P = MC/(1 + 1/e_P).$$

11.3 A firm believes that its price elasticity of demand is -5 and its advertising elasticity of demand is 0.5. If its marginal cost is £2 for all levels of output, calculate the profit-maximizing price and show that when profits are maximized the firm will spend 25p on advertising for each unit of output sold.

11.4 A firm that is a price maker produces its output in two plants. Draw a diagram to show its profit-maximizing position and the allocation of its output between the two plants. Show also how the firm's position is affected by the introduction of a subsidy of a fixed amount per unit of output produced in one of the plants.

11.5 A firm produces a product with two characteristics. There are a number of other products with the same characteristics but in different proportions. Using a characteristics diagram, analyse the effect of 'vertical' and 'horizontal' product variation on the demand for the firm's product.

11.6 A market stallholder sells only two products – cabbages, which he buys from a wholesaler at 10p each, and leeks, which he can buy for 5p each. He finds that the lower the price he charges his customers for cabbages, the more leeks he can sell. Analyse the conditions under which he would be willing to sell cabbages for less than 10p each.

CHAPTER TWELVE
COMPETITION AND MONOPOLY

Introduction

In the chapters that follow, we widen the discussion to take account of the influence of other firms on the behaviour of an individual firm, which requires us to examine the behaviour of firms in the context of their market environment. In economics a number of models relating to differing market conditions have been developed. Some of them, in particular those of perfect competition and monopoly, form a major plank of a standard introductory course in economics, and will no doubt be familiar to most readers. We nevertheless start with a review of these basic models in this chapter, since the issues and models discussed in subsequent chapters are essentially elaborations and developments of these traditional theories.

To begin with, therefore, we need to appreciate the links between the various models of firms' behaviour, and in Table 12.1 we attempt to bring out these links by examining the answers to a set of questions that can be posed about any model of the firm. The questions are not intended to be comprehensive, since at this stage we only seek to emphasize the links and differences between the main types of model.

Moving across the table from left to right we move from traditional models (encompassing the models of **perfect competition** and **monopoly**) to **oligopoly** models. Oligopolistic markets are simply markets in which there are only a few sellers, and one of their most important distinguishing features for analytical purposes is that the actions of one firm have a significant effect on the position of its competitors and may therefore provoke some reaction. Since how competitors will react cannot always be predicted accurately, an element of uncertainty is introduced into the outcome. In most other respects, however, the approach is similar to that of traditional models.

The move across to the next column and **managerial** models is more fundamental in its implications, since it takes explicit account of the separation of ownership from control, discussed in Chapter 8 above, and the opportunities that presents for departures from profit maximizing behaviour. The objective function is therefore defined in more general terms but, in

Table 12.1

	Traditional models	Oligopoly models	Managerial models	Satisficing models	Behavioural models
Who makes decisions?	Entrepreneur	Entrepreneur	Management	Management	Management
What is firm's objective?	Profit maximization	Profit maximization	Maximizing utility rather than profit, but subject to profit constraint	Achieving a satisfactory target figure for at least 2 variables	Achieving a compatible set of target figures for major operating variables
What is the state of knowledge?	Certain	Uncertain	Uncertain	Uncertain	Uncertain

order to emphasize the effects of changing the objective functions, some models in this category return to the certainty of traditional models.

One advantage of managerial models is that they retain the concept of the maximum so, at least in the absence of uncertainty, we still get well-defined solutions. As we have already emphasized, however, for many economic agents (including firms) rationality may be bounded because of deficiencies in information and computational capacity, and that may lead to **satisficing** behaviour. With no maximum in satisficing models, covered in the next column, solutions become far less determinate. Nevertheless, certain models can be represented in the traditional graphical format, an example of which is presented in Chapter 16.

The final step in the table is to the last column covering **behavioural** models. Satisficing behaviour is also a characteristic of these, but there is a major difference in emphasis compared with all other models since behavioural models are concerned primarily with analysing the decision-making process *within* the firm, in contrast to the emphasis in other models towards providing a framework within which the firms' responses to *external* stimuli (such as changes in costs or demand) can be analysed.

Perfect competition

The term 'perfect competition' was, perhaps, ill chosen for this model since the man in the street would probably interpret it to mean that firms are engaged in a perpetual price war. As we will discover, that is precisely what does *not* happen. Unfortunately, there are few good examples of what perfect competition means in practice. A reader might find something close to a perfect market if he lives in a town where small stallholders are massed together to sell products such as fruit and vegetables, which are consumed on a very regular basis by the typical would-be purchaser. Under such circumstances comparing products is a virtually costless operation for the buyer (it requires only a small sacrifice in terms of time), and he or she is therefore unlikely to pay over the odds at one stall for an identifiable product that can be bought more cheaply at another.

An interesting example on a larger scale is the Stock Exchange, which brings together information on a great number of companies in a manner that, in principle, makes for perfectly informed behaviour by both buyers and sellers of stocks. In the great majority of cases a single offer to buy or sell a stock will not affect the price set by the market, and this price should reflect the most up-to-date information about both the current and expected performance of a company, which (assuming there is no insider trading) is equally well known to all market participants. Participants are indifferent about which company they are involved with, since every share is impersonally evaluated according to well-established criteria such as price–earnings ratios. Each participant's objective is to make as much profit as possible out of his dealings, and buying and selling decisions can be transacted almost instantaneously.

We can compile a list of assumptions for a perfectly competitive market that closely parallel the key points in the above illustration. These are as follows:

(1) the representative firm operates on a small scale in relation to the overall market;

(2) the products of all firms supplying the market are regarded as virtually indistinguishable by consumers, and can therefore be treated as identical;

(3) the individual firm is, consequently, a price taker in so far as it cannot affect the market price by altering the amount that it produces. The same goes for individual consumers, who cannot buy on a scale sufficient to affect the market price;

(4) the *industry* displays freedom of both entry and exit in so far as there are no impediments either natural (for example, high fixed costs) or artificial (for example, patents) upon the ability either of new firms to enter the industry or of existing firms to leave the industry;

(5) the sole objective of every firm is to maximize its profits; indeed, as we shall see, that is necessary for its survival;

(6) the decisions of both buyers and sellers are taken in full knowledge of all information that is relevant to those decisions.

This appears, on the face of it, to be a fairly exhaustive list of assumptions, but they give the model its special characteristics. In particular, since the firm is a *price taker* (assumption (3)), its demand curve is horizontal as in Figure

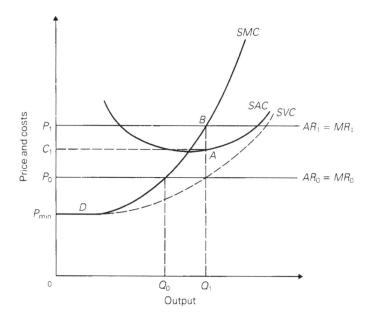

Figure 12.1

12.1. Further, since this means that it can sell as much as it likes at the given price, it has no need to spend resources on making its product known, whilst the need for its product to be identical to those of other producers (assumption (2)) rules out the possibility of product variation. In fact, the only decision the firm has to make is on the quantity of its output. However, although the individual firm is a price taker, the industry demand curve is assumed to be downward sloping in the normal manner. The relationship between the firm and industry is illustrated in Figure 12.2, but for the moment, with the help of Figure 12.1, we concentrate on the individual firm.

The short run

Since each firm has a unique objective, namely profit maximization, its optimal output is where marginal cost equals marginal revenue in the usual way, but which in this case, since the firm is a price taker, also equals price. In Figure 12.1, therefore, where SAC and SMC are standard short-run average and marginal cost curves of the form discussed in Chapter 10 above, with a market price of P_1, and hence the coincidental average and marginal revenue curves denoted by $AR_1 = MR_1$, the profit-maximizing output is Q_1, where the marginal cost curve cuts the average/marginal revenue curve, or in other words where marginal cost equals price. In addition, to meet what we described above as the second-order conditions, the marginal cost curve must cut the marginal revenue curve from below, which means, since the latter is horizontal, that the firm's marginal cost curve must be upward sloping at the maximum profits output as in the diagram.

Also, in the case illustrated, we may note that average cost, at the profit-maximizing output, is C_1, so the firm obtains a profit of C_1P_1 per unit of output and its total profits are shown by the area of the rectangle C_1P_1BA. However, that is only one of a variety of possible situations the firm could find itself in the short run. A second case illustrated is where the market price is P_0. In that case, the optimal output is Q_0, which is again that at which marginal cost equals price, but this time price is less than average cost and so losses are being made. Here Q_0 is the optimal output in the sense that it is the output at which the firm's losses are minimized, but in this situation the firm would need to consider whether it was worthwhile to continue in production or whether it should stop immediately. As previously indicated, continuing operation in the short run is worthwhile as long as revenue is sufficient to cover the costs that are avoidable in the short run. With a price of P_0 this is obviously the case for the firm in the diagram, since price exceeds average variable costs, shown by the dashed curve SVC, but, if price fell below P_{min}, an immediate shut-down would be advisable.

Short-run supply curves

The fact that the firm's output is determined where marginal cost equals price, as long as price exceeds average variable cost, means that we can read off from the marginal cost curve above point D, where the marginal cost curve diverges from the average variable cost curve, the quantity of output per period the firm is willing to supply at any price. Thus, as we have seen, with a price of P_0 the firm is willing to supply Q_0, whilst if the price is P_1 it is willing to supply Q_1. In other words, the marginal cost curve above point D constitutes the firm's **supply curve**.

So far as the industry as a whole is concerned, one requirement of perfect competition is freedom of entry and exit (assumption (4)). As we have already indicated, however, apart from when immediate closure is advisable, exit from an industry is likely to be more of a long-run decision and similar considerations apply to entry. Acquiring the equipment and possibly the expertise to enter a new industry is essentially a *long-run* operation rather than something that can be accomplished in the short run. Hence, the number of firms is normally assumed to be fixed in the short run but variable in the long run. This means that, since the industry supply at any price is simply the sum of the supplies of all individual producers, we can derive the short-run supply curve for the industry simply by summing horizontally the supply curves of every firm currently in the industry.

The nature of the relationship between the firm and industry supply curve is illustrated in Figure 12.2, where S_i, in Figure 12.2a, is the supply curve of some representative firm i whilst S in Figure 12.2b is the industry supply curve aggregated across all firms. Moreover, since the marginal cost curves of

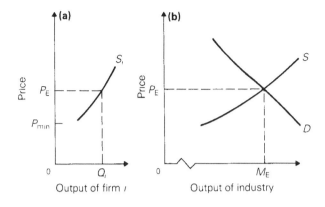

Figure 12.2

the individual firms are upward sloping, the same must also apply to the industry supply curve, although its slope will be less than the slopes of individual marginal cost curves because of the effects of aggregation.

The industry supply curve is of particular interest because it enables us to complete the model, at least as far as the short run is concerned, by showing how the price faced by individual firms is determined. In fact it is simply the price established by the market, and is thus the price at which the market for the product is in equilibrium. As the reader will be aware, this is the price at which demand and supply are equal. In Figure 12.2b, therefore, with the demand curve D the market equilibrium price is P_E, and by going back to Figure 12.2a we can see that firm i's contribution to the industry output of M_E is Q_i.

The long run

In the long run, the analysis of a perfectly competitive equilibrium has to take account of the possibility of the movement of firms into and out of the industry, to which, it will be recalled (assumption (4) above), there are no barriers. Since an equilibrium situation is one in which no economic agent wishes to change the quantity he is buying or selling, a perfectly competitive long-run equilibrium can only be established when no existing producers in the industry wish to make further adjustments to their output and, at the same time, no firms wish to enter or leave the industry.

The first of these conditions requires each firm to be producing a profit-maximizing output, with no possibility of increasing profits further by adjusting plant size. For each firm, therefore,

$$MR(= P) = SMC = LMC. \tag{12.1}$$

195

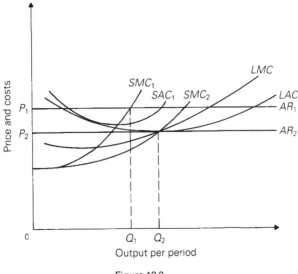

Figure 12.3

This is clearly not the case where the firm illustrated in Figure 12.3 has short-run average and marginal cost curves SAC_1 and SMC_1 respectively and when the market price is P_1. Its profit-maximizing output is then Q_1, where

$$P_1 = SMC > LMC.$$

The firm would therefore plan to increase its productive capacity in the long run, and, because that would shift its short-run marginal cost curve to the right, increase its output. Hence, if all firms in the industry were reacting in the same way, there would be a tendency for the industry supply curve also to shift to the right.

The second condition for long-run equilibrium is also not met at the firm's original output of Q_1 because price exceeds its average cost and it is making profits. These profits would be a source of attraction to firms outside the industry and, since there are no entry barriers, they would not hesitate to enter. This would have the effect of adding to the tendency for the supply curve to move to the right. The extra supplies thus generated, however, cannot be absorbed by the market at the existing price, so the price would tend to fall. Nevertheless, the process of adjustment would continue until a situation is reached at which condition (12.1) above is met and there is also no further incentive for new firms to enter the industry. This occurs when all profits have been competed away so that price has been reduced to the level of average cost. The firm must, therefore, be in a situation where

$$P = LMC = LAC. \tag{12.2}$$

This means – and here it will be recalled that costs are defined to include the 'normal' profits necessary to keep firms in the industry – that, in the long run, competition is such that firms are only just able to maintain their position in the industry, and it also provides a justification for the assumption (assumption (1)) that firms' sole objective is to maximize their profits.

In terms of Figure 12.3, condition (12.2) is when the product price has fallen to P_2 and the firm produces an output of Q_2. Further, it can be observed that the firm is then producing at the minimum point of its long-run average cost curve. This is because at any other point on that curve when it is maximizing its profits either

$$P = LMC > LAC,$$

in which case profits are being earned and new firms are still attracted into the industry, or

$$P = LMC < LAC,$$

in which case the firm would be making a loss and would be seeking to leave the industry. In long-run equilibrium, therefore, the firm must be at the minimum point of its average cost curve.

Moreover, since at this point it is also the case that

$$SMC = LMC,$$

and therefore that

$$SAC = LAC,$$

we can write as a general condition for long-run equilibrium in a perfectly competitive industry

$$P = MR = SMC = LMC = SAC = LAC. \qquad (12.3)$$

This condition appears highly unusual in that it involves a large number of variables having the same value. Moreover, it may be observed that, since the price is the same for all firms, they must all have the same minimum level of average costs. However, we may note that, even if that is the case, their minimum levels of average cost may occur at different outputs. Secondly, it can be argued that where firms operate at different levels of efficiency, competition will ensure that they end up with the same level of average cost.

Consider, for example, what would happen if one firm initially had a lower long-run average cost curve than other firms. This would suggest that some input employed by that firm was more productive than comparable inputs employed by other firms. The owner of that input could then threaten to transfer it to another firm unless its remuneration was increased. The firm employing it would be obliged to agree and, as a result, its average cost curve would be shifted upwards until it was on a par with others. At that point further threats to transfer the more productive input would be pointless, and, in this way, competition in input markets would have been combined with competition in product markets to ensure that the conditions for long-run equilibrium expressed in (12.3) are attained.

The long-run industry supply curve

We can now proceed to examine the nature of a perfectly competitive industry's long-run supply curve by considering the effects on the long-run equilibrium position of a shift in its demand curve. Thus Figure 12.4 illustrates a situation in which a perfectly competitive industry is initially faced with the demand curve D_1, and is in long-run equilibrium with a price of P_0 and an output of M_0, whilst S_1 is its short-run supply curve. If the demand curve now shifts to D_2, the market price rises and firms in the industry adjust along their short-run supply curves until a short-run equilibrium is reached with a price of P_1 and an output of M_1. The profits earned in this situation attract newcomers into the industry which, as indicated above, generates additional output by shifting the short-run supply curve to the right and reduces the price again. The question then is, how far does the price fall? In fact this is one of those cases where we cannot make a definite prediction, but we can list the possibilities.

The first arises when all the inputs required by the industry are available with perfectly elastic supplies. This might be the case where, for example, the industry accounts for a small proportion of the total market for the inputs concerned. In this situation the expansion of the industry has no effect on input prices; incoming firms can therefore produce at the same level of costs as existing firms, and hence the new long-run equilibrium is reached only when the product price has fallen to its original level of P_0. Output by then will have increased to M_2, but since at a price of P_0 the original firms would wish to produce no more than they had produced in the initial situation, in the long run all the extra output produced following the shift in the demand curve (M_0M_2) is provided by new firms. Also, since the increased output is provided without any long-run increase in price, supply is perfectly elastic and the supply curve is the horizontal line LS in the diagram.

In many cases, however, the supply of some inputs may be less than perfectly elastic. For example, extra supplies of some raw material may be obtainable only at a higher price. Alternatively, the managers of incoming firms may be less knowledgeable about the industry's activities than the managers of established firms. In that case it is managerial expertise that is in relatively inelastic supply and that can therefore command a higher price when the industry expands. In either case there is upward pressure on the cost curves of both established and new firms, and as a result the new long-run

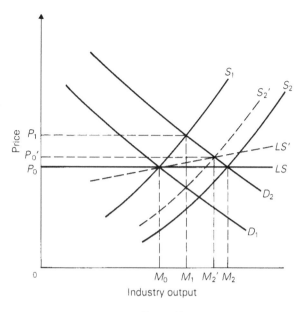

Figure 12.4

equilibrium price has to be higher than the old one. Thus in Figure 12.4 a new long-run equilibrium price of P_0' might be established with an output of M_2', producing the upward-sloping long-run supply curve LS'.

The other possibility would arise if the expansion of the industry enabled suppliers to provide inputs at a lower price than before. In that case (not shown on the diagram), firms' cost curves would be shifted downwards, the new long-run equilibrium price would be less than P_0 and the long-run supply curve would be downward sloping. This case, which is perhaps less likely than the other two, can only arise if there are **external economies of scale**. At a perfectly competitive equilibrium there are no further internal economies of scale to be exploited since, as we have seen, all firms produce at the lowest points of their long-run average cost curves. Moreover, for similar reasons, there are no internal economies to be exploited in input-supplying industries that are also competitive. It would therefore seem reasonable to conclude that the long-run supply curves are, in practice, likely to be horizontal or upward sloping rather than downward sloping. But, whatever their precise form, the unimpeded entry and exit of firms in the long run will ensure that they are more elastic than their short-run counterparts.

Efficiency and perfect competition

One final aspect of perfect competition that needs to be noted is its efficiency in producing an optimal allocation of resources. We have already observed that any profit-maximizing firm, which must include all those operating under perfectly competitive conditions, will in any case seek technological efficiency, in the sense of maximizing the output obtainable from any bundle of inputs, and will also seek to employ the bundle of inputs that minimizes the cost of producing its desired output. But perfect competition is also efficient in two broader senses. In the first place, given that in long-run equilibrium all firms produce at the minimum points of their average cost curves, the total costs of producing the industry's product are minimized since there is no way in which output can be redistributed between producers without increasing costs. Secondly, it involves a situation in which all firms are producing where price is equal to marginal cost.

The equality of price and marginal cost is significant because, if we take the cost to the producer of making one additional unit of output as the cost to society of that unit, and if we further take the highest price that a potential consumer is prepared to pay for that unit of output to be an indicator of the value to society of the production of that unit, then a comparison of marginal cost and price tells us whether or not production of the unit of output in question is a beneficial or detrimental use of scarce resources. Where price exceeds cost at the margin, more production is desirable, but where marginal cost exceeds price it clearly is not. Hence the greatest possible net benefit is obtained where the last or marginal unit is only just beneficial and that is where marginal cost and price are equal.

In some cases, which we consider in more detail in Chapter 22, costs and benefits arise that are not fully reflected in the costs borne by producers and the prices paid by consumers, but in the absence of such externalities the output produced under perfect competition will be that which maximizes net community benefit, since for all producers marginal cost equals price. Moreover, again in the absence of externalities, in a perfectly competitive *economy* the free movement of firms in the pursuit of profits leads to a situation in which resources are being used in their most beneficial employment throughout the economy.

Nevertheless, in identifying the potential efficiency of perfect competition, we must not lose sight of the limited applicability of the perfectly competitive model in the real world. Apart from the fact that the six basic requirements for a perfectly competitive market set out at the start of our discussion are rarely met in full, an important requirement for a perfectly competitive equilibrium is for individual firms to have upward-sloping long-run marginal cost curves. If that requirement is not met, there can be no determinate maximum profits output as long as the marginal revenue curve is horizontal. In addition, the firm's profit-maximizing output must be small enough, relative to the output of the industry as a whole, to ensure that output adjustments by the firm have an insignificant effect on total industry supply and, consequently, on the market price. This is clearly unlikely to be the case where there are economies of large-scale production and, indeed, our earlier discussion of cost functions suggested that long-run marginal and average cost curves may not in all cases start rising at some stage as output increases.

In cases where long-run marginal cost curves don't eventually rise, price-taking, profit-maximizing firms will seek to expand their output more or less indefinitely in the long run. But if a number of firms attempt to do that (and all firms in an industry are likely to face similar technical conditions), the price at which output can be sold will fall and less efficient firms will be forced out of the industry. Then, as the number of firms falls, each surviving firm may become large enough, in relation to the industry as a whole, for its output decisions to start to have some effect on market price. In other words, they become price makers rather than price takers and competition is no longer perfect in the strict sense. Moreover, in extreme cases, the number of firms in an industry can be reduced to one, and that is the situation we consider next.

Monopoly

A monopoly exists in theory where a firm is the only supplier of a good or service for which there are no direct substitutes. Whilst potential entry may not be ruled out in principle, it does not take place in practice because a monopoly is protected by extremely effective barriers to entry. Thus a monopoly can be regarded as the other extreme case in the spectrum of market structures.

A monopoly may arise as a result of *natural* forces, or it may be artificially created. By a **natural monopoly** we mean a sitution in which there are such extensive economies of scale involved in the supply of a commodity that duplication of the entire supply system would be hopelessly uneconomic. The classic examples of this situation are the public utilities, all of which either are, or were, nationalized in the UK. Thus more than one electricity grid, or gas pipe network, or rail network would be expected to raise costs much more than revenue. Notice, however, that the same argument cannot be applied to every individual part of the supply system as is commonly supposed. Whilst it is only sensible to have a single gas main running down each road, there is no reason why the gas itself cannot be stored in a large number of competing plants, which obtain it from competing gas suppliers, and fed into the network at a price to be negotiated between the supplier of the gas and the owner of the network monopoly.

The state may also choose to award an exclusive right to supply to one body, most commonly through franchises or patents. There are many variants of the former. The Post Office, for example, is not overall a natural monopoly, but has always been run as a state monopoly in order to ensure safe delivery of official correspondence. Many professional bodies, such as lawyers, are given exclusive rights to provide specific services, and also the right to govern who enters their ranks. These monopoly rights tend in practice to be permanent, although there is no economic rationale why this should be the case. An interesting exception is that of the provision of local bus services. Until recently these were controlled through a licensing system which effectively gave specific operators exclusive rights to supply particular services, but these have now been thrown open to the forces of competition.

All advanced economies award patents giving an exclusive right of supply for a period of years to the originator of an idea, the belief being that without such protection the effort put into inventing would rapidly fall away. Since patents cannot be renewed, the monopoly power that it confers can be eroded by new entry as soon as the patent expires, but this may prove difficult in practice since the process (for example photocopying) may at least initially become synonymous with the provider, in this case Xerox.

An alternative way of acquiring a monopoly is to become the sole discoverer of, say, an essential raw material. Whilst it is clearly open to other firms to find a competing supply, the monopoly is safe until such time as this occurs.

There is also an inevitable tendency for some *de facto* monopolies to be created by arrangements amongst initially competing firms. In some cases these firms are amalgamated, either as a result of an agreed merger or as a result of a successful takeover bid. In such cases competition cannot be restored without breaking the new firm down into its constituent parts. In other cases the firms form a cartel (see discussion on pp. 235–7) whereby mutually agreed pricing and output policies are designed to replicate artificially those that would be chosen by a single seller. Each firm does, however, retain its individual status, and hence is able at any time to withdraw from the cartel and pursue an independent course of action.

The tendency to cartelize and the frequent merger booms (an especially notable one is just coming to an end at the time of writing) reflect a simple fact of life, namely that, whereas it normally takes decades for what starts out as an entrepreneurial firm to grow sufficiently large to dominate a market, the requisite size can be reached within weeks through mergers or takeovers. Equally, where there are too many medium-sized firms for any to have any real expectation of acquiring monopoly power, a cartel instantly bestows such power upon them all.

Whilst a monopoly may be generated in any of the above ways, it is important to have two reservations constantly in mind. First, there are very few private monopolies in existence using the textbook definition of a single seller, and it is for that reason that monopoly policy (anti-trust) defines a monopoly far less rigidly. In the UK, the original definition only required a monopoly to supply at least one-third of a market, and this figure was reduced under the 1973 Fair Trading Act to at least one-quarter. Secondly, even the more common public utility monopolies can find themselves competing strongly against one another, even when each has the exclusive right of supply over its own product. Thus gas and electricity compete not merely against each other in the UK, but also against the coal industry and the privately organized oil industry. Likewise, the railways compete strongly against privately operated road transport.

This line of argument can be extended to produce the claim that there is no such thing as a textbook monopoly. For example, no matter how ingenious and desirable a new patented product may turn out to be, there is almost certainly going to be an alternative, albeit less economic, way of producing it if the monopoly abuses its position too far. This suggests that the monopoly model can be viewed as another limiting case of market behaviour which serves as a benchmark against which other, more complex, theories of the firm can be compared. However, the incentive for firms to behave in a manner similar to that of a monopolist suggests that the model may also have wider applications.

The basic model

Whilst a perfectly competitive industry consists of a large number of small firms, a monopoly is by definition both firm *and* industry. As a consequence it is faced by a demand curve that slopes downwards from left to right in the customary manner. The monopolist is therefore a **price maker** and the relevant analysis of profit maximization for that type of firm developed in the last chapter applies without modification. Hence, in Figure 12.5, if D is the monopolist's demand curve, MR its associated marginal revenue curve and SMC its short-run marginal cost curve, the short-run profit-maximizing output is Q, where the marginal cost curve cuts the marginal revenue curve from below, and P is the price at which it is sold. The monopolist may also seek to increase his profits by advertising and varying his product, but again the conditions for profit maximization with respect to these variables are exactly as in the previous chapter and need not be repeated. There are, however, certain issues arising from the basic price–output decision illustrated in Figure 12.5 that are worth considering further.

First of all, a popular misconception is that monopoly power gives the firm an ability to earn large profits. However, that depends on the relative positions of the cost and revenue functions. In the case illustrated, price is considerably in excess of average costs (SAC) at the profit-maximizing output, but with less demand and higher costs the firm's profitability could be considerably reduced. Indeed, monopolists have been known to make losses. In fact, a distinguishing feature of monopoly is not so much its absolute level of profits, but its ability to retain them in the long run because of the protection to its position afforded by barriers to entry. This means that the distinction between the short and long run is of less significance in the case of monopoly than in perfect competition as, in the absence of movements in its cost function of the market demand function, the only long-run adjustment the monopolist needs to make is to ensure that short-run marginal cost is equal to long-run marginal cost.

An alternative approach to monopoly power, which was proposed by

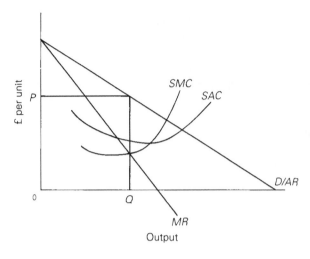

Figure 12.5

Lerner in the 1930s (Lerner, 1934), is to consider the extent to which the monopolist can raise his price above marginal cost. Accordingly, Lerner suggested that monopoly power could be measured by

$$\frac{P - MC}{P},$$

which, since marginal cost (*MC*) is usually positive, yields an index between 0 and 1.

Lying behind this index is the idea that the more competition a firm has the more elastic its demand, since it will be recalled from expression (11.5) above that, when the firms is maximizing its profits,

$$\frac{P - MC}{P} = -\frac{1}{e_P}.$$

Firms facing a lot of competition from rivals producing close substitutes to their own products thus face a highly elastic demand curve, which restricts their ability to raise price above marginal cost. The value of the Lerner index in their case is, therefore, close to zero. Indeed, in the limiting case of perfect competition where demand is infinitely elastic, the index has a zero value. In contrast, more monopolistic situations are marked by the absence of close substitutes and a less elastic demand, allowing a greater divergence between price and marginal cost and producing a value of the Lerner index closer to unity.

Another important feature of monopoly is the absence of a supply curve. In the case of perfect competition we were able to derive a determinate

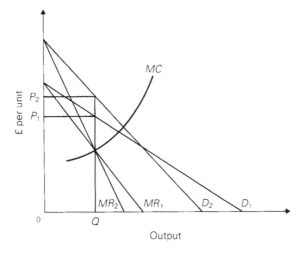

Figure 12.6

relationship between the amount the firm was willing to supply and price, which was independent of the form of the demand function. In the case of monopoly, the amount the firm is willing to sell at any price, or the price at which it is willing to sell any output, depends as much on demand conditions as on the form of its cost function. This is illustrated in Figure 12.6, in which the profit-maximizing situations arising with two different demand curves D_1 and D_2 can be compared. In both cases, the profit-maximizing output is Q because both marginal revenue curves cut the marginal cost curve at the same point. However, the profit-maximizing price is higher with D_2 than D_1 essentially because D_2 is less elastic than D_1 at the profit-maximizing output.

This can be shown in more formal terms since, when output is Q,

$$MR_1 = MR_2 = MC.$$

Hence

$$P_1(1 + 1/e_1) = P_2(1 + 1/e_2) = MC,$$

where e_1 and e_2 are the relevant elasticities of demand, or

$$P_2 = P_1(1 + 1/e_1)/(1 + 1/e_2).$$

With $e_1 < e_2 < -1$,

$$(1 + 1/e_1)/(1 + 1/e_2) > 1$$

and

$$P_2 > P_1.$$

Profit-maximizing behaviour is thus consistent with selling Q at a price of P_1 in one situation and of P_2 in another, so no unique relationship between quantity and price, which would constitute a supply curve, exists.

This lack of a supply curve, it will be realized, applies not just to a single firm monopoly but to any situation in which a firm is a price maker. Likewise, all price makers enjoy some degree of monopoly power as measured by the Lerner index. Further, barriers to entry may also, in many cases, provide some partial degree of protection to their profits in the long run. All this merely serves to emphasize the point that, although-single firm monopolies may be comparatively rare, some degree of monopoly power is more widespread. Indeed, it is only in the rather special case of perfect competition that it is completely absent. In the following chapters we discuss models dealing with situations in which firms are to some extent monopolistic but are also in competition with other similar firms. However, there are also some further issues arising from their monopolistic position to be discussed and these are considered first in the next chapter.

Exercises

12.1 'A permanent increase in the demand for the output of a perfectly competitive industry will not necessarily lead to a permanent increase in the output of individual firms in the industry.' Explain this statement.

12.2 What does the model of perfect competition predict will be the effect of a reduction in agricultural subsidies on the farming industry?

12.3 To what extent is it true to say that perfect competition leads to an efficient allocation of resources?

12.4 Explain why a monopolist does not have a supply curve.

12.5 If a tax of a given sum per unit of output is imposed on a product sold in a competitive market, it is normally supposed that, in the short run at least, price will rise by less than the tax. Is the same true of monopoly?

CHAPTER THIRTEEN
MONOPOLY: FURTHER ISSUES

Introduction

In this chapter we consider a variety of issues arising from the existence of monopolistic situations. First of all, having noted the potential optimality of perfect competition in the last chapter, we consider how monopoly compares with perfect competition in that respect. Secondly, we extent our analysis of the monopolist's behaviour to deal with the phenomenon of price discrimination. This is essentially found in monopolistic markets because it requires some restriction of competition, which has the effect of limiting the access of some buyers to lower-priced markets. This restriction may arise from relatively natural causes (for example, geographical), or from the seller's ability to separate arbitrarily one group of buyers from another. Then, thirdly, we consider the problems of regulating monopoly, and finally we begin to take account of the fact that firms may have some degree of monopoly power, but may still have to face competition from other firms producing similar products. So far as this chapter is concerned, we concentrate on what is referred to as **monopolistic competition** since this still falls within the general category of classical models as set out in Table 12.1 above, but we widen the discussion to oligopolistic markets in the next chapter.

Dead-weight losses

In certain respects, the long-run outcome of monopoly compares unfavourably with that of a perfectly competitive industry. This can be illustrated by considering the case of a competitive industry, operating under constant cost conditions, that is subsequently monopolized without, initially at least, disturbing the cost structure of the industry and where the demand curve for the industry's product also remains unchanged. The long-run supply curve of the competitive industry can then be taken to be the long-run average and marginal cost curve of the monopolist, as indicated in Figure 13.1.

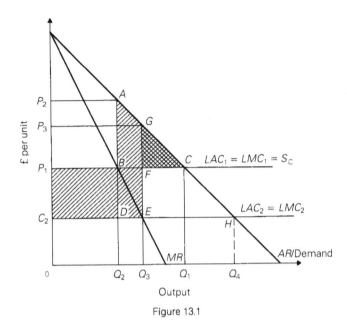

Figure 13.1

In the competitive situation, we can see from the diagram that, with the supply curve, S_C, an output of Q_1 is produced and sold at a price of P_1. The monopolist, however, facing the same situation (that is, with a long-run average cost curve of LAC_1) maximizes his profits by reducing output to Q_2 and raising price to P_2, thereby creating profits represented by the area P_1BAP_2. This represents the appropriation by the monopolist of part of the surplus previously enjoyed by consumers. On the assumption that £1 gained by the producer can be treated as identical to £1 lost by a consumer, the aggregate surplus to society as a whole is unaffected by this **transfer** of. consumers' surplus. There is, however, an additional loss to consumers of the triangle ABC, which arises because they are being denied access to the consumption of the Q_1Q_2 additional units of output that they would have bought in the competitive situation. Because consumers are willing to pay a price in excess of the marginal costs of producing these units of output, they can be produced with positive net benefits to society, represented by ABC, which are lost in the monopoly situation. These lost benefits constitute a **dead-weight** loss, since there are no compensating gains elsewhere.

It may also be noted, however, that when a monopolist takes over a competitive industry he may be able to rationalize its operations in such a way as to achieve significant cost savings. Under such circumstances the firm's long-run average cost curve might fall, for example to LAC_2 in Figure 13.1. Profit maximization then requires the monopolist to increase his output to Q_3 and to reduce his price to P_3. Compared with the competitive situation, the dead-weight loss from the restricted output (now reduced to CFG) is offset, to a greater or lesser extent, by the gain from the cost savings on the output produced ($= C_2 P_1 FE$), with the net effect being determined by the relative size of these two areas. But although this position might represent an improvement over the initial competitive equilibrium in terms of the overall net benefits to society, there would still be a dead-weight loss, measured this time by the triangle EGH, arising from the monopolist's restriction of his output to Q_3, because additional positive benefits could, in this situation, be obtained by increasing output to Q_4 where price, which indicates the amount consumers are willing to pay for marginal units, is equal to marginal cost.

In general, dead-weight losses are an inescapable feature of a monopolist's profit-maximizing behaviour. Hence, even where a monopolistic structure has advantages over a competitive structure – where, for example, it allows technical economies of scale to be exploited – with a profit-maximizing monopolist the outcome, at best, will be a second best situation that can potentially be improved upon by devoting more resources to the monopolized product.

X-inefficiency

An additional source of welfare loss in a monopolistic situation can arise because, as suggested in Chapter 12 above, the lack of competitive pressure allows the monopolist to pursue, to some extent at least, other than profit-maximizing objectives. The precise effect of this depends on the nature of these other objectives, which might involve simply a preference for a 'quiet' life, or a preference for the use of a particular type of input, but in either case it could lead to costs per unit being higher than if the firm's sole objective was maximum profits. It would, therefore, lead to some inefficiency in the use of resources. As a form of shorthand, this type of inefficiency has been termed X-inefficiency by Leibenstein (Leibenstein, 1966; Comanor and Leibenstein, 1969), who was one of the first to examine its implications.

In terms of Figure 13.2, the X-inefficient firm can be characterized as operating along the long-run marginal cost curve LMC_2, rather than LMC_1 which would apply if costs were being minimized. If the firm then attempted to maximize its profits with these higher costs, it would produce an output of Q_2 and set a price of P_2, rather than the efficient monopolist's output and price of Q_1 and P_1 respectively. Output is thus both further restricted and also sold at a higher price. The issue to consider, therefore, is what dead-weight loss arises, in addition to that which has already been identified with the triangle ABC, from this X-inefficiency.

As in the previous case, the loss of consumers' surplus arising from the change in price from P_1 to P_2 is measured by the area $P_1 P_2 EA$. However, if we also recall that the consumers' surplus is the difference between what consumers are willing to pay for particular units of output and what they

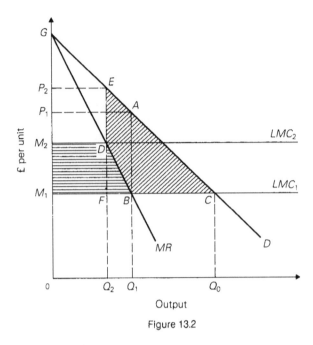

Figure 13.2

actually do pay, we can see that this loss in consumers' surplus can also be expressed as

$$Q_2EAQ_1 - Q_2DBQ_1 = BDEA,$$

since the area under the demand curve Q_2EAQ_1 reflects the maximum amount consumers are willing to pay to increase their consumption of the product from Q_2 to Q_1, and the area under the marginal revenue curve Q_2DBQ_1 is the extra amount they actually would pay given the chance, since it is the extra revenue the firm would receive. $BDEA$, the area below the demand curve and above the marginal revenue curve between the outputs of Q_2 and Q_1, thus indicates the additional loss of consumers' surplus from the restriction of output from Q_1 to Q_2.

Now, in the case above, some of the loss of consumers' surplus constituted a transfer to the owners of the firm in that it was offset by increased profits. In this case, however, the firm's profits are reduced. On the Q_2 units of output that the efficient monopolist actually produces, profits are M_1M_2DF less than in the efficient monopoly case by virtue of the higher costs of production. But in addition, the inefficient monopolist also forgoes potential profits of FDB, the area between the marginal revenue curve and the *efficient* marginal cost curve between the outputs of Q_2 and Q_1 because of his reduced output. The total reduction in profit is therefore M_1M_2DB, as indicated by the horizontally shaded area, and the question is, does this necessarily involve a net loss to society?

At first sight it might appear that it must involve some loss, because the resources used to produce Q_2 units of output could, if they were used more efficiently, be used to produce more output. However, as Parish and Ng (1972) have pointed out, the fact that the firm's managers have *chosen* not to operate with maximum efficiency suggests that they benefit in some way from the X-inefficiency. At this point, the distinction between owner-managed and other firms is relevant because, if the X-inefficient firm is managed by its owners, they are choosing to sacrifice profits to allow them a more relaxed working life, more leisure or whatever. Presumably, therefore, the utility gain from the latter must be at least as great as the loss of utility from reduced profits, and so there can be no net loss additional to that suffered by consumers. However, where ownership is divorced from control, the loss of profit is borne by shareholders, whilst the benefits of X-inefficiency are enjoyed by the managers. In this case there can be no certainty that the managers would be willing to sacrifice as much as M_1M_2DB if they had to pay it out of their own earnings. In this latter case, therefore, there may be some additional dead-weight loss in addition to that represented by the diagonally shaded area $ACBDE$ already identified.

Price discrimination

So far, we have assumed that the monopolist sells all his output for a uniform price. In practice, this may not be the case because the monopolist is able, and finds it profitable, to practise **price discrimination**. The basic analysis of monopoly can easily be extended to cover this eventuality, as we shall now see.

In general terms, price discrimination occurs when a producer sells a specific product to at least two distinct buyers at different prices that do not reflect differences in the cost of supply. Essentially it can arise whenever buyers' willingness to pay different amounts for an identical good or service can be turned to the seller's advantage. Where the seller is a profit-maximizing firm, the potential advantage is, of course, increased profits.

In Figure 13.2, at an output of Q_2 the marginal buyer is willing to pay a price of P_2 in order to acquire the last unit of output. The shape of the demand curve tells us that previous buyers were willing to pay much higher prices. Therefore, if all buyers are charged a uniform price of P_2, the monopolist is effectively forgoing the opportunity to obtain the revenue indicated by the area EP_2G, which represents the consumers' surplus available to him if he can charge each buyer the maximum price per unit that that buyer is willing to pay for each unit.

Successful discrimination, as will become clear when we discuss the formal models, requires three things to be true. In the first place, the monopolist must be able to deal with his buyers separately. Secondly, there must be differences in the prices buyers are willing to pay, and thirdly the seller must have the market power to exploit these differences. Alternatively, it may be said that successful discrimination rests both upon the ability of the seller to select his clientele and upon the prevention of resale by the customer who buys cheaply to the customers who pay higher prices. Since it is extremely difficult to resell most services, it is much easier to practise price discrimination for services as compared to goods. It is also considerably easier to discriminate where markets are physically separated, such as home and abroad. In the latter circumstances, the monopolist is discriminating only between a few large markets, as is also true where, for example, a firm sells part of its production to another manufacturer for incorporation in his own products, and part direct to the general public at much higher prices (as is true, for example, for car parts). It may be possible, however, for a monopolist to discriminate on an individual basis; for example, an eminent surgeon may be able to charge an enormous range of prices to patients of varying means, secure in the knowledge that the operations cannot be resold.

The positive benefits to the monopolist are as follows:

(1) for any given level of output, any form of discrimination enables a monopolist to acquire for himself part of the consumers' surplus that would be denied to him were he to sell his entire output at the same price, and

(2) a monopolist never finds it pays him to produce beyond the output level at which marginal cost and marginal revenue are brought into equality. But the effect of successful discrimination is to raise marginal revenue relative to price, since MR must fall more slowly where the lower price is being charged only on the marginal unit sold rather than on the entire amount sold. As a result, it may become profitable to expand output beyond the single price equilibrium.

On a more formal note we can distinguish three degrees of price discrimination. **First degree** price discrimination is what can be referred to as perfect price discrimination, since the monopolist is able to extract from each customer the highest price that that customer is prepared to pay for each successive unit. In other words, he acquires the entire consumers' surplus. It also means that the demand curve becomes the firm's marginal revenue curve rather than its average revenue curve. Hence the efficient monopolist in Figure 13.2, with the marginal cost curve LMC_1, would increase his output to Q_0, which is the optimal output from the point of view of the community. With first degree price discrimination, therefore, in the absence of X-inefficiency, the dead-weight losses normally associated with monopoly disappear. However, this is at the expense of a transfer of the entire consumers' surplus to the monopolist. Nevertheless, in practical terms, first degree discrimination is unlikely because of the knowledge about his customers required by the monopolist, but the example of the surgeon above

Price discrimination

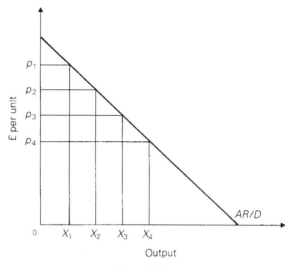

Figure 13.3

illustrates the possibility of its successful implementation in the service sector.

Second degree price discrimination occurs when a customer is offered a variety of prices according to the quantity he is willing to consume. For example, he might be asked to pay one price for the first 100 units consumed, a somewhat lower price for the second 100 units, a somewhat lower price again for the third 100 units, and so forth. Such a pricing schedule might, for example, lend itself to the provision of gas or electricity by way of a multi-part tariff. The monopolist is enabled to obtain part, but no longer the whole, of the consumer surplus, as indicated in Figure 13.3, where X_1 is sold at p_1, X_1X_2 at p_2, X_2X_3 at p_3 and so forth.

Third degree price discrimination occurs where different prices are charged in different markets. In Figure 13.4, the model incorporates a monopolist operating in two markets, in both of which the firm is faced with a downward-sloping demand curve. It is, however, an extremely simple matter to convert one of the markets into a perfectly competitive market where the firm is a price taker, or to add on as many different markets as we wish, since the economic principles remain unaffected.

In Figure 13.4, parts (a) and (b) incorporate average and marginal revenue curves for two independent markets, whilst part (c) is the aggregation of the other two parts. The AR_T curve is the horizontal aggregation of AR_1 and AR_2 and is thus the average revenue curve with which the firm is faced when it does *not* discriminate between the markets. Likewise, the MR_T curve is the horizontal aggregation of MR_1 and MR_2. The marginal cost curve appears only in part (c). This is because costs of production are a function of total output and are independent of its distribution between markets. Marginal cost thus applies only to *total* sales.

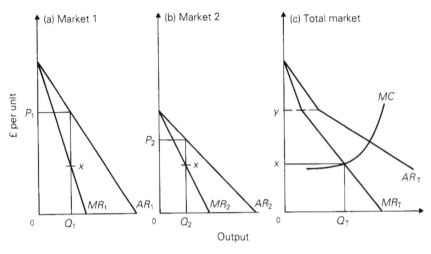

Figure 13.4

The profit-maximizing output is now determined where MC cuts MR_T, and thus involves a total output of Q_T, but this must also be allocated between the two markets in such a way as to *keep marginal revenue equal in both markets* at the level of marginal cost. Thus we conclude that he should sell quantity Q_1 in market 1 and quantity Q_2 in market 2, where $Q_1 + Q_2$ adds up to Q_T.

Now the logical implication of this situation is that the monopolist must derive as much additional revenue from selling the final unit of output in one market as in the other. Clearly, if this were not so, and the monopolist intended initially to allocate his output in such a way as to leave MR higher in one market than in the other for the final unit produced, it would pay him to transfer part of his output from the market where the MR was relatively low to the market where it was relatively high. Furthermore, he should continue to do so only up to the point where the MR is equated in both markets, since beyond that point further transfers of output would cause total profits to fall.

This does *not*, however, imply that the selling price ends up the same in both markets, and this can be seen in Figure 13.4. If the two sets of AR and MR curves are identical, then clearly the equating of MR in each market must produce identical outputs and identical prices. But where the demand curves are dissimilar, which is to say that the elasticity of demand is different in each market for any given price, the equating of MR in each market results in different prices irrespective of how much is sold in each market.

In more formal terms, profit maximization requires

$$MR_1 = MR_2 = MC$$

but since

$$MR_1 = P_1\left(1 + \frac{1}{e_1}\right)$$

and

$$MR_2 = P_2\left(1 + \frac{1}{e_2}\right),$$

where e_1 and e_2 are the relevant price elasticities of demand, the profit-maximizing prices can be represented as

$$P_1 = \frac{MC}{\left(1 + \frac{1}{e_1}\right)}$$

and

$$P_2 = \frac{.\ MC}{\left(1 + \frac{1}{e_2}\right)}$$

P_1 is, therefore, greater than P_2 if

$$\left(1 + \frac{1}{e_1}\right) < \left(1 + \frac{1}{e_2}\right)$$

which requires

$$\frac{1}{e_1} < \frac{1}{e_2} \quad \text{or} \quad e_1 > e_2.$$

If we recall again that these price elasticities are *negative*, the above condition actually requires e_1 to be closer to zero than e_2, and hence demand to be less elastic in market 1 than in market 2.

Regulation of monopolies

The fact that monopolistic behaviour can impose welfare losses on society raises the issue (assuming that breaking up all monopolies into competing sections is a somewhat impractical task) of how monopolies can be regulated to restrain their exercise of market power to the detriment of the community. Two approaches to this task are available in normal circumstances, the first

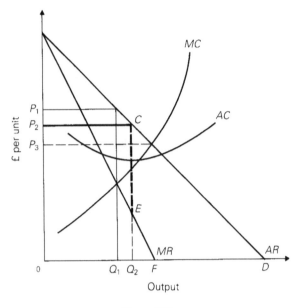

Figure 13.5

of which is to regulate the monopolist's price, and the second of which is to impose taxes of varying kinds upon the monopoly.

Price regulation

Here the government may fix a price below that which the monopolist would have chosen in the absence of regulation. As can be seen by reference to Figure 13.5, this will result in the monopolist producing a larger than intended output and earning lower than intended profits.

Left to his own devices the monopolist could choose to produce Q_1 at a price of P_1 in the usual way. But suppose the government now introduced a maximum price set at P_2 per unit. This would have the effect of creating a new demand curve P_2CD, such that price would remain constant over the section P_2C, but could be set at any lower level thereafter in order to attract more customers. Since AR is constant along P_2C it is necessarily also equal to MR, whilst the rest of MR where it is positive, corresponding to the upper part of section CD or AR, is shown as EF on the MR curve. There is therefore a discontinuity on the MR curve between C and E, which arises because demand suddenly becomes less elastic.

At the imposed maximum price of P_2 the monopolist will, in the case illustrated, produce an output of Q_2. Thus price is lower, output is higher and profits are lower (otherwise price P_2 would have been chosen in the first place) than in the absence of regulation.

It is also worth noting that, if the government were to try to push the price down to a price below P_3 (the price at which the marginal cost curve cuts the demand curve) in the expectation of inducing a yet larger supply of output at an even lower price, it would not obtain the expected outcome. At such prices the monopolist would supply the output at which marginal cost is equal to price, and that would be less than the total demand. This might lead unsatisfied customers to bid for extra supplies in an unofficial (black) market, and as a result at least some of the available supply would be sold at a price above the regulated price.

The problem for the government in this approach is, therefore, to fix the price ceiling at an appropriate level, usually in the absence of detailed information about the relevant cost and demand function. An obvious aim would be to try to fix it at a level that allows the monopolist to earn reasonable rather than excessive profits. If, however, in these circumstances the monopolist is led to believe that any increased profitability would lead to a reduction in the maximum permitted price, the firm might be tempted, in the absence of any controls on cost, to appropriate the benefits from new profitable opportunities by allowing X-inefficiency to develop, thus raising costs. In an attempt to discourage such tendencies, a retail price index minus X formula has been adopted to regulate the prices of recently privatized natural monopolies in the UK, which at least provides them with an incentive to reduce their costs in real terms. One problem with this approach, however, is that the ceiling applies to an index of prices rather than to any individual price, so it also provides an incentive for firms to increase their revenue through more effective price discrimination by raising prices in the more inelastic markets by more than the permitted average and those in more elastic markets by less.

Public ownership

Another possible approach to the regulation of monopolies is through public ownership, and until the 1980s that was the approach adopted in the UK as well as other countries for the more basic natural monopolies like electricity, water, telephones and gas. This approach has the potential advantage that the government can prescribe pricing procedures more directly. Because of the scale on which they operate, the industries concerned are normally operating along the falling part of their average cost curve, as depicted in Figure 13.6. Left to its own devices, the monopoly would produce where $MC = MR$ in the usual way but, from the viewpoint of maximizing the welfare of the community, the ideal output, for reasons explained above, is that where price equals marginal cost. In the diagram this would involve an output of Q_2 and a price of P_2, which would result in the firm suffering a loss of $C_2 P_2$ per unit, the amount by which average cost exceeds price at the desired output.

An obvious problem in this case is that the loss has to be financed from somewhere, and, unless it can be financed out of the profits of other public

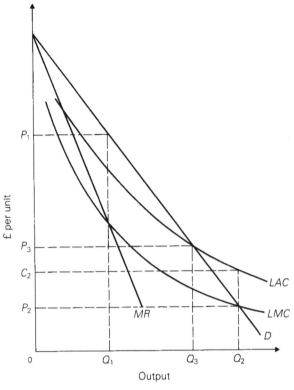

Figure 13.6

enterprises, it has to be financed out of taxation. This solution may not appeal to the government on the grounds that it would require (additional) taxes to be imposed on other goods and/or services, which would involve dead-weight losses in just the same way as when a monopolist raises his price relative to marginal cost. In addition, the government may not feel that the redistribution of welfare from tax-payers in general to the users of the products of a particular nationalized industry is a particularly desirable one. For these and other reasons the government may require a publicly owned industry to set prices high enough to cover its costs. Indeed, in the United Kingdom, successive governments since 1961 have taken the view that, where possible, nationalized industries should earn a surplus to enable them to finance at least part of their investment programmes, and to that end has set them profit targets.[1]

· In this kind of situation, particularly in the kind of situation depicted in Figure 13.6, there is a conflict between efficiency and profit targets. In the simple case of a single-product monopolist, the most straightforward response is to raise price to P_3 (= average cost) if the requirement is simply to break even, or higher if there is some specific profit target to meet. However, nationalized industries are typically multi-product enterprises, and as such the average cost of individual products is not precisely measurable because of the existence of joint costs. In these circumstances it has been shown that an approach that minimizes the dead-weight losses from higher prices is for the enterprise to behave like a price-discriminating profit maximizer by raising prices differentially, with the largest increases on the products with the more elastic demand, until the profit target is met (see Baumol and Bradford, 1970).

An alternative approach, which is used in some cases, is to use *second* degree rather than third degree price discrimination in the form of two-part (or multi-part) tariffs. These involve either a standing charge, which is levied irrespective of the level of consumption, combined with a single price for all units consumed, or a relatively high price for the first few units consumed combined with a lower price for subsequent units. Like all price discrimination, this has the effect of transferring some consumers' surplus to producers, but in this context, if the lower price (or the price per unit) is related to the marginal cost of production, it provides a potential means of financing the losses that would arise with uniform prices set at the marginal cost level and hence largely avoids the dead-weight losses that arise with other approaches.

Regulation via taxation

Alternatively, attempts may be made to regulate monopolies through the imposition either of a lump-sum tax or of a per-unit tax. A lump-sum tax is imposed irrespective of output, and hence can be straightforwardly treated as an increase in the firm's fixed costs. By implication, such a tax cannot affect the firm's marginal cost curve, and hence cannot affect the profit-maximizing price and output. All that happens, therefore, is that the monopolist's profit is reduced by the amount of the tax itself, but the customer consumes as much as before at the same price as before. The dead-weight losses to the community are, therefore, no less than before, and all that happens is that some of the monopolist's profits are transferred to the government. The imposition of a per-unit tax would, however, cause the tax bill to rise progressively with increases in output, and the average cost curve would rise parallel to itself by the amount of the tax. Since a per-unit tax affects variable costs, the marginal cost curve would also increase and would therefore intersect the unchanged MR curve at a lower output than before. The price would accordingly be higher than before, and profit would be lower. In this case, therefore, not only is the firm affected adversely through a reduction in its profit, but consumers must also pay more for a smaller supply of the product. Given that the object of regulating the monopoly is to allow the consumer to buy more at a lower price than in the absence of regulation, a per-unit tax that has the opposite effect would be a most appropriate instrument of regulation.

Indeed, to induce the firm to move in the required direction, a per-unit subsidy is necessary. By itself, however, that would also have the effect of increasing the monopolist's profits. Therefore, if fiscal measures were to be used to regulate monopoly, the ideal would be to combine a subsidy, which would induce the monopolist to produce more at a lower price, with a lump-sum tax, which could be used to prevent the monopolist from having excess profits.

Monopolistic competition

The theory of monopolistic competition arose from attempts in the 1920s and 1930s to develop models to deal with situations lying between the extremes of perfect competition and monopoly. Chamberlin, in his original use of the term in his pioneering book on the subject (Chamberlin, 1933), used it to embrace both industries in which the number of firms is large and industries in which the number of firms is small. However, in current usage, the term tends to be confined to the large group case, which in fact is the one to which Chamberlin made the most distinctive contribution, whilst the term oligopoly is used for situations where the number of firms is small.

On this definition, monopolistic competition is actually much closer to perfect competition than monopoly. In fact it differs from it in one major respect. Whereas the industry is assumed to consist of a large number of small firms, each of which is run by an entrepreneur who pursues the goal of profit maximization under conditions of perfect knowledge, and whereas there is considerable freedom of entry into, and exit from, the industry, each firm nevertheless cannot be regarded as a price-taker. This rises from the fact that each firm produces a product that is regarded by consumers as being in some meaningful way different from the products made by all the other producers. In essence every producer in the industry sets out to satisfy a specific consumer requirement, but does so in a way that is similar to, but never identical with, the way chosen by any other producer. Differences between products may either be real (for example, every brand of beer tastes different from all others) or largely imaginary, (as in the case of washing powders with almost identical chemical formulae), but this distinction is unimportant provided that consumers treat the products of different firms as being less than perfect substitutes for one another.

Considerable importance is to be placed upon the assumption that no individual producer is in a position to supply more than an insignificant share of the total market, since this implies that other firms within the industry remain more or less unaffected by any action taken by an individual producer (a feature that distinguishes the model from oligopoly). This allows an individual producer considerable scope in pursuing independent policies; that is, it confers upon each producer an element of monopoly power with respect to his own particular product. Nevertheless, this power is very limited in comparison to that available to a monopolist, since a monopolistically competitive firm has close substitutes for its product to which its customers will turn if it attempts, for example, to raise its price sharply, whereas a monopoly has no close substitutes at all.

A producer under monopolistic competition can exercise this limited market power in all of the ways distinguished in Chapter 13. He can alter his price, the extent to which he promotes his product, and the degree to which his product is differentiated from all others on the market. In practice, the distinguishing element of a product may prove to be its perceived quality rather than its price, the variety of shapes and sizes in which it is available, or the specific locations in which it can be obtained. One obvious difficulty that arises out of this discussion is that the concept of the industry has become blurred at the edges. In both perfect competition and monopoly there is only a single product on offer, whilst in monopolistic competition there is a whole variety of products. Whilst the term 'product group' was often used in order to overcome this difficulty, we will continue to use the term 'industry' below, redefining it slightly to mean a group of similar but differentiated products. In terms of our exposition, however, we are obliged as a consequence to confine ourselves to a 'representative' firm and to leave out any graphical representation of the industry.

In order to simplify the analysis it is helpful to make certain additional assumptions at this point. These are that:

(1) each firm has already decided upon the optimal degree of product differentiation and extent of sales promotion, thus allowing us to concentrate solely upon the effects of price changes upon profits; and
(2) each firm operates along identical cost and revenue curves (whilst recognizing that this is unlikely to be true in practice since every product is different and is hence likely to cost a different amount to produce).

Although Chamberlin analysed in detail the process by which an equilibrium in monopolistic competition might come about, it is sufficient for our purposes to concentrate our attention on the long-run equilibrium position, which is illustrated in Figure 13.7. This contains elements of the pure monopoly case, in that profits are maximized where the marginal cost curve cuts the downward-sloping marginal revenue curve, but it also reflects the effects of free entry, which, as in perfect competition, reduces the firm's profit to zero. Hence, as in the diagram, the representative firm's long-run equilibrium output is at Q, where $LMC = MR$ and where in addition the firm's average revenue curve just touches its long-run average cost curve so that price equals long-run average cost.

Excess capacity

One particular feature of this long-run equilibrium that attracted considerable attention in the early days is that the downward-sloping demand curve must touch the average cost curve at an output less than that at which

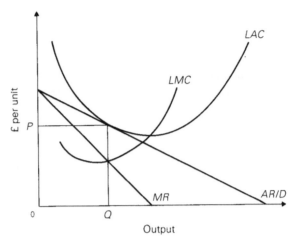

Figure 13.7

average costs are at a minimum. This appears to suggest that, in contrast to perfect competition, monopolistic competition in an industry leads to an inefficient use of resources in the sense that the same total output can be produced at a lower cost by a smaller number of firms. In other words, long-run equilibrium seems to involve excess capacity. However, the situation is not so simple as it appears at first sight.

In the first place, it is only unambiguously true in the rather special case where there are no selling expenditures. With positive selling expenditures, which are, of course, part of the firm's costs, the average (total) cost curve can be disaggregated into average production costs and average selling costs. With a given level of selling expenditures, the average selling cost curve (ASC) is a rectangular hyperbola, as in Figure 13.8, like any other fixed-cost curve. When such a curve is added vertically to a conventional long-run average production cost curve (APC) as in the diagram, the lowest point of the aggregate curve (LAC), which is associated with an output of Q_2 in the diagram, is to the right of the lowest point of the average production cost curve at output Q_1. Hence, as in the diagram, the point at which a downward-sloping demand curve touches LAC need not be to the left of the point at which the firm's average production costs are a minimum, although it could be if selling expenditures were relatively small. Hence it is not necessarily the case that the same output can be produced more cheaply with a smaller number of firms.

Secondly, the long-run equilibrium depicted in Figure 13.7 theoretically relates to a situation where the industry has a particular range of products. If concentrating output in fewer firms led to a smaller range of products being available, the losses to consumers from the restriction to the choice of available products could offset the benefits of reduced production costs. If on

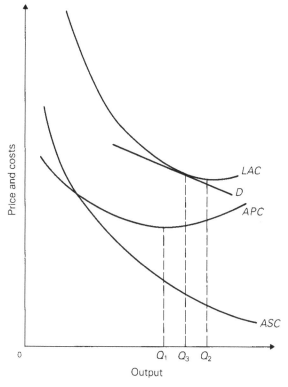

Figure 13.8

the other hand, starting from the kind of equilibrium illustrated in Figure 13.7, it was possible for output to be concentrated in fewer firms, and costs to be thereby reduced, without reducing the number of individual products, then it can be argued that it would happen anyway. If, say, firm A is in a position to produce firm B's product more cheaply by producing it alongside its own product, A would be in a position to make a successful takeover bid for B (in other words, it would be able to offer a price for B that would more than compensate B's owners and still leave itself with enhanced profits) with a view to closing B's production facilities down and concentrating production in its own plant. Firm A could therefore be expected to make such a bid as part of its normal profit-maximizing behaviour. This implies that the original 'equilibrium' would not be a true equilibrium as it would lead to further changes to the number of firms in the industry and ultimately, as the opportunities for cost savings were exploited, to outputs and prices. Moreover, as a result of adjustments of this nature, once firms start producing more than one product, the existence of joint costs, as we have already seen, is likely to mean that average cost in relation to any particular product becomes undefinable and hence so does the output at which average costs are a minimum.

Other problems

A more fundamental criticism of the model arises from its assumption that firms in the industry are virtually unaffected by the individual actions of other firms. This can only really be the case where one firm is an equally close competitor to a large number of other firms. However, since product differentiation means that individual firms' products are likely to differ from each other in the proportions in which they combine various characteristics, our earlier analysis of product characteristics suggests that any individual firm's product is likely to be a closer substitute to some than to others. This means that the effect of its actions is likely to be greater on some competitors than others. Moreover, in these circumstances the effect is likely to be significant. For example, if a fish and chip shop lowers its prices it could have a significant effect on the trade of a similar shop in the next street, even though the effect on shops farther away is negligible. This is also means that, before our fish and chip shop proprietor makes a decision to change his prices, he would need to consider precisely how his rival might react, because that would be an important factor in determining the final outcome. These problems are tackled explicitly in oligopoly models, which we consider next, but the fact that they can arise in situations where there are a large number of firms that are small in relation to the size of the industry suggests that the assumptions of the monopolistic competition model relate to rather an extreme case in exactly the same way as those for perfect competition.

From one point of view, however, this need not matter. Any theoretical model presents a simplified view of the real world, but the simplifications can be justified if the model provides a basis for making predictions about the effects of relevant changes. Thus the perfectly competitive model is based on extreme assumptions, but it does yield a supply curve, which is useful, in conjunction with the demand curve, in the analysis of competitive markets and how they react to changes in external factors. With monopolistic competition, firms are price makers, as in monopoly, so they have no determinate supply curve. Hence there can be no aggregate industry supply curve. Further, even at the individual firm level, it is difficult to predict how it will respond to a simple change like an increase in demand becauses of the conflicting ways the relevant factors operate in determining the overall effect. Indeed, considerations of this kind have led one commentator to conclude that from this point of view the theory of monopolistic competition is almost theoretically empty (see Archibald, 1961). However, an important contribution of the theory as developed initially by Chamberlin was to emphasize the importance of advertising and product variation in the analysis of the firm, and in recent years these aspects of his work have been the subject of renewed interest, particularly in the light of the development of the analysis of the characteristics of products.[2]

Notes

1 This policy was first set out in a government White Paper, *The Financial and Economic Objectives of the Nationalised Industries*, Cmnd 1337 (London: HMSO, 1961).
2 See particularly Archibald and Rosenbluth (1975) and a recent survey of work in this area by Waterson (1989).

Exercises

13.1 A firm supplies two markets, demand being more elastic in one than the other. Assuming that the firm aims to maximize its profits,

(i)   show how the price and output in each market are determined;
(ii) indicate the likely effects on both markets of a downward shift in the demand curve for the market with the less elastic demand.

13.2 A firm producing instant coffee sells its output in two forms, as a branded product, for which it is faced with a downward-sloping demand curve, and as an unbranded product, for which it is a price taker. Show how its total output will be distributed between the two forms. Under what conditions would the firm be willing to sell its product in the unbranded form at a price below average cost?

13.3 In the UK the regulation of certain recently privatized natural monopolies has restricted price increases to a fixed number of percentage points below the increase in the index of retail prices. (The so-called $RPI - X$ formula). Is this an effective means of restraining monopoly power?

13.4 What predictions can be made about the effects on individual firms and the industry, under conditions of monopolistic competition, of

(i)   a shift in the demand curve for the industry's product,
(ii) a tax of a given sum on each unit of output produced.

To what extent does your analysis support the assertion that the theory of monopolistic competition is empirically empty?

CHAPTER FOURTEEN
OLIGOPOLY

Introduction

As we have indicated above, the theory of the firm is sensibly approached first by analysing the extreme possibilities in the form of perfect competition and monopoly, and then by turning to analyse the gap in between these models. The model of monopolistic competition was a worthy attempt to fill the gap, but itself ultimately foundered largely on the basis of the unreality of its assumptions and its limited powers of prediction.

In point of fact, an alternative avenue for exploration did already exist, since a number of models had been developed during the nineteenth century that had never received widespread recognition. Curiously, these were characterized by a greater degree of mathematical sophistication than those that appeared subsequently. However, the failure on the part of the established models to provide a satisfactory conceptual framework compatible with the significantly increased empirical data on firms' behaviour, published mainly during the 1930s, rekindled interest in these half-forgotten models of duopoly (two-firm) behaviour, whilst simultaneously inducing certain economists to develop totally new approaches. These new and rediscovered approaches are generically known as **oligopoly** models.

'Oligopoly' literally means 'few sellers'. However, it is not ultimately the number of sellers in a market that is the critical factor but the relationship between the sellers. The most sensible approach is, therefore, to concentrate upon the interdependent nature of decisions made by firms within a particular market, irrespective of precisely how many firms there may be. What is meant by interdependence is that a behavioural change on the part of one firm has a significant effect upon the other firms' positions, and therefore forces the other firms in the industry to reconsider their own behaviour (though they may opt not to change it). In other words, in contrast to what happens under perfect competition and monopoly, each firm is forced to consider whether or not to react to a behavioural change by any other firm, and to consider in turn whether a positive reaction will induce a counter-reaction. For its own part, the firm that triggered off this chain reaction must make some estimate of the likely reactions of its rivals and must consider whether it will end up any better off when the whole process has run its full course.

The key to understanding this chain reaction lies in the one significant departure that sets off oligopoly models from those analysed previously, namely the dropping of the assumption that knowledge is certain. An oligopolistic market is characterized by uncertainty because no one firm can be sure what its competitors will do if it changes its behaviour. If it acts in isolation, then it is forced to work its way logically through all the possible eventualities, and to try to pin down the likeliest reaction to any behavioural change. For obvious reasons, firms are not altogether enthusiastic about the effort required by this approach, and seek constantly to improve their knowledge base in other ways. It does not take much thought on their part to realize that collusion offers the most direct route towards this objective, and we will therefore have much to say about this practice in subsequent pages.

In the meantime we need to recognize that there is no unique way to set up an oligopoly model. The great bulk of those referred to here do, however, share the same approach as those previously encountered. That is, they involve the construction of a model based upon a tightly defined set of assumptions, which are assembled to yield predictions about how the firms will behave when subjected to external changes. Like their predecessors, they also stand or fall according to their ability to predict firms' actual behaviour in the real world.

There is a tendency to discuss oligopoly problems in the context of **duopoly**, which refers to an industry containing only two firms, since this greatly simplifies the exposition without detracting from the central problem of interdependence between firms. Nevertheless, duopoly as a market structure is unusual in the real world, so we also need to be aware of the extent to which the conclusions of the duopoly models extend to the multi-firm case.

A second distinction that needs to be raised at this juncture concerns that between identical (homogeneous) products and differentiated products. Given that the latter can only be discussed by introducing a number of additional variables into the models, we will follow the customary practice – that is, we discuss first a number of models dealing with homogeneous products, and then consider the effects of introducing product differentiation.

When products are homogeneous, there clearly needs to be some mechanism for ensuring that every firm ends up by charging the same price as its competitors, otherwise it may find itself unable to sell anything at all. There are three possible ways of arriving at price equivalence:

(a)   to let the market determine the price (as in perfect competition), leaving firms to concentrate upon adjusting their outputs;

(b)   to initiate collusive price-fixing agreements;

(c)   to allow one firm to take on the role of price leader, with other firms following whatever price is set.

In the sections that follow we will be considering all of these alternatives, but our initial attention will be concentrated upon models that fit into category (a) above. Clearly, the element of uncertainty in this case cannot relate to the price variable, but must concern one firm's lack of knowledge about how the other firm(s) will respond when it places its own output on the market. The other firm(s) might either do nothing, increase output or decrease output. One firm's assessment of its rivals' reaction in this respect is embodied in the concept of **conjectural variations**, which are a fundamental characteristic of oligopoly models. In order to introduce the role of conjectural variations as simply as possible, we will begin by examining models of duopoly.

Classical duopoly models

A number of duopoly models were developed by European economists during the nineteenth century. The best known are those by Cournot, Bertrand and von Stackelberg. It was not, however, until they were translated into English that they came to be appreciated fully for their innovatory features. The classic model is that developed by Cournot in 1838, which eventually appeared as *Researches into the Mathematical Principles of the Theory of Wealth*, published by Macmillan in 1897.

The Cournot model

The Cournot model in its original form involves competitive behaviour between two rival sellers of identical bottles of spring water produced at zero cost at mineral springs owned by the two rivals. The duopoly is sustained by an exclusion order placed upon potential new suppliers by the local authority.

Given that neither supplier has individually any control over price, each supplier's concern is to determine an optimal level of output taking account of his rival's reactions to changes in his output and the ultimate effect of these changes on the product price. The distinguishing feature of this model is, however, that each supplier conjectures that his rival will maintain his existing level of output. Hence each supplier seeks to adjust his output to the level that maximizes his profits *whilst leaving the rival supplier's sales unchanged.*

For simplicity, the demand curve in the model can be expressed as the linear equation $Q = 300 - 30P$, where Q is the quantity sold and P is the price. This appears in Figure 14.1 as the line DD. Supplier A, in choosing his

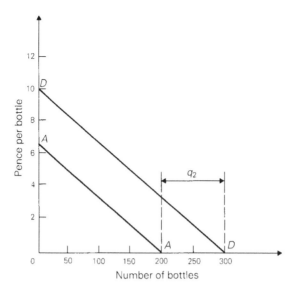

Figure 14.1

optimal price–output combination, assumes that B will continue to supply his existing level of output q_2. His potential sale at any price therefore represents the total market demand at that price, Q, less q_2, or $(Q - q_2)$. The demand curve for supplier A is accordingly represented in Figure 14.1 as the line AA, in the case where $q_2 = 100$.

AA is supplier A's average revenue curve as well as his demand curve in the usual way, and his marginal revenue curve in this linear case therefore bisects the horizontal axis at $\frac{1}{2}(Q - q_2)$. The profit-maximizing output is determined in the usual way where $MC = MR$, but there are zero costs of supply so MC is always equal to 0. Profits are therefore maximized where $MR = 0$, that is, where the marginal revenue curve cuts the horizontal axis at $\frac{1}{2}(300 - q_2)$, which would be at an output of 100 bottles in the case shown. Hence, in order to identify supplier A's optimum output q_1, it is only necessary to know q_2 and to solve the formula $q_1 = \frac{1}{2}(300 - q_2)$. In the absence of a specific value for q_2 it is, however, possible to determine q_1 for any given value of q_2, and to plot the corresponding values as in Figure 14.2. Since q_2 can range from 0 to 300, q_1 can range accordingly from 150 to 0. This is labelled A's **reaction function**, since it depicts graphically how supplier A reacts to any output level chosen by supplier B.

By following precisely the same reasoning, but substituting supplier B for supplier A as we go, B's reaction function can also be derived as the equation $q_2 = \frac{1}{2}(300 - q_1)$, which appears in Figure 14.2 for all values of q_1 between 0 and 300.

The equilibrium position is denoted by point X above where the two reaction functions intersect. Point X is an equilibrium because, once it has

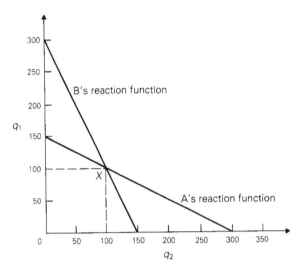

Figure 14.2

been attained, neither supplier would want to adjust his output further, and indeed it is the only point compatible with *both* suppliers maximizing profits whilst leaving their rival's sales unaffected. At any other point on A's reaction function, B would want to adjust his output and, likewise, at any other point on B's reaction function A would want to change his output. The output level corresponding to point X is found by solving the simultaneous equations that represent the reaction functions. Thus we have

$$q_1 = \tfrac{1}{2}(300 - q_2) \quad \text{or} \quad q_1 + \tfrac{1}{2}q_2 = 150$$
$$q_2 = \tfrac{1}{2}(300 - q_1) \qquad q_2 + \tfrac{1}{2}q_1 = 150,$$

which yields a value of 100 for both q_1 and q_2. Thus total sales amount to 200 bottles. The price per bottle can be calculated by substitution into the formula for the demand curve, which is $Q = 300 - 30P$, where Q is equal to 200. Price per bottle is therefore equal to $3\tfrac{1}{3}$p, and each supplier has a total revenue of £3$\tfrac{1}{3}$. In the absence of any supply costs, revenue and profit are identical, and total profit therefore stands at £3$\tfrac{1}{3}$ for each supplier and £6$\tfrac{2}{3}$ in total.

The above solution is static in the sense that it explains why, at a particular point in time, each supplier would be happy with a situation in which they both sell 100 bottles. It is also interesting to trace the dynamic process whereby point X in Figure 14.2 is reached, particularly since this exposes the most serious flaw in the model, namely that the suppliers do not learn by experience. In Figure 14.3, B is initially the sole supplier, and is producing 150 bottles at point U, his profit-maximizing output given that $MR = MC = 0$. This output is chosen on the assumption that A will not

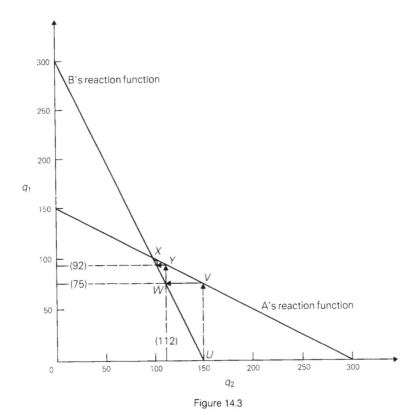

Figure 14.3

produce any output in the forthcoming period since he has not done so during the previous period. But A now enters the market and, expecting B to continue to sell 150 bottles, he chooses to produce 75 bottles. In this turn B, now expecting A to continue to sell 75 bottles, reduces his output to 112 bottles, which causes A to increase his output to 92 bottles and so on. Eventually the path plotted out by the arrows will converge on the point X where the reaction functions cross, and this will be true irrespective of where the process begins.

During this process of convergence upon point X both suppliers persist in believing that each can adjust his output without provoking some reaction from the other, even though experience rapidly shows this to be untrue. Clearly, we would expect suppliers to recognize their interdependence in the real world and to amend their behaviour accordingly.

Once interdependence is recognized, the possibility of collusive behaviour arises. We will be discussing collusive behaviour in detail below. By way of introduction, we may note briefly that, in the above model, collusive behaviour results in the two suppliers wishing between them to serve the total available market demand given by the equation $Q = 300 - 30P$. Since profits are maximized where $MC = MR$, and since MC is always zero, then optimum output is where the MR curve cuts the horizontal axis at the output 150. The price is then found by substitution from the equation $150 = 300 - 30P$. Price therefore equals 5p per bottle. Total revenue now becomes £7.5, with total profits of the same magnitude in the absence of any costs. Each supplier therefore can earn a profit of £3.25 if the total sales are divided equally between them, which is 42p more than the profits he obtained whilst acting independently.

The basic model can be extended in a number of directions; that is, it can be subjected to a new set of conjectural variations. For example, A might assume that B will match any changes in his (A's) output in order to maintain his market share and vice versa. Again reaction curves can be drawn up and an equilibrium found, exactly as in the Cournot model. All such solutions remain non-collusive. It is also a simple matter to extend the number of firms in the market. Were there three suppliers in the market, then each would supply according to the formula $q_1 = \frac{1}{2}(300 - q_2 - q_3)$ or its equivalent, giving $q_1 = q_2 = q_3 = 75$ and a total output of 225. In effect, the larger the number of suppliers, the larger the communal output.

The Stackelberg model

Another interesting early duopoly model was that developed by von Stackelberg (1952). In this model each firm must choose whether to be a leader or follower, where a leader is a firm that chooses its optimal output on the basis that the rival firm will take the leader's output as unalterable, and where a follower is the firm that takes the rival firm's output as unalterable and fixes its optimal output on that basis. Since both firms are free to choose which kind of firm to be, there are three possible ways in which they can combine. First, one firm chooses to be a leader while the other chooses to be a follower. This combination readily produces a stable equilibrium solution. Second, both firms choose to be followers. Since each firm acts on the assumption that its rival's output is unalterable, this is a repeat of the Cournot model, and also produces a stable equilibrium solution. The third possibility is that both firms elect to be leaders, which precludes a stable equilibrium until such time as either one firm agrees to switch from a role as leader to a role as follower, or both firms collude in order to maximize their joint profits. Obviously equilibrium may take some considerable time to establish since each firm will initially be trying to force the other into playing the follower role.

Von Stackelberg suggested that the third possibility is likely to prove most popular, with each opting initially for the role of leader, since the greatest possible level of profit for a single firm is clearly that obtained where that firm is the leader and its rival the follower. But where both firms compete fiercely to acquire the role of leader, they are likely to depress each other's profitability below that available even in the role of follower. Nevertheless, this is unlikely to continue for all that long since the firms will soon come to

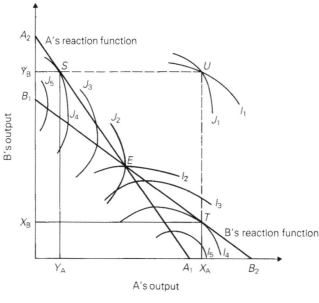

Figure 14.4

realize that collusion is the answer to both their problems, with neither forced to take on the follower role.

The formal model is illustrated in Figure 14.4, which is based upon the standard Cournot diagram with its equilibrium at E. Superimposed upon this are a series of iso-profit curves, the value of which rises as they move towards the situation where one duopolist is the role seller. I_4 therefore represents the highest profit that A can earn given B's reaction function, and J_4 the highest profit that B can earn given A's reaction function. Also A's iso-profit curves I_1–I_4 are horizontal where they cross his reaction curves because that is by definition the point at which A's profits are maximized for any output of B. Likewise, B's iso-profit curves J_1–J_4 are vertical where they cross his reaction curves.

Initially both duopolists are happy with the Cournot equilibrium, but subsequently A chooses to become the leader and sets out to maximize his profit whilst assuming that B will remain a follower. A's optimum position is therefore at T where A produces X_A and B produces X_B. Conversely, were B to choose to become the leader, with A adopting the role of follower, B would move to S where B produces Y_B and A produces Y_A.

In effect, the Stackelberg model introduces learning behaviour into the Cournot model since, in the circumstances described above, one, but not both, of the duopolists, noting that the other always treats his rival's output as unalterable, eventually raises his output accordingly and thereby induces the other to produce considerably less. However, where both duopolists simultaneously choose to become leaders they will both increase their output and the result will be a movement from E to U, where neither makes much profit at all. Since the firms are showing considerably more sophistication in their behaviour than in the simple Cournot model, it is reasonable to assume that they will rapidly seek to reach agreement on a mutual reduction of output in order to maximize their joint profits.

Conclusions on classical duopoly models

It is perhaps questionable whether these classical models have much to tell us about the real world. As we have already noted, the Cournot and related models based on the assumption of fixed conjectural variations suffer from their assumption that firms do not learn from experience but continue with those conjectures even when proved wrong by events. The Stackelberg model does provide the basis for a more sophisticated approach, but then has a rather indeterminate outcome.

More recently, attempts to develop the conjectural variation approach have explored the possibility of consistent conjectures (see, for example, Laitner, 1980; Bresnahan, 1981; Perry, 1982). These occur when firms' assumptions about their rivals' reactions turn out to be accurate. In that case, it is more plausible to assume that conjectural variations remain unchanged in the light of experience, and there is more reason to believe that the equilibrium determined by the point of intersection of the reaction functions (if there is one) might actually be reached. Precisely what conjectures are consistent in any situation can be determined mathematically from the firms' cost functions and the industry demand function and hence depend on the form of those functions. However, whilst the approach is an interesting one, there is no obvious reason why, in conditions of uncertainty, firms' conjectures about their rivals' behaviour will, initially at least, be consistent with their actual behaviour. It is possible, of course, but it might be more satisfactory to assume that there might be a process of adjustment as firms seek to move towards a consistent set of conjectures, but whether consistent conjectures will eventually materialize can only be examined in the context of a more dynamic model.

Models of collusive oligopoly

Our previous analysis of the Stackelberg model leads us inevitably towards a consideration of situations where agreements between firms can be mutually beneficial. It is hard to dispute the fact that the simplest way to deal with uncertainty about how rivals will react to one's own behaviour is to ask them! Collusion amongst legally independent firms is known as a cartel, the sole justification for which is that its members make more profit by acting jointly than they would, in aggregate, by acting independently. However, although

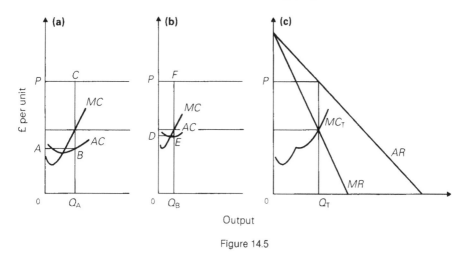

Figure 14.5

this is necessarily true for cartel members in aggregate, it is not necessarily true, as we shall see, for each and every member, a fact that renders cartels inherently unstable.

Joint-profit-maximizing cartels

In this section we continue to concentrate upon the situation in which all firms produce an identical product. The job of determining the joint-profit-maximizing price and output is delegated to the cartel administration, which to this end is empowered to obtain the necessary cost and revenue information from firms in order to construct an industry MC curve and industry AR and MR curves.

Initially we will examine this model under conditions of duopoly, although we will take account subsequently of a potential increase in the number of firms all producing the same product. In Figures 14.5a and 14.5b appear the average and marginal cost curves of the duopolists, of which the former is the more efficient producer. In Figure 14.5c their combined marginal cost curve MC_T, which is formed by adding together the sales associated in each firm with any given level of MC, is superimposed upon the industry average and marginal revenue curves.

The objective of the cartel is to maximize its members' joint profits. This objective is attained when a combined output of Q_T is produced where MC_T and MR are equal, and where this output is allocated between the duopolists such that the final unit supplied by each firm is produced at the same marginal cost.[1] This latter condition is necessary otherwise it would be possible to reduce total cost by reallocating output to the cheaper of the two producers. This equality of MC is satisfied where firm A produces Q_A and firm B produces Q_B. The selling price for both is fixed at P, which is the price at which the joint-profit-maximizing output can be sold. The combination of price P and output Q_T yields a total profit equal to the sum of the profits earned by firms A and B, respectively $ABCP$ and $DEFP$. The more efficient producer, firm A, necessarily sells more output and earns more profit than firm B.

The sum of $ABCP$ and $DEFP$ is necessarily greater than the sum of the profits that could be earned by the duopolists were each to act as a wholly independent entity, unless by chance they happened to produce the same outputs. Nevertheless either firm, or indeed both, might feel that the available share of the jointly earned profits is potentially less than could be earned in isolation. In other words, although the firms might agree in principle that jointly earned profits are advantageous to both, they might not agree upon the method by which they are to be shared out. It can thus be seen that a collusive agreement is necessarily subject to an element of instability in so far as there is no way of knowing in advance whether all parties to it fully intend to abide by the agreed method of distributing jointly earned profits.

One obvious method of distributing such profits is for each party to place individually earned profits into a central pool from which they are redistributed according to some agreed formula. This might result in firm B receiving less, but it also might conceivably earn more profit than it actually earns on the basis of its share of output. Such a method will succeed provided that each party believes that his share of the pool is greater than the amount that he could have earned through independent action. It is obviously possible that an individual firm's opinion concerning this matter will vary over time, so that an agreement may subsequently be abrogated or a new agreement formed. Much will depend upon how each firm expects future trends in the industry to develop, since if, for example, one firm expects profits to rise whereas the other expects profits to fall, then it will be very difficult to reach an agreement satisfactory to both parties.

No fundamental problems arise should one wish to incorporate into the above model the possibility of the industry consisting of more than two firms. Clearly one can still conceive of a joint-profit-maximizing equilibrium irrespective of how many firms are participants to a collusive agreement. On the other hand, as the number of firms party to an agreement increases, so does the probability that at least one firm will be dissatisfied with its share of the jointly earned profits. Moreover, as the number of firms increases, the more individual firms perceive themselves to be in the position of price takers, in the sense that changes in their own output have a negligible effect on price. Looking at the situation facing the individual firms in Figure 14.5 from that point of view, they would see an opportunity to increase their profits by increasing their output to the point where marginal cost is equal to price. If a number of firms simultaneously attempt to exploit such opportunities, the whole cartel arrangement is liable to collapse.

Quite apart from these considerations, it has to be recognized that it is much harder to define the joint-profit-maximizing output in practice than in theory. For example, the summation of each cartel member's MC curve is

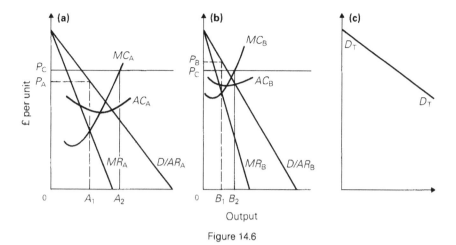

Figure 14.6

unlikely to be done with precision, and the estimation of the elasticity of demand may be wide of the target. Once the price is agreed upon, there may be considerable resistance to changing it. If profits are excessively high, this may be noticed by government agencies and trigger off an investigation into the cartel. It may be felt that excessive profits will attract new entrants who will have to be allowed to join the cartel, and hence to reduce all existing members' market shares and profits.

It can be seen that there are many pitfalls to be overcome before a collusive agreement can operate successfully over anything other than the short term, and it is for this reason that collusive agreements, such as the market-sharing model described below, make do with something less than joint-profit maximization as their objective.

Market-sharing cartels

The behaviour pattern of these cartels is broadly similar to that of the joint-profit-maximizing cartel above. The allocation of market share is designed to enable each firm to earn at least as much profit as it expects to earn through independent action. In Figure 14.6c, total demand is allocated between firm A (Figure 14.6a) and firm B (Figure 14.6b) such that firm A can sell one third more than firm B at any price. The firms' respective cost curves also appear in Figures 14.6a and 14.6b.

Acting independently, firm A would choose to supply A_1 at a price of P_A, whereas firm B would choose to supply B_1 at a price of P_B. However, given that the product produced by both firms is identical, they must clearly charge the same price if the agreement is to hold good, and it becomes necessary to settle upon a price acceptable to both parties somewhere between P_A and P_B. P_C is one such price, but even if both firms agree initially to honour it they will again both be tempted to cheat. This is because at price P_C firm A's

237

optimum output is A_2 and firm B's optimum output is B_2. However, if either or both firms do decide to cheat, overproduction will result and stocks will accumulate. This may result in a price-cutting war in an effort to dispose of surplus stocks. The probability of widespread cheating can be reduced by the imposition of fines upon those firms that exceed their allocated market shares, the proceeds being used to compensate those firms whose market shares have been reduced. Nevertheless, as in the previous case, the agreement will be subject to continual stress, especially as the number of firms involved increases.

Dominant-firm price leadership

It is possible for price leadership to be manifested as an explicit form of collusion. Given that cartels are illegal in the UK it is, however, more likely to appear as a pattern of behaviour that cannot be pinned down as collusive. If, for example, one major petrol retailer raises his price by 10p, and the other major retailers promptly follow suit, it may be taken to mean *either* that the price-raiser is the tacitly acknowledged leader of a price-fixing cartel *or* that the circumstances of the market are such as to produce a particular price that all major suppliers would choose *independently*. In either case, the price is adopted by all firms because it suits them so to do, possibly because the market place is a less uncertain place to operate in if there is little or nothing to choose between firms with respect to price. It has to be recognized, of course, that any firm that follows the price fixed by a competitor may be forgoing the chance to make more profits. On the other hand, it greatly reduces the odds of making very little profit.

One thing is certain, and that is the existence of price leadership in the real world. Cartels of the kind described above are not all that common because some power has to be vested in a central agency which may have the job of allocating market shares. In the case of price leadership, all decisions are taken independently, and in general there will be no attempt to follow anything other than price, thereby allowing wide variation in non-price methods of competing for market share. Price leadership may appear in a variety of forms, the most relevant of which in relation to a situation where firms produce identical products is dominant-firm price leadership. In essence it describes a situation in which all the firms in the industry are prepared to follow the price set by one of their number, which is in a dominant position because of its size and ability to produce more cheaply than its rivals, even though this price does not maximize their own profits, on the grounds that satisfactory profits are better than a price war that they cannot win.

The underlying principle of the dominant-firm model is that the dominant firm derives its demand curve by subtracting from the industry demand curve the sales that all the other firms within the industry would want to make at each price level that the dominant firm might conveivably set. Given this

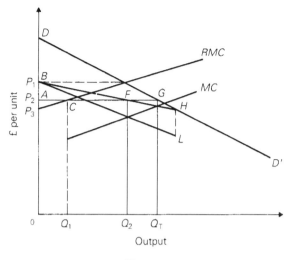

Figure 14.7

assumption, and also an accurate estimate of both its own and other firms' marginal cost curves, the dominant firm can readily select the price that will maximize its profits, as depicted in Figure 14.7.

In Figure 14.7, the market demand curve is DD'; MC is the dominant firm's marginal cost curve; and RMC is the marginal cost (supply) curve of all other firms within the industry. At a price P_1 the smaller firms will want to supply the whole market, as they will for any price above P_1 given that they are free to sell whatever they like at the price fixed by the dominant firm. Hence the dominant firm would be able to sell nothing until the price dropped below P_1, and its demand curve accordingly commences at B. At a price of P_2 the smaller firms will want to supply a quantity AC, leaving CG units to be supplied by the dominant firm. CG is equivalent to the distance AF, so F must be a point on the dominant form's demand curve. Since in the case illustrated the demand curve is linear (because RMC and DD' are drawn as linear curves), it must join DD' at H, which is equivalent to price P_3, the lowest price at which the smaller firms will be willing to supply anything at all. For this reason the section HD' of DD' is supplied only by the dominant firm and therefore constitutes part of that firm's overall demand curve $BFHD'$.

The marginal revenue curve corresponding to BH is BL, and the dominant firm will be maximizing its profits where BL is intersected by MC, which yields a price of P_2 and an output of Q_2. At that price, the smaller firms will supply the output Q_1, which, when added to Q_2, represents the total demand of Q_T units at price P_2.

It may nevertheless be very difficult for a firm to play a dominant role unless it is simultaneously the lowest-cost firm in the industry. This is because any attempt by a relatively high-priced firm, no matter how large compared to its competitors, may not persuade its lower-cost brethren of the desirability of a price rise. It is also the case that any dominant firm must weigh up the odds of its retaining that position in the long run when it may be threatened either by expansion among some of its existing competitors or by the potential entry of a similarly sized firm. It may well be, therefore, that the optimal strategy for a dominant firm is to make as much profit as possible as quickly as possible and to accept philosophically a steady reduction in its market share over time.

Differentiated products

If we now move on to consider oligopolistic situations where firms produce differentiated products, we will find that some of the themes of the discussion relating to identical products recur. But first we should note the additional factors to be considered when product differentiation is introduced.

The most obvious is that it is no longer necessary for all producers to sell at the same price. Brand loyalty, locational advantages and the like enable a firm to sell at a higher price than its rivals without losing all its sales. Secondly, since information about a firm's prices is likely to be more easily obtainable by its competitors than information about its output, price changes are more likely to be the subject of conjectures than output changes. Thirdly, product differentiation opens up the possibilities of non-price competition, in that firms can attempt to improve their positions through the use of advertising campaigns and product 'improvements'.

If we ignore for the moment such possibilities, all this suggests we could set out a Cournot-type model for oligopoly with product differentiation, but substituting conjectures about prices for conjectures about outputs. However, since such an exercise is so similar to that involved in the original Cournot model, we leave that to the reader. Instead, apart from noting in passing that such a model is open to precisely the same criticisms as the earlier models based on given conjectural variations, we move straight on to what seems to be (in textbooks at least) the most popular model of non-collusive oligopoly with differentiated products, which is known as the **kinked demand curve model**.

The kinked demand curve model

This model was developed simultaneously by Sweezy (1939) and Hall and Hitch (1939), although for rather different purposes. Hall and Hitch, for example, set out to explain why, given a price based on average cost, it should tend to be 'sticky' over time in oligopolistic industries. The key to the model lies in Figure 14.8, which depicts the situation of a 'representative' firm in the industry. This diagram contains two demand curves, D_1 and D_2, and their

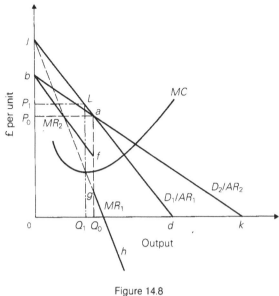

Figure 14.8

corresponding marginal revenue curves. The demand curves cross at point a, representing the *current* price and output, which in the case illustrated are P_0 and Q_0 respectively. The model addresses itself to answering the question why the firm should choose to keep that price and output unaltered even when its costs are changing.

The two demand curves incorporate different reactions by competitors to price changes by our representative firm, which we will call firm A. D_1 then illustrates what happens to the firm A's sales if its rivals follow suit on price changes, whereas the more elastic curve D_2 shows what happens if they leave their prices unaltered. The kinked demand curve model then suggests that A will conjecture that D_1 applies if it reduces price, whilst D_2 is the relevant demand curve for price increases.

The justification for these conjectures is straightforward. If A raises its price in isolation, many of its customers will immediately transfer their custom to what are now cheaper sources of supply. This will be to the benefit of rival producers because they will now be able to sell more at an unchanged price. Since these additional sales will be put at risk if they follow A's price increase, they can be expected to leave their prices unchanged. When raising its price, therefore, A can expect to move up the demand curve D_2 towards b. When, however, A lowers its price it will attract customers from its rivals and leave them worse off. They will therefore, it is argued, follow the price reduction in order to retain their customers. This communal price reduction will obviously expand the total market beyond its previous output level, and A will share in the benefits of that, but it will not in the end win much extra custom from its rivals. Hence the expected effect of a reduction in A's price on its sales is likely to be rather less than the effect of an increase, and will involve a move down D_1 rather than D_2.

If we put these two cases together we find that they define the demand curve bad, which is kinked at a. Further, corresponding to this kinked demand curve is a marginal revenue curve that has a discontinuity at the current level of output between f and g. This simply reflects the fact that the elasticity of D_1 is rather less than that of D_2, and hence that the gap between P and MR is greater along D_1 than along D_2. Hence at the kink in the demand curve, where there is a sudden change in the elasticity of demand, there is a corresponding change in marginal revenue.[2] It follows then that, as long as A believes its demand curve is of this kinked form, and as long as its marginal cost curve passes through the discontinuity in the marginal revenue curve, it will perceive that it cannot increase its profits by changing its price. Increases in price will lead to a reduction in sales with which the loss in revenue is greater than the reduction in cost (since $MR > MC$), but reductions in price, whilst increasing sales, would produce an increase in revenue on those sales that is less than the cost of producing the extra output (since $MR < MC$). Firm A will, therefore, conclude that its most profitable course of action is to leave its price unchanged at P_0. Morerover, this would continue to be the case if A's costs were to vary, as long as the marginal cost curve continues to pass through the gap fg. In other words, its costs may vary quite appreciably without there being any change in its perceived optimal price–output combination. It may be noted further that, even if A's demand curve is shifted to the right, the price may still remain unaltered, although the amount sold necessarily rises, provided the marginal cost curve passes through the discontinuity of the new marginal revenue curve.

The model thus provides an explanation of why prices in oligopolistic industries, characterized by strong rivalry and fairly volatile costs, might be sticky. Its biggest weakness lies in its inability to explain how the price P_0 came to be established in the first place, but it has also been doubted whether, in fact, prices in oligopolistic industries are all that sticky (for example, see Stigler, 1947). Some justification for those doubts can be obtained from further examination of Figure 14.8.

Collusive outcomes

From Figure 14.8 we can see that if the demand curve D_1 applies at all prices rather than just those below P_0, firm A would be able to increase its profits by reducing its output to Q_1, where the marginal cost curve cuts MR_1, and raising its price to P_1. But this increase in profits can be realized only if A's competitors raise their prices by a corresponding amount, so the question is whether there are any circumstances in which they would find it in their interests to do that. Now clearly, if A was a truly representative firm, its competitors would be starting off from a similar initial position to that illustrated in Figure 14.8. Whilst none of them would benefit by raising their prices in isolation, all could benefit from a general increase in prices. If they were asked, therefore, they might all agree to raise their prices simultaneously by an appropriate amount.

Further, although in practice such explicit collusion is often illegal, the same outcome could emerge in a different way. If firm A were to raise its price from P_0 to P_1 independently of its rivals, the latter might enjoy some short-run gains but might also conjecture that, if they didn't follow suit by raising their prices, firm A would quickly reduce its price back to P_0 and the opportunity for longer-term increased profitability for everyone would be lost. Hence they would decide to follow the price increase. Once firm A's price had become established at P_1, and if all the other firms were in a similar position, there would be no further opportunity for increasing profits by raising prices and P_1 would become an equilibrium price. The firms may then assume that they faced a kinked demand curve, but this time kinked at the higher price of P_1. If, however, this equilibrium is disturbed by a cost increase that they all experience, such as for example a new wage agreement or an increase in the price of some key raw material, opportunities for profitable price increases again emerge and the whole adjustment process could be repeated.

What all this implies is that, in the absence of explicit collusion, a form of price leadership might emerge. It would not require one firm to be dominant, as in our earlier model, but merely to be willing to take the lead. Moreover, it need not always be the same firm that makes the first move. As long as the general conditions are appropriate for an increase in price, the argument is that, as soon as one firm takes the lead, the others will follow. This kind of price leadership is often referred to as **barometric** price leadership, because it relies on the general atmosphere of the industry being conducive to price adjustments, and it is certainly a type of price leadership that can often be observed amongst oil companies, banks and building societies, to name just a few examples.

Non-price competition

Another line of thought arising from the kinked demand curve model is that, if firms are inhibited from changing their prices competitively in some way because of their conjectures about rivals' reactions, they will turn instead to non-price forms of competition, such as advertising and product variation, either separately or in combination. However, it can be argued that similar considerations to those underlying the kinked demand curve may apply here as well. If firm A increases its advertising expenditure, and that expenditure is successful in attracting more buyers, there may be some increase in the total market for the product but the main gains will be at the expense of rival's products. Competing firms can, therefore, be expected to match any increase in advertising expenditure in an attempt to retain their market share for exactly the same reasons that they would match any price reductions. In the end, all firms would be faced with higher advertising costs, but not much to show for it in terms of extra sales or profits. Conversely, if A reduced its advertising expenditure, it would lose sales to its competitors who, having benefited from the situation, would appear to have little incentive to match A's reduced level of expenditure. So, again, it can be argued that changes in either direction from the status quo are likely to be unprofitable.

However, it can also be argued that firms are likely to be more willing to risk an increase in advertising expenditure than a price reduction. A price reduction is, in a sense, a crude weapon that can easily be matched by rivals, whilst advertising has a more qualitative dimension that can less easily be countered. If a firm, therefore, has a good advertising idea or a new improved product to market, it might be willing to embark on an advertising campaign to exploit the situation even in the almost certain knowledge that its action would provoke retaliation from competitors, whilst remaining reluctant to engage in a price war. The qualitative dimension to advertising may also lead firms to be less willing to act collusively, either formally or informally, to reduce advertising expenditures than to raise prices. Hence the issues raised in the preceding two sections are likely to be a less constraining influence on advertising and product behaviour than on price changes.

Uncertainty and the theory of games

In the introduction to the discussion of different market structures in Chapter 12, and again in the introduction to this chapter, we suggested that, in contrast to perfect competition and monopoly, oligopolistic markets are characterized by uncertainty, because no one firm can be sure what its competitors will do if it changes its behaviour. But in fact, in the models we have discussed so far, uncertainty is not a very prominent feature. Indeed, in models based on specific conjectural variations, firms behave as if they are certain about their rivals' reactions, and, as we have seen, continue to act on that belief even when proved wrong by events. Further, in most of the other models we have discussed, firms have taken steps to reduce the uncertainty by acting in a collusive or semi-collusive manner. Whilst acting to reduce the uncertainty is a natural response to it by risk-averse economic agents, it may not always be possible, which raises the question of how we can deal more generally with the uncertainty faced by firms in oligopolistic situations.

A possible approach suggested by the analysis of uncertainty in Chapter 7 is to assume that a firm, for example, in evaluating the effects of a price reduction, makes some assessment of the probability of its rivals reacting in particular ways and uses these probabilities to estimate the **expected value** of the effect on its profits.[3] Alternative moves can then be estimated in the same way and the one offering the greatest increase in expected profits selected. Or, if the firm is risk-averse, the exercise could potentially be carried out in terms

Table 14.1

	(a) A's pay-off matrix				(b) B's pay-off matrix		
	A_1	A_2	A_3		A_1	A_2	A_3
B_1	2	-4	-7	B_1	3	5	6
B_2	5	0	-3	B_2	-2	0	2
B_3	7	6	10	B_3	-4	-1	5

of expected utilities. However, this general approach would imply that rivals' reactions were reasonably random events that are independent of the firm's own actions, in the same way as the results obtained from shaking an unbiased dice, which is unlikely to be the case.

A rather different approach is provided by the **theory of games**, which, following the pioneering work of von Neumann and Morgenstern (1947), has been applied to an increasing range of economic problems. The starting point of game theory analysis is a *pay-off* matrix, which, in the oligopoly context, could set out the effects on the firm's profits of various *strategies* or changes it might make to its decision variables, with a variety of different reactions by rival firms. Thus Table 14.1(a) shows a hypothetical pay-off matrix for A in a simplified situation when it is faced with the choice of three strategies A_1, A_2 and A_3 – which might be lowering its price, keeping it constant or raising it – and where there are three possible responses by its rival B, shown as B_1, B_2 and B_3. Thus, if A plays strategy A_1 and B's reaction is B_1, A's profits increase by 2, and similarly for the other entries in the table.

In the absence of any information about B's behaviour A might choose A_1, on the grounds that the worst that can happen in that situation is better than the worst that can happen in any other situation. This is referred to as a **maximin** strategy. Similarly, if B's pay-off matrix is as shown in Table 14.1(b), B, acting in the same way, would choose B_1. The resultant pay-offs would be 2 for A and 3 for B. Further, once these strategies had been revealed there would be no incentive for either party to reconsider their decision, so an equilibrium would be obtained.

It can also be seen that, in the case illustrated, the same position would be reached if each behaved in Cournot fashion by assuming the other firm's strategy remains unchanged. For example, if the starting strategies are A_2 and B_2 then A, assuming B will stick with B_2, will change to A_1 because that is the best he can do with B on B_2. But once A has moved to A_1, then B, on the assumption that A will stick with that, chooses B_1. After that change, however, neither party can see the possibility of greater pay-offs given the other's behaviour, so an equilibrium is again reached. In the game theory context, a situation in which A's choice is optimal given B's choice *and* B's choice is optimal given A's choice is referred to as a **Nash equilibrium** after the mathematician who popularized it, but as we have seen it is equivalent in the oligopoly context to a Cournot type of equilibrium.

Such equilibria do not always exist, and if they do exist they need not be unique, but with the figures in Table 14.1 there are also other possibilities. First of all there is the possibility of collusion. If A and B agree to adopt strategies A_3 and B_3 respectively, the total pay-off is 15, which is greater than the total pay-off available from any other pair of strategies. But that might prove to be an unstable result because, with A choosing A_3, B can improve his position by reneging on the agreement and choosing B_1 instead. In fact, with the figures in Table 14.1(b), B would always prefer B_1 because it offers him better pay-offs in all situations than those from any other strategy.[4] However, in the case in the table, A could forestall such a move by offering B two extra units of profit to continue with B_3, leaving himself with 8 and B with 7, which is still better than either could do with any other strategies. But if A's pay-off with A_3/B_3 was only 6, whilst collusion to adopt these strategies would still yield the greatest combined pay-off, both firms would be tempted to try and improve their positions by changing the strategy.

From this we can see that the theory of games approach endorses some of the conclusions of our earlier analysis, particularly with respect to the incentives to collusion and the potential instability of that collusion, but does so with an approach that is less restricted by preconceived conjectures. However, it has not, in the main, succeeded in producing a more determinate theory of oligopoly than the traditional approach, In our simplified example the conclusions we were able to draw, although illustrating some of the possibilities, were specific to the numbers in the pay-off matrix. Further, as the number of firms increases, the solutions become more complex and less determinate because of the possibility of collusive coalitions between sub-groups of firms within the industry. Nevertheless, the theory of games has been found to provide a useful framework within which oligopolistic, and indeed other forms of economic behaviour, can fruitfully be studied.

Notes

1   This is identical to the profit-maximizing position of a multi-plant monopolist.
2   Here it should be recalled that $MR = P(1 + 1/e)$.
3   Expected profits can be worked out as in expression (7.11) above.
4   In this case, B_1 is said to dominate all other strategies.

Exercises

14.1   How would you identify an oligopolistic industry in practice? Use your criterion to identify one or more oligopolistic industries in the UK. From casual observation, to what extent do you think the behaviour of firms in the industry (or industries) you have identified corresponds to that described in any theoretical model of oligopolistic behaviour you have met?

14.2 The (inverse) market demand curve for a given product can be represented by the equation

$$P = 32.50 - 0.05Q,$$

where P is the price in £s and Q the quantity demanded.
Compute the output and price of the product:

(i) when it is supplied by a single profit-maximizing producer who can produce at a constant marginal cost of £2.50;

(ii) when it is supplied by two producers who can both produce output at a constant marginal cost of £2.50 and both act as assumed in the Cournot model;

(iii) when it is supplied by three producers with the same marginal costs and behaving in the same way as those in (ii).

Compare your answers and comment.

14.3 Suppose there are two firms, A and B, in a particular industry. They produce identical products but for any level of output A's marginal costs are lower than B's.

(i) Analyse the determination of price, total output and its distribution between the two firms when they collude with the object of maximizing their joint profits.

(ii) What difference would it make if instead the firms agreed to divide the market between them?

14.4 Analyse the determination of price, output and its distribution between the two firms in Exercise 14.3 above if there was no explicit agreement but firm B allowed firm A to act as price leader. Compare the position in this situation:

(a) with that in Exercise 14.2(i), and

(b) with that arising if both firms acted competitively by producing where price equals marginal cost.

14.5 Explain the limitations of the kinked demand curve model of oligopoly.

14.6 What grounds are there for supposing that collusion will be the natural outcome of any oligopolistic situation unless it is prevented by law?

CHAPTER FIFTEEN
BARRIERS TO ENTRY AND CONTESTABLE MARKETS

So far in our discussion of monopoly and oligopoly it has been assumed that the existence of barriers to entry prevents the erosion of monopoly profits by new competitors in the long run. However, in practice not all monopolistic and oligopolistic industries are protected by such barriers, and where they exist they are not always completely insurmountable. This means that the likely reactions of potential entrants to an incumbent firm's behaviour may have as much effect on its actions as the reactions of existing competitors. In this chapter, therefore, we consider in more detail the nature of entry barriers and how they might affect the behaviour of firms. We also consider how monopolistic firms behave in the absence of entry barriers on the basis of the recently developed theory of **contestable markets**.

Barriers to entry

The issue of barriers to entry originally arose in the literature as a side-effect of the analysis of traditional models of the firm. In essence, the issue was concerned with whether it would be desirable for a firm to forgo some of its potential short-run profits if it could thereby guarantee itself a higher level of profitability in the longer run. Whilst the maximization of short-run profits obviously has its attractions as an objective, it might lead to the entry of new firms into the market, with the result that, in the longer run, prices and hence (assuming normal cost conditions) the profits of established firms will be depressed. If, in accordance with the discussion of firms' objectives in Chapter 8 above, established firms consider that the longer-run effect upon their profits is sufficient to reduce the net present value of their future profits, they will naturally seek ways of preventing entry of new firms from taking place.

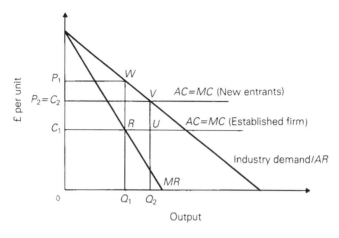

Figure 15.1

The limit price

A key concept in the analysis of entry barriers is that of the limit price. This is best explained by reference to Figure 15.1. Suppose there is one established firm in the industry which can operate at a level of average cost equal to C_1. The pursuit of short-run profit maximization therefore results in the choice of output Q_1 and price P_1. Potential entrants, on the other hand, are assumed to be less efficient and hence will all find themselves operating at an average cost equal to C_2. At a price of P_1 they will, however, be able to make a profit of P_1C_2 per unit, and entry will therefore take place. This in turn will deprive the established firm of part of its market, and have the effect of shifting its demand curve to the left. This process will continue as entry proceeds until the demand curve and its associated MR curve have moved sufficiently to the left such as to produce a profit-maximizing price of P_2, which is equal to C_2. At this point no further entry will take place since no profits can now be earned by potential entrants. For this reason price P_2 is known as the **limit price**. It may be noted that at this price the established firm, unlike potential entrants, will continue to make profits. Its unit profit margin is, however, much reduced as compared with its pre-entry level. This ability of established firms to retain at least some element of profit in the post-entry longer run is related to the existence of the barriers to entry, which enable them to operate along a lower average cost curve than potential entrants.

The question thus arises whether it will pay the established firm to try to prevent any form of entry by new firms through the expedient of holding down its price in the short run below its profit-maximizing level. Clearly, any price set in excess of P_2 will attract entry, and an entry-prevention strategy will therefore require the establishment of the price at P_2. Such a price will result in the established firm selling an output of Q_2, both in the short run and, in the absence of entry, also in the long run.

On the face of it such behaviour might appear perverse. If an established firm can earn a profit of P_1C_1 per unit in the short run, and of P_2C_1 per unit in the longer run after entry has taken place, why would it ever choose an entry-preventing strategy that yields a constant per unit profit of P_2C_1? The answer clearly lies in a comparison of output levels rather than just of profit per unit. An entry-preventing firm sells a constant output of Q_2 at a unit profit of P_2C_1 (equal to area UVP_2C_1). A short-run profit-maximizing strategy will indeed initially yield a higher total profit of RWP_1C_1, but as soon as entry commences this will begin to shrink rapidly. By the time the industry settles into a new equilibrium at price P_2 the established firm will only be left with an output of considerably less than Q_2, thereby reducing significantly its longer-run profitability as compared to the entry-prevent strategy. Hence, in deciding whether to adopt an entry-preventing strategy, the firm will have to consider whether the reduced profits in the short run are more than compensated for, in present value terms, by the expected higher profits in the long run.

A final point of interest arising from this discussion is that it must clearly follow that the structure of an industry will be significantly affected by the choice of established firms between the above two strategies. Where an entry-preventing strategy is chosen, the number of firms within an industry will be considerably smaller as compared to where entry is free, and the level of concentration will accordingly be much higher.

The nature of entry barriers

As we will discover below, there is some ambiguity about what precisely qualifies as an entry barrier. Attention continues, for the most part, to be focused upon the interpretations placed upon the term by Bain (1956) and Sylos-Labini (1962). Sylos-Labini concentrated almost exclusively upon homogeneous oligopoly, whereby all firms, whether actual or potential, produce perfectly substitutable commodities while operating along identical average cost curves. Consequently, the only exploitable barrier to entry arises from access to economies of scale. Bain, on the other hand, broadened the definition to encompass in addition the possible existence of competing products (the product differentiation barrier to entry) and the possible existence of a variety of average cost curves along which different firms operated (the absolute cost advantage barrier to entry).

According to Bain, the entry conditions of any industry would fall into one of four categories:

(1) *easy entry*: this is where there are no barriers to entry whatsoever, and there can therefore be no incentive to prevent entry since any lowering

of price by existing firms below the average cost of potential entrants necessarily also lowers it below their own.

(2) *ineffectively impeded entry*: this is where there are partial barriers to entry that allow an established firm to operate at a slightly lower level of average cost than potential entrants.

(3) *effectively impeded entry*: this is where there are substantial barriers to entry that allow an established firm to operate at a considerably lower level of average cost than potential entrants.

(4) *blockaded entry*: this is where there are such substantial barriers to entry, and average cost differentials between an established firm and potential entrants are so great, that the established firm's profit-maximizing price is below the average cost of potential entrants.

In the circumstances of (1), established firms are best advised to maximize short-run profits, since the ease of entry is guaranteed to erode them away quite rapidly. The same conclusion applies in (4), since short-run profit maximization will not attract any entry. In the circumstances of (2), profits will eventually be competed away, and such small profits as are available in the short run are therefore best obtained whilst the opportunity exists. Clearly, therefore, only in the case of effectively impeded entry can any strategy other than short-run profit maximization prove worthwhile, and in this case limit pricing would appear to be justified since it allows established firms to make respectable short-run profits without sacrificing too much profit in the long run.

The four-fold categorization of entry barriers proposed by Bain has long been used for investigating the empirical significance of such barriers in different industries. Each barrier is categorized as high, medium or low in any given industry, and an overall assessment is subjectively formed as to whether, taking all three together, the overall entry barrier to the industry is high, substantial or moderate-to-low. Subsequent work, largely derived from an approach first employed by Comanor and Wilson (1967), involves the use of proxy variables for the entry barriers, using, for example, the advertising/sales ratio as a proxy for the product differentiation barrier.

Whilst the detailed empirical work is not the concern of this book, it is nevertheless worth observing that there has never been widespread agreement about what precisely constitutes a barrier to entry. Stigler, for example, defined a barrier to entry as 'a cost of producing (at some or every rate of output) which must be borne by a firm which seeks to enter an industry, but is not borne by firms already in the industry' (1968, p. 67). Such a definition excludes economies of scale as a barrier to entry since, provided entrants have access to the same operating processes as established firms, they will obtain the same economies of scale by operating them. Ferguson (1974, p. 10), who considers that 'the main non-legal barriers to entry are increasing returns to any input, including advertising', agrees with Bain about the barrier effect of economies of scale, but disagrees about absolute cost advantages. Thus whilst advertising is always considered by Bain to constitute a barrier to entry, it constitutes a barrier to entry according to Ferguson only if it produces economies of scale; and is disregarded by Stigler provided any firm, whether established or a potential entrant, can employ it on equal terms.

Brozen (1975) takes a more restrictive view altogether, arguing that neither advertising, product differentiation nor economies of scale constitute barriers to entry. Whilst it is obviously true, for example, that advertising can in principle constitute a barrier to entry, it might also permit potential entrants to gain relatively cheap access to potential customers and hence assist, rather than deter, entry. It has also been suggested that economies of scale may assist rather than deter entry. The heart of this argument is that if a new manufacturing unit needs to be built on a large scale in order to be efficient, then if demand rises beyond the capacity of established firms they may be reluctant to open a new unit for fear that the initial large increase in capacity will create excess supply, and hence force down the price fetched by the output of their existing units. A potential entrant, on the other hand, will be concerned solely with the profitability of the new unit, and may therefore be far readier to build it than the established firms.

The Sylos' postulate

The issue of the role played by economies of scale is very much tied up with what has long been known as the Sylos' postulate.[1] This states that potential entrants will select their strategies in the belief that established firms will adopt a policy that is highly unfavourable to entrants, namely that of holding their output constant in the face of entry. Furthermore, established firms will expect them to behave accordingly. Acting on this belief, new entrants will expect the post-entry price to fall, since entry will create circumstances of excess supply. Hence a potential entrant will enter only where he expects the post-entry price to exceed his average cost of production. Even assuming the potential entrant expects to operate with a similar level of average cost to established firms, the latter can keep the price above their average cost by the amount it is expected to fall as a consequence of entry without such entry taking place. Where a potential entrant expects to suffer cost disadvantages compared to established firms, the price set by the latter will accordingly be higher without attracting entry.

It can be seen as a general proposition that the extent of actual entry depends upon the view taken by potential entrants of the probable post-entry behaviour of established firms. The Sylos' postulate must ultimately be viewed as only one such pattern of behaviour, and either the established firms, or potential entrants, or indeed both might make alternative assumptions. This line of argument has strong parallels with the theoretical models of oligopoly previously discussed, but with one interesting difference. Whereas previously we considered the attitude only of rivals towards other firms already within the industry, we have now extended the analysis to cover the attitudes of established firms towards potential entrants.

One may proceed a stage further by noting that we have so far assumed that the potential entrant's strategy is concerned only with the reactions of established firms. Where, however, there are a number of potential entrants, both established firms and potential entrants must take account of the effect upon total supply and price should there be multiple simultaneous entry. If established firms expect the latter to occur, it would justify maintaining the pre-entry price above the level that would forestall entry by a single potential entrant without expecting entry to take place. Such a strategy implies an element of risk on the part of established firms, since a determined entrant who was prepared to supply at a lower price, even at the cost of making short-run losses, could thereby attract a substantial share of the market and leave established firms with huge amounts of unsold output on their hands if they responded to entry by maintaining their output. Such a strategy could potentially damage the established firms more than the entrant, and has led to the suggestion that the limit price should be more realistically defined as the price that is financially more damaging to the entrant in the longer run than to established firms.

There are, in any event, difficulties with the concept of limit pricing in so far as established firms are obliged to choose between two well-defined alternative strategies, namely short-run profit maximization and limit pricing. It is often argued that the cause of profitability might best be served by a policy of retarding rather than of forestalling entry. Quite apart from anything else, a potential entrant might well be willing to suffer short-run losses if he believed that the market was likely to grow rapidly in the longer run, and hence would permit him to operate profitably without damaging established firms to the point at which they would prefer a price war to peaceful coexistence. Ultimately, if for whatever reason the established firms believe either that some entry will take place come what may, or alternatively that whilst entry can be forestalled it will be hugely unprofitable to secure such an outcome, their best strategy may be to reduce their output as soon as actual entry occurs.

By implication, much depends upon whether entry is expected to be sporadic or on a large scale, and upon whether new entrants are expected to be combative or cooperative. Where collusion of any kind is customary, it may be best for established firms and new entrants to get together in order to determine what strategy is in their mutual best interests. Rigid adherence to the Sylos' postulate would not seem sensible under such circumstances.

We can state, by way of summary, that limit pricing is the optimal strategy only under circumstances of effectively impeded entry, but as we have indicated above such circumstances may rarely be found in practice. As indicated, if the market is expanding rapidly it may not be sensible to forestall entry. Equally, if the new entrant is not expected to increase the existing capacity significantly, the established firms' profitability may not be sufficiently affected as to warrant entry-preventing behaviour on their part. Entrants may also suffer few, and possibly no, cost disadvantages, and if technology is changing at all rapidly the entrant may conceivably be able to operate at a lower average cost than established firms through the operation of more up-to-date and efficient plant. Given all of these reservations, it can reasonably be concluded that the limit pricing model is distinctly lacking in its general applicability.

Furthermore, it requires that the established firms all behave in exactly the same way when faced by potential entry, which suggests the need for at least some degree of collusion to be present. Where products are homogeneous, such an assumption may appear to be reasonable, but its validity must be in question where products are differentiated. It is true that product differentiation appears as a barrier to entry in the limit pricing model, but in so far as the degree of differentiation varies from firm to firm, some may feel much less threatened than others by potential entrants, and hence may feel less urgency in responding to the pressure for the setting of a limit price.

As a final consideration, it is worth remembering that there can be a wide range of possible reasons, other than that they are limit pricing, for the failure on the part of established firms to maximize their short-run profits. Deciding between alternative explanations is ultimately an empirical matter, and it has to be said that the evidence has always been far from conclusive one way or the other. The empirical work has tended to concentrate upon determining the relationship between barriers to entry and profitability, since a close correlation between these variables is more likely to lend support to the limit pricing hypothesis than to other explanations of non-profit-maximizing behaviour. However, even the existence of a close correlation would fall well short of absolute proof, especially since, as indicated above, established firms may be seeking to retard rather than to forestall entry.

Contestable markets

Introduction

In recent years the role played by entry has taken on something of a new form in the context of what are known as perfectly contestable markets. This shares certain of the characteristics of the model of perfect competition, but has much wider appeal because it can be applied across the entire spectrum of industry structures through oligopoly to monopoly. Like the models of perfect competition and monopoly, the perfectly contestable market is not so much a description of real world structures but rather a benchmark for a desirable structure, yet at the same time one that is far more flexible and applicable than those that preceded it. Some idea of how the three benchmark models compare can be obtained by reference to Table 15.1.

Table 15.1 Characteristics of benchmark models of competition

	Perfect competition	Pure monopoly	Perfectly contestable
Firms' objective	Profit Maximization	Profit Maximization	Profit Maximization
Number of firms	Many	One	Immaterial
Size of firms	Small	Large	Immaterial
Product homogeneity	Yes	Yes	Not necessarily
Long-run profit	Zero	Positive	Zero
Entry/exit barriers	None	Significant	None

The ways in which perfectly contestable markets differ from other market models, including oligopoly, overcome many of the drawbacks of these models. For example, the contestable markets theory allows for the possibility that the circumstances of every industrial market are not necessarily always ideally met by a perfectly competitive structure (airframe manufacture, for example). Second, the theory overcomes the dependence of the oligopoly models previously described upon the reaction patterns (conjectural variations) of incumbent firms already within the industry. Rather, the emphasis is placed upon incumbents' reactions to potential competition as a result of entry. Third, the theory attacks the proposition that any change in an industrial structure away from monopoly and towards perfect competition is likely to cause resource allocation to become progressively more efficient.

The behaviour of perfectly contestable markets is sharply discontinuous in its welfare attributes as compared to the traditional view that welfare improves gradually in line with increasing competition. Any contestable market must exhibit the ideal behaviour to be expected under perfect competition. Hence two competitors are sufficient to trigger off contestable market behaviour.

A final critical point to be made by way of introduction to contestable markets is that, whereas traditional models start out by taking the structure of an industry as exogenously given, and then proceed to investigate how each structure affects the determination of prices, output and so forth, the contestable market model assumes that each industry's structure is determined endogenously by technical conditions reflected in the cost functions of firms..

Entry and exit characteristics

As denoted in Table 15.1, there are no entry barriers in a contestable market. This is to be taken to mean not simply that entry is necessarily costless, but rather that an entrant can produce products that consumers will treat as comparable to those of incumbent firms with respect to such matters as quality, and that the existing price levels are sufficiently attractive as to suggest to the potential entrant that he can make a worthwhile profit. In other words, the entrant must be able to operate with a cost structure comparable to that of incumbent firms and cannot be prevented from attaining it. In addition, there must be absolute freedom of *exit* in a contestable market so that any entry costs can always be recouped when a firm leaves the industry.

A critical requirement here is the absence of *sunk* costs, which are costs that cannot be recovered on exit from the industry. For example, mining operations involve considerable initial expenditures on the drilling of mineshafts, tunnelling and the like, which cannot, in most cases, be recovered on exit from the industry because the facilities created have little value in alternative use. It is physically impossible to transfer them to another site and they are unlikely to have any value in alternative uses on their existing site. Indeed, they are likely to be a positive hindrance if the site is put to some other use, and can constitute a source of danger to the general public. In this kind of situation, entry into the industry is deterred, not only because potential entrants know they cannot recover their sunk costs if entry proves unprofitable, but also because it gives incumbent firms an advantage since the avoidable costs to them of continuing in operation are likely to be much lower than the costs faced by a firm starting from scratch. These sunk costs also restrict exit in that firms may find it profitable to continue in production even though the return on their initial investment is less than could be obtained in other industries. Other activities may require comparable initial capital expenditure, but if the equipment involved can be readily switched to another use or resold for more or less the same as its purchase price, firms can leave the industry without loss, and for that reason are likely to be tempted to enter more readily.

In other words, the essential characteristic of a contestable market is its susceptibility to *hit-and-run* operations. Potential entrants always have the opportunity of entry on a short-term basis and then leaving as soon as prospects appear to be deteriorating. It is for this very reason that any contestable market, irrespective of its structure and of any monopolistic elements within it, cannot be in equilibrium with profits being earned. The instant that profits manifest themselves, an entrant who can produce the same product as cheaply as incumbent firms is likely to offer to sell at a slightly lower price than the incumbent firms; to make a slightly reduced, but nevertheless satisfactory profit; and quite possibly to exit at some speed. The policy implications of this are that the case for the regulation of monopoly is much reduced, since it follows that even a monopolist in a contestable market cannot earn excess profits. It also follows that no incumbent firm or firms can allow X-inefficiency to creep into their operations, since if they do a potential entrant will spot the fact that even if the incumbent(s) are making little profit, he can move in and, by virtue of operating at minimum cost, be able to earn profits even at a price slightly below that of incumbent firms.

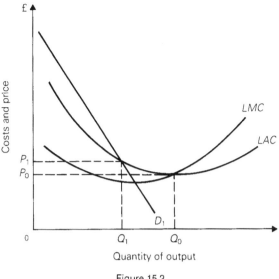

Figure 15.2

Welfare considerations

Finally there is an important welfare consequence associated with a contestable market, which arises because contestability not only induces firms to produce where price equals average cost, but also encourages them to produce where price equals marginal cost. This can be explained with the help of Figure 15.2. Assuming all the existing firms in an industry and all potential entrants are faced with the long-run average cost curve LAC illustrated, it should be clear from the diagram that any firm producing an output other than Q_0 (at which average costs are minimized) for which the price would have to be higher than P_0, could be undercut either by other firms already in the industry or by new entrants producing Q_0 and selling it at price P_0. All firms will, therefore, seek to produce Q_0 and sell at P_0 and, since at the lowest point on the average cost curve marginal cost is equal to average cost, all will be producing where price equals marginal cost. The equilibrium output of the industry will, therefore, tend to be the optimal output from the point of view of resource allocation, as well as from the point of view of minimizing total costs, irrespective of whether the number of firms in the industry is large or small.

Strictly speaking, in the case illustrated, there would be some deviation from this optimum if the total demand at price P_0 is not an exact multiple of Q_0. However, if in practice, as suggested in Chapter 11 above, there is some range of output at which average costs are at their minimum level, this is unlikely to be a serious problem. Probably of more practical significance is the special case where the total industry demand curve is like D_1 in the diagram, which cuts LAC to the left of its minimum point. In that case, with perfect contestability, equilibrium would involve one firm producing an output of Q_1 and selling at P_1. Price would then be greater than marginal cost, but even then output would be rather less restrictive than if the monopolist faced no threat of entry.

Implications for industry structure and regulation

As we have indicated above, the only firms that can hope to survive in a contestable market are those that are the most efficient irrespective of their size, and that do not attempt to take advantage of their market power by raising their prices above the level at which entry is attracted. It therefore follows that the structure of an industry in long-run equilibrium is that which results in minimum average costs. What this means is that the 'ideal' industry structure must always be realized in practice, and that there is no need to analyse market behaviour as such since this is predetermined by the ideal structure.

One may object that the above is only true under circumstances of perfect contestability, and that these may rarely occur in practice. It is impossible to know the exact consequences of minor deviations from perfect contestability, but it does seem plausible that there are many cases in which the industry structures to be found approximate to the contestable outcome. Certainly, there is a remarkable similarity between the structures of a specific industry in all advanced economies, and it may reasonably be presumed that this reflects the vulnerability to entry of any individual country's industry that becomes relatively inefficient, particularly vulnerability to foreign competition. This suggests that contestability theory can be used to predict the expected industrial structure in such an economy with considerable accuracy.

This conclusion is not affected by the existence of multi-product rather than single-product firms. Where a supplier operates across a range of markets, it can survive in any individual market under contestable conditions only where it is as cheap as its single-product competitors, whether they be incumbents or potential entrants.

Regulation need not, therefore, take account of this latter issue. Nor indeed need it take account of the objection that is commonly raised in support of regulation that entrants are deterred by the need to undertake fixed costs on a scale comparable to that of an incumbent. The critical point, as noted above, is that fixed costs are not necessarily the same thing as sunk costs. Capital investment will not be deterred provided the capital can be resold for close to the purchase price, since in that case such losses as might occur will appear to be worthwhile given the potential profits available to the entrant.

Transport offers a classic illustration of this point, since it is clearly always possible for a multi-vehicle company either to switch vehicles from one route to another or to lease surplus vehicles, without in either case creating any sunk costs. This is one of the reasons that in recent years have been strongly advanced for deregulation of airline and bus/coach services. Furthermore, the wide applicability of the contestable market doctrine can be seen in the recent deregulation of financial markets.

Clearly the existence of significant sunk costs would indicate circumstances in which regulation was quite possibly needed. In their absence, however, contestability is a *substitute* for regulation. Competition between firms already within a market, or more obviously its absence, is no longer the issue. The consumer will be protected provided potential entrants exist. For this reason the *absence of entry* and a high level of concentration are just as likely to indicate consumer sovereignty as the opposite circumstances, since there will be no entrants when entry is *no longer worthwhile*. This turns conventional principles of regulation on their heads, since the consumer will suffer if the regulation is successful rather than vice versa.

In conclusion, we may note that contestability raises two distinct issues. The first of these is normative, in that it is proposed that the yardstick for regulation should be switched from a 'behaving as if competitive' to a 'behaving as if contestable' basis. Regulation thus becomes concerned with removing artificial barriers to contestability; to improving contestability when the existing industry structure is not conducive to it; and taking action in cases of so-called 'non-sustainability', which is where the market is contestable but the appropriate equilibrium has not come about.

The second issue is concerned with the positive question as to whether entrants' costs are or are not sunk in practice. The literature on entry barriers traditionally takes the view that an entrant will be involved in sunk costs, and that exit will be a drawn-out and expensive process. The incumbents' prices, on the other hand, can be rapidly lowered so as to make entry unprofitable. Perfect contestability, by way of contrast, requires that there be no sunk costs, and treats implementation of price changes by firms, and the reaction to such changes by consumers, as processes that require a considerable period of time to elapse. As we have indicated above, there are certainly some industrial sectors where sunk costs are small or can be avoided,[2] but the *generality* of the contestability hypothesis has yet to be proved empirically one way or the other.

Notes

1 This idea originated in the work of Sylos-Labini, but it was first given this title in F. Modigliani (1958).
2 J. E. Davies (1986), is a case study of the liner shipping industry, which he argues is very close to being a perfectly contestable market.

Exercises

15.1 What do you understand by the term 'barriers to entry'? Give examples and explain their potential role in market behaviour.

15.2 'Firms will always prefer to fix their prices at an entry-preventing level rather than the short-run profit-maximizing level.' Consider whether this statement is true or false.

15.3 What are the important characteristics of a contestable market? Give some examples.

15.4 To what extent is the allocation of resources in a perfectly contestable market optimal?

15.5 To what extent do you think that the market for local bus services is perfectly contestable? Do bus operators in localities known to you behave in the manner suggested by the theory of contestable markets?

CHAPTER SIXTEEN
ALTERNATIVE APPROACHES TO
THE THEORY
OF THE FIRM

Introduction

It was argued in Chapter 8 that in *managerial* firms – that is, firms in which there is some divorce between ownership and control – managers may have some opportunity, particularly where competition is restricted, to pursue their own objectives at the expense of profits and thus may not seek to maximize profits. Our subsequent analysis has so far ignored this possibility except for the brief discussion of X-inefficiency in the context of monopoly. An important strand in the more recent developments in the theory of the firm has, however, been concerned with exploring the implications of alternative objectives to profit maximization for the behaviour of firms and in this chapter we consider some of these developments.

In general terms, as suggested in Chapter 8, we can think in terms of a firm's managers seeking to maximize their utility subject to the constraints imposed by the need to earn sufficient profits to meet the shareholders' requirements, but an important first step in this approach is to identify the key variables that determine managerial utility. Since managers derive satisfaction from things like their salaries, the status their jobs confer, the perquisites that go with their jobs, their working environments and degree of security, we could include all these as possible variables in the utility function. However, since many of these are not easily measurable, it is useful to try and represent them in the utility function by more easily observable proxy variables. In one of the earliest developments of this approach, Baumol (1962) suggested that all the variables contributing to managerial utility vary directly with the size of the firm as measured by turnover or sales revenue. Managerial utility can then be regarded simply as a function of total sales revenue and the objective of the firm taken to be the maximization of sales revenue subject to the constraint that profits are sufficient to keep shareholders happy. We consider this model first and then go on to consider further elaborations of the general approach.

Sales revenue maximization

The essentials of Baumol's model can most easily be examined with the help of a diagram showing total cost and total revenue curves. Hence Figure 16.1 shows possible total cost and total revenue curves for a typical price maker denoted as TC and TR respectively. Also shown is a profit curve (π) showing, for each level of output, the difference between total revenue and total cost. The output at which revenue is a maximum in the case illustrated is Q_1, whilst the profit-maximizing level of output is Q_3. However, the firm's choice of output also depends upon the level of profit required to keep shareholders happy, and three possible cases are shown in the diagram. When the required level of profit is π_1, it is less than the profit earned at the revenue-maximizing output of Q_1 and so that is the output produced. If, however, the required level of profit is π_2, the profit at Q_1 is insufficient to meet this requirement, and the maximum revenue it can obtain with a profit of π_2 is at output Q_2, so that is the chosen output in this case. It should also be apparent from the diagram that as the required level of profit rises the output that maximizes revenue subject to obtaining the required profit falls and, in the case illustrated, when the required profit level rises to π_3 the only way the firm can meet it is to maximize its profits and produce an output of Q_3. Similarly, of course, if the firm's opportunities to earn profits above the level required by shareholders are restricted by competitive conditions, the possibility of pursuing other than a profit-maximizing objective will also be limited. However, in a less competitive environment this model predicts that firms will produce an output greater than the profit-maximizing output, which will have to be sold at a lower price.

The model can be elaborated further to take account of advertising behaviour and the like, but the simple case illustrated in Figure 16.1 is sufficient to demonstrate one interesting feature of the model relating to the response of the firm to a profits tax. If such a tax is imposed, whether it is a lump-sum or proportional tax on profits, the profits potentially available to shareholders are the net-of-tax profits, which are less than the gross profits by the amount of the tax. If, in the diagram, the dashed curve π^* represents the net-of-tax profits after a tax has been imposed, it can be seen that when π_1 is the required level of profits the firm has to reduce its output to Q_1^*, and if π_2 is the required level of profit output has to be reduced to Q_2^*. This is in marked contrast to the more traditional profit-maximizing model, which predicts that firms do not change their output following the imposition of a profits tax, because the output at which before-tax profits are maximized is also the maximum profits output after tax. In the Baumol model the tax leads

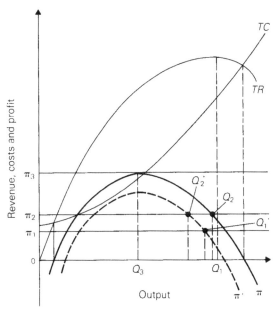

Figure 16.1

to a change in output unless either competitive pressures are such that the firm is forced into profit-maximizing behaviour to meet shareholders' requirements, or, at the other extreme, after-tax profits are more than enough to meet shareholders' requirements when sales revenue is maximized.

The expense-preference model

One obvious criticism of Baumol's model is that it relies on an oversimplified managerial utility function, which, because it contains only one independent variable, does not allow any account to be taken of the trade-offs between objectives that are likely to be an important feature of managerial and indeed any economic decision-making. A later development by Williamson, now sometimes referred to as the **expense-preference** approach, takes explicit account of such trade-offs and so is worth considering further.

The basis of Williamson's approach is that the variables in the managerial utility function are enhanced by certain types of expenditure. In his basic model he identifies three types of expenditure that he thinks are particularly relevant. These are expenditure on staff, reflecting the idea that a manager's salary and status are greater the more staff he has under his control; expenditure on managerial perks, expense accounts, company cars and the like; and discretionary profit. The latter is simply the profit left over after all costs have been covered, all tax liabilities met, and the shareholders paid adequate dividends. This residual is then at the disposal of managers and can be spent on prestigious investment projects, the sponsorship of sporting or cultural events, contributions to political parties and the like, or be used to build up reserves.

Simplifying a little, to facilitate a diagrammatic analysis, we will ignore expenditure on managerial perks, so that the utility function that managers seek to maximize, subject to meeting the shareholders' minimum profit requirements, can be expressed as

$$U = U(S, D), \tag{16.1}$$

where S is the staff variable and D is discretionary profit. S can in fact be interpreted in a variety of ways. It could, for example, be the total labour force or it could be staff in a particular category, such as 'headquarters' staff or 'professional' staff. It could also be defined in terms of expenditure rather than numbers, but for present purposes we will define it in terms of numbers. Discretionary profit is simply actual profit less the profit required to keep shareholders happy. The latter Williamson takes to be a fixed sum, as in the Baumol model. Williamson also assumes that S is a variable in the demand function operating like advertising and product variables to increase the demand for the firm's product at any given price (they could alternatively be treated as an input into the production process). With this particular formulation, for each level of S a specific demand and marginal revenue curve can be derived and the firm's objective requires that, at the chosen level of S, marginal cost equals marginal revenue.

We can, therefore, first of all find the profit that is obtained at each level of S when marginal cost and marginal revenue are equal. We can then subtract the profits required by shareholders to obtain the value of D at each level of S and plot the relationship between S and D. The latter will be of the form illustrated by the curve DP_1 in Figure 16.2, rising to a maximum at the profit-maximizing value of S, which is S_0 in the diagram, and declining thereafter. If then, as seems reasonable to suppose, the firm's utility function can be represented by conventional, downward-sloping, convex-to-the-origin indifference curves, its optimum position is at T_1, where one of the firm's indifference curves is tangential to DP_1, involving the employment of S_1 staff and discretionary profits of D_1.[1] Moreover, it can be seen that, as long as the indifference curves are downward sloping (that is, an increase in S yields positive utility), the preferred position must involve more than the profit-maximizing level of staff, and, as long as they add to demand, a greater output.

Having derived the firm's optimum position we can go on to consider the effects on that position of particular changes. Of particular interest in that respect is, as in the previous model, the effect of a tax on profits, because again such a tax is predicted to have some effect on the firm's position. In this

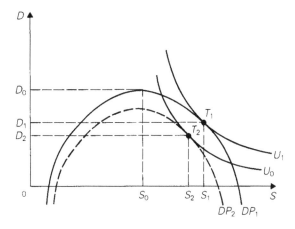

Figure 16.2

case, however, a distinction can be made between a lump-sum tax and a proportional one.

In Figure 16.2 the effect of a lump-sum tax is simply to displace the curve DP_1 downwards by the amount of the tax, for example to the position indicated by the dashed curve DP_2, and is thus similar to the effect on the consumer of a simple income change. In the diagram, the firm's preferred position moves to T_2, where the indifference curve U_0 is tangential to DP_2. The precise effect on S and D thus clearly depends on the exact form of the curves, but so long as both variables in the utility function are normal, which seems a reasonable assumption, T_2 must be below and to the left of T_1, suggesting a reduction in both S and D. In addition, the reduction in S leads, in Williamson's formulation, to some reduction in the demand for the firm's product and hence its output. So, again, contrary to the traditional model, this model predicts an output change as a result of a lump-sum profits tax.

The same is also the case with a proportional tax on profits, except that the direction of change is more ambiguous. The effects of a proportionate tax on profits on the DP curve, at least where D is positive, is indicated by the dashed curve DP_3 in Figure 16.3. It will be noted that this is flatter than DP_1 (the curve in the no-tax situation) because, in absolute terms, the greater the profits the higher the tax payments. This means that the proportional profits tax has a *substitution* as well as an income effect. Further, since the effect is to reduce the cost of staff relative to discretionary profits (staff costs being deductible for tax purposes), the substitution effect tends to *increase* the firm's use of staff. The income effect, however, operates as in the previous case (again assuming staff is a normal good) in the opposite direction. The net effect therefore depends on the relative sizes of the two effects. The diagram illustrates the case where the income effect dominates, and hence where the tax leads to a reduction in the staff employed (and hence in

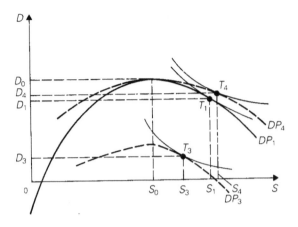

Figure 16.3

output). The opposite result is, of course, equally likely, but the important point is that the Williamson model again points to the possibility of an output change.

We have looked at the model in a fairly simplified form, but clearly it can be elaborated and its supporters argue that it does offer useful insights into the behaviour of the firm. Moreover, the fact that the predictions of the theory differ from those of the traditional model would seem to provide a useful basis for testing the model empirically. However, in practice it is not easy to measure with any degree of precision the relevant variables. Nevertheless, Williamson (1963), in one of his early papers on this approach, did carry out some empirical tests that he thought were at least suggestive of some support for his hypothesis.

Some problems and developments

Both the Baumol and Williamson models can be criticized because they provide no explanation of what determines the shareholders' required level of profits. In an attempt to fill this gap Yarrow (1975) has argued that the shareholders in general are interested in maximizing the value of their holdings, which requires the firm to maximize its profits, and that the main obstacle preventing them from forcing firms to act in line with their preferences is the cost of mobilizing shareholders to vote for directors pledged to follow profit-maximizing policies or of organizing takeovers by more profit-oriented concerns. In practice, the magnitude of these costs may be somewhat uncertain but, if they can be denoted by M, the minimum level of profits required to forestall hostile action by shareholders is $\pi^* - M$ where π^* is the maximum profits attainable. As soon as actual profits fall below this critical level it becomes worthwhile for the shareholder to act because the expected gains, in terms of higher profits, exceed the costs, but so long as they remain above this level such action is not worthwhile. Discretionary profits for any level of S can then be expressed as

$$D = \pi_{act} - (\pi^* - M), \qquad (16.2)$$

where π_{act} are the actual profits earned.

This modification has a significant effect on the predictions of the Williamson model, particularly that relating to the effect of a lump-sum tax on profits. Whilst such a tax obviously reduces the profits obtainable at any value of S by the amount of the tax (T), it also reduces the required level of profits (which is now $(\pi^* - T - M)$) by the same amount because $\pi^* - T$ is now the maximum profit attainable. The expression for discretionary profits, therefore, can be written as

$$D = (\pi_{act} - T) - (\pi^* - T - M),$$

but the tax terms cancel out to produce

$$D = \pi_{act} - (\pi^* - M),$$

which is the same as (16.2).

This means that the curve DP_1 in Figure 16.2 remains unaffected by the tax and the firm can continue with the combination of S and D at T_1. The prediction of the model, that a lump-sum profits tax has no effect on the firm's output, now turns out, therefore, to be the same as in the profit-maximizing case.

The case of a proportional tax is a bit more complex and is perhaps best explained with the help of a numerical example. Thus, in Table 16.1, the first column of figures represents the situation in which profits are maximized. The figures in the second column show the case where higher expenditure on S reduces profits to 80 and in the third to 60. If $M = 40$, the minimum profits required by shareholders in the no-tax situation are 60, leaving the discretionary profits shown in the third row of the table. The second part of the table shows the effect on the figures of introducing a profits tax of 20 per cent. Since this reduces the maximum profits attainable by 20, it reduces the minimum required level of profits to 40 and gives the managers more discretionary profits in cases 2 and 3. This extra discretionary profit arises because, when the firm reduces its profits by increasing its expenditure on S, it reduces its tax liability and, so long as shareholders' requirements are already met, the resultant tax savings add to discretionary profit.

More generally, the expression for discretionary profits taking account of the proportional tax is

Table 16.1

		1	2	3
(i)	*No profits tax*			
	Gross profits (*G*)	100	80	60
	Required profits when *M* = 40 (*R* = 100 − *M*)	60	60	60
	Discretionary profits (*D* = *G* − *R*)	40	20	0
(ii)	*With 20% profits tax* (*t* = 0.2)			
	Gross profits (*G*)	100	80	60
	Net profits *N* = *G*(1 − *t*))	80	64	48
	Required profits (*R* = 80 − *M*)	40	40	40
	Discretionary profits (*D* = *N* − *R*)	40	24	8

$$D = \pi_{act}(1 - t) - [\pi^*(1 - t) - M]$$

$$= [\pi_{act} - (\pi^* - M)] + [\pi^* - \pi_{act}]t,$$

which is the same as (16.2) when $\pi_{act} = \pi^*$, but *increases* as t increases when $\pi_{act} < \pi^*$.

In diagrammatic terms, therefore, the effect is to produce a new discretionary profits curve like DP_4 in Figure 16.3 lying above DP_1, except at the latter's maximum point, rather than below. This removes some of the ambiguity from the earlier prediction because the income and substitution effects underlying the move to the new preferred position of T_4 both operate to increase the level of S.

However, whilst it is possible in this way to refine the specification of the model, a more fundamental weakness of the whole approach adopted in these managerial models (which also applies to traditional models) is that it assumes all parties to be well informed about the opportunities available to the firm. In practice, of course, even managers are unlikely to have accurate information about all the firm's activities, and shareholders are likely to be considerably less informed. In fact, the firm provides a good example of what are referred to as **principal–agent** problems.

Within a firm the relevant principals are the owners of the firm (the shareholders) and the agents are the managers who run the firm on behalf of the principals. An important feature of principal–agent problems, which is particularly relevant to the firm, is that there is **asymmetric information**, in that the principal knows rather less about the situation facing the firm than his 'agent'. This provides the agent with an opportunity to pursue his own objectives, but it also provides the principals with an incentive to seek ways of influencing and controlling the behaviour of management. As we have seen, managers' decisions can be affected by minimum profit requirements, but another possible approach is through the negotiation of contracts that provide an incentive to pursue objectives more in line with those of the principals or shareholders. This is another area in which much work has been done by economists in recent years.[2] Unfortunately, space does not permit us to consider it further here, but the reader may well meet it again in more advanced courses.

Models of satisficing behaviour

One related problem arising from all this, which we have already hinted at in various places, is that, when the full range of decision variables available to the firm is taken into account, finding their optimal values, whether from the point of view of profit maximization or more general utility maximization, becomes quite a formidable computational task. In addition, a firm's knowledge of all the relevant relationships, particularly with respect to the form of its demand function and the effect on it of advertising and product changes, is likely to be extremely rudimentary. In these circumstances it has been argued that firms may be content with **satisficing** rather than maximizing behaviour and, following the work of Simon (see particularly Simon, 1955 and 1959), a number of models have been developed along these lines.

At the heart of satisficing models lies the proposition that firms are more concerned with staying in business than with achieving some ideal outcome. Since the managers operate in a highly uncertain world and cannot cope simultaneously with all of the variables that need to be controlled, they prefer to play safe, adopting a set of yardsticks that promise reasonably satisfactory profits in the long term, and a maximum of stability in relations with customers, suppliers and competitors. There is, understandably, an enormous range of variables that can be combined in a satisficing model. One that almost always appears is survival, and there is considerable reference to security, safety margins and liquidity. In order to illustrate how such a model is constructed we have chosen to sketch out the Margolis 'deliberative' model (derived from Margolis, 1958).

The Margolis deliberative model

According to Margolis, the objective of profit maximization is rarely attainable because uncertainty and ignorance are omnipresent. When management choose to pursue a particular line of action they are aware that a more profitable choice might well exist. However, they do not feel it worth the effort to discover the most profitable choice of action because their primary concern is to protect themselves from the unknown while seeking ever-higher profits.

Management behaviour is, however, rational rather than random or imitative when due allowance is made for the need to make decisions under conditions of less than perfect foresight. By restricting themselves to the pursuit of satisfactory rather than maximum profits, management are able to concentrate upon known facts such as actual sales, prices and inventory movements. They are then able to fix their profit objective (aspiration) in the light of these facts at a realistic and attainable level. The profit aspiration level is determined by two principal criteria. In the first place it must be high enough to assure the continued survival of the firm, and in the second place it must be equal to, or greater than, current normal profits. The aspiration level therefore flexes upwards over time.

Now, where an objective is expressed in the form of an aspiration level its attainment can result from the pursuit of a whole range of alternative courses of action. Which alternative happens to be chosen by management depends, for example, upon the background of staff and the firm's administrative structure, but primarily upon the firm's current experience. The outcome of the firm's activities in one period provides hard information about market conditions, which can be carried forward to form the basis of decisions made in the ensuing period. In this manner, an ever-increasing pool of knowledge can be built up within the firm that permits sequential decision-making based exclusively upon past and present production and marketing data. Not unnaturally, the greatest emphasis is placed upon the most recent data since these are the most certain guide to future outcomes.

Firms are understandably anxious to avoid those courses of action that might cause the firm to sustain heavy losses. Margolis argues that business conventions, which tend to emphasize relationships with known outcomes, are useful devices for the elimination of potentially disastrous courses of action. Such conventions are admittedly 'inefficient' in the sense that they restrict management's scope for action in the pursuit of profit maximization, but this inefficiency is to be regarded as the price paid to reduce uncertainty. Margolis goes on to illustrate how such business conventions can be employed to good effect by reference to break-even charts. He argues that management do not have the necessary information for the accurate estimation of marginal cost and marginal revenue curves. What they have instead is a forecast based upon current prices, sales and inventories, and strategic rules based upon past experience. Figure 16.4 illustrates a conventional break-even chart, containing linear cost and revenue functions, which are based upon the assumption that both total cost and total revenue increase at a constant rate in line with rising output levels. Each distinct revenue curve is based upon a different constant selling price, the steepness of the curve increasing in line with increases in the selling price. Profits are measured as the vertical distance between a given revenue curve and the cost curve at any output level.

At any constant selling price there is a maximum quantity that can potentially be sold. Potential sales obviously decline as price rises. Assume initially that the firm sets a price P_1 equal to the slope of OR_1 in the expectation (without accurate knowledge of the demand curve) of selling Q_1.

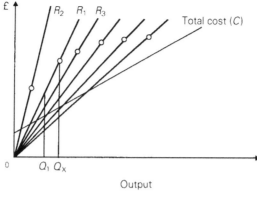

Output

Figure 16.4

In the event it discovers that at price P_1 there is excess demand for its product, as indicated by the distance Q_1Q_x in the diagram.

If the firm is meeting its initial profit aspiration level at price P_1, it may then raise its aspiration level in recognition of the excess demand at the prevailing price. Clearly, profits can be increased, but the unresolved question is whether to raise the price, to lower the price or to leave it unchanged and expand output. In the case of a price increase, the major difficulty is that the exact position of the demand curve along its upper reaches is unknown to the firm, and the possibility exists that, at the chosen price, sales will turn out to be lower than anticipated, hence leading to a decline in profits. On the other hand, there are negligible risks associated with a simple expansion of output at the prevailing price, until the existing demand at that price is fully satisfied.

Pursuit of this latter policy enables the revised aspiration level to be met. However, the increased profit level thereby comes to be regarded over time as no more than satisfactory, and a further increase in the aspiration level will be adjudged desirable. Since demand is fully satisfied at the prevailing price P_1, profits can only be increased via either a price increase or a price decrease. In order to distinguish the preferred alternative one begins by measuring the existing profit level in Figure 16.4, given by the vertical distance between OR_1 and C at output Q_x. One can then find the output levels that yield the same profit at prices P_2 (along OR_2) and P_3 (along OR_3). These output levels are indicated as Q_2 and Q_3 respectively in Figure 16.5. Since the price–output combinations identified in the diagram yield the same level of profits, they lie on the same iso-profits curve, which is shown as the curve π_x in the diagram. Now whilst the firm may not know precisely what happens to its demand curve at prices above and below P_1, it may have sufficient information at its disposal to make a judgement as to whether the loss of sales from an increase in price to P_2 is likely to be less than Q_xQ_2, in which case it will increase its profits, or whether it is likely to be greater. Similarly, it might be able to come to a view on whether the extra sales from a reduction in price are likely to be

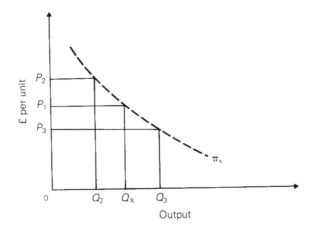

Figure 16.5

greater or less than Q_xQ_3 and thus whether it will yield more or less profits. It can then decide whether and how to alter its price on the basis of these judgements.

However, there are obvious limitations upon the extent to which profits can be increased by repeated adjustments in price. Margolis therefore argues that a firm will increasingly concentrate upon changing the ingredients of the marketing operation. One obvious course of action is to redesign the existing product and to market it as a range of products of varying qualities at different prices. This can prove more profitable than changing the price of a single product because it enables the firm to exploit the different sections of the demand curve that are sequentially discovered. It can also reduce the risk implicit in altering the price of a product when the exact shape of the demand curve is unknown. In Figure 16.6, the firm sells Q_x at price P_1 and subsequently introduces a poorer-quality variant of the same product at price P_2. Assuming that as many people as before continue to buy the original product, the total revenue curve now kinks at point Y and proceeds along YZ.

If some customers switch from the original to the cheaper variant of the product, then the revenue curve simply kinks below point Y along OR_1. This strategy is clearly more profitable than the equivalent volume of sales at price P_2 (along OR_2). Furthermore, it remains profitable for the firm to introduce further variants of the product provided that the slope of the resulting kinked total revenue curve always remains greater than the slope of the total cost curve.

An additional benefit of this latter course of action is that customers may well prove more amenable to quality changes than to price changes in a uniform product. Furthermore, any given variant of the basic model can always be withdrawn from production should its introduction lead to a reduction in overall profitability.

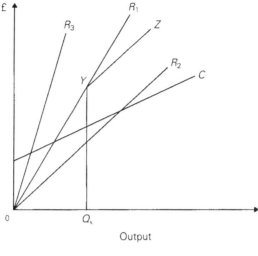

Figure 16.6

The behavioural theory of the firm

Many of the ideas introduced in satisficing models reappear in a rather different context in what is known as the behavioural theory of the firm. Unlike managerial and satisficing models, all of which are essentially substitutes for traditional models, behavioural theory is viewed as a complementary model. Traditional models exist in order to explain the way in which the price system functions as a mechanism for allocating resources among markets, but largely ignore resource allocation within the firm. Behavioural models, on the other hand, focus upon the internal decision-making structure of the firm.

Rather than taking the firm's objective as given, behavioural models set out to analyse the process whereby firms decide upon their objectives. These are multiple rather than single, since firms consist of individuals who do not fit into neat little slots, but rather have needs and goals that do not tally exactly with those of the employing institutions. However, in any situation where multiple objectives exist, the need arises to strike some kind of balance between them, and this implies the existence of conflict. Behavioural theorists are interested to discover how such conflict arises, what form it takes, and how it is resolved.

One of the best-known models, by Cyert and March (1963), views the firm as run by salaried managers who have certain personal objectives that they pursue in their day-to-day work. These objectives encompass doing well for themselves, their departments and their firm. However, desire to promote their own departments, even at the expense of other departments within the firm, inevitably creates conflicts both between individuals and between

273

departments. Such conflicts clearly need to be resolved in order to run the firm more or less to everyone's satisfaction.

In practice, the conflict situation will encompass more than just the managerial group, since the latter are not freed from all external constraints upon their behaviour. Cyert and March accordingly introduce the concept of the **coalition**, which is defined to include everyone who has reason to expect anything from the firm. The composition of the coalition varies over time, but in general incorporates the firm's managers, shareholders, customers, employees and creditors. Cyert and March go on to suggest that most of the coalition members tend to take no great interest in the specific objectives of the firm provided that they receive a satisfactory stream of *side-payments* from the firm. In other words, the managers of a modern corporation can buy off interference from shareholders, employees and customers, and thus remove a possible source of conflict in the setting of the firm's objectives.

However, this still leaves conflicts between individual managers and between departments within the firm. The idea of side-payments is again useful, because certain managers can be rewarded with higher salaries or greater prestige in return for their agreement not to participate in the decision-making process. Nevertheless, most managers will expect to have a hand in decision-making, especially when the annual budget plans are up for discussion or when the firm is considering branching out in new directions. Cyert and March consider that bargaining over objectives will generate one set of objectives that are *quantitative* and another set that are *qualitative*.

Qualitative objectives have no operational content, and do not require specific action to be taken if they are to be fulfilled. They are intended to be bland and general so that no one can disagree with them. Quantitative objectives, however, need to be translated into specific courses of action. Cyert and March suggest that the following five goals are the most important:

(1) the production goal, concerned primarily with keeping machinery fully utilized and with minimizing disruptive change-overs from one product to another;
(2) the inventory goal, concerned primarily with avoiding stock shortages of either raw materials or finished goods;
(3) the level of sales goal, defined in terms either of output or of revenue;
(4) the market share goal, concerned primarily with the firm's standing in its various markets relative to its competitors;
(5) the profit goal, concerned primarily with satisfying the ongoing need to pay dividends and to fund the firm's future growth, and serving as a guide to the firm's performance.

Production managers want to plan long production runs in order to ease production scheduling and to keep down costs. But if sales are poor this results in large stocks of finished goods, which pleases the sales force because they will be able to meet new orders directly from stock, but which conflicts with the interests of the financial managers who regard the holding of excessive inventories as unprofitable since it ties up valuable working capital. To a greater or lesser extent all managers are supportive of the profit goal, but in the majority of cases they are willing to sacrifice some part of potential profit in order to achieve other goals.

There is an **aspiration level** associated with each of the quantitative objectives outlined above. An aspiration level signifies a desire on the part of management to improve upon, repeat, or fall short of the previous year's performance during the following year. Given the variability of the environment within which the firm has to operate one might well expect aspiration levels to fluctuate widely over time. Cyert and March, however, expect aspiration levels to fluctuate relatively little. They argue that the stability of aspirations arises largely from the methods by which decisions are taken within corporations. There is an observed tendency for corporations to become bureaucratic and to establish sets of written rules concerning the conduct of substantial areas of the firm's operations. These rules are laid down after lengthy discussions by committees, and, once established, tend to be treated with some reverence, despite the fact that the firm's environment may be undergoing rapid change. These rules are often financial in nature, appearing in the form of budgets and operating standards that greatly constrain the scope of the individual manager for unorthodox behaviour.

However, aspirations are not necessarily unrealistic. No manager will want to commit himself to targets that are almost certain to be beyond his reach, nor will management allow subordinates to commit themselves to targets that present no real challenge. Hence, if a firm produces an unusually good or bad performance, extra care will be taken to adjust aspirations accordingly. This is of much greater importance where the firm falls well short of meeting one or more of its quantitative goals, and when this happens **search behaviour** will be instigated in order to discover the cause of the failure. There is much less likelihood that a firm will search out ways of improving its efficiency so long as targets are, by and large, being met, despite the fact that aspirations may frequently fall well below what could potentially be achieved were the firm to respond to smaller variations in market conditions. This in turn is likely to lead to inconsistencies between objectives, since the response to a crisis situation is generally going to produce much larger adjustments to those objectives that are way off target than to those that remain broadly satisfactory.

In circumstances in which aspiration levels mostly change slowly, but in which the firm's environment fluctuates a good deal, one would expect the firm to perform either considerably better or considerably worse than it had anticipated. By implication there must either be excess resources to absorb or a shortfall to be made good. This is dealt with through the concept of **organizational slack**. Cyert and March argue that members of the coalition are often paid in excess of their opportunity costs. Wages, salaries and profits are generally higher than they need to be in order to keep managers, workers and shareholders happy. Alternatively, prices may be kept below what the market will bear. This is due in part to the difficulties inherent in trying to assess accurately the correct level at which various financial magnitudes should be set, but it may also reflect an indifference on the part of the firm to holding down costs to their lowest possible level.

There are thus several unutilized sources of profits: first, in the surplus payments to coalition members; secondly, where factor inputs of all types are not being utilized either fully or efficiently; and thirdly, where the firm pursues sub-optimal pricing, production or marketing strategies. Thus, at times when the firm does much better than expected, it allows slack to develop so as to absorb the difference between aspiration and actual performance. Should the firm subsequently fall upon hard times it can make up the difference between aspiration and actual performance by eliminating previously accumulated slack. In a sense, therefore, slack is simultaneously both desirable because it provides a cushion to fall back upon in hard times, and undesirable because it is created through inefficiencies of various kinds.

We can conclude by applying the logic of the preceding discussion to the five quantitative goals set out above. The firm has an aspiration level with regard to each individual goal. Although the goals are incompatible, it is possible to satisfy them all simultaneously provided that the firm is satisficing rather than profit maximizing. The holding of excessive inventories does not necessarily conflict with the profit goal, although it clearly does so at times when the profit goal is not being achieved. In the latter event, search behaviour will be initiated and continued until some source of slack has been identified and eliminated, thereby increasing profits into line with aspirations. However, no real attempt is likely to be made to eliminate more slack than is strictly necessary in order to meet the profits goal. The firm sub-optimizes at all times.

Notes

1 Mathematically, the firm's optimum position is where
$U = U(S,D)$ is maximized subject to

$$R(Q, S) - C(Q) - w_S S - D \geq \pi_R,$$

where $R(Q, S)$ is the firm's total revenue, $C(Q)$ is its production cost, w_S is the cost per unit of S and π_R is the minimum required profit. Using the Lagrangian multiplier approach it can be shown that this requires

$$R_Q = C_Q \quad (\text{or } MC = MR)$$

and
$$- U_S/U_D = (R_S - w_S),$$

where U_S/U_D is the marginal rate of substitution between S and D and $(R_S - w_S)$ is the extra D available when an extra unit of S is used (which is negative on the downward-sloping section of DP_1).

2   For a useful survey of the principal–agent literature see Rees (1985).

Exercises

16.1 'It is only necessary to consider alternatives to the traditional assumption that firms aim to maximize their profits when analysing the behaviour of firms *not* subject to vigorous competition.' Explain and discuss this statement.

16.2 The managers of firm A seek to maximize the firm's revenue subject to earning the 'normal' profits incorporated in its average cost curve. If that average cost curve over the relevant range of output is an upward-sloping straight line, compare:

(i)   its output and price, and
(ii) its response to a subsidy of *s* per unit

with that of a profit-maximizing firm with the same cost and revenue functions.

16.3 Suppose the managers of the firm in Exercise 16.2 above were replaced by managers with a utility function

$$U = U(Q, D),$$

where Q is output and D discretionary profit. Assuming the required profits are again as in Exercise 16.2, compare:

(i)   the managers' preferred price and output with those in Exercise 16.2 and,
(ii) the firm's response to the subsidy of *s* per unit with your answers to Exercise 16.2(ii).

16.4 Think of a plausible alternative managerial utility function and explore, as far as you can, its implications for the behaviour of the firm.

16.5 Evaluate the potential role of *satisficing* approaches to the theory of the firm.

CHAPTER SEVENTEEN
THE FIRM'S DEMAND FOR INPUTS IN COMPETITIVE MARKETS

Introduction

So far, we have been analysing the behaviour of firms, and the effects of differing competitive conditions on that behaviour, largely from the point of view of the firm as a supplier of goods and services. Equally important, however, is the role of firms on the demand side of markets, which arises because of their need to buy goods and services to use as inputs into the production process. Clearly, a firm's behaviour in input markets cannot be independent of its behaviour in product markets, since ultimately the quantity of inputs it buys is determined by the level of output it wishes to produce. Indeed, analysing the behaviour of firms in input markets really involves no more than looking at a different aspect of the behaviour that has been the focus of attention in previous chapters. Nevertheless, it does provide an opportunity to extend the discussion to some of the more specific features of input markets and to take into account some competitive situations that we have not so far considered. Before getting on to that, however, we need first to develop the more basic analysis of the profit-maximizing firm's demand for inputs when it operates in competitive input markets.

The link between the behaviour of firms in product markets and their behaviour in input markets is most clearly seen in the case of profit-maximizing firms. So far, given that we have characterized both costs and revenues as functions of output, we have also defined profit (the difference between the two) as a function of output and expressed the profit-maximizing conditions in terms of output variables. However, since the firm's production function relates output to the quantity of inputs employed, both revenue and costs can be expressed as functions of inputs. Profits can, therefore, be defined in similar terms, and profit-maximizing conditions can be expressed in terms of input variables. Hence, an important part of our task in this chapter is to identify these conditions and to examine some of their implications.

The analysis of a firm's behaviour in input markets might appear to be intrinsically more complex than the analysis of its behaviour in product markets, since, whilst firms may, as we have assumed in much of the preceding discussion, produce a single product, without exception they all use a number of inputs – different types of labour and materials, a variety of types of equipment, and so on. Indeed, as we have seen, the very notion of production involves inputs being combined in order to produce an output. The analysis of a firm's behaviour in input markets ideally, there-fore, should take into account the interaction between the various inputs involved in production and the need to make simultaneous decisions about what to buy in input markets. We consider how this can be done later in the chapter, but initially, in order to establish certain basic principles and ideas, we consider briefly the somewhat unrealistic case of a firm with only one variable input.

Profit maximization with one variable input

The conditions under which profits are maximized when expressed in terms of a single variable input are basically similar to those applying to the case with a single output variable. Just as profit maximization requires the costs incurred in producing the marginal unit of output to be equal to the additional revenue obtained from selling that output, it also requires the cost incurred when an extra unit of input is employed to be equal to the revenue obtained from selling the extra output produced. Similarly, just as the second-order conditions for profit maximization, when expressed in terms of output, require the marginal cost of output to be increasing at a faster rate (or declining at a slower rate) than marginal revenue, the same applies to the relationship between the cost and revenue associated with the employment of extra units of inputs.

The extra output produced when an additional unit of input is employed is simply the marginal product of that input. Hence, the additional revenue obtained from selling that output is the marginal product of the input multiplied by the marginal revenue of output, which is a measure of the rate at which revenue per unit of output is increasing at the margin. Multiplying these two magnitudes together produces what is called the **marginal revenue product** of the input, so profit maximization requires, provided the second-order condition noted above is satisfied, the marginal revenue product of an input to be equal to its marginal cost. Hence, if Y is the variable input used in the production of X, the basic (first-order) profit-maximizing condition can be expressed as

$$MRP_Y = MP_Y \cdot MR_X = MIC_Y, \qquad (17.1)$$

where MRP_Y, MP_Y and MIC_Y are the marginal revenue product, marginal product and marginal cost of input Y respectively and MR_X is the marginal revenue of product X.

If the firm operates in competitive input markets, it is a price taker in those markets and can buy as much as it desires at the ruling market price. The marginal cost of any input is then equal to its price and we can write condition (17.1) as

$$MP_Y \cdot MR_X = P_Y,$$

where P_Y is the price of input Y. This latter expression can then be seen to be formally identical to the standard condition for a profit-maximizing output, since if we divide both sides of the equation by MP_Y we obtain

$$MR_X = P_Y/MP_Y,$$

and it will be recalled that P_Y/MP_Y is equal to the marginal cost of output (MC_X). Hence, as suggested in the introduction to this chapter, in looking at the firm's profit-maximizing employment of inputs rather than output, we are simply looking at profit maximization from a different angle.

It is also no more difficult to illustrate the conditions under which (17.1) is met as in the corresponding output case. With the firm a price taker in the market for input Y and the marginal cost of input Y equal to its (constant) price, a marginal input cost curve showing the relationship between the quantity of Y employed and its marginal cost can be represented by a horizontal line. Thus when the price of input Y is R_1 in Figure 17.1, the relevant marginal cost curve is MIC_1. In the same diagram, the marginal revenue product curve for Y (MRP) is shown as a mainly downward-sloping curve, and the reason for this is also straightforward. Given that the marginal revenue product of Y is the marginal product of Y multiplied by the marginal revenue of X, the shape of MRP will depend on how both behave as Y increases. However, as we saw in Chapter 9 above, the law of diminishing returns suggests that when the quantity of one input is increased while the quantities of all other inputs remain unchanged, the marginal product will sooner or later decline. In addition, we also know that the marginal revenue of output is constant if the firm is also a price taker in its product market, or declining as output, and thus the use of the variable input, increases when the firm faces a downward-sloping product demand curve. We may therefore conclude that the marginal revenue product itself must decline as the employment of Y increases, at least when the marginal product of Y declines, and that the marginal revenue product curve can be drawn as in Figure 17.1.

It is, however, important to remember that reflected in this curve are both the technical conditions of production, which determine the rate at which the marginal product declines, and the conditions in the market for the final product. The importance of the latter reflects the fact that the firm's demand for inputs is essentially a *derived demand* and it would not be worthwhile for

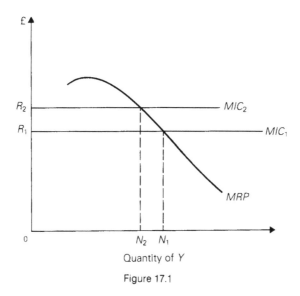

Figure 17.1

the firm to employ any inputs unless sufficient revenue for the sale of its products could be expected.

With the marginal revenue product curve in Figure 17.1, however, and MIC_1 the marginal input cost curve, it can be seen from where they intersect that condition (17.1) is satisfied when N_1 of Y is employed. Further, since at this level of employment the marginal revenue product is falling at a faster rate than marginal input cost, we can confirm that N_1 is the profit-maximizing level of employment of Y. Moreover, the diagram suggests that if the price of Y increases to R_2, the marginal input cost curve becomes MIC_2, and the firm's profit-maximizing employment of Y falls from N_1 to N_2, where MRP intersects MIC_2.

It would seem, therefore, that MRP can also be taken to be the firm's demand curve for input Y. However, there are two qualifications to be made to that conclusion. First, it would only apply if the firm made no consequential adjustment to the quantities of the other inputs it used. If it adjusted them also, then those adjustments would have some effect on the position of the marginal revenue product curve for Y and thus on its optimal employment. The effect that this might have on the firm's position is considered in the following sections. The second qualification arises from the fact that, in the case where the firm is a price taker in the product market, the marginal revenue product curve is constructed on the assumption of a constant product price. If, however, an input price change faced by one firm is also experienced by all of its competitors in the product market, they would all be induced to adjust their use of Y and as a result all would be making some change to their output. In these circumstances the market price of the firms' product may also be affected, with further consequential effects on the profit-maximizing position of our individual firm. The relevant adjustments can be traced in the context of the restricted situation illustrated in Figure 17.1, but, to avoid undue repetition, detailed discussion is deferred until they can be put in the context of the more multivariate analysis of the following sections.

Profit maximization with two variable inputs

One important feature of profit maximization that provides a useful starting point for the analysis of this section is that it must involve producing whatever output is produced at minimum cost. This provides a starting point because the cost of producing any output is simply the sum of the cost of all the inputs employed in producing that output, and we have already examined the conditions under which such input costs are minimized. As is often the case, extending the analysis to incorporate two variable inputs is sufficient to reveal most of the features of the multi-input situation whilst keeping the analysis within the scope of diagrammatic techniques. Moreover, it will be recalled from the discussion of Chapter 9 above that, in the two-input case, cost-minimizing input combinations can be characterized diagrammatically, as in Figure 17.2.

In this diagram, M_0N_0, M_1N_1 and M_2N_2 are constant cost lines representing the input combinations that can be obtained for different given outlays, whilst Q_0, Q_1 and Q_2 are isoquants showing the input combinations that can be used to produce their respective levels of output. The input combinations that minimize the costs of production Q_0, Q_1 and Q_2 are then located at T_0, T_1 and T_2, where the isocost curves are tangential to the isoquants. The scale expansion path (*SEP*) drawn through all such points of tangency then indicates how a cost-minimizing firm would vary its use of inputs as it increases the (scale of) its output. Since a profit-maximizing firm needs to minimize its costs, it must operate at some point on this curve. One of our tasks, therefore, in seeking to analyse the implications for the firm's demand for inputs of profit-maximizing behaviour in the two-input case, is to find some means of identifying the point on this scale expansion path at which profits are maximized, and thence to analyse the effects of changes in market conditions on that point.

The conditions under which profits are maximized in this two-input case simply involve an extension of the conditions applying in the single-input case and require, subject to the relevant second-order conditions being satisfied,[1] the marginal cost of each input to be equal to its marginal revenue product. If, for the time being, we concentrate on the case in which the firm is a price taker in all the markets in which it operates (which would be the case if all these markets were perfectly competitive), we can denote the conditions for maximum profit as

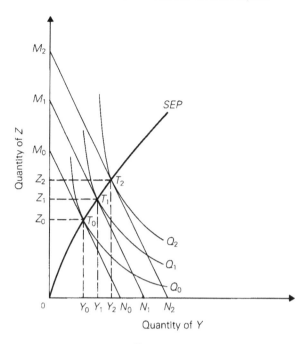

Figure 17.2

$$p \cdot MP_Y = r_Y \qquad (17.2)$$

and
$$p \cdot MP_Z = r_Z \qquad (17.3)$$

where MP_Y and MP_Z are the marginal products of X and Y respectively. Of these conditions, (17.2) can again be illustrated by a point in a diagram like Figure 17.1 above where the marginal revenue product curve for input Y (MRP_Y) cuts a horizontal marginal input cost curve from above. However, we also need to consider how this position might be affected by varying the quantity of Z.

In Chapter 9 above, it was suggested that increasing the quantity of Z would displace the total product curves for Y, in Figure 9.2, upwards. However, it needn't necessarily increase the marginal product of Y, reflected in the slope of the total product curve. In fact we can distinguish between the **complementary** case, in which increasing the use of Z increases the marginal product of Y, and the so-called **anti-complementary** case, in which an increase in Z reduces the marginal product of Y. In most cases inputs are likely to be complementary (think, for example, of the effect on the marginal product of five men digging a trench equipped with only four shovels when a fifth shovel is found), but anti-complementarity can arise when inputs are very close substitutes. For example, the employment of more semi-skilled labour in a firm might reduce the productivity at the margin of skilled labour if the semi-skilled workers were to take over some of the latter's tasks.

283

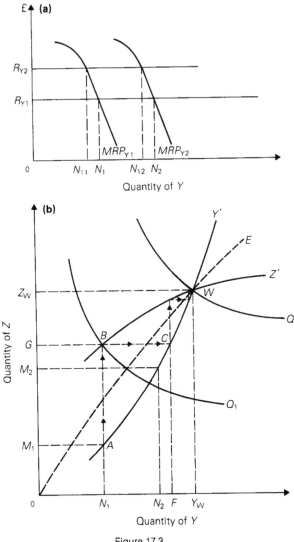

Figure 17.3

In the complementary case, an increase in Z would thus have the effect of pushing the marginal revenue product curve for Y in Figure 17.1 upwards, which would increase the optimal level of employment. The implications of this are shown in more detail in Figure 17.3. In Figure 17.3a, MRP_{Y1} is the marginal revenue product curve for Y when M_1 of Z (in Figure 17.3b) is employed. If R_{Y1} is the price of A, then condition (17.2) above is satisfied when N_1 of Y is employed. If the quantity of Z is now increased (to M_2 in Figure 17.3b), then the marginal revenue product curve for Y is moved upwards and, if its new position is MRP_{Y2}, the quantity of Y needed to satisfy condition (17.2) is increased to N_2. Increasing Z further will have similar effects. Hence the curve Y^* can be traced out, in Figure 17.3b, showing, for each quantity of Z, the optimal quantity of Y, which is, of course, the quantity satisfying condition (17.2). Reversing the process, a similar curve showing the optimal quantity of Z for any quantity of Y, satisfying condition (17.3), can also be traced, and that curve is labelled Z^* in the diagram.

With condition (17.2) satisfied at all points on Y^* and condition (17.3) satisfied at all points on Z^*, both conditions are met at point W where the two curves intersect. W therefore indicates the firm's profit-maximizing position, and the isoquant passing through W, labelled Q_2, indicates the consequent level of output. A check that W lies, as we would expect, on the scale expansion path, shown in Figure 17.3b as the dashed line OE, can be made by dividing (17.2) by (17.3). This gives

$$MP_Y/MP_Z = (MRTS_{YZ}) = r_Y/r_Z,$$

which, it will be recalled, is the distinguishing feature of all points on the scale expansion path, OE.

However, we have so far concentrated on the first-order conditions for profit maximization. The second-order conditions, which distinguish maxima from other possible stationary values, require the marginal revenue products of each input to be declining relative to their marginal cost as before, and, in addition, the slope of Y^* in Figure 17.3b to be greater than the slope of Z^*. This latter requirement can be deduced mathematically,[2] but a more intuitive explanation can be obtained from the diagram. In Figure 17.3b, it can be seen that with N_1 of Y employed, the optimal use of Z would be G. This suggests that if the firm was initially at point A on Y^*, employing M_1 of Z with N_1 of Y, it would be able to increase its profits by following the arrowed path in the diagram to point B, located vertically above A on Z^*, which would require an increase in its use of Z to G. Similarly, having reached B, it would be able to increase its profits further by moving to C, since the optimum quantity of Y to employ with G of Z is F. The process could continue by a series of similar steps until point W is reached. The reader can check for himself, however, that if the relative positions of Y^* and Z^* were reversed, with Z^* having a greater slope than Y^*, a series of similar moves would take the firm away from the point of intersection of the two curves rather than towards it. The profit-maximizing position is thus found only where Y^* intersects Z^* from below, as at W in Figure 17.3b.

The profit-maximizing quantities of inputs in the anti-complementary case can be determined in a similar manner. In fact the only substantial difference is that the curves Y^* and Z^* are negatively sloped, reflecting the adverse effect of an increase of one input on the marginal product of the other. The possibilities in that case are illustrated in Figure 17.6 below, and there again, as in both cases illustrated, as long as Y^* is steeper than Z^* (relative to the

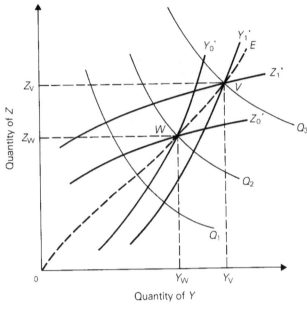

Figure 17.4

horizontal axis), the point of intersection between the two curves determines the profit-maximizing quantities of the two inputs and the required level of output.

The comparative statics of profit maximization

The effects of a product price change

Diagrams like Figure 17.3 above also provide a convenient basis for analysing the effects of various price changes on the firm's position. For example, if the price at which the firm could sell its final product were to increase, the effect in Figure 17.3a would be to displace all the marginal revenue product curves upwards, so that the optimal employment of input Y for any level of Z would be greater. If, therefore, in Figure 17.4, Y_0^* is the curve showing the optimal employment of Y for each quantity of Z at the initial price, the curve showing the same relationship at the new higher product price lies to the right of the old one, for example like Y_1^*. Similar considerations apply to the corresponding curve for input Z, except that it is pushed upwards to Z_1^*. These new curves intersect at V, which is farther along the scale expansion path than the original point of intersection W, and this suggests that the firm increases its use of both inputs and also its output. Moreover the reader can check that the same is normally true in the

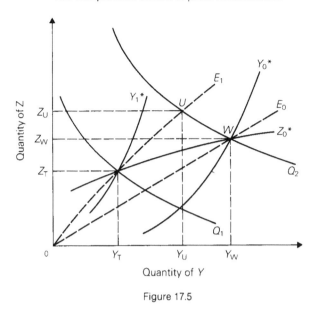

Figure 17.5

anti-complementary case. However, if the adverse effect of one input on the marginal product of the other is a particularly strong one, one of the inputs may be inferior. In that case its use would decline as output increased.

The effects of an input price change
(product price constant)

The effects of an increase in the price of an input can be analysed in similar fashion to that of a product price change, although the greater range of possible outcomes requires this case to be examined in more detail. The complementary case is shown in Figure 17.5. It can be confirmed from Figure 17.3a above that raising the price of input Y from R_{Y1} to R_{Y2} will reduce the optimal employment of Y for any level of Z, and thus move the curve tracing out these optimal employment levels in Figure 17.5 to the left, from Y_0^* to Y_1^*. Nothing has happened to change the optimal employment of Z for any level of Y, so Z_0^* in Figure 17.5 applies both before and after the change. The profit-maximizing position, therefore, moves from W to T, involving less employment of both inputs and also less output. Further, the total change can be disaggregated into two effects, which correspond to the substitution and income effects of consumer theory, but which in this context are referred to as **substitution** and **scale** effects.

The substitution effect shows the effect on the demand for inputs of the input price change if output is kept constant. Thus in the diagram, if the dashed curve OE_1 is the scale expansion path resulting from the new relative prices, the substitution effect of the price change involves a movement along the Q_2 isoquant from W to U, and thus a reduction in the use of Y from Y_W to

Y_U coupled with an offsetting increase in the use of Z from Z_W to Z_U.

The scale effect, corresponding to the consumer's income effect, is then represented by the movement from U to T and involves a reduction in (the scale of) output and a consequent reduction in the quantities of both inputs employed to Y_T and Z_T respectively. It will be noted that both substitution and scale effects operate in the same negative direction on the firm's demand for Y, but in opposite directions on its demand for Z.

The possibilities in the anti-complementary case are illustrated in Figure 17.6. The effect of the increase in the price of Y on the curve showing the optimum quantity of Y associated with each level of Z is exactly as in the previous case, moving it to the left from Y_0^* to Y_1^* in the diagram. Again, therefore, it can be seen that, in both cases illustrated, the profit-maximizing employment of Y falls. We are thus able to predict that a profit-maximizing firm's demand for an input will always fall as its price rises. In contrast to the case of consumer's demand, there appear to be no Giffen-type exceptions to this general result even though we have not ruled out the possibility of inferior inputs. In fact, the main difference between the anti-complementary cases illustrated in Figure 17.6 and the complementary case in Figure 17.5 is in the effect on the demand for the other input, Z, whose price is unchanged. In the latter, the firm's demand for Z falls, but in the anti-complementary cases, illustrated in Figure 17.6, it always rises because of the nature of the scale effect. However, in the anti-complementary case there is some ambiguity in the effect on output. The profit-maximizing output might fall, as in the complementary case, and that is the case illustrated in Figure 17.6a, but on the other hand it could rise, as in Figure 17.6b. It all depends on the slope of the isoquants relative to Z_0^*. If Z_0^* slopes downwards more steeply than the isoquants, then output is increased rather than reduced as a result of the increase in the price of Y.

However, it so happens, for reasons that are not readily susceptible to intuitive explanation, that the seemingly perverse or **regressive** effect on output in Figure 17.6b occurs only when Y is an inferior input.[3] This means that, as the firm increases its output, when it moves along the scale expansion path from U to T its use of Y actually falls. As a result, despite the perverse change in output, the scale effect on the demand for Y is in the same direction as in all other cases, and reinforces the substitution effect. The profit-maximizing firm's demand for any input will therefore always, without exception, vary inversely with its price.

The difference between this case and the corresponding analysis of the individual consumer discussed in Chapter 3 above arises because of the different objective pursued by the consumer, coupled with the budget constraint which constrains him to spend the same total sum of money on goods and services before and after the price change. The profit-maximizing firm does not aim to produce the highest possible output, which would be the diagrammatic equivalent of maximizing utility in the production context. Neither is it normally assumed to be bound by a budget constraint. Indeed,

The comparative statics of profit maximization

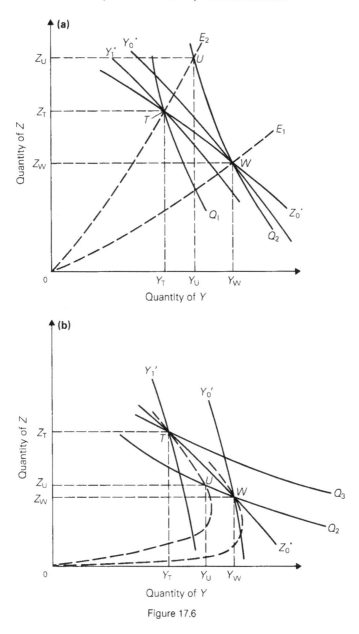

Figure 17.6

the analysis of the profit-maximizing firm implicitly assumes that its total expenditure on inputs can readily be adjusted to the new profit-maximizing level following an input price change, and this might involve an increase or a reduction depending on the particular condition under which the firm operates. The effect of all this, however, is to ensure that, whatever the inputs involved and their relationship to other inputs, the firm's demand for an input will always fall when its price rises. Moreover, we shall see below that this conclusion does not have to be modified when possible product price changes arising from the input price change are taken into account.

The effects of a change in an input price
(product price varying)

In the preceding analysis it has been assumed that the product price would remain unchanged as firms adjust to the input price change. Whilst that would be the case if an individual firm affected by the input price change bought its supplies of the input concerned from a market that was separated from those used by its competitors in the product market, if all or a number of its product market competitors were also affected by the input price change there might be some consequent effect on the product price. To consider the effect of this on the firm's behaviour we will concentrate our attention on the complementary case illustrated initially in Figure 17.5 above and leave the reader to carry out for him/herself the corresponding analysis for the other two cases and observe the differences and similarities.

As we have already seen, Figure 17.5 shows that as the price of input Y rises, with the product price constant, the firm's profit-maximizing position moves from W to T, involving less use of both Y and Z and less output, so we can now consider the effect on T of the likely product price adjustment. If all, or a substantial number, of the firms in the industry are reducing their output in the same way as the firm illustrated in Figure 17.5, there will be a significant reduction in the supply of the firms' product X to the market and consequently an excess demand for it. The price of X therefore rises to restore market equilibrium, with an effect on individual firms similar to that already discussed above. The curves satisfying conditions (17.2) and (17.3) are displaced outwards, moving their point of intersection farther away from the origin along OE_2. This change is illustrated in Figure 17.7, which is essentially the same as Figure 17.5 with the effect of the product price adjustment added. Thus Y_1^* and Z_0^* intersecting at T are the curves satisfying (17.2) and (17.3) after the input price change but at the original product price, whilst Y_2^* and Z_2^* are the corresponding curves reflecting the product price adjustment. These new curves intersect at V, which then indicates the new profit-maximizing demands for the inputs when all the necessary adjustments have been made.

The actual position of V relative to T depends on the price elasticity of demand for the product X, because that determines how much its price needs to rise to restore market equilibrium. The more elastic the demand, the smaller the adjustment would have to be and therefore the closer V would be to T. Indeed, in the limiting case with a perfectly elastic market demand, the product price does not change at all and the profit-maximizing position remains at T. The opposite extreme case involves perfectly inelastic demand and in that case the product price would have to rise sufficiently to induce the

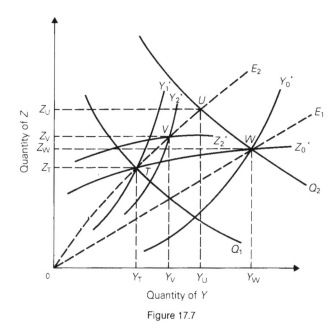

Figure 17.7

firm to produce the same output of X as before any of the price changes. In the case illustrated in Figure 17.7, with the initial position at W, that would involve producing an output of Q_2. In other words, the product price would have to rise sufficiently to take point V to the point of intersection between OE_1 and the Q_2 isoquant at U.

The overall effect of the product price change is thus to offset to some extent the effects of the increase in the input price. In fact, in terms of the substitution and scale effects identified above, the product price change has the effect of reducing the size of the scale effect except when product demand is perfectly elastic. However, even in the extreme case of inelastic product demand where the scale effect is reduced to zero, the firm still ends up employing less of the input whose price has risen than before because of the negative substitution effect. We are thus again able to make an unambiguous prediction that, in competitive markets at least, there must be a reduction in an individual firm's demand for an input whose price rises. However, in the complementary case illustrated in Figure 17.7, the effect on the demand for the other input, Z, is now more ambiguous. It may fall, as when the price of X remains constant, but only if the demand for the final product is sufficiently elastic.

Imperfect competition in the product market

In this final section we note briefly how the analysis of the preceding sections needs to be modified when there is less than perfect competition in the firm's product market but the firm still trades in competitive input markets. In this context, the most straightforward case is where the firm is a monopolist in its product market. In such a case, the required amendments are related entirely to the fact that the firm faces a downward-sloping demand curve for its product and thus also experiences declining marginal revenue when its output increases. The latter is, of course, reflected in the calculation of the marginal revenue products of its inputs, which are obtained by multiplying marginal revenue rather than price by the relevant marginal product, and hence also in the slope of the individual marginal revenue product curves. In addition, the first-order conditions for maximum profit become

$$MR_X \cdot MP_Y = r_Y \qquad (17.4)$$

and
$$MR_X \cdot MP_Z = r_Z \qquad (17.5)$$

and this change will also have some effect on the shape of the curves reflecting these conditions. In particular, in the case where Y and Z are complementary, an increase in the use of Z, which increases the marginal product of Y (MP_Y), will also, because it leads to an increase in output, reduce the marginal revenue of that output (MR_X). If the negative effect on MR_X is proportionately greater than the positive effect on MP_Y, then the marginal revenue product of Y ($= MP_Y.MR_X$) falls rather than rises. The curve reflecting (17.4) will thus be negatively rather than positively sloped, as in the anti-complementary case, and similar considerations might apply to the curve reflecting (17.5). Apart from this, however, the determination of the profit-maximizing position is exactly as in previous cases.

The analysis of the effects of an input price change is also largely as in the competitive case. However, in the monopoly case there is no requirement for any separate consideration of product price adjustments resulting from input price changes. They are already fully accounted for in the marginal revenue component of the marginal revenue curves and are thus fully reflected in the basic curves of the analysis. With oligopoly rather than monopoly in the product market, however, the situation is less clear-cut, as in that case any price adjustments would also reflect the particular oligopolistic strategies the firms were pursuing. However, if the oligopolist's actions were based on a demand curve reflecting an accurate forecast of rivals' reactions, the situation would be identical analytically to that of the monopolist.

Notes

1 If the production function is $q = f(y, z)$, these require its direct second-order partial derivatives, f_{yy} and f_{zz} to be negative (which is the case if their marginal revenue product curves are downward sloping) and

$$f_{yy} \cdot f_{zz} - (f_{yz})^2 > 0.$$

2 The slope of Y^* relative to the horizontal axis is $-f_{yy}/f_{yz}$, whilst the slope of Z^* is $-f_{yz}/f_{zz}$. With f_{yy} and f_{zz} both negative but f_{yz} either positive or negative depending on whether the inputs are complementary or anti-complementary, the condition

$$f_{yy} \cdot f_{zz} - (f_{yz})^2 > 0.$$

requires $\quad -f_{yy}/f_{yz} > -f_{yz}/f_{zz},$

which implies that Y^* must be steeper than Z^*.

3 A necessary condition for these results, which were first pointed out in J. R. Hicks (1946), is that an increase in the use of Z has a proportionately greater negative effect on MP_Y than MP_Z.

Exercises

17.1 A profit-maximizing firm which is a price taker in both input and product markets has only one variable input. Analyse the effects on the firm's use of the variable input and its output of an increase in the price of the input

(i) when the increase in price applies only to that firm

(ii) when the increase applies also to all other producers of the product.

17.2 Show how the response of a firm using one variable input to an increase in the price of that input, when it is a price maker in its product market but a price taker in its input markets, depends on the technical conditions of production and the elasticity of demand for the firm's product.

17.3 Extend the analysis of the effects of an increase in the price of an input in Exercise 17.1 above to the case of a firm with two variable inputs.

17.4 Extend the analysis of the effects of an increase in the price of an input in Exercise 17.2 above to the case of a firm with two variable inputs.

17.5 'With an inferior good a consumer's demand may rise as its price rises but with an inferior input this cannot be the case.' Explain.

CHAPTER EIGHTEEN
IMPERFECTLY COMPETITIVE INPUT MARKETS

Introduction

In the last chapter it was assumed that firms buying inputs were price takers in input markets, which would be the case if the numbers of buyers in those markets was sufficient to ensure reasonably competitive conditions. In this chapter we consider some of the consequences of relaxing that assumption. However, in extending the analysis to imperfectly competitive input markets we need to take into account not only competitive conditions between buyers, but also competitive conditions between sellers. As a preliminary therefore, it is useful to remind outselves of which particular types of economic agent are involved in supplying inputs.

So far as labour inputs are concerned, the predominant suppliers are individual consumers or households. Moreover, it will be recalled from our earlier discussion of labour supply decisions, in Chapter 4, that an individual's supply curve for labour can be either upward sloping, suggesting a willingness to supply more labour at higher wage rates, or backward bending, suggesting the opposite, depending on the strength of the individual's preference for leisure as opposed to more income. Nevertheless, so far as the market as a whole for a particular type of labour is concerned, the effect of any individual's backward-sloping supply curve is likely to be offset by the desire of more people to enter that particular occupation as its wage rate rises relative to that obtainable in other jobs. Whatever the shape of individual supply curves, therefore, the overall market supply curve is still likely to be an upward-sloping one. However, such a supply curve can only be derived in situations where all individuals in a particular labour market are price takers and are thus unable to influence the wage rate on offer. In practice some individuals have unique talents or special skills that enable them to exercise some monopoly power, but, more importantly, many wage rates are determined by collective bargaining between trades unions and either individual firms or employers' organizations. Our discussion, therefore, needs to include some analysis of labour markets and wage determination in situations involving collective bargaining.

Individuals and households are also involved in the supply of other inputs in that they may supply firms with material inputs or professional services. They are also an important source of finance, but undoubtedly the most important sellers of non-labour inputs are other firms. Again, in earlier chapters, we have analysed in some detail the factors determining the terms under which firms are willing to produce and supply to the market particular quantities of goods and services. For example, we have seen that in competitive industries these can be summarized in a supply curve that is definitely upward sloping in the short run, and is probably more likely to be upward sloping in the long run than any other shape, even though it can be expected to be rather more elastic in the long run than in the short run. We have also seen, however, that, when firms have some degree of monopoly power in the markets in which they sell their output, no determinate supply function as such can be defined as firms will seek to use whatever monopoly power they have to exploit the particular demand conditions facing them. The lack of a supply curve in some input markets therefore constitutes another problem to be considered.

In order to impose some sort of order on the discussion, in this chapter we concentrate on the general case of a buyer with some monopoly power in a market faced with competitive sellers who might either be individuals, households or firms. We then consider in the following chapter the more specific problems of the labour market, particularly those arising because of the institution of collective bargaining, together with the related problem of inputs supplied by firms with monopoly powers. Throughout, firms are assumed to be profit-maximizing. It would not be too difficult to extend the analysis to firms with wider utility-maximizing or even satisficing objectives as considered above, but many of the problems arising would not be dissimilar to those arising with profit-maximizing firms.

Monopsonistic buyers with competitive sellers: basic analysis

The term monopoly strictly means a single seller; the corresponding term for the case of a single buyer is **monopsony**. The monopsonistic buyer when faced with competitive sellers is, like a monopoly seller, a price maker rather than a price taker because his decisions affect the market price. Hence if, as suggested above, the aggregate market supply curve of competitive sellers, whether they are households or firms, is an upward-sloping one, as in Figure 18.1a, the monopsonist has to pay a higher price the more of the input he wishes to buy. Now, assuming that the monopsonist cannot discriminate between sellers and has to pay a uniform price for each unit of input, so far as he is concerned the market supply curve (S in the diagram) is his average input cost (AIC) curve. We noted, however, in the previous chapter that the marginal input cost curve is more relevant from the point of view of determining the profit-maximizing use of inputs, and this is, as before, labelled MIC in Figure 18.1a. In general, as illustrated in the diagram, marginal input costs are both higher and rise more rapidly than average input costs because the additional cost incurred in the employment of extra inputs includes both the price that has to be paid for the extra inputs and the additional amounts that have to be paid for the quantity originally purchased.

In fact, the relationship between marginal and average input cost can be shown to be of similar form to that between average and marginal revenue, since total input costs (TIC) can be expressed as

$$TIC = PQ$$

where Q is the quantity of the input employed and P is its market price ($= AIC$) and hence

$$MIC = \mathrm{d}(TIC)/\mathrm{d}Q = P + Q\mathrm{d}P/\mathrm{d}Q$$
$$= P(1 + Q/P\mathrm{d}P/\mathrm{d}Q),$$

but, given that the elasticity of supply (e_s) of the input is $P/Q\mathrm{d}Q/\mathrm{d}P$, we can write

$$MIC = P(1 + 1/e_s). \tag{18.1}$$

With an upward-sloping supply curve, $1/e_s$ is positive and is greater the lower the elasticity of supply. Hence we may conclude that the marginal input cost is greater than the average input cost by an amount that is greater the more inelastic the supply.

Given the supply and marginal input cost curves as illustrated in Figure 18.1a, with a given usage of all other inputs, the relevant marginal revenue product curve for input Y can also be derived, and the optimal employment of Y is determined in the usual way where the latter curve cuts the marginal input cost curve. Hence in the two-input case depicted, when Z_1 of input Z (in Figure 18.1b) is employed, the marginal revenue product curve for input Y is MRP_1 and the optimal employment of Y is Y_1. Similarly, with more Z, such as Z_2, in the complementary case illustrated, the marginal revenue product curve of Y is MRP_2, and the optimal use of Y increases to Y_2, requiring a higher price to be paid. Hence, as in the last chapter, the curve Y^* can be generated, showing the optimal employment of Y for each level of Z. Similarly, the curve Z^* can be derived showing the optimal employment of Z for each level of Y. As in previous cases, the overall profit-maximizing position is at the point of intersection of the two curves (M) so long as, to

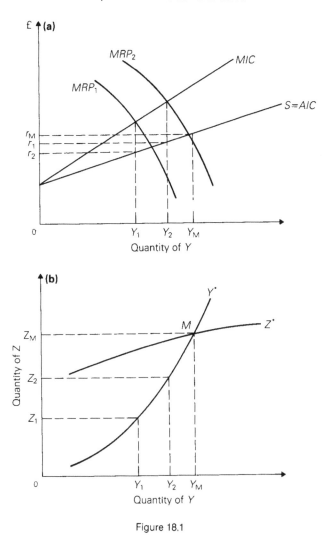

Figure 18.1

meet the relevant second-order conditions, Y^* is steeper than Z^*. Thus in Figure 18.1b, profits are maximized when Y_M of Y and Z_M of Z are employed, and, by going back to Figure 18.1a, it can be seen that the price paid for Y is then r_M per unit.

The problem of the demand curve

Having reached this point in the corresponding analysis of the firm's behaviour in competitive markets (and as in that chapter the analysis of the anti-complementary case is the same apart from the negative slopes of Y^* and

Z^*), we went on to consider the effect of a change in the price of input Y on the firm's position in order to enable us to make deductions about the form of the firm's input demand curve. We were able to do this, however, because in the competitive case a profit-maximizing use of the input always involved the input price being equal to marginal revenue product. With a monopsonistic buyer of an input, however, using expression (18.1),

$$MRP = MIC = P(1 + 1/e_s),$$

so the relationship between the input price and marginal revenue product also involves the elasticity of supply of the input. One consequence of this is that the amount the monopsonist is willing to pay for a given quantity of an input depends not just upon the quantity required but also upon the elasticity of supply.

This is demonstrated in Figure 18.2, where, with a given quantity of other inputs, MRP is the monopsonist's marginal revenue product curve for Y. With that marginal revenue product curve, Y_M of input Y would be employed whether the marginal input cost curve was MIC_1 or MIC_2 since both intersect MRP at T. However, because the supply curve from which MIC_2 is derived (S_2) is less elastic than S_1, the divergence between S_2 and MIC_2, and thus MRP, is greater in the vicinity of T than that between S_1 and MRP. The firm is thus willing to pay less for Y_M of Y when faced with the supply curve S_2 than when faced with S_1. Hence it is impossible to derive an input demand curve for a monopsonist because there is no unique relationship between the quantity demanded and the price the monopsonist is willing to pay.

Our search for a monopsonist's input demand curve has so far concentrated on a situation with a given marginal revenue product curve and, by implication, a fixed quantity of other inputs, but it should be clear that the unpredictability demonstrated in Figure 18.2 carries over to a more multivariate situation. In fact, the diagram shows the rather special case in which the illustrated reduction in the price of Y from r_1 to r_2 leads to no change in the optimal employment of Y. With a smaller increase in the elasticity of supply for Y, however, the gap between MIC_2 and S_2 in the relevant range would be smaller. MIC_2 would then intersect MRP below and to the right of T, suggesting an increase in the firm's optimal employment of Y for the given employment of Z. Equally, with a larger change in the elasticity of supply for Y, MIC_2 would intersect MRP above and to the left of T, suggesting a decrease in the optimal employment of Y with the given Z. This means that a lower input price will under some conditions move the curve showing the optimal employment of Y for each quantity of Z (Y^* in Figure 18.1) to the right and in others to the left. Indeed, it is also possible for the new curve to intersect the old one and thus be to the left of it for some values of Z and to the right of it for others. Again, therefore, no general prediction can be made about where it will intersect Z^* relative to the original profit-maximizing position and hence no demand curve can be derived.

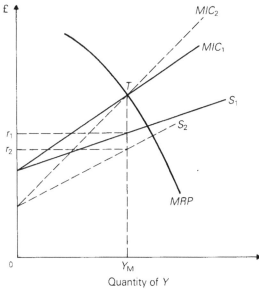

Figure 18.2

This absence of a demand curve corresponds directly to the absence of a supply curve for a monopoly seller. It will be recalled from our earlier discussion that there is no unique relationship between the quantity supplied by a monopolist and the price of his product, because that price also depends on the product's price elasticity of demand. The profit-maximizing monopolist thus seeks to take the opportunity provided by a more inelastic demand to charge a higher price for a given output. The monopsonistic buyer likewise seeks to exploit a situation in which the supply of an input is relatively inelastic by paying a lower price for it.

The effect of monopsony on input use

A second parallel to the case of the monopoly supplier is found (in comparison with the competitive case) in the restriction in the quantity of the input bought by the monopsonist and the corresponding dead-weight loss of welfare. If we consider a situation in which the firm is a monopsonist in the market for Y but faces competitive conditions in the market for Z, the restriction on the amount of Y used is demonstrated in Figure 18.3. In Figure 18.3b the firm's demand for Y and Z is indicated as in Figure 18.1b by point M at the intersection of Y^* and Z^*, and from the supply curve in Figure 18.3a we can see that the price paid for input Y is r_M. Also in that diagram MRP_M is the monopsonist's marginal revenue product curve for Y when Z_M of Z is

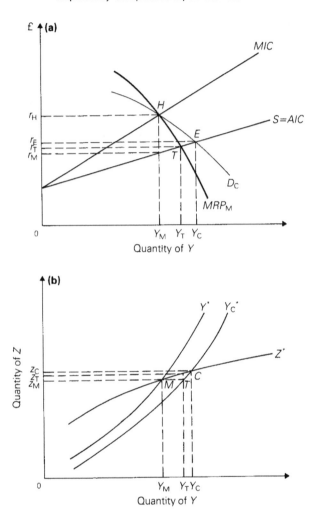

Figure 18.3

employed, and it is drawn to cut *MIC* when Y_M of Y is employed, because in that profit-maximizing position the marginal revenue product of input Y is equal to its marginal cost.

The curve MRP_M is, however, also of significance because it represents the demand curve for Y that would arise with competitive buyers so long as the total amount of Z available, shared between them all, was Z_M. As such it would be the horizontal sum of their individual demand curves taking account of any consequent product price changes. This curve then suggests that, with competitive buyers, the demand for Y would be restricted to Y_M only if the price of Y was increased to r_H. However, that price could only be the competitive equilibrium price if the supply curve passed through H. With the supply curve S, the competitive supply exceeds the demand at that price and so the price falls until a competitive equilibrium is reached at point T where MRP_M intersects the supply curve. Y_T is then employed at a price of r_T. Competitive buyers, therefore, in an equivalent situation to our monopsonist and employing the same quantity of Z, would buy more of Y and pay a higher price for it.

However, a full competitive equilibrium would also involve a different quantity of Z, because we can see from Figure 18.3b that the firm's optimal use of Z associated with Y_T of Y is Z_T rather than Z_M. In this complementary case an increase in the use of Z will further increase the competitive demand for Y. Nevertheless, we can locate the final competitive equilibrium by deriving from Figure 18.3a the competitive employment of Y that would arise with each possible use of Z, which can be found from points like T where the relevant MRP curve cuts the supply curve, and by plotting the resultant relationship between the quantities of Z and Y in Figure 18.3b. This relationship is represented by the curve Y_C^*, drawn to the right of Y^* to reflect the tendency of competitive buyers to buy more Y with any quantity of Z, and passing through T since we have already seen that, with Z_M of Z, Y_T would be the desired employment of Y in the competitive case. Point C, where Y_C^* cuts Z^*, then indicates the combination of Y and Z that would be employed if our monopsonist was replaced by competitive buyers, all other things being equal, and the difference in the use of inputs between points M and C indicates the extent to which the use of both inputs is restricted by monopsony in the market for Y. Further, going back to Figure 18.3a, we can see that the equilibrium price of Y associated with the use of Y_C of Y is r_E.

Moreover, the overall implication of the preceding paragraphs is that the competitive industry's demand for Y, when it can make appropriate adjustments in its use of Z, increases from Y_M to Y_C as the price of Y falls from r_H to r_E. This suggests that its demand curve for the use of Y under these conditions is the curve D_C in Figure 18.3a. This curve we can call the **equivalent competitive demand** curve, as it is the demand curve that would arise if our monopsonist were to be replaced by a set of competitive buyers equivalent to the monopsonist in every other respect. In the complementary case illustrated, it is flatter than the marginal revenue product curves derived for particular quantities of Z (like MRP_M) because it takes account of the fact that a lower price of Y induces firms to employ more of Z as well as more of Y, and this further enhances the demand for Y.

The anti-complementary case, which we have so far ignored, can be analysed on similar lines, but the fact that, in this particular case, increasing the use of one input reduces the marginal product of the other makes only one significant difference to the general picture. This arises because the equivalent curves to Y^*, Z^* and Y_C^* in Figure 18.3b are negatively rather than positively sloped, as in the corresponding analysis in the last chapter. As a result, whilst point C would still be located to the right of M, it would lie below it rather than above it. In this case, therefore, the effect of monopsony in the market for Y is to reduce the demand for Y, as in the complementary case, but to increase the demand for Z. Again, however, an equivalent competitive demand curve can be derived corresponding to D_C in Figure 18.3 that bears the same relationship as that curve to the individual marginal revenue product curves because, whilst an increased use of Y in this case reduces the firms' use of Z, that reduction would again have favourable effects on the demand for Y.

Whilst we have derived the equivalent competitive demand curve in the context of the two-input model, it is evident that corresponding curves can be derived however many other inputs are involved in the firm's production processes. These more general equivalent demand curves will be found useful in the following chapter, as well as in investigating the dead-weight losses arising from the existence of monopsony, which is our more immediate task.

Dead-weight losses with monopsony

These dead-weight losses can be identified with the help of Figure 18.4, which reproduces the features of Figure 18.3a above that are necessary for this purpose. Hence, as before, Y_M is the monopsonist's profit-maximizing demand for Y for which he pays r_M, whilst in the equivalent competitive situation Y_C would be used at a price of r_E. The monopsonist, of course, restricts his demand for Y in order to increase his profits and, in the diagram, the increase in his profits arising from his ability to buy Y_M at a price of r_M rather than r_E is represented by the rectangle $r_M r_E FG$. However, these gains are partly offset by the loss of profits potentially obtainable from the employment of $Y_M Y_C$ additional units of Y, which are represented in the diagram by the triangle HFE, since D_C reflects at each point the revenue obtainable from an additional unit of Y (with appropriate adjustments to the employment of other inputs) and r_E the cost of each additional unit. The monopsonist's net gains from restricting his use of Y can therefore be expressed as

$$r_M r_E FG - HFE.$$

The other parties to the transaction are the suppliers of input Y who, as a result of the situation of monopsony, have to accept a lower price for Y and thus supply less of it. Their losses are the loss of producers' surplus or economic rent (that is, the difference between the price received for any unit supplied and the minimum price that the supplier is prepared to accept to supply it) arising from the reduced price of Y, which is represented in the diagram by the area

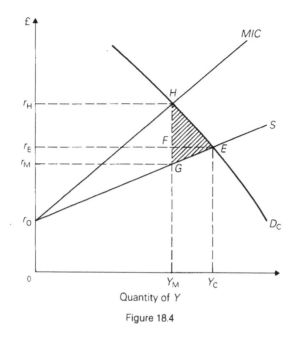

Figure 18.4

$$r_M r_E EG = r_M r_E FG + GFE.$$

From this we can see that part of this loss ($r_M r_E FG$) is also the gain to the monopsonist from the reduction in the price of Y, but there is an uncompensated loss of $HFE + GFE$ represented by the shaded triangular area in the diagram. This then is the dead-weight welfare loss arising from monopsony in the market for Z, and as such it is directly comparable to the dead-weight loss arising with monopoly in the product market. It is, moreover, additional to any dead-weight loss that might arise through any monopoly power the buyer of Y might have in his product market, and it is also additional to any similar dead-weight losses arising because of any monopsony in other input markets, which for the purposes of identifying the dead-weight losses arising from monopsony in the supply of Y have been assumed to be competitive. However, because our equivalent competitive demand curve is defined to take account of adjustments to other inputs, the shaded area in the diagram covers the losses arising from the distorting effects of monopsony in the markets for Y on the demands for all other affected inputs as well as on the demand for Y.

Price discrimination and monopsonistic markets

One further point of similarity with the case of the monopoly supplier that we need to note is the possibility of price discrimination. If the monopsonist buys his supplies of any given input in segregated markets, there is no necessity for him to pay the same price in each, and in most cases it would be profitable for him not to do so. If perfect discrimination is possible, the monopsonist is able to pay for each unit of input the minimum price the supplier is willing to accept for that unit.

In terms of Figure 18.4, that would mean that the supply curve would also be the monopsonist's marginal input cost curve, and so the latter would be willing to extend his employment of Y to Y_C, the competitive level. The dead-weight losses identified above would thus be eliminated, although the distribution of the benefits between buyers and sellers would be rather different from the distribution arising with competitive buyers buying at the uniform price of r_E. In that case the supplier's economic rent would be $r_0 r_E E$, but with a perfectly discriminating monopsonist all that rent would be appropriated by the buyer. This directly corresponds with the situation arising with a perfectly discriminating monopolist supplier discussed in Chapter 13 where, it will be recalled, the dead-weight loss arising from a restricted output was eliminated but the monopolist was able to appropriate all the consumers' surplus. In both cases, whilst perfect discrimination might therefore, in general terms, lead to a more efficient allocation of resources, the resultant effect on the distribution of benefits is particularly detrimental to those discriminated against.

Similar considerations apply with less than perfect discrimination. If the monopsonist has two separate markets (1 and 2) in which he can obtain supplies of input Y, profit maximization requires that the marginal input cost in each market be equal to marginal revenue product or

$$MIC_{Y1} = MIC_{Y2} = MRP_Y.$$

But, using expression (18.1), this means that

$$r_{Y1}(1 + 1/e_{S1}) = r_{Y2}(1 + 1/e_{S2}) = MRP_Y \tag{18.2}$$

and that
$$r_{Y1} = MRP_Y/(1 + 1/e_{S1})$$

and
$$r_{Y2} = MRP_Y/(1 + 1/e_{S2})$$

from which we may deduce that

$$r_{Y1} < r_{Y2} \quad \text{if} \quad e_{S1} < e_{S2}$$

and vice versa.

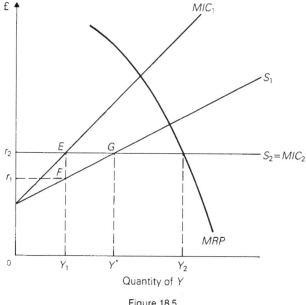

Figure 18.5

The effects of this kind of discrimination are illustrated most straight-forwardly in a diagram like Figure 18.5, which depicts a situation in which an infinitely elastic supply of Y is obtainable in market 2, and a less elastic supply in market 1. The supply curve for the less elastic supply, S_1, might therefore be the supply curve of competitive local producers, whilst S_2 could reflect the conditions in a wider market not accessible to local suppliers. It can then be seen from the diagram that condition (18.2) above is satisfied if the firm uses a total of Y_2 of Y, of which Y_1 is obtained from the first market at a price of r_1 while the remainder is obtained in the second market at the higher price of r_2. Note that, despite the lower price in market 1, it would not pay the firm to increase its purchases of Y from that source because marginal input cost (MIC_1) would then be greater than the marginal input cost from the alternative source of supply (MIC_2).

In the absence of discrimination, the total use of Y would also be Y_2, but all suppliers would receive r_2. The ability to discriminate, by enabling the firm to buy Y_1 units of Y at a lower price, reduces its input costs and thereby increases its profits by the rectangle r_1r_2EF and, of course, the suppliers lose a corresponding amount. However, the suppliers' total loss is greater than the monopsonist's gain because at a price of r_2 they would be willing to supply Y^* rather than Y_1, which would yield them an additional economic rent of FEG. Moreover, this loss of FEG constitutes a dead-weight loss, because it represents output that market 1 producers would be willing to supply for a price less than or at the limit no more than the prevailing market price in market 2.

A necessary condition for this kind of discrimination is for the local suppliers in market 1 to have no access to the higher-priced other market. That might occur because of artificial impediments to trade, like tariffs, but it may also be due to items like transport costs. Thus local suppliers might be able to supply our monopsonist for less than the 'world' price because their transport costs are considerably lower, but cannot compete on the world market because their own production costs, when added to the transport costs involved, are too high. This sort of situation can clearly arise when Y is some produced input, but it may also arise when Y is a particular type of labour. In this case the discrimination may take a form that many would find morally unacceptable. For example, for social reasons women may be less mobile than men and therefore the supply of female labour in any given locality may be less price elastic than male labour. Hence a monopsonist employer would find it profitable to discriminate against female workers by paying lower wages. Similarly, a firm may find it equally profitable to discriminate between its workers on grounds of race. In this kind of situation, such discrimination need not necessarily imply sexual or racial prejudice (although it would suggest no strong aversion by the monopsonist to sexual or racial inequality); it would merely be a question of the employer exploiting the differing elasticities of supply of the different groups of workers with a view to increasing its profits. As such it provides an example of a case where there may be a clash of interests between profit-making and ethical principles.

Exercises

18.1   Show how a profit-maximizing monopsonist can exploit his monopsony power in order to lower the price he pays for an input and to increase profits.

18.2   Explain why no demand curve can be derived for a monopsonistic buyer of an input. Why is this case similar to that of a monopolistic seller?

18.3   What dead-weight losses arise with monopsony

(i)   in the case where there is one variable input

(ii)   in the case where there are two variable inputs?

18.4   A monopsonist has two sources of supply for input Y. With both he is faced with an upward sloping supply curve but their elasticities are different. Draw a diagram to show the profit-maximizing quantities and prices for each source. How would these prices be affected by a tax on the inputs obtained from one of the sources of supply?

CHAPTER NINETEEN
BILATERAL MONOPOLY AND COLLECTIVE BARGAINING

Introduction

In the last chapter the emphasis was on imperfect competition amongst buyers of input. In this chapter we turn our attention to imperfect competition between sellers of inputs. First we consider the case where the inputs are supplied by monopolistic profit-maximizing firms, and then we go on to consider the particular problems arising in labour markets where monopolistic elements are introduced through collective bargaining. In considering the problem of supplies by a monopolistic firm, our earlier analysis of monopoly has already adequately covered the case of a monopolist selling to price-taking buyers, whether they are competitive firms or individuals buying for private consumption. We can, therefore, concentrate here on the case where a monopolistic seller is trading with a monopsonistic buyer – a situation often referred to as **bilateral monopoly** because there is monopoly on both sides of the market. When we turn to labour markets, however, we will broaden the discussion to include both competitive and monopsonistic buyers.

Bilateral monopoly with one firm as a price taker

On the face of it, bearing in mind that a monopolist has no supply curve and a monopsonist no demand curve, the situation of bilateral monopoly might not seem to be a promising area for fruitful analysis. However, by considering situations in which one of the parties behaves as a price taker, which is the equivalent, in the present context, to a firm acting as a follower in an oligopolistic market where there is price leadership, we can begin to get some idea of the range of possible outcomes.

In Figure 19.1, in which firm S sells product Y to firm B for use as an input,

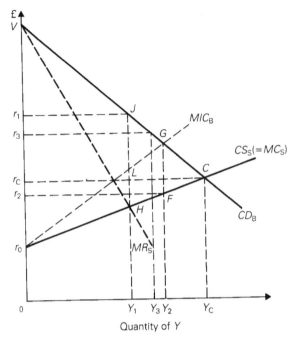

Figure 19.1

in the case where **B**, the buyer, acts as a price taker, then if CD_B is B's equivalent competitive demand curve as derived in the previous chapter it is also the demand curve faced by firm S and MR_S is its marginal revenue curve. Similarly, if CS_S is the supply curve firm B faces when S acts as a price taker, B's marginal input cost curve is MIC_B. However, since in this case the price-taking seller seeks to produce an output at which marginal cost is equal to price, this supply curve is simply S's marginal cost curve. Hence, in the case where B is acting as a price taker, S, seeking to maximize his profits given B's behaviour, reacts as in the standard monopoly analysis by producing an output of Y_1, where $MR_S = MC_S$, and selling it to B at a price of r_1. Conversely, when S acts as the price taker, B, as in the standard monopsony case with an upward-sloping supply curve, offers to buy Y_2, where MIC_B cuts its demand curve, at a price of r_2.

Joint profit maximization

In the situation illustrated in Figure 19.1, there are some differences in the output produced in the two cases, but rather larger differences in the price at which Y is traded and in the profits earned by each firm. Thus in the first case considered, with B the price taker and S fixing the price, S's profits from the production of Y (ignoring any fixed costs) are $r_0 r_1 JH$ ($= Or_1 JY_1 - Or_0 HY_1$),[1] whilst the buyer's profits defined equivalently are $r_1 VJ$

308

$(= OVJY_1 - Or_1JY_1).^2$ Conversely, with their roles reversed, S's profits are reduced to r_0r_2F, whilst the buyer has r_2VGF.

However, it may also be recognized that in neither of these two cases are the combined profits of buyer and seller maximized. The combined profit, which in terms of the diagram is most easily seen as the area between CD_B and CS_S to the left of the vertical drawn at the relevant level of Y (thus with Y_1 of Y it is r_0VJH) is at a maximum (equal to r_0VC) when Y_C of Y is traded. The latter is the quantity of Y that is produced and used when B and S are combined into one single profit-maximizing firm. It is also the amount of Y that would be used if the firms colluded with the object of maximizing their joint profits. Moreover, it can be argued additionally that it is the use of Y that tends to emerge when the firms are neither combined nor colluding but rather are negotiating with each other as independent entities. This is based on the grounds that, if the combined profits at Y_C are greater than the combined profits with any other level of Y, whenever the actual amount of Y traded is greater or less than Y_C there exist a number of possible contracts that can be negotiated between the two parties that would leave both better off.

This can easily be shown, again with the help of Figure 19.1. Suppose initially B is acting as a price taker and using Y_1 of Y, which he buys at a price of r_1. In these circumstances a reduction in the price of Y to r_C would induce him to increase his use of it to the required level of Y_C, and thus increase total profits. That would not be acceptable to S, however, because, with $MR_S < MC_S$, his own profits would fall. But with the lower price of r_C, B's profits would have increased by r_Cr_1JC and would thus have increased sufficiently to allow him to pay S a lump sum of r_Cr_1JL for the right to buy Y at the lower price of r_C. That sum would fully compensate S for the lower profit per unit of Y and still leave B better off than before.

Alternatively, S, having observed that B is not willing to buy more than Y_1 when the price is r_1, could offer to sell additional units of Y at a lower price. If that lower price was r_C, then B would be willing to buy Y_1Y_C extra units at that lower price and his surplus would increase by LJC whilst S's would increase by HLC. As a variation on that theme, S could secure more of the surplus for himself by offering, first, an intermediate price of, say, r_3 at which B would be willing to buy Y_1Y_3 extra units, before offering further units at r_C.

Similar arrangements, also offering greater profits to both parties, are available when the roles of the two agents are reversed such that the seller is the price taker and starts off by selling Y_2 at price r_2. A characteristic of all these arrangements is that the firms move away from the idea of having a uniform price per unit of Y and use instead some form of two-part or multi-part tariff, and it will always be the case that whatever the initial price and output, provided it is not Y_C, there is some multi-part pricing system that can be negotiated that is beneficial to both parties.

Uniform price contracts

It can also be shown, however, that whenever the use of Y is less than (or greater than) Y_C, there are likely to be beneficial contracts available with uniform pricing as well as with multi-part pricing. Again, we can consider a situation in which B, acting as a price taker, initially buys Y_1 of Y at a price of r_1. This situation is shown in Figure 19.2, which is the same as Figure 19.1 but contains, in addition, information about the firms' profits in the form of iso-profit curves.

We have met these curves before in our discussion of oligopoly, from which it will be recalled that they are simply curves connecting points yielding the same level of profits to the firm concerned. Some idea of their shape for firm B in the present context can be obtained if we consider what happens to B's profits as, with a given price of r_1, it increases its use of Y from zero. Since the demand curve shows B's preferred use of Y at any price, it must follow that the maximum profits attainable with a price of r_1 are at point J where Y_1 is used. It must therefore be the case that as the firm moves along the horizontal line r_1J, increasing its use of Y at the given price, profits increase until point J is reached and then start to decline. In moving along r_1J, therefore, B will cross iso-profit curves representing successively higher levels of profits until it reaches J. At that point a curve representing the highest possible profits attainable with the given price is tangential to r_1J, and if the use of Y is further increased, progressively lower iso-profit curves will be met. Further, since profits must be increased if any given quantity of Y is obtained at a lower price, we can conclude that B's iso-profit curves are convex upwards and horizontal at their point of intersection with CD_B, exactly as in Figure 19.2. For similar reasons the seller's iso-profit curves are concave upwards, and are horizontal at their point of intersection with the seller's marginal cost/supply curve. From the latter we can infer that, at point J (with r_1 the price of Y), S is on an iso-profit curve that is downward sloping because J is well to the left of his marginal cost curve (it will actually be tangential to CD_B at J since J is the profit-maximizing price–quantity combination along CD_B, where $MC_S = MR_S$).

With these curves we can now see that if the buyer and seller were to negotiate on the basis of price and quantity, rather than price alone, the area between $\pi_1^{\,B}$ and $\pi_1^{\,S}$ provides a range of possible price–quantity combinations that give both parties greater profits than at J. In the diagram, V indicates one such price–quantity combination, but at V there remain further unexploited opportunities for mutual gains so the bargaining process is likely to go further. In fact, the limit to the opportunities for further gains to both parties is reached at T, where the firm's iso-profit curves are tangential to each other. Once a point like T has been reached, any further change must leave at least one of the two firms worse off, and thus is less acceptable.

T, however, is not a unique point within the area enclosed by $\pi_1^{\,S}$ and $\pi_1^{\,B}$, because there are a number of other points of tangency between the two sets

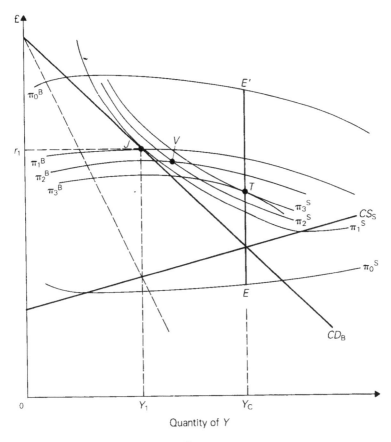

Figure 19.2

of iso-profits curves. There are also others outside the area enclosed by π_1^S and π_1^B that might be reached if the bargaining process started at some point other than J. In fact, the ultimate limits on the bargaining process are determined by the need for the firms to stay in business. Too high a price for Y would make B's profits negative, whilst too low a price could drive S out of business. If π_0^S and π_0^B are the iso-profit curves associated with zero profits for each party, then any point of tangency between those two curves provides a potential contract that cannot be improved upon for both parties. If, therefore, the bargaining process is efficient, in the sense that all opportunities for mutual gain are exhausted, it will lead to such a point of tangency. In the diagram the curve EE' is drawn through all such points of tangency between π_0^S and π_0^B and, since it indicates all the possible outcomes of an efficient bargaining process, it is referred to as a **contract curve**.

Contract curves crop up in a number of situations and we will meet them again in later chapters, but one thing we can say about the contract curve EE' in Figure 19.2, which need not be true in other cases, is that it must be a vertical line because whatever the price charged for Y the joint-profit-maximizing position must involve the use of Y_C of Y. This may not seem intuitively obvious but it can easily be shown. The buyer's total revenue (R_B) is a function of his own output, which, in turn, is a function of the quantity of all the inputs he uses. If, to allow some degree of generality without introducing too many variables, we consider a situation in which the buyer's inputs are Y and labour (the quantity of which we can denote as L), we can express his total revenue function as

$$R_B = R(Y, L),$$

and, if the price of Y is fixed at some arbitrary level r^* whilst the wage rate is w, B's profits can be expressed as

$$\pi_B = R(Y, L) - r^* Y - wL.$$

Similarly, if the seller's costs are denoted by

$$C_S = C(Y),$$

his profits are

$$\pi_S = r^* Y - C(Y).$$

The combined profits of both firms can then be expressed as

$$\pi_J = \pi_B + \pi_S = R(Y, L) - r^* Y - wL + r^* Y - C(Y)$$
$$= R(Y, L) - wL - C(Y),$$

and are thus independent of the value of r^*. We must, therefore, conclude that the maximizing level of combined profits is also independent of r^* and depends only on Y and L. Further, since for any level of L it must be located where the marginal revenue from the use of an additional unit of Y (that is, B's marginal revenue product as expressed in CD_B in the diagram) is equal to the marginal cost of producing an additional unit of Y as reflected in CS_S, the optimum use of Y must involve a situation like that in Figure 19.2 where Y_C of Y is produced.

The upshot of all this is that in this bilateral monopoly case we can predict that firms will tend to trade that quantity of Y at which their joint profits are maximized, but we cannot predict the price at which it can be traded except to say that it needs to be a price that will not force either firm out of business.

There is one qualification to all this that we ought to note before concluding, which is that pure bilateral monopoly, like pure monopoly and pure monopsony, is an extreme case and for that reason may not be all that usual. Few supplying firms sell their output to one customer only, and few buying firms are completely dependent on one source of supply. One of the nearest equivalents to a bilateral monopoly situation in the United Kingdom in recent years has been in the market for coal, since around three-quarters of the output of British Coal has been purchased by the Central Electricity Generating Board.[3] That, however, has still left a significant volume of sales to other users and export markets have also been available for competitively priced coal. Similarly, coal has been available in foreign markets and the CEGB has also been in a position to increase its use of alternative fuels. This is of some significance because with more than one buyer or seller some of the problems raised in our discussion of oligopoly in Chapter 14 begin to raise their heads. In particular, whilst the joint-profit-maximizing position would still be a situation in which, potentially, all those involved could be better off than in any other, the transactions costs involved in reaching it increase with the number of firms in the negotiations, and so do the opportunities open to individual firms to gain by breaking the original agreement. The outcome thus becomes less determinate until the number of firms involved on each side becomes large enough to establish competitive conditions. In that case, with the same supply and demand curves as in Figure 19.1 and 19.2, we would again predict an output of Y of Y_C, but this time we would also be able to predict a determinate price of r_C.

Collective bargaining

We now turn to the particular problems of labour markets arising from the fact that wages are often fixed by collective bargaining rather than the more impersonal forces of the market, and consider the implications of such collective bargaining for the level of wages and the level of employment in the firms concerned. By collective bargaining we mean any arrangement by which the wage rates for a whole group of workers are fixed through negotiations between representatives of that group and representatives of management. This covers a wide range of possible situations because, clearly, such negotiations may cover anything from plant bargaining involving a small group of workers in one particular plant to negotiations at a national level between trade union leaders (or officials of some professional associ- ation) and employers' representatives covering the bulk of workers in a particular industry or occupation. However, one aim of all such collective bargaining is undoubtedly to secure higher wages and better working conditions than could be obtained through individual negotiations, and to start with we can consider the effect that this might have on situations with competitive and monopsonistic buyers of labour services respectively.

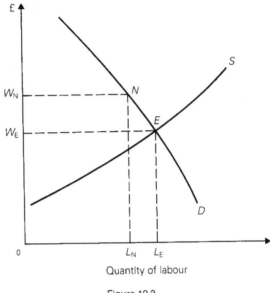

Figure 19.3

Collective bargaining with competitive markets

The competitive situation, which is quite straightforward, is illustrated in Figure 19.3 where D is the relevant market demand curve for a particular type of labour, whilst S is the supply curve. The normal market equilibrium then involves a wage rate of W_E and the employment of L_E units of labour. If, however, as a result of collective bargaining, the wage rate rises to W_N, the demand for labour falls to L_N and there is an excess supply of labour. Now since in this situation most of those unable to find work at the negotiated wage rate W_N are willing to work for less than the negotiated wage, some firms may be tempted to offer work at less than W_N. Whether in these circumstances the negotiated wage can be maintained will depend on the extent to which the labour organizations involved are in a position to impose effective sanctions on defaulting employers, either by calling their workers out on strike or through overtime bans and the like. But if the negotiated wage is maintained, it will be maintained at the cost of some unemployment compared with the market-determined wage.

Collective bargaining with monopsony

With monopsonistic buyers of labour, the situation is a little different. Without collective bargaining, the wage rate and level of employment are determined, as in the previous section, by the point at which the marginal labour input cost curve (MIC_L) is cut by the firm's marginal revenue product for labour curve (MRP_L). Hence in Figure 19.4, L_M is employed at a wage

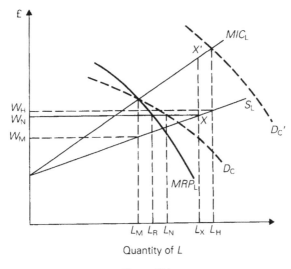

Figure 19.4

rate of W_M. If, however, as a result of collective bargaining the wage rate is raised to W_N, the monopsonist is able to employ as many or as few workers as he requires at that wage rate, at least as long as his total demand does not exceed L_X, which, given the supply curve in the diagram, represents the maximum amount of labour available at a price of W_N. The supply curve for labour now facing the firm, therefore, lies along the horizontal line $W_N X$, after which it continues up the original supply curve above X as before. The marginal input cost curve accordingly also lies along $W_N X$ and then continues along the original marginal input cost curve above X'. (As usual, the kink in the supply curve produces a discontinuity in its associated marginal curve.) For any desired level of employment below L_X, therefore, the profit-maximizing monopsonist is in the same position as a price taker in a more competitive situation and acts accordingly. If he is unable to alter the other inputs employed, he will move to where MRP_L, his marginal revenue product curve for labour given the fixed quantity of other inputs, cuts $W_N X$ and will employ L_R units of labour.

Alternatively, if he is able to vary his employment of other inputs, he moves to where his equivalent competitive demand curve, D_C, cuts $W_N X$ and thus increases his use of labour to L_N. If, however, the relevant demand curve cuts the firm's effective supply curve at a point above X, as is the case with demand curve D_C', then L_H is the optimum level of employment with a wage rate of W_H and the firm's position is unaffected by the negotiated rate. But where the monopsonist is forced to pay higher wages as a result of collective bargaining, because of the change in the supply conditions facing him, it is always profitable for him to employ more rather than fewer workers at the higher rate. Nevertheless, it needs to be recognized that this is a once and for all effect of the introduction of collective bargaining. Once a system of negotiated wage rates has been established, any increases in the negotiated rate are, other things being equal, at the expense of employment, just as in the competitive situation.

Determination of negotiated wage rates

Whilst the above analysis indicates the potential effects of collective bargaining on the quantity of labour employed, it suffers from the limitation that it does not provide any insight into how a particular negotiated wage rate is determined. Obviously, in any actual negotiated rate there may be some element of compromise between the wage rate preferred by the employers and that preferred by the union. Profit considerations presumably dictate that employers will seek the lowest possible wage consistent with being able to recruit adequate quantities of labour of an acceptable quality, but what the preferred rate of union negotiators might be is a more open question.

One crude hypothesis is that union negotiators seek the highest possible wage rate consistent with the firm staying in business. They would then seek to push the wage rate up until the firm's costs have risen to the level that just reduces its profits to zero. What level that might be depends, of course, on the firm's competitive position and the extent to which its competitors are subject to the same increase in labour costs. This approach, however, might be deemed unsatisfactory on the grounds that it implies that union negotiators completely ignore the effects of higher wage rates on the demand for their members' labour, and there are various ways in which such effects might be taken into account.

One is to suggest that union negotiators seek to maximize **expected** wages rather than actual wages. To consider the implications of this proposition it will help to simplify by assuming that labour is supplied only in standard week-units, so that, for those employed, weekly earnings are equal to the negotiated weekly wage rate W and there are no complications arising from variable hours. In these circumstances there will be some probability s, where $0 < s < 1$, of an individual being out of work. If when out of work the individual is eligible for state benefits of B per week, his expected weekly earnings can be expressed as

$$E = (1 - s)W + sB.$$

Since increasing W also increases s by an amount depending on the elasticity of demand for labour, union leaders, on this hypothesis, seek to increase the wage rate only up to the point where the positive effects of increasing W on expected earnings begin to be offset by the negative effects arising from the increase in the probability of being unemployed. It might also be argued that such an approach should, additionally, take account of the extent to which individual workers might be risk-averse and therefore require increased

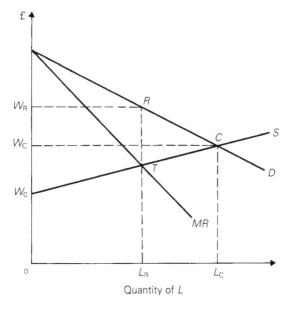

Figure 19.5

expected earnings to compensate for increased risk. In that case the union's objective would need to be expressed in terms of maximizing the expected **utility** of the workers rather than their expected earnings, and it may be doubted whether union negotiators could have sufficient information about the utility functions of their members to make that an operational concept.

Another, perhaps more fruitful, approach is to treat a union, and by implication any other body involved in negotiating the wage rates of its members, as a kind of firm. As such, it can be viewed as seeking to maximize the economic rent earned by its members, which is the direct equivalent of maximizing profits in a firm. This economic rent, which is the difference between the sum of money that the workers receive for a particular amount of work and the minimum sum they are willing to accept to supply that amount of work, is maximized when the extra revenue received when the marginal unit of labour is employed (the addition to the workers' total earnings) is equal to the minimum amount that that unit must receive to induce it to work. Since the latter is shown by the supply curve in Figure 19.5, and the addition to the workers' total earnings by the marginal revenue curve associated with the labour demand curve D, we may conclude that economic rents are maximized when the wage rate is fixed to secure the level of employment at which the marginal revenue curve cuts the supply curve. In terms of Figure 19.5, therefore, this means fixing the wage rate at W_R where L_R workers are employed. The workers' economic rent is then represented by the area $W_0 W_R R T$ in the diagram.

Developing further the idea of a union as a sort of firm, we may note that in unions, as in many firms, there may be some separation between the 'owners' of the union (its members) and its management (the union leaders). Like the directors of firms, union leaders are accountable to their membership, who, if dissatisfied with their leaders' performance, may be able to vote them out of office. Subject to the constraints imposed by the need to avoid that eventuality, the leaders may nevertheless have some opportunity to pursue policies reflecting their own preferences. For the purposes of our analysis, these preferences can be expressed in the usual way in the form of a utility function, so we need to consider what variables might be involved.

Clearly the wage rate (or rates) secured by its members constitutes one important variable (or set of variables) because, other things being equal, higher wage rates are likely to be regarded as preferable to lower wage rates, if only because the ability to negotiate high wage rates may be regarded as a sign of successful union leadership. Another important variable is likely to be the number of jobs available to union members, since that largely determines the size of the union, and union leaders (like the managers of firms) might feel they have more power and prestige running a larger organization than a smaller one. There will undoubtedly be other variables in the utility function, such as working hours and working conditions generally, but some useful insights into the effects of collective bargaining can be obtained by considering a union seeking to maximize its utility when utility is a function of these two variables and can thus be written as

$$U = U(L, W), \tag{19.1}$$

where L is the number of jobs, which can again be assumed to involve a standard working week. This function can be assumed to have the same general properties as those of individuals discussed earlier, which means that it can be represented by a series of downward-sloping, convex to the origin indifference curves in a diagram with L and W on the axes, as in Figure 19.6. In more practical terms this means that the union's utility is increased if L and W increase, but that it is willing to trade off jobs for higher wages and vice versa, but at a diminishing rate.

If the firms continue acting as price takers once the wage rate has been negotiated, the choices open to the union are the points on the firms' demand curve arising from that behaviour. Hence with the demand curve D in Figure 19.6, and a utility function represented by the curves U_1, U_2 and U_3, the union's preferred position is at P where U_2 is tangential to the demand curve, and which involves a wage rate of W_P and employment of L_P. In the case illustrated, W_P is above the competitive wage W_C but below the rent-maximizing wage W_R, but whether it is above or below either depends on the strength of the union leaders' preferences for higher pay as opposed to jobs. Nevertheless, wherever P is located, it needs to be recognized that, whilst it indicates the union's preferred wage, the firms it is negotiating with may

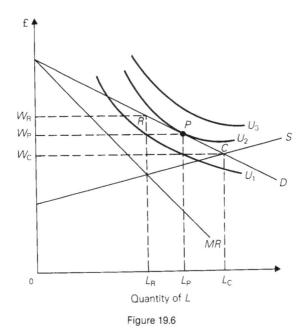

Figure 19.6

prefer something less, and both parties may eventually agree on a wage rate that is some compromise between their respective preferred rates. However, it can be shown that, even if W_P was conceded by the employers, that need not be the end of the bargaining process because there might exist some other potential wage–job combinations preferable to both parties.

Bargaining solutions again

To show this we can again add information about the firm's profits to the diagram in the form of iso-profit curves (It is perhaps most straightforward to think in terms of negotiations with a single firm, although exactly the same arguments apply when there is a group of firms seeking to maximize their joint profits.) If we superimpose these curves onto a diagram also containing the union preference function, as in Figure 19.7, where one of the union's indifference curves is tangential to the firm's demand curve at P, we can see that there are possible wage–job combinations to the south-east of P in the 'eye' formed by the iso-profit curve π_1 and U_1, which give both the firm more profits and the union more utility.

To reach such combinations, however, a more comprehensive bargaining process is required than has been considered so far. In our previous discussion, we have assumed that unions and firms negotiate over the wage rate only, leaving the firm to decide for itself how many workers it wishes to employ at that wage rate. In those circumstances the demand curve indicates its optimal employment levels. However, to persuade the union to move to

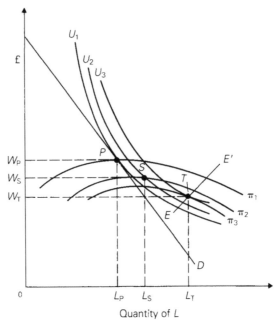

Figure 19.7

points such as S or T, involving lower wages than P, the firm must give a commitment to employ the extra workers involved. In other words, the negotiations have to cover explicitly the level of employment as well as the wage rate. Once employment levels are included in the negotiations, the opportunities for mutually beneficial agreements can be exploited. Hence both firm and union should find it easy to agree to move from P to S in the diagram, because both are better off at S.

But again, as in Figure 19.2, there are still further unexploited opportunities for mutual gains, so the bargaining process is likely to go further, with the limit to the opportunities for further gains to both parties being reached at points like T where one of the union's indifference curves is tangential to one of the firm's iso-profit curves. Any movement beyond T, however, must involve at least one party becoming worse off and so would be less readily acceptable. As before, T is not a unique point because there are a number of other points of tangency between indifference curves and iso-profit contours. The curve EE' is therefore drawn, as before, through all such points of tangency as T. However, in this case, in contrast to the situation of bilateral monopoly discussed above, EE' need not be vertical. So long as the union leaders are concerned to maximize utility rather than some monetary return, no equivalent to joint profits can be defined and therefore no unique joint optimum level of employment can be defined either. However, if the union was concerned more specifically to maximize its members' economic rents, the solution is exactly as in Figure 19.2.

Subject to that qualification, points on EE' have the same significance as before in that, if the bargaining process is an efficient one in the sense that all opportunities for mutual benefit are exploited, it must lead to a point on EE'. Precisely which point on EE' is reached depends on the precise circumstances involved in the negotiations, the strengths of the parties, and so on. Bargaining theory attempts to probe further into the likely outcome of bargaining, but our analysis is sufficient to reinforce and extend the conclusion of our earlier simple model that collective bargaining in a monopsonistic situation can lead to higher wages and more employment, because it opens up the possibility of negotiations going beyond the constraints imposed by the demand curve. Indeed it suggests that, even with competitive buyers of labour, collective bargaining could lead to higher wages and more employment.

Notes

1   Or_1JY_1 is the total revenue S receives from the sale of Y_1 units at the price of r_1, whilst Or_0HY_1, the area under S's marginal cost curve, is the variable cost arising from the production of Y_1.
2   For B the total revenue from the use of Y_1 of Y $(= OVJY_1)$ is the area under CD_B which is its marginal revenue product curve, whilst Or_1JY_1 is the cost of buying that amount of Y.
3   This situation will be changed under the plans for the privatization of the industry.

Exercises

19.1   When two firms sell to third parties collusion is usually deemed to be against the public interest. When they sell to each other there seems to be a case of encouraging them to collude. Why?
19.2   Assess the argument that in the absence of collusion bilateral monopoly will tend to have a joint-profit-maximizing outcome. What can be predicted about the price(s) at which the parties trade?
19.3   Show that collective bargaining to increase wages need not always reduce employment.
19.4   If a trade union is considered to be a utility-maximizing agent, what other variables, in addition to those referred to in the chapter, do you think might contribute to its utility?
19.5   The profit-maximizing firm's demand curve for labour is defined by the profit-maximizing use of labour at each wage rate. Why then might the firm be willing to move to points off its demand curve in a bargaining situation?

CHAPTER TWENTY
SOCIAL WELFARE: BASIC CONSIDERATIONS

Introduction

Our main concern in the previous chapters has been with the behaviour of individual economic agents under various conditions, and with some of the implications of that behaviour for the allocation of resources in an economy. The primary emphasis has been on the *positive* aspects of that behaviour in that the concern has been with analysing the choices the agents actually make. In places we have, however, introduced some more *normative* elements into the discussion, particularly in the comparison of perfect competition and monopoly where we raised the question of whether the allocation of resources was 'better' from the point of view of the broader community in one case than the other. This kind of question is of general interest because of its implications for economic policy, and indeed a primary motivating force in the development of economics as an academic discipline has always been the desire to provide a more satisfactory analytical framework for the consideration of policy issues. However, discussion of these matters requires more careful consideration than we have attempted so far of the criteria by which one situation might be considered better or worse than another. This is a particular concern of what is usually referred to as **welfare economics** and that is the focus of interest in the remaining chapters of the book.

In this and the following chapter we will be concerned with the development of certain basic ideas that can be applied in the appraisal of the allocation of resources produced by any sort of economic system. After that we examine the market system as a means of allocating resources in the light of these ideas, identify the problems likely to arise and consider some of the implications of the analysis for the role of government and economic policy.

The social welfare function

The question of whether one allocation of resources is better or worse than another from some broad community viewpoint can ultimately only be decided with reference to the way the community concerned ranks alternative situations in its order of preference. As a starting point, therefore, some consideration needs to be given to the characteristics of the utility functions of communities, which, in this context, are usually referred to as **social welfare functions**, just as we have examined the main characteristics of the utility functions of other economic agents in earlier sections of the book. Then, in the next chapter, following the pattern of the earlier discussions, we can examine the conditions under which the welfare of a community, with limited resources at its disposal, is at a maximum.

At the outset we do, of course, need to recognize that there may be considerable differences between the social welfare functions of individual communities, but we can consider what common properties they might all share (just as we did with utility functions). In the nature of things the properties conventionally attributed to social welfare functions are potentially more contentious than those ascribed to utility functions, but despite this they are considered to be sufficiently general to apply to any community of two or more people. Our analysis thus encompasses the whole range of communities from households, at one extreme, to the world-wide community at the other. Nevertheless, in so far as our particular concern is to cast light on issues of economic organization and policy within a national economy, it makes some sense to think more specifically in terms of the nation state as the relevant community.

Much of recent welfare economics has involved the use of a social welfare function, the most basic properties of which are based on the ideas of Vilfredo Pareto, an Italian economist and sociologist of the late nineteenth and early twentieth centuries. This social welfare function rests on three propositions, which are essentially ethical in nature.

The first of these is that the welfare of a community depends solely on the welfare of the individual members of that community and no one else. This means that we can express the social welfare function of a community with n members in general terms as

$$W = W(w_1, w_2, \ldots, w_n), \tag{20.1}$$

Where W is the welfare of the community as a whole and the terms $w_1, w_2, \ldots$ w_n denote the welfare, or some general measure of well-being, of individual members of the community. This proposition does not rule out concern for people in other communities, because the welfare of each individual member of the community may be diminished or enhanced by the situation faced by people in other communities, but it does imply that the community, which as suggested above might be a nation, has no collective interest over and above the individual interests of its members. Whilst this is a proposition that many people would be happy to go along with, it is not necessarily one that would command universal assent.

The second proposition is that the individual welfare variables in (20.1) should reflect the individuals' own evaluation of their welfare rather than that of anyone else. The approach is thus individualistic. In practice, laws are in force in most countries that are not strictly compatible with this proposition since they restrict the individual's ability to consume certain goods and services (for example, drugs and pornography) and compel the consumption of others (for example, education services). As it happens, the basic welfare propositions would not be significantly affected if some other person's evaluation (for example, that of a dictator) was considered to be the relevant one, provided this did not affect the other properties of the welfare function. Nevertheless, the notion that, unless there are specific reasons to the contrary, individuals should be free to act in the light of their own personal assessments of their own welfare is a fundamental one in market-oriented economies, and therefore needs to be taken into account in appraising the potential efficiency of such economies. In addition, if it is the individual's view of his or her own welfare that is important, then the welfare we are concerned with can be regarded as being synonymous with the individual utility we were concerned with earlier in this book, suggesting that we can write our welfare function as

$$W = W(U_1, U_2, \ldots, U_n), \qquad (20.1a)$$

where $U_1, U_2, \ldots, U_n$ denote the utility of individual members of the community.

It might be objected that the welfare or well-being of an individual depends on a wider range of variables than those associated with utility in that, as well as depending on such obviously economic variables as the quantities of particular goods consumed and the amount of leisure enjoyed, it will also depend on a whole range of political and environmental variables, ranging from the weather and the disposition of his/her neighbours to the personal and political freedom he or she enjoys. In our earlier analysis of consumers' behaviour it was reasonable to regard these factors as given and constant, or, if they were not constant, as having a fairly random effect on an individual's behaviour. In the context of welfare economics it is sometimes reasonable to make the same kind of *ceteris paribus* assumption, but in comparing different economic systems, or in comparing different ways of organizing a given economy, the possibility that some of these variables might be affected cannot be ignored. Thus a reorganization that gives everyone more income and leisure might not improve the welfare of the community if at the same time it limits individual freedoms or requires the abandonment of cherished cultural traditions.

With these qualifications in mind, we can go on to the third. Paretian

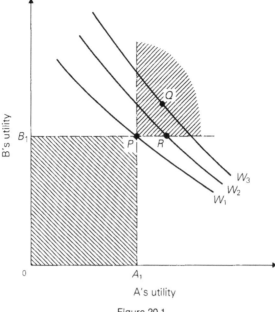

Figure 20.1

proposition, which is that any change that increases the welfare of at least one person in the community without reducing the welfare of any other also improves total welfare.[1] Such a change is often referred to as a **Pareto improvement**. The proposition also implies that any change that reduces the welfare of at least one person without improving that of any other also reduces total welfare. Whilst this proposition is relatively uncontroversial, it might appear to be of limited use since there must be many more potential changes in which some people gain and some lose than changes with which there are no individual losers or gainers. However, it does provide a basis from which discussion of the diagrammatic representation of the social welfare function can start.

If, to facilitate diagrammatic analysis, we consider a community of two persons, A and B, we can plot their respective utilities on the axes of a graph as in Figure 20.1. Since any situation in our community would involve each individual enjoying a certain amount of utility, it can be represented by a point on that graph. Thus a situation in which A has utility of A_1 and B of B_1 can be represented by point P. As in the construction of indifference curves, we do not need to be able to measure utility in precise cardinal units to be able to do this; all that is required is some (ordinal) index of utility that increases as the individual's utility increases. If, then, the welfare of the community is increased when at least one person is made better off without anyone being made worse off, it follows that all points such as Q or R lying within, or on the boundary of, the shaded area lying above and to the right of P must represent a situation yielding more welfare to the community than P. Correspondingly, all points within, or on the boundary of the shaded area lying below and to the left of P must involve lower levels of welfare. If, therefore, we are seeking points yielding the same level of social welfare as at P, they must lie in the unshaded parts of the diagram. Accordingly, in the same way that in earlier chapters we have drawn indifference curves through points yielding the same levels of utility and isoquants through points with the same output, we can construct, through P, a welfare contour connecting points in the diagram yielding the same level of social welfare as at P, and we can conclude from Figure 20.1 that it must be downward sloping like the curve labelled W_1. Further, since the diagram suggests that social welfare is higher at Q and R than at P because no one has any less utility at these points than at P and one or both has more, we may conclude that Q and R must be on welfare contours representing higher levels of social welfare such as W_2 and W_3.

How steep or flat these curves are then depends on what gain in utility to B the community regards as sufficient to compensate for a given loss of utility by A, and this reflects the community's preferences just as the precise form of an individual's indifference curves depends upon his or her own preferences. In the case of indifference curves, however, we were able to argue that there were good reasons for assuming them to be convex to the origin as well as downward sloping. As it happens, convexity of the welfare contours is not so crucial for our present analysis as convexity of indifference curves was in Chapter 2. Nevertheless, it is useful to consider further the factors likely to influence the shape of welfare contours in order to see if anything further can be said about their shape, even though it constitutes something of a digression.

Welfare contours and their shape

In considering further the form of a community's welfare contours, let us, for the moment, ignore the problems of measuring utility and treat it as a conventionally measurable variable. If, then, U_A and U_B are measured in the same units, the negatively sloped 45° line JK in Figure 20.2 represents different distributions of some given total utility. Further, if the community has no particular preference for any distribution and regards all those on JK as equally preferable, JK would also constitute a welfare contour, and higher and lower welfare contours would be represented by lines parallel to JK.[2] If, however, the community regards some distribution of utility on JK, such as that at G, as preferable to all the others, then G itself must lie on a welfare contour that lies above JK other than at G where it would be tangential to it; it would also seem reasonable to suppose that points closer to G will lie on higher welfare contours than those further away. All this implies that the individual welfare contours are convex to the origin as drawn in the diagram.

Moreover, there are some possible additional properties that can be mentioned. In the first place, the fact that in many economies there is some

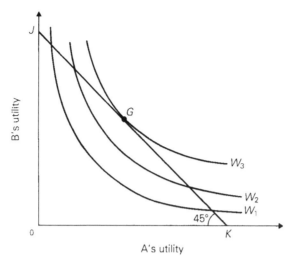

Figure 20.2

attempt to redistribute income from the better-off to the less well-off might be taken to indicate a preference for equality. In that case G would be at the mid-point of JK where the utilities of A and B are the same. Similarly, all other welfare contours would be tangential to a negatively sloped 45° line at their mid-points as in Figure 20.3, and all these points of tangency would lie on the positively sloped 45° line OE in the diagram. Moreover, the greater the preference for equality, the greater the degree of convexity of the welfare contours, since the lower A's utility relative to B's, the greater the extra income he would need to receive to compensate for a further reduction in A's income.

It has further been suggested that the welfare contours might be symmetrical about OE, as is also the case in Figure 20.3. This property would reflect a situation in which the community's view of a particular distribution of welfare is not affected by the identity of the individual with the higher level of utility. Thus in Figure 20.3, where $A_S = B_R$ and $A_R = B_S$, R and S lie on the same welfare contour because the distribution of welfare is the same in the two cases, although A has the higher level of welfare at S and B at R.

A symmetrical welfare function might appeal to conventional notions of fairness, but philosophical thinking on the nature of social justice has taken the argument further. The American philosopher Rawls, in his highly regarded work on social justice (Rawls, 1971), has argued that inequality in a society is justified only to the extent that it benefits the *least advantaged* members of that society. Under this criterion a Pareto improvement, which made someone better off without making anyone worse off, would not be regarded as a welfare improvement unless the least advantaged were among the beneficiaries. Thus in Figure 20.4 a movement from Q to S would not improve social welfare because there would be no benefit to B with the lesser

327

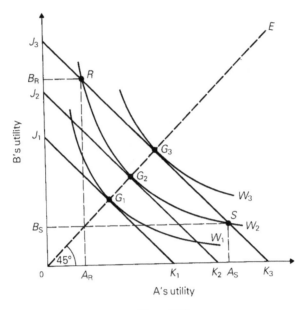

Figure 20.3

initial utility. This implies that S lies on a lower welfare contour than Q. However, a movement from Q to S' could be regarded as an improvement in welfare because, although B's share of the total welfare is in fact also less than that at Q, the gain to B might be considered sufficient to compensate for the greater inequality. In this case, therefore, the welfare contour through Q would be upward sloping, to pass between S and S', rather than downward sloping. Similar arguments can be applied to the welfare contour passing through R, where A is the more disadvantaged member of the community.

Overall, therefore, with a Rawlsian social welfare function each welfare contour would consist of two upward-sloping segments meeting on the 45° line as illustrated, and the slope of each segment would ultimately depend on how much inequality would compensate for a marginal increase in the welfare of the least disadvantaged.

It might be argued that the Rawls principle, and also to a lesser extent the notion of symmetry, assumes that members of a community are typically far more concerned with the welfare of their neighbours than they appear to be in practice. The justification for them, however, is that they reflect basic principles for the organization of society that even the most self-centred persons might support if they were uncertain about their future position. Against that it can be argued that the question of what individuals would choose in such an uncertain situation is somewhat irrelevant, because in any established society some individuals are already relatively advantaged and some disadvantaged, and that is likely to influence their views on the desirability of more or less equality. Hence, whether the more advantaged

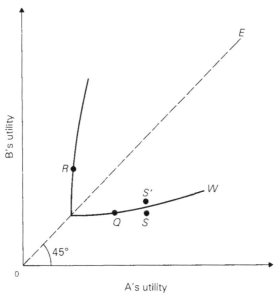

Figure 20.4

would accept that a change that benefited them without affecting the worse-off would actually reduce the welfare of the community, and whether they would accept that the welfare of the community would be unaffected if they were to swap places with the disadvantaged, is very much an open question. Indeed, it might also be questioned whether in practice individuals have any real preference for equality. In many countries the redistribution of income through the tax–benefit system is more to ensure minimum standards of living for the poorest members of the community rather than to promote equality, and could thus be interpreted as an aversion to some of the worst consequences of inequality rather than a definite preference for equality. If this is the case, then the welfare contours would only be convex in the more extreme regions of inequality rather than over the whole of their length.

In any case, whatever our views on these issues, there is a limit to the extent to which precise geometrical properties can be attributed to the welfare contours if the variables on the axes – individual levels of utility – cannot be measured in terms of some objectively defined unit. One conclusion of Chapter 5 was that small changes in an individual's utility are potentially measurable in money terms to a reasonable degree of approximation, suggesting that the slopes of the welfare contours, reflecting the loss in utility to B that the community is willing to accept for a gain of 1 unit of utility to A, are in principle capable of measurement. However, even though individual utility might be measurable in monetary terms, there can be no guarantee that the monetary unit of measurement represents the same amount of utility to A as it does to B. This means that equality of welfare (as opposed to income or wealth) is practically impossible to define, and situations involving symmetric but unequal distributions of welfare are likewise impossible to identify. Nevertheless, if a community does have some aversion to inequality, given that the more extreme forms of it are more readily identifiable, the willingness of the community to sacrifice the welfare of the less well-off members of the community in order to increase the welfare of the better-off may at some stage begin to decline, giving some convexity to the welfare contours. However, there do not seem to be strong grounds for assuming that they will necessarily be convex over all possible distributions of welfare.

The Pareto optimum

Given our social welfare function, however loosely defined, our next task is to consider the conditions under which the community's welfare is maximized. But if, as suggested above by the third of our Paretian propositions, social welfare is increased if the welfare of at least one member of the community is increased without reducing that of any other, it must be the case that one property of the position of maximum welfare, the community's most preferred position, is that there is no possibility of any further Pareto improvement. Such a situation is referred to as a **Pareto optimum**.

Essentially Pareto optimality simply involves efficiency in the use of resources. If a community is not at a Pareto optimum, by definition someone can be made better off without anyone being made worse off. This suggests that resources are not being used in their most efficient way because potentially more social welfare can be obtained from them. But, once a Pareto optimum has been reached, the opportunities for further efficiency gains of that nature are exhausted. As we shall see below, however, there is likely to be more than one Pareto optimum available, and these differ in their distribution of welfare between members of the community. We are thus able to make a distinction between the efficiency aspects of welfare maximization and the distributional aspects. In the following chapter, therefore, where we consider these matters in more detail, we consider first the efficiency problem, which involves an investigation into the properties of a Pareto optimum, and then go on to consider the issue of an optimal distribution of welfare.

Notes

1   In mathematical terms, this means that all the partial derivatives of the welfare function are non-negative (i.e. $\partial W/\partial U_i \geqslant 0$, $i = 1, 2, \ldots, n$).

2   This implies a social welfare function of the form

$$W = U_1 + U_2 + \ldots + U_n,$$

which is referred to as a utilitarian welfare function on the grounds that economists in the utilitarian tradition were (allegedly) primarily concerned with total welfare.

Exercises

20.1 To what extent is it reasonable to assume that the welfare of a community depends solely on the welfare of the individuals who make up that community?

20.2 What qualifications, if any, would you wish to make to the proposition that 'individuals are the best judges of their own welfare'?

20.3 Can the Paretian social welfare function be defended from the charge that it favours the status quo?

20.4 'Efficiency is a goal for raising pigs, not for the social life of a community of people.' Discuss.

20.5 What distributional value judgements might be incorporated into the Social Welfare Function?

CHAPTER TWENTY-ONE
THE MAXIMIZATION OF WELFARE

Introduction

An important consideration to bear in mind throughout our discussion of welfare issues is that the social welfare function, which is central to our concern, is derived from the utility of members of the community, depending largely on what they consume. This, in turn, is determined by what is produced, and therefore depends on the productive resources available and the technical conditions of production. Consequently, there are various levels of efficiency to be considered. To start with, resources have to be used with maximum efficiency in production, otherwise more output is capable of being produced to the potential benefit of consumers. Secondly, the output produced needs to be allocated efficiently to consumers. Thirdly, the efficiency with which the product mix meets the demands of consumers has to be considered. Having considered all these aspects of efficiency we can then turn to the distributional issues.

In what follows, to permit a diagrammatic exposition, we consider all these dimensions to the determination of maximum welfare in the context of an economy using two inputs, L and K, in the production of two goods X and Y,[1] which are then used by two consumers A and B. As usual, the results obtained from the analysis of this case are general in that they can be extended to situations with a larger number of inputs, products and consumers, but the diagrammatic approach has the advantage that it helps to provide a clearer understanding of what lies beneath the various conditions.

Efficiency in production

In our discussion of production we distinguished between technical and economic efficiency. Technical efficiency simply required the maximum output of a particular product to be obtained from the employment of a particular set of inputs. Clearly that kind of efficiency is essential for Pareto

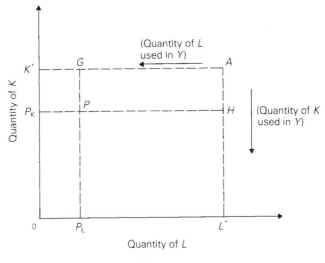

Figure 21.1

optimality, because without it there would be scope for someone to get more utility from the extra output of the product attainable from greater technical efficiency in the use of the resources employed in its production. However, once this kind of efficiency has been achieved, there remains the question of whether there are potential welfare gains from changing the proportions in which the inputs are combined in the (technically efficient) production of particular goods. This involves an aspect of economic efficiency, since it raises the question of the relative costs of different input combinations, and is our main concern in this section.

The conditions under which inputs are allocated efficiently in this latter sense can be investigated with the help of what is called, after the economists who developed it, the **Edgworth–Bowley box** diagram, or the Edgworth box for short. This diagram may seem formidable at first sight, but in reality it is no more than an extension of the standard type of diagram that has been used extensively in our earlier discussion of production and utility functions. The basic elements of this diagram, when used in a production context, are shown in Figure 21.1, which illustrates a situation in which the two inputs, L and K, are used in the production of goods X and Y.

This diagram depicts a situation in which the total inputs available are L^* of L and K^* of K, which, when the quantities of L and K are measured on the horizontal and vertical axes respectively, can be represented by point A. Now consider a situation in which, of the total resources available, P_L of L and P_K of K, represented by point P, are used in the production of X. Since the inputs not used in the production of X must be available to producers of Y, it follows that a total of $P_L L^*$ of L and $P_K K^*$ of K can be used in the production of Y. However, since $P_L L^*$ measured on the horizontal axis is the same as GA on the opposite side of the rectangular 'box' OK^*AL^*, and P_KK^* is the same as HA, it follows that we can also measure the inputs available for the production of Y from point A in the top right-hand corner of the box OK^*AL^*, with the quantity of L measured horizontally along AK^* from right to left and the quantity of K measured vertically down AL^* (in the directions indicated by the arrow). Point P thus indicates both the resources used in the production of X, measured conventionally from 0, and the resources available for the production of Y, measured from A, and therefore represents one possible allocation of the resources between the production of the two products. Similarly, every other point in the box OK^*AL^* (including those on the perimeter) represents another possible allocation. Whilst, therefore, the inputs employed in the production of X are measured conventionally from O, point A can be interpreted as the relevant 'origin' when measuring the inputs employed in the production of Y. This feature is made more explicit in Figure 21.2a, where the analysis is taken a stage further, by labelling these two points O_X and O_Y respectively.

Apart from these amendments, Figure 21.2a also includes information about the output of X and Y obtainable from each possible allocation of inputs. The curves labelled x_1 to x_5 are the isoquants derived from the production function for X, and thus show the technically efficient input combinations that can be used to produce x_1 to x_5 units of X respectively. Similarly, y_1 to y_5 are the isoquants representing the production function for Y, and show the combinations of inputs, measured from O_Y, required to produce the specified quantities of Y.[2] These curves enable us to deduce the technically efficient outputs represented by each point on the diagram in addition to the allocation of inputs. Thus, with the allocation of inputs at P, x_2 of X and y_2 of Y can be produced, whilst at Q, y_1 of Y ($< y_2$) and x_5 of X ($> x_2$) is produced. The Edgworth box diagram is thus essentially a device that enables us to represent no fewer than eight variables on a two-dimensional plane, since in Figure 21.2a we are able to show the total quantities of the two inputs available O_XL^* and O_XK^*, the quantities of L and K employed in the production of X and in the production of Y and the resultant outputs of X and Y. More importantly, however, it enables us to deduce the conditions under which a given allocation of inputs is an efficient one.

In terms of our Pareto criteria, inputs are allocated efficiently when it is not possible to increase the output of X without reducing the output of Y (and vice versa). Otherwise someone can gain from the extra output of X (or Y) without anyone being made worse off. Looked at from that point of view, it can be seen from Figure 21.2a that resources are not allocated efficiently at P, since by moving to V, for example, which involves the transfer of some additional units of input L to the production of X in exchange for the transfer of some units of K to the production of Y, more X would be produced (x_3) without any adverse effect on the production of Y. Moreover, whilst the allocation of resources is more efficient at V than P, it still does not represent a point of maximum efficiency, because there is still scope for increasing the

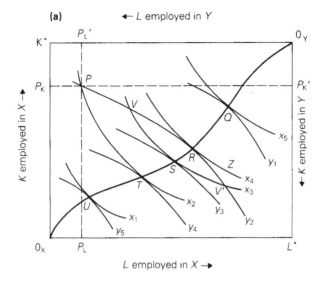

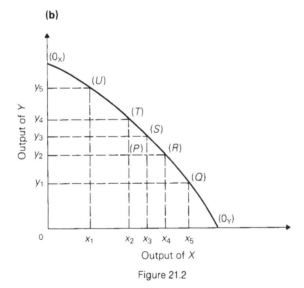

Figure 21.2

output of X further (to x_4) without reducing the production of Y, by moving
to point R.

However, once point R has been reached, further reallocations of
resources, such as for example to V' (or Z), would only lead to a reduction in
the output of X (or Y) and hence would not yield any further efficiency gains.
We may therefore deduce that the allocation of resources is efficient at R,
because it yields the maximum output of X attainable when y_2 is also
produced, given the total resources available. For similar reasons we may

deduce that T represents another efficient allocation of the available resources, since at that point the maximum output of Y (y_4) obtainable with x_2 of X would be produced. Moreover, it should be clear from the diagram that what distinguishes points such as R and T from points like P, V and V', at which the allocation of inputs is relatively inefficient, is that at the efficient points the X and Y isoquants are tangential to each other and thus have the same slopes. Further, as we may recall from p. 134 that the slope of the isoquants relative to the horizontal axis is the negative of the marginal rate of technical substitution of L for K, which we denoted as $MRTS_{LK}$, we may deduce that inputs are allocated efficiently when the marginal rate of technical substitution is the same in the production of both X and Y, or

$$MRTS_{LK}{}^X = MRTS_{LK}{}^Y. \tag{21.1}$$

Of course, R and T are not the only points where condition (21.1) holds. Q, S and U are others identified on the diagram and many more could be found by drawing in more isoquants. Indeed, if all possible isoquants were shown, a continuous curve could be drawn through all the points at which the isoquants are tangential. This curve, called a **contract curve**, is denoted in Figure 21.2a by the thick line drawn through $O_X UTSRQO_Y$. All points on this curve thus represent possible efficient allocations of the available inputs. By contrast, some improvement in efficiency is always possible at points off the contract curve because more of one, or both, products can be obtained from an appropriate reallocation of inputs.

Whilst the different output combinations available from the efficient use of the inputs can be deduced from Figure 21.2a, they can be shown more directly by constructing a **production possibility curve**. A production possibility curve, drawn on a diagram with quantities of the two goods produced plotted on the axes, indicates the maximum output of Y obtainable for each possible output of X (and vice versa). Since obtaining the maximum amount of one product for a given production of the other requires efficient use of the available inputs, each point on the contract curve has a corresponding point on the production possibility curve. Hence, in Figure 21.2b, which shows the production possibility curve derived from the contract curve in Figure 21.2a, the point labelled (Q), where y_1 of Y and x_5 of X is produced, corresponds to point Q in Figure 21.2a, and other corresponding points are labelled similarly. It will be noted that the point in Figure 21.2b corresponding to O_X in the box diagram is where the production possibility curve reaches the Y axis, because at O_X no resources are being used in the production of X, thereby allowing the maximum possible output of Y to be produced. Similarly, at O_Y the opposite applies, yielding the greatest possible output of X. In addition, it can be noted that, whilst the main purpose of Figure 21.2b is to highlight the output combinations attainable when inputs are being used efficiently, points off the contract curve in Figure 21.2a, such as P, also have their corresponding points in Figure 21.2b, but these are inside the production possibilty curve.

The form of the production possibility curve, like that of the contract curve, reflects the form of the underlying production functions, and it is possible to show that, if both the production functions exhibit constant or decreasing returns to scale, the production possibility curve will normally be convex to the origin.[3] With sufficiently strongly increasing returns to scale in one or both production functions, however, the production possibility curve might be convex to the origin. Since the precise shape of the curve does not materially affect the present discussion, we do not attempt to demonstrate these properties in this text. Nevertheless, as is usually the case, the slope of the curve does have some meaningful economic interpretation and we do need to consider what that is.

The slope of the production possibility curve actually reflects the amount of Y that needs to be given up to produce an additional unit of X when inputs are being used efficiently. Alternatively, it can be interpreted as that amount of Y that 1 unit of X can be transformed into by a reallocation of productive resources. In the light of this, it has been given the technical term the **marginal rate of transformation of X into Y**, which can be denoted as MRT_{XY}, and in line with this terminology the production possibility curve itself is sometimes called a **transformation curve**. More usefully, however, we may note that

$$MRT_{XY} = MC_X/MC_Y,$$

since, for example, if at some point $MRT_{XY} = 3$, indicating that giving up 1 unit of X enables 3 more units of Y to be produced, a necessary implication is that production of a marginal unit of X requires 3 times the inputs required to produce a marginal unit of Y. Hence we may conclude that in such a case

$$MC_X = 3 \cdot MC_Y$$

or

$$MC_X/MC_Y = 3 = MRT_{XY}.$$

Further, if MC_X rises relative to MC_Y as the production of X increases relative to Y, the production possibility curve will be concave to the origin. Since, as suggested above, that will normally be the case unless there are strongly increasing returns to scale in the production of one or both products, we have drawn our production possibility curves to be concave, although as already stated that is not crucial to our present analysis.

Efficiency in consumption

Having considered the conditions under which a given bundle of goods is produced efficiently, our next task is to consider the conditions under which the allocation to consumers of the goods produced is efficient. Given the properties of our Paretian welfare function, it will be recognized that this allocation is efficient if it is not possible, through a reallocation of the goods, to increase the utility of one individual without reducing the utility of others.

In the case where there is a given quantity of two goods to be allocated to two consumers, the analysis of efficiency conditions is very similar to that of efficiency in production and uses the same basic tools of analysis. Thus we can again use an Edgeworth box diagram, but this time the quantities of consumer goods rather than inputs are measured on the axes and, within the box, utility functions are represented rather than production functions. Figure 21.3a, therefore, depicts a situation in which a total of OX_1 of good X and OY_1 of good Y is available for allocation between consumers A and B, so that all points within the box $O_A Y_1 O_B X_1$ represent possible allocations of the available resources between our two consumers with the quantities of goods consumed by A measured from O_A and the quantities consumed by B from O_B. The utility functions of the two individuals can thus be represented by the indifference curves $a_1, a_2, \ldots, a_4$ and $b_1, b_2, \ldots, b_4$ respectively.

As in the production case, the goods are allocated efficiently where the indifference curves are tangential to each other. At other points, like P in Figure 21.3a, it is always possible for one individual to be made better off without the other being made worse off, or indeed for both to be made better off, if A were to give up some X in exchange for some of B's Y. However, there would be no possibility of such mutually beneficial exchange at points such as S and T where the indifference curves are tangential. Again, as in the production case, there are a number of points of tangency, so another contract curve can be drawn through all the efficient allocations in the diagram. At each point on this curve the slopes of the two consumers' indifference curves, reflecting their marginal rates of substitution of X for Y (MRS_{XY}) are equal, so we may write as a condition for the efficient allocation of goods for consumption

$$MRS_{XY}{}^A = MRS_{XY}{}^B. \tag{21.2}$$

Extending the analysis, a utility possibility curve can be derived from the box diagram corresponding to the production possibility curve in Figure 21.2b, showing the maximum amount of utility obtainable by B for any given level of A's utility and vice versa. Such a curve is illustrated in Figure 21.3b. However, in contrast to the case with production functions, since there are no grounds for suggesting that the utility functions might possess particular properties like homogeneity that might restrict the shape of the utility possibility curve, no general propositions can be made about its shape except

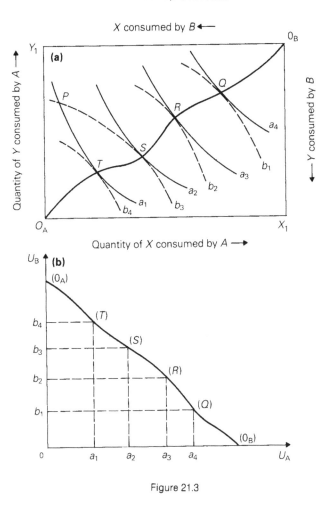

Figure 21.3

that it will be downward sloping as long as both X and Y are 'goods' to both individuals rather than 'bads'. In that case, since moves along the contract curve will be accomplished only if some of both goods are transferred from one individual to another, the recipient must gain some utility at the expense of his partner.

Efficient product mix

The previous section indicated the conditions under which a *given* combination of X and Y would need to be allocated to secure efficiency in consumption, but did not rule out the possibility that someone could be made better off without anyone being made worse off by changing the combination of goods produced. In this section we need to consider the conditions under

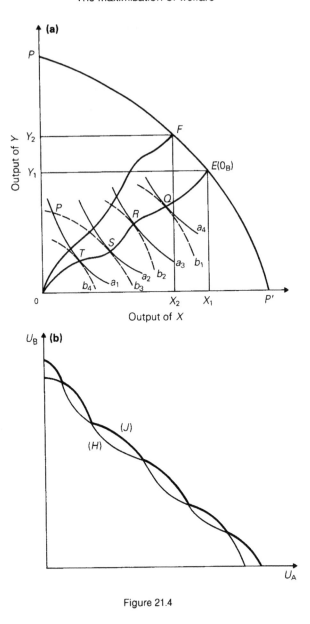

Figure 21.4

which the bundle of goods produced, or the product mix, is an optimal one.

As long as the bundle of goods featured in Figure 21.3, namely $O_A X_1$ of X and $O_A Y_1$ of Y, is produced efficiently so that condition (21.1) is satisfied, it constitutes one of the possible output combinations on the overall production possibility curve. Hence, Figure 21.3a can be extended, as in Figure 21.4a, to take account of other efficient production possibilities. In the latter diagram, PP' is the production possibility curve defined as in Figure 21.2b, and E is the point at which X_1 of X and Y_1 of Y is produced. The rectangle OY_1EX_1 thus constitutes the Edgworth box of Figure 21.3a, and the indifference curves and contract curves from that diagram are also shown in Figure 21.4a. But the latter diagram also shows the corresponding Edgworth box when the bundle of goods at F, involving X_2 of X and Y_2 of Y, is produced and the contract curve (OF) arising in that case. Further, just as a utility possibility curve can be drawn showing the utility combinations attainable along the contract curve OE when the bundle of goods at E is consumed efficiently, a similar utility possibility curve can be drawn representing the utility combinations along OF, and indeed the process can be repeated for all possible output combinations along PP'.

A selection of such utility possibility curves is shown in Figure 21.4b. From that diagram it should be clear that there are points on individual utility possibility curves, such as that labelled (H) that are not Pareto-optimal in its fullest sense. Although by definition both conditions (21.1) and (21.2) are satisfied at such points, it is still possible to increase the utility of A (or B) without reducing the utility of the other member of the community by changing the product mix and moving on to another utility possibility curve. However, further Pareto improvement is not possible once a point on the outer frontier of the area covered by utility possibility curves such as that labelled (J) has been reached. This outer frontier constitutes what is termed the **utility possibility frontier** and can be obtained geometrically by drawing an envelope curve, shown in Figure 21.4b as a thick line, round the outer limits of the family of utility possibility curves. Since this frontier includes all the points from which it is not possible to increase one person's welfare without reducing that of others, it represents the locus of all possible Pareto optimum positions. Further, since conditions (21.1) and (21.2) are satisfied at all points on each individual utility possibility curve, the question remaining to be considered is what additional condition distinguishes the points on the utility possibility frontier from those on utility possibility curves inside the frontier.

The answer to this question is that at points on the utility possibility frontier the marginal rate of transformation between the two products is equal to the marginal rate of substitution, which, given that condition (21.2) applies to all members of the community, means that

$$MRT_{XY} = MRS_{XY} \qquad (21.3)$$

where $$MRS_{XY} = MRS_{XY}^A = MRS_{XY}^B.$$

Condition (21.3), which is sometimes referred to as a **top-level** optimum since it presupposes that the **lower-level** condition (21.1) and (21.2) are already met, can most easily be demonstrated numerically. Suppose all members of the community are willing to accept 2 units of Y as compensation for losing 1 unit of X. If in these circumstances the resources used to produce the marginal unit of X can be used to produce 3 additional units of Y when

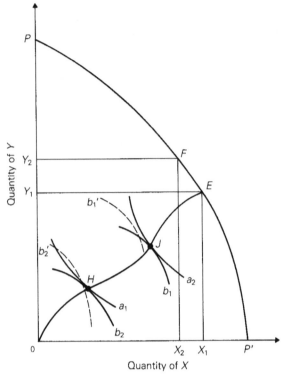

Figure 21.5

switched to the production of that product (that is, $MRT_{XY} = 3 > MRS_{XY} = 2$), the consumers can be more than compensated for the loss of the unit of X and so at least one of them can be made better off without making the other any worse off. The situation is thus clearly not Pareto-optimal. However, if only 2 additional units of Y could be produced following the transfer of resources (that is, $MRT_{XY} = 2 = MRS_{XY}$), the individual forfeiting the unit of X could only just be compensated for his loss and there is no scope for making anyone better off. The situation, therefore, is already Pareto-optimal.

A diagrammatic illustration of all this is provided in Figure 21.5. If production is initially at E on the production possibility curve (so that condition (21.1) is satisfied), points H and J on the contract curve OE, defined as in Figures 21.3a and 21.4a, represent possible distributions of the available output when condition (21.2) is also satisfied. The diagram is drawn so that the slopes of the individual indifference curves at H are less than the slope of the production possibility curve at E ($MRT_{XY} > MRS_{XY}$), whilst at J the slopes of the indifference curves are the same as the slope of the production possibility curve at E ($MRT_{XY} = MRS_{XY}$). If the bundle of goods produced is now changed to that at F, involving less X and more Y, then the origin for B's indifference curves is shifted to F and the indifference curves themselves are correspondingly displaced upwards and to the left.

In the diagram, the new positions of b_1 and b_2 are indicated by the dashed curves b_1' and b_2'. By contrast, the location of A's indifference curves with their origin at O is unaffected. It can be seen from the diagram that at H the change in the relative position of B's indifference curve from b_2 to b_2' opens up the possibility of one or both individuals moving to a higher indifference curve, whereas at J the relative movement of the indifference curves is such that one individual can obtain the same utility as before only if the other receives less. In Figure 21.4b, therefore, the point corresponding to J in Figure 21.5, labelled (J), must be represented by a point on the utility possibility frontier, whilst the point in Figure 21.4b corresponding to H in Figure 21.5, labelled (H), must be represented by a point inside it. Hence we can see again that Pareto optimality requires the slope of the individuals' indifference curves to be the same as that of the production possibility curve, and that condition (21.3) applies.

Variable inputs

So far, our analysis has assumed a fixed bundle of inputs to be allocated between uses. It remains to consider the implications for Pareto optimality of relaxing this assumption. Since with more inputs available the dimensions of the production box are increased and more of both goods can be produced and consumed, the community's production possibility curve is pushed outwards, reflecting these enhanced production and consumption opportunities. But the extra production naturally involves some cost in the form of reduced leisure when more labour inputs are required and reduced consumption when additional capital or material inputs are required, since the production of such intermediate products requires the use of resources that might otherwise be devoted to the production of goods for consumption. The question to be examined therefore concerns the conditions under which the supply of inputs is Pareto-optimal. As we shall see, it turns out that extending the analysis to allow for a variable supply of inputs does not involve any new conditions but simply involves a broadening of the interpretations of previous conditions and the diagrams that were used to derive them.

Consider, for example, Figure 21.4a when X can be used as an input in the production of Y as well as a consumer good. With a given amount of other productive resources, PP' can again be taken to indicate the possible bundles of X and Y available for final consumption. Thus if P' of X and no Y is produced, P' of X is available for final consumption, whereas if all the available X is used in the production of Y there is none available for final consumption but instead there is P of Y. Point E then, as before, reflects a situation in which X_1 of X and Y_1 of Y is available for final consumption, but in this case the implication is that some of the $P'X_1$ of X given up is used in the production of Y. Nevertheless, in both cases $P'X_1$ is being given up to allow the production of Y_1 of Y, and hence the difference between the two cases is minimal. Moreover, as previously, the bundle of final output is optimal if it is distributed efficiently between members of the community, requiring condition (21.2) to be met, and if the marginal rate of transformation of X to Y is equal to the community marginal rate of substitution, or in other words if condition (21.3) holds.

Exactly the same arguments apply if X is leisure rather than some variable material input. The production of Y, in so far as it requires labour inputs, requires the sacrifice of leisure, which, of course, is a potential source of utility to individuals. If, therefore, P' is the initial stock of leisure available (the total time available), then at E the community enjoys a total of Y_1 of Y and, having used up X_1P' labour hours in the production of Y, X_1 hours of leisure. Possible distributions of the available Y and leisure are represented by points inside the box OY_1EX_1, and the usual optimal conditions apply.

In this case, however, we can see that the marginal rate of transformation has another possible interpretation. Since it is by definition the extra Y produced when an extra unit of leisure is given up, it is also the marginal product of labour in the production of Y. Indeed, this must be expected because PP' is really no more than the total product curve relating the output of Y to quantity of X employed, but in this case the latter is measured along the horizontal axis to the left from P' rather than in the conventional direction.

Overall, therefore, the introduction of variable input supplies requires nothing new in the way of optimal conditions. It can be dealt with simply by interpreting X in conditions (21.2) and (21.3) as something that is used potentially for production purposes as well as in consumption.

The welfare optimum

The previous sections have suggested that in any community there are likely to be a range of Pareto optimum situations represented by points on the utility possibility frontier. These situations differ basically in the distribution of welfare or utility between members of the community. However, if as suggested in the previous chapter communities have a welfare function that ranks different distributions of welfare, then some characterization of the situation in which community welfare is maximized is possible.

In our earlier discussion it was suggested that a community's welfare function could be represented diagrammatically by a series of welfare contours drawn through equally ranked distributions of welfare. These are shown as the curves W_1, W_2 and W_3 in Figure 21.6, and if UU' is the community's utility possibility frontier, then point T, where a welfare contour is tangential to the utility possibility frontier, indicates the position of maximum welfare. At this point A and B will enjoy levels of utility

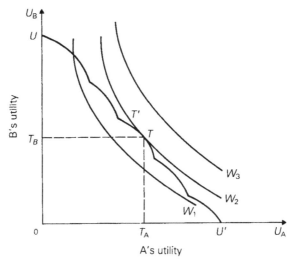

Figure 21.6

represented by T_A and T_B respectively, but the fact that T is a point on the utility possibility frontier also implies that the three basic conditions for Pareto optimality derived above are satisfied. However, since the latter can be expressed in terms of equalities between marginal concepts, it is useful to consider to what extent the situation at T can be described in similar terms.

Since T represents a point of tangency between the welfare contours and the utility possibility curve, the slopes of the two curves are equal, so we need to consider what is measured by these slopes. We can examine the slopes of the welfare contours in exactly the same way as we looked at the slopes of indifference curves and isoquants in earlier chapters. For a small movement along the welfare contour W_2 from T to T' in Figure 21.6, B enjoys a gain in utility, which can be denoted by ΔU_B, whilst A suffers a change in utility (which is actually a loss), which can be denoted correspondingly by ΔU_A. The slope of UU' in the vicinity of T is thus approximated by $\Delta U_B/\Delta U_A$. However, if total community welfare is unchanged.

$$\Delta U_A \cdot MW(U_A) + \Delta U_B \cdot MW(U_B) = 0,$$

where $MW(U_A)$ and $MW(U_B)$ represent the community's valuation of the effect of a marginal increase in the utility of A and B respectively on community welfare. Rearranging we get

$$\Delta U_B/\Delta U_A \ (= \text{slope of welfare contour}) = -MW(U_A)/MW(U_B).$$

The slopes of the welfare contours thus reflect the relative weights the community attaches to utility changes affecting A and B respectively with particular distributions of welfare.

So far as the slope of the utility possibility frontier is concerned, it needs to be remembered that a point on this curve is also a point on a utility possibility curve. Since movements along such a utility possibility curve can be achieved by transferring one (optimally produced) unit of any commodity such as X from A to B, the gain in utility to B is represented by MU_X^B and the (negative) change to A by MU_X^A. The slope of the relevant utility possibility curve, which is the same as the slope of the frontier at T, is then simply $- MU_X^B/ MU_X^A$. It should be noted that this is the same as $- MU_Y^B/MU_Y^A$, since, if condition 21.2 holds,

$$MU_X^A/MU_Y^A = MU_X^B/MU_Y^B,$$

which can be rearranged to give

$$MU_X^B/MU_X^A = MU_Y^B/MU_Y^A,$$

thus confirming that movement along a utility possibility frontier can be achieved by transferring one unit of *any* commodity from A to B or vice versa.

Using these results, we may conclude that at T

$$MU_X^A/MU_X^B \; (= MU_Y^A/MU_Y^B) = MW(U_B/MW(U_A), \qquad (21.4)$$

or again by rearrangement

$$MU_X^A MW(U_A) = MU_X^B MW(U_B).$$

The left-hand side of this expression can be interpreted as the effect on community welfare, or the social value, of A receiving an extra unit of X, whilst the expression on the right-hand side is the corresponding social value of an extra unit of X to individual B. Since condition (21.4) can also be rearranged to produce a similar expresson for good Y, we may conclude that the distribution of welfare is optimal if the social value of an extra unit of any good is the same for A and B and thus that

$$MU_i^A MW(U_A) = MU_i^B MW(U_A), \quad i = X, Y. \qquad (21.5)$$

Extending the conditions

To sum up so far, we have identified four basic conditions for maximizing community welfare. The first, expressed in condition (21.1) as

$$MRTS_{LK}^X = MRTS_{LK}^Y,$$

is a condition for efficient production. The second, expressed in (21.2) as

$$MRS_{XY}^A = MRS_{XY}^B,$$

is a condition for efficient consumption, whilst the third, expressed in (21.3) as

$$MRS_{XY} = MRT_{XY},$$

is a condition for an efficient product mix. We have just added to that condition (21.5), which is a condition for an efficient distribution of welfare and requires that

$$MU_X^A MW(U_A) = MU_X^B MW(U_B).$$

Moreover, although we have defined these conditions in the context of a two-input, two-good and two-consumer model, it can be shown using mathematical procedures that they can be generalized without significant modification to cover any number of inputs, goods and consumers. In its more general form, condition (21.1) requires the marginal rate of technical substitution for each pair of inputs to be the same. Similarly, condition (21.2) when generalized requires the marginal rate of substitution between each pair of goods to be the same for all consumers. Condition (21.3) then likewise has to apply to all pairs of goods,[4] whilst condition (21.5) needs extending to cover all consumers.

Some qualifications

Having defined the conditions under which welfare is maximized, our next main task is to consider the circumstances under which these conditions might be met. Before going on to that, however, there are certain quali-fications to our main results that need to be noted. First of all, although Figure 21.6 has been constructed to show a single unique welfare optimum, the possibility of more than one such optimum cannot be ruled out. Given that the only restriction on both the utility possibility frontier and the welfare contours is that they are downward sloping, W_2 in the diagram could be tangential to the utility possibility frontier at more than one point. If that arises because the welfare contour runs along the utility possibility frontier over some range of utility distributions, then it creates no additional problems. Indeed, it would ease the problem of actually achieving a welfare optimum because there would be a range of equally acceptable positions rather than a unique optimum.

However, in cases like that illustrated in Figure 21.7, additional compli-cations do arise. In this diagram it will be seen that, although there is a point

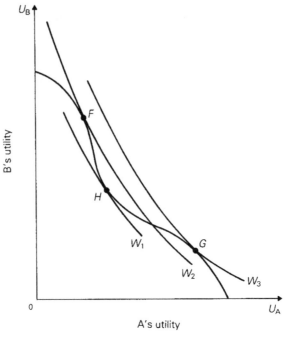

Figure 21.7

of tangency between the utility possibility frontier and the welfare contour W_2 at F, F does not represent the best possible position because G, where all the optimal conditions are also met, is on a higher welfare contour. This reflects the fact that the conditions deduced above are essentially conditions determining *local* welfare optima and therefore need not preclude further welfare improvement when other local optima exist. A further problem is that, where a number of such local optima exist, other points of tangency between welfare contours and the utility possibility frontier will also be found, such as that at point H. All the marginal conditions specified above apply at H, but it is a point of minimum rather than maximum welfare along the utility possibility frontier. This reflects the fact that our marginal conditions are strictly only the first-order conditions for a maximum, and these are the same as the first-order conditions for a minimum and other stationary values.[5] The satisfaction of the marginal conditions will reflect a position of maximum welfare only if all the relevant second-order conditions are also met.

The full statement of all these conditions, even in our simple two-good, two-input, two-person case, is mathematically somewhat involved, but it can be seen from Figure 21.7 that one of its requirements is for the welfare contours to be more convex to the origin than the utility possibility frontier. Nevertheless, this seems to suggest that, even if we do not know whether the relevant second-order conditions are satisfied or not, we can be reasonably

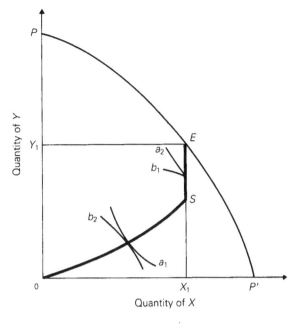

Figure 21.8

certain that, if the (first-order) marginal conditions are not satisfied, some welfare improvement is possible. However, even that conclusion needs qualifying.

Strictly, it only applies when all inputs are used in the production of each good and all consumers consume some of each good. Whilst it may be reasonable to assume that this is the case in our limited two-product world, it does not seem to be a very realistic assumption to apply in a multi-commodity world. After all, only a limited section of the population buys economics textbooks and, more generally, it must be the case that most consumers buy only a limited range of all the goods on offer. This does not detract from any of our discussion about the nature of the welfare function, but it does affect the specification of our optimal conditions.

Some indication of how it can affect them can be seen if we consider a situation in our two-good world like that in Figure 21.8, which is similar to Figure 21.4a except that the contract curve meets the side of the consumption box OY_1EX_1 at point S and then runs vertically up X_1 to E. Points between S and E then represent situations in which individual A consumes all the available X but shares the available Y with B. The distributions of the available output are optimal because, given the way the indifference curves are drawn, there is no way of redistributing the available supplies without making at least one of the two individuals worse off. However, as can be seen from the diagram, the slopes of the individuals' indifference curves need not be equal, as welfare improvements would not be possible as long as A's indifference curve was steeper than B's. In other words, the efficiency condition along the stretch of the contract curve between S and E is that

$$MRS_{XY}{}^A > MRS_{XY}{}^B.$$

Correspondingly, product-mix efficiency would require

$$MRS_{XY}{}^A > MRT_{XY} > MRS_{XY}{}^B.$$

This is an example of what is called a **corner solution**, and when such corner situations appear some of the conditions for a Pareto optimum need to be modified.

Similar considerations apply if the underlying utility and production functions are not the smooth functions we have taken them to be but contain kinks or discontinuities. However, to avoid undue complications to our analysis, we will ignore such complications and continue to assume that, to a reasonable degree of approximation, a welfare optimum can be characterized by the marginal conditions deduced above. Whilst this may seem to be a somewhat heroic assumption in the light of the preceding paragraphs, it has been shown that most of the key conclusions in our subsequent analysis are reasonably robust and are not affected by the relaxation of this assumption.

Notes

1 An efficient use of resources would not involve the production of 'bads' (products yielding negative utility – see Chapter 2) unless they were unavoidably produced in the process of producing other goods. Such possibilities are ignored for the moment, but are considered further in the next chapter.

2 The conventional production function diagram for Y is thus rotated through 180° and superimposed on that for X.

3 The single exception arises when, with constant returns to scale in the production functions of both products, the contract curve takes the form of a diagonal of the box. In that case, the production possibility curve will also be linear. The reader is invited to consider for him/herself why that might be the case.

4 Alternatively, as indicated in Chapter 2, Y can be a numeraire good (which might be money), in which case the general form of condition (21.3) is that the marginal cost of each good in terms of Y must be equal to the consumer's valuation of that good in terms of Y.

5 This is directly analogous to the case of the profit-maximizing firm, since marginal revenue equals marginal cost at the firm's minimum profit output as well as when profits are maximized.

Exercises

21.1 'The Edgworth-Bowley box is simply a device for increasing the number of variables that can be represented on a two-dimensional diagram.' Discuss.

21.2 If two goods X and Y can be produced using two inputs, and the production functions for both exhibit constant returns to scale, draw an Edgworth box diagram showing all possible allocations of fixed quantities of the two inputs between the production of X and Y and locate within it one point on the contract curve. Now starting from that point show how the efficient allocation of the inputs between uses must change when the output of X is increased a little with a corresponding reduction in the output of Y. Hence show that the contract curve must be concave to the diagonal of the box except when it coincides with that diagonal.

21.3 Consider how the analysis of Exercise 21.2 might be extended to deduce the shape of the resultant production possibility curve.

21.4 To what extent is it true to say that the welfare of a community must be increased if it moves from a point inside the production possibility curve to one on it?

21.5 Explain carefully the conditions which are met on a utility possibility frontier which need not be met on a utility possibility curve.

21.6 Explain why a Pareto optimum position is not necessarily a welfare optimum. What additional conditions are satisfied at the latter?

21.7 'The various marginal conditions are neither necessary nor sufficient for a Pareto optimum'. Is this statement true or false? Explain why.

CHAPTER TWENTY-TWO
SOCIAL WELFARE AND MARKETS

Introduction

In the last chapter, we derived the theoretical conditions under which the social welfare of a community is maximized without reference to the way in which resources in an economy might be allocated in practice. But given that we are in the western world operating in economies that rely to a large extent on markets to allocate resources, it is appropriate to begin this chapter by considering the extent to which resources might be optimally allocated in a market economy. We can then go on to identify the main obstacles to the achievement of an optimal allocation of resources in such an economy. In all this we will be concerned with the outcome of economic agents operating through markets and can, therefore, draw extensively on the analysis of the behaviour of economic agents in previous chapters. On the basis of that discussion we will conclude the book by considering briefly the implications for the role of government suggested by our analysis and by noting some of the problems arising.

The invisible hand theorem

The belief that markets provide an efficient means of allocating scarce resources is a long-standing one and the more analytical interests of economists in the idea can be traced back to Adam Smith, who argued in his *Wealth of Nations* that economic agents operating through markets were led by an invisible hand to produce an outcome of potential benefit to society that was no part of their original intention. In a sense, this might be regarded as saying no more than the obvious, because it would be irrational for any economic agent to trade through markets unless he received some benefit, and if all the agents benefit through trade then, clearly, given our discussion of the nature of the welfare function, so must the community as a whole. However, welfare economics, as developed over the last hundred years, has produced the more specific proposition that, under certain circumstances, optimizing behaviour by economic agents operating through markets leads to a Pareto-optimal allocation of resources. Moreover, this proposition can easily be demonstrated by referring back to the various optimum conditions derived in the last chapter.

In that chapter, it was shown first of all that inputs would be allocated efficiently between uses if the marginal rate of technical substitution between any pair of inputs was the same in all uses. In the two-input, two-good case considered in the diagrammatic analysis of that chapter, this condition was expressed in equation (21.1) as

$$MRTS_{LK}^{X} = MRTS_{LK}^{Y}.$$

Now, if the producers of X and Y are firms acting as price takers in the markets in which they buy their inputs, the analysis of Chapter 9 suggests that they would all be concerned to minimize their costs by using an input combination along the scale expansion path of its isoquant diagram, like the points on OS in Figure 9.6 where isoquants are tangential to the constant cost curves reflecting the relative prices of the inputs. At all such points, therefore,

$$MRTS_{LK} = P_{L}/P_{K},$$

and, if all producers of X and Y are adjusting their input quantities to meet this condition, we may deduce that

$$MRTS_{LK}^{X} = P_{L}/P_{K} = MRTS_{LK}^{Y}, \qquad (22.1)$$

and the condition for efficient production is automatically satisfied.

Similarly we have seen in Chapter 2 that price-taking, utility-maximizing consumers buy bundles of goods for which the marginal rate of substitution between any pair of them is equal to their price ratio, and hence in the two-good, two-consumer case we can deduce that

$$MRS_{XY}^{A} = P_{X}/P_{Y} = MRS_{XY}^{B}, \qquad (22.2)$$

and hence that the condition for efficient consumption (21.2) is also met.

Thirdly, we have seen in Chapter 12 that price-taking, profit-maximizing producers produce outputs at which marginal cost is equal to price, so that

$$MC_{X}/MC_{Y} = MRT_{XY} = P_{X}/P_{Y},$$

and hence in general terms, with conditions (21.1) and (21.2) already met, it must also be the case that

$$MRT_{XY} = P_X/P_Y = MRS_{XY}, \qquad (22.3)$$

where $$MRS_{XY} = MRS_{XY}^A = MRS_{XY}^B,$$

and thus condition (21.3) for an efficient product mix is satisfied.

Finally, if X is an input as well as a consumer good, price-taking, profit-maximizing producers use the quantity of X for which the marginal revenue product of X in the production of Y is equal to its price, or

$$MP_X \cdot P_Y = P_X,$$

or $$MP_X = P_X/P_Y.$$

But, as argued above, in this context

$$MP_X = MRT_{XY},$$

so with consumers maximizing their utility we would again have

$$MRT_{XY} = P_X/P_Y = MRS_{XY},$$

and the condition for an efficient product mix is satisfied.

We can thus demonstrate that, with utility-maximizing, price-taking agents operating through markets, the invisible hand of market forces leads to a Pareto-optimal allocation of resources. However, as will be shown below, the conditions under which this result can be achieved turn out to be quite restrictive. Moreover, even when the invisible hand works to produce an optimal allocation, there are no grounds for concluding that the distribution of welfare between individuals is likely to be such that a welfare optimum will also be achieved.

Given that each individual's utility depends on the goods and services he consumes and the leisure he enjoys, the level of utility attainable is constrained in a purely market economy by the value of the goods and services he can supply to the market. This, in turn, is determined by the nature of the labour services he can offer and by the price they command in the labour market (that is, his human capital) and by the value of other assets (material capital) at his disposal that can be sold to provide purchasing power or, in the case of durable assets, hired to others. This inevitably leads to inequalities, in that those endowed with scarce skills that the market values highly – like leading sportsmen, pop stars or successful businessmen – and those well-endowed with material assets can spend more than those with more modest endowments. Moreover, such inequalities may tend to increase over time, as those with high earning capacities are able to earn more than they need to spend to live comfortably. They can thus acquire additional capital assets that further enhance their earning power and may also, ultimately, enhance the spending power of their descendants. In contrast, those at the other end of the income scale are hard put to meet their normal day-to-day living expenses and have nothing left over to permit the accumulation of wealth.

Since the ability to develop scarce skills is, to some extent at least, an accident of birth, and access to inherited wealth is entirely an accident of birth, the resultant distribution of wealth at any time, if left entirely to market forces, would seem to be more a matter of chance than conscious choice. Moreover, since the distribution of welfare at any time in an efficiently operating market system is uniquely determined by the initial distribution of wealth, the resultant distribution of welfare is also largely a matter of chance and the likelihood of it being the community's preferred one would thus appear to be fairly small. Whilst, therefore, a market system may be seen as having the potential to allocate resources efficiently, it may nevertheless fail to produce a welfare optimum as defined in condition (21.5) above. Indeed, the fact that governments in market-based economies normally take some steps to redistribute incomes provides an indication of the extent to which markets, when left to themselves, fail to produce an acceptable distribution of welfare in their economies.

Moreover, as we have already hinted, markets may also fail even to allocate resources efficiently because the restrictive conditions required to satisfy the invisible hand theorem are not met in practice, so we must now consider these conditions in more detail.

Conditions for optimal allocation

The existence of equilibrium

One important requirement for conditions (22.1)–(22.3) above to be satisfied is that a situation of **general equilibrium** exists. This requires all markets concerned to be in equilibrium simultaneously. If one market is not in equilibrium for some reason, then at least one of the agents operating in that market would be seeking to revise his buying or selling plans either because he is prevented from carrying out his initial (optimizing) plans or because unforeseen opportunities for further gains have arisen. In either case the relevant marginal rate of substitution would not be equal to its correspond-ing price ratio, and thus at least one, and possibly more, of the conditions for an optimal allocation of resources would be violated, leaving unexploited opportunities for Pareto improvement.

Much of the analysis of the earlier chapters of the book has in fact rested on an assumption that individual markets tend to move towards a definable equilibrium, but it was sufficient for the purposes of that analysis for that equilibrium to be a *partial* equilibrium in the market concerned, with a given situation in other related markets, which need not themselves necessarily be in equilibrium. Whilst it may be reasonable to assume that individual markets tend to such partial equilibrium (although it may be doubted whether that is always the case), it does not follow that it can equally be assumed that a market economy tends to a position in which all markets are simultaneously in equilibrium. Indeed, before it can be assumed that a market economy tends towards such a general equilibrium situation it has first to be established that such a general equilibrium can exist, or that there is a set of prices capable of generating equilibrium in every single market, and, secondly, that such an equilibrium is stable in that after any disturbance the system moves back towards the equilibrium rather than away from it.

Proving the existence and stability of general equilibrium in a multi-market economy would take us well beyond the scope of this text. It can, however, be stated that it has been shown that a stable equilibrium can exist in a competitive economy, but is less certain in an economy with more monopolistic elements. Moreover, irrespective of whether a general equilibrium is theoretically possible, casual observation of the world around us suggests that in practice it may not be a very common experience. In a dynamic world, individual markets are subject to a variety of shocks, some random and some not so random, which means that change rather than static equilibrium is the norm. Further, in many markets, because of rigidities of various sorts, the adjustment to changed conditions can often be a long drawn out and painful one. Indeed, the levels of unemployment experienced in the UK and elsewhere in recent years would suggest that to assume a market economy is typically anywhere near a general equilibrium position would be an extremely heroic assumption.

Competitive conditions

One important condition for the allocation of resources through markets to be efficient is that economic agents are price takers in all the markets in which they operate. Whilst this condition is met in **perfectly competitive** markets, we have observed that in practice very few markets are perfectly competitive. In most there is some degree of market imperfection, providing certain agents with some degree of monopoly power that they can exploit. We have already seen (in Chapter 13) that monopoly power can lead to a restriction of the output of the good or service whose production is monopolized, but we can get a more general picture of the effect of monopoly on the overall allocation of resources by looking at its effects on the two-good model we have been using in our welfare analysis.

In that model, it will be recalled that if good X is produced by a profit-maximizing monopolist, the output of X is restricted to the point at which

$$MC_X = MR_X,$$

and as we have seen, with a monopolist

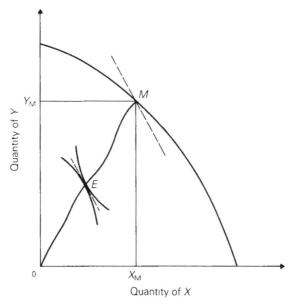

Figure 22.1

$$MR_X < P_X.$$

With price-taking consumers this implies that

$$MRT_{XY} < P_X/P_Y = MRS_{XY}. \qquad (22.4)$$

and thus that the condition for an efficient product mix is not met. In diagrammatic terms, the economy would be at a point such as M in Figure 22.1, where the slope of the production possibility curve is less than the slopes of the individuals' indifference curves at point E on the contract curve, which represents the current distribution of welfare. To achieve an efficient product mix, MRT_{XY} has to rise relative to MRS_{XY}, which requires the output of X to rise relative to that of Y. This reduces everyone's marginal rate of substitution between X and Y and, so long as the production possibility curve is concave to the origin, raises MRT_{XY}. In other words, in comparison to a Pareto-optimal allocation, monopoly in the production of X leads to too few resources being devoted to the production of X and too many to the production of Y.

At this stage, the observant reader might object that the inequality in expression (22.4) could also become an equality by raising the price of Y relative to the marginal cost of Y. In other words, it appears that a monopoly in the production of Y could counter-balance the adverse effects on the allocation of resources of a monopoly in the production of X. However, it is not quite so simple as that for two reasons.

First of all, it will be recalled from Chapter 13 that the extent to which a profit-maximizing firm can raise its price above marginal revenue depends on the elasticity of demand for its product. More specifically it was shown that

$$MR = P(1 + 1/e).$$

With monopoly in the production of both X and Y,

$$\frac{MC_X}{MC_Y} = \frac{P_X(1 + 1/e_X)}{P_Y(1 + 1/e_Y)},$$

and hence we can see that the marginal cost ratio ($= MRT_{XY}$) can only be equal to the price ratio if the price elasticity of demand for both products is the same. Clearly that would be a rather special case, and there are no theoretical or empirical grounds for assuming that it could happen other than by chance.

More importantly, however, if the output of both products is restricted, we might suspect intuitively that there might be some inefficiency in the allocation of resources even when the product mix efficiency condition is satisfied. Moreover our intuitive instincts can be confirmed by considering the implications of monopoly in the use of final output on the use of inputs. A profit-maximizing monopolistic producer of X, which is a price taker in input markets, employs input Z up to the point where its marginal revenue product equals its price or where

$$MRP_Z{}^X = MP_Z{}^X \cdot MR_X = P_Z, \tag{22.5}$$

or $$MP_Z{}^X \, (= MRT_{XZ}) = P_Z/P_X(1 + 1/e_X) > P_Z/P_X. \tag{22.6}$$

This is simply another way of saying that the monopolist produces where marginal cost equals marginal revenue, since if P_Z is the cost of employing one extra unit of Z, and $MP_Z{}^X$ is the extra output of X that one unit of Z produces, the cost of producing 1 extra unit of output (MC_X) must be $P_Z/MP_Z{}^X$, which using (22.5) is equal to $MR_X < P_X$.

The important implication of (22.6), however, is that less Z is applied in the production of X than is optimal, since with diminishing marginal product more employment of Y is required to convert the inequality into an equality. Similar considerations must also apply to other inputs used in the production of X. Further, with monopoly in the production of Y, the same would also apply to Y, so in aggregate fewer resources would be devoted to production than with perfectly competitive markets. Such an outcome need not imply disequilibrium (and thus the involuntary unemployment of the inputs concerned) in the sense defined in Chapter 19, but the effect of monopoly would be to reduce the overall demand for the inputs concerned and hence their (equilibrium) market prices. The implication of our analysis, however, is that the resultant equilibrium position is not Pareto-optimal in that, if more inputs were used in the production of the monopolized products, some members of the community could become better off without others being made worse off.

In addition, it must be noted that the discussion of this section has so far concentrated on the case of profit-maximizing monopolists. Since such a monopolist would be concerned to minimize the cost of producing any output, the condition for efficient production (21.1 above) would be satisfied at least so long as the firm was a price taker in input markets. However, we noted in Chapter 13 that monopolists may take advantage of competitive constraints to pursue other objectives, which could involve X-inefficiency. As we have seen, this usually leads to further output restrictions and, since it also implies that more than the cost-minimizing quantities of at least some inputs are being used, the conditions for efficient production are also violated.

Externalities

A third important requirement for the validity of the invisible hand theorem is that all relevant costs and benefits are fully reflected in the prices of traded goods. This requirement is not met if any agent's activities, whether in production or consumption, have a direct effect on the utility of another agent. Such spillover effects are known as **externalities** and there are many ways in which they can arise. For example, productive activities sometimes involve the release of noxious effluents, which may escape as a gas into the atmosphere or poison streams and sterilize land. Other agents then suffer reduced enjoyment of the environment or may simply face higher costs for their own activities because the quality of the natural resources available to them has been reduced. An externality exists in this sort of case if those affected cannot obtain compensation for the losses suffered. Of course, not all externalities need be harmful. A firm with attractively designed buildings and landscaped grounds may enhance people's enjoyment of the local environment, as indeed may an individual householder with a well-tended garden. If the firm or individual concerned cannot charge those who benefit from the extra utility they enjoy then again an externality exists, albeit a beneficial one.

The actions of some economic agents, or groups of agents, may also have an effect on others indirectly through prices. For example, if it was discovered that cabbages possessed some previously unsuspected health-giving property, the demand for cabbages would rise and, as a result, their price would tend to rise relative to other vegetables. This would have the effect of increasing the incomes and thereby the utility of cabbage producers. However, effects of this nature, sometimes referred to as **pecuniary externalities**, do not prevent the attainment of a Pareto-optimal allocation of resources and therefore need not detain us here. Spillover effects acting more directly on the utility of economic agents, however, do prevent the attainment of a Pareto-optimal allocation of resources, because their existence implies that decisions are taken that do not take account of all the relevant costs and/or benefits.

The way in which direct externalities can prevent the attainment of a Pareto-optimal allocation of resources is shown in a simplified manner in Figures 22.2 and 22.3. In Figure 22.2, the curves DD' and SS' reflect the normal market demand and supply curves for a competitively produced good X, whilst FF' represents the cost per unit of output imposed on non-users of the product that might arise, for example, from the disposal of some polluting effluent from the production process. In this situation the industry supply curve reflects only the marginal costs actually incurred by suppliers, which can be referred to as their **marginal private costs**. The costs borne by the community as a whole (called the **marginal social costs**), however, include both the private costs of the suppliers and the costs their actions impose on others. These are therefore reflected in the marginal social cost curve in the diagram (MSC), which is obtained by adding FF' vertically to SS'. This suggests that the Pareto-optimal output of X is Q_0, where $MSC_X = P_X$, whilst the actual market equilibrium output is Q_1, where $MSC_X > P_X$ (and hence where $MRT_{XY} > MRS_{XY}$, assuming $MC_Y = P_Y$) and is thus in excess of the optimal output.

Where the externalities take the form of benefits rather than costs, the opposite occurs. This can be seen from Figure 22.3, which is the same as Figure 22.2 except that it illustrates a situation in which there are external benefits per unit of output as represented by the curve BB'. In this case the demand curve for the good reflects the marginal private benefits of purchasers and ignores the benefits accruing to others. Aggregate social marginal benefits are thus reflected in the curve labelled MSB, which is obtained by adding DD' and BB' vertically, and suggests that the Pareto-optimal output is Q_0, which, in this case, is greater than the market output of Q_1.

To a large extent, the existence of externalities reflects property rights, because if, in the case illustrated in Figure 22.2, those adversely affected by the production of X were entitled to compensation from the producers of X (in other words, they had property rights in an unpolluted environment), all the costs imposed by the production of X would be borne (or **internalized**) by the producers and they would then produce the optimal output. Similarly, if, in the case illustrated in Figure 22.3, those producing the external benefit were entitled to charge for the benefits provided, those benefits would be internalized and an optimal output would again be produced. This suggests that one solution to the problem of externalities might be a legal one involving the definition of property rights to internalize all external costs and benefits. However, this solution would only be appropriate if the costs involved in levying charges and enforcing property rights were negligible, which is not always the case in practice. Moreover, it has been argued, initially by Coase (1960), that whatever the initial distribution of property rights, if the initial market equilibrium output (for example Q_1 in the cases

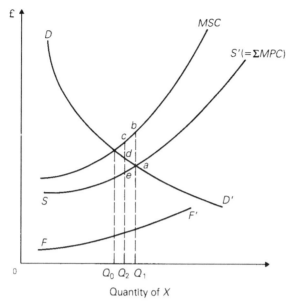

Figure 22.2

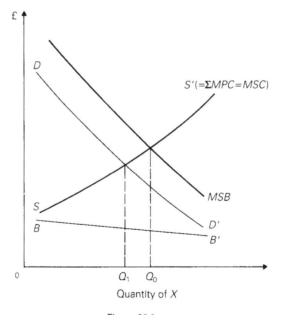

Figure 22.3

illustrated) diverges from the Pareto-optimal output then the agents concerned can be relied upon to take the necessary corrective action to ensure an optimal output.

This can be shown by referring back to Figure 22.2. In the case illustrated there, when Q_1 is produced the costs imposed on those suffering from the externality are ab, whilst the profit on that unit to any producer is zero since the price producers receive is only just sufficient to cover marginal cost. If, therefore, those affected by the externality were to offer the producers a positive sum of money greater than zero, but less than ab, *not* to produce that last unit of output, both parties would be better off. Similarly, with a slightly lower output of Q_2, the costs imposed on external parties by the last unit of output would be ce, whilst the net profit to the producers would be only de. Hence again, if the sufferers were to offer producers a sum less than ce but greater than de, both would be better off. Indeed, similar considerations would apply to any output of X greater than Q_O. It is therefore argued that, because agreements can be entered into to reduce output to the benefit of both parties whenever output exceeds Q_0, in a properly operating market economy in which all agents can pursue their own advantage without constraint, such agreements will be negotiated and hence the invisible hand will ultimately operate to reduce output to the optimal level Q_0. Similar arguments can be used to show that in the case illustrated in Figure 22.3 mutually beneficial bargaining will take place to internalize the external benefits and increase output from Q_1 to Q_0.

However, the situation is unlikely in practice to be as straightforward as this suggests. With one producer and one sufferer or beneficiary from the externality, it is relatively easy for the two parties to get together and come to some mutually beneficial agreement. But even in that case some costs would be involved. The negotiations take time: written documents may need to be drawn up and legal advisors may also be required. In other words, there would be some **transactions costs**. But clearly, as the numbers of producers and consumers involved in the situation increases – and the problems of acid rain and the aftermath of the Chernobyl disaster provide a graphic illustration that the external effects of some activities may be very widespread – the transactions costs increase and constitute a barrier to effective negotiations. Nevertheless, the existence of transactions costs need not themselves prevent the attainment of a Pareto-optimal position. Transactions costs are real resource costs, including as they do the cost of labour, capital and materials, which have value in alternative uses. Hence, if the transactions costs involved in reducing output from Q_1 to Q_0 exceed the value of the benefits obtained from reduced pollution there is no scope for any Pareto improvement through bargaining, and from that point of view the original output of Q_1 would be the optimal output unless some less costly way could be found to internalize the externality.

However, a further and more fundamental problem is that, even where transactions costs are not sufficiently great to prevent mutually beneficial negotiations, any individual agent has an incentive not to take part in the bargaining process. By opting out of the bargaining process and leaving it to others, that agent might be able to avoid any commitment to contribute to the compensation required to reduce the harmful externality and still enjoy the benefit of the reduced output. Moreover, even if the individual is involved in the negotiations, he has an incentive to understate the damage the externality does to him, because in that way he may be able to reduce his share of the compensation that has to be paid to reduce output. There is thus an incentive for individuals in these situations to **free-ride** and to try to enjoy the benefits of reduced pollution for little or no costs. Further, since all affected by the externality have the same incentive, the negotiating process might not even get off the ground, allowing the externality to continue in existence.

Public goods

The basic reason why the bargaining approach to the removal of an externality breaks down is the concept of a **public good**. A product is classed as a public good if its use by an economic agent does not reduce the amount available to others, and clearly the enjoyment of the benefits arising from the removal of an externality by one person does not reduce the benefits available to others. A more traditional example of a public good is the light in a lighthouse, since its use by one ship in its vicinity in no way diminishes the light available to others. Much of our analysis so far has in fact been concerned with **private** goods like loaves of bread. With such goods, if one individual consumes more then less is available for consumption by others. Consumption is therefore **rival**, whilst with public goods consumption is **non-rival**.

With many public goods there is also the problem that it is difficult to exclude those not willing to pay for their provision, which is usually referred to as the property of **non-excludability**. With an ordinary private good, such as a bar of chocolate, non-payers can easily be excluded from its benefits because the seller can simply refuse to hand it over until payment has been received. In contrast, with a public good like our lighthouse, or national defence services, the exclusion of non-payers from the benefits is virtually impossible, or at least extremely costly, and it is this non-excludability that is an important reason for the failure of market provision. If individuals can enjoy the benefits of a public good without paying for it they have every incentive to free-ride, and if everybody is attempting to free-ride it becomes impossible for the supplier to recoup his costs, leaving him with no alternative but to withdraw from the market. Moreover, even if producers of public goods could exclude non-payers, it is most unlikely that market provision would be Pareto-optimal.

The conditions for Pareto-optimality are not quite the same for public goods as for the private goods considered so far. Since public goods use resources like labour and materials, which have value in alternative uses, the conditions for optimal production are as before but some modification is required to the conditions involving consumption. In the basic case considered in Chapter 21, with X a private good, the marginal unit of X produced could have been consumed by either A or B, and the optimal provision of X required the marginal benefit to both to be the same and to be equal to the marginal cost of provision. Or, as expressed in expression (21.3),

$$MRS_{XY}^A = MRS_{XY}^B = MRT_{XY}.$$

With the marginal unit of a public good, the marginal benefit must again be equal to marginal cost for optimal provision, but this time *both* individuals can benefit from the marginal unit of provision, so it is the **sum** of individual benefits that is important. Hence, if X is now a public good and Y, as before, a numeraire private good, the 'top-level' condition for Pareto-optimality becomes

$$MRS_{XY}^A = MRS_{XY}^B = MRT_{XY}. \tag{22.7}$$

This optimal position can also be illustrated with the help of Figure 22.4. In that diagram d_A and d_B are the individuals' demand curves for the public good, whilst MC is the marginal cost curve for the production of that good. When Q_1 is produced it can be seen that A is willing to pay p_1^A for the marginal unit whilst B is willing to pay p_1^B. The total value of that unit to the community is thus $p_1^A + p_1^B$, which in the diagram is P_1. For greater or smaller outputs the value to the community of the relevant marginal unit can be determined in the same way, and the curve D traces out those marginal values for different levels of output. Alternatively, D can be obtained by adding the two individual demand curves vertically, and it is akin to the market demand curve for a private good in that it indicates what the community is prepared to pay at the margin for particular quantities of output. More importantly for present purposes, it indicates that the optimal output of the public good is where D cuts the MC curve and Q_0 of the public good is provided. Such an allocation could be achieved if it was possible for producers to charge each consumer the maximum amount he or she was willing to pay for the marginal unit of the public good and to increase output until

$$P_X^A + P_X^B = MC_X. \tag{22.8}$$

If the consumers have different preferences this could require them to pay different amounts, and it would be difficult for producers to know how much to charge each consumer. Moreover, since it costs producers nothing to supply additional consumers, any non-zero price would be acceptable to the producer. But once consumers become aware of this they have an incentive to offer a low price rather than one that reflects their true valuation of the

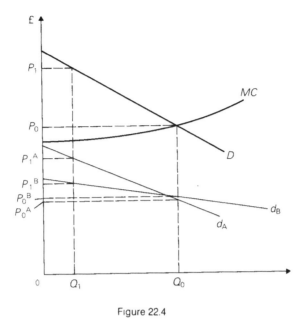

Figure 22.4

product. In other words, free-riding will again occur, and with everyone having an incentive to behave in the same way a natural outcome is for the market to fail.

Government and market failure

We have now noted a number of reasons why in practice markets may fail to provide an allocation of resources and distribution of welfare that satisfy the conditions derived in Chapter 21. All this leads to the idea that an important task for governments to undertake is to seek, where possible, to remedy the failures of the market. They may attempt to do this in a variety of ways: for example, through the regulation of private markets with a view to constraining the behaviour of individual agents; through influencing the outcome of market behaviour by a judicious use of taxes and subsidies; by seeking more direct control of the behaviour of key firms by taking them into public ownership or by taking over the responsibility for the provision of particular goods and services and thus replacing market provision by public service provision. The latter is frequently adopted as the solution to market failure in the case of public goods because governments can use their powers of taxation, backed up by the threat of penalties for non-payment, to ensure that all members of the community make an appropriate contribution to the cost of provision. Hence defence services and the maintenance of law and order are invariably the responsibility of government. However, governments are also frequently involved in the provision of educational, health and social services. Here market provision would not fail completely because they are not pure public goods in the sense defined above, but they are provided through the public sector so that individuals' access to them is not constrained by income in the way that access to goods and services provided through the market is constrained, and also because of their possible external benefits.

An obvious difficulty in all these cases is that government intervention in the economy creates problems of its own. Whilst the detailed analysis of such problems is the subject of the more specialist area of study of public sector economics, it is nevertheless important at this stage to have some appreciation of the main sources of difficulty. Of these, the need to raise revenue from taxation to finance government activities is of particular relevance to the discussion of the obstacles to the achievement of an optimal allocation of resources. A second problem, or group of problems, arises from the difficulty the government faces in obtaining relevant information about individual preferences, whilst a third set of problems arises from the institutions of government themselves. We discuss each of these in turn below.

Taxation

All taxes have some effect on the allocation of resources because they involve reductions in the spending power of the agents subject to taxes and increases in the spending power of others. Not all taxes, however, need prevent the achievement of a Pareto-optimal allocation of resources. In fact, so far as public goods are concerned, the ideal form of tax would be to impose a tax on each individual equal to the prices in expression (22.8) above, reflecting the benefits at the margin from the provision of the relevant public good. However, governments may find it just as difficult as private producers to determine the prices to be levied on each individual consumer. Moreover, if condition (22.8) was met, the price received per unit would be the marginal cost rather than the average cost, and hence the total cost of providing the public good would not be fully met if, because of indivisibilities, marginal cost was below average cost.

A second non-distortionary form of revenue is from taxes levied to overcome other deficiencies in the market allocation of resources. For example, one way of dealing with harmful externalities is to levy taxes on producers equal to the difference between marginal social cost and marginal private cost. This possibility is illustrated in Figure 22.5, which reproduces the essentials of Figure 22.2 above. Thus SS' is the producers' supply curve reflecting their marginal private costs and DD' is the market demand curve, so that without intervention Q_1 is produced and sold at a price of P_1. With the harmful externality raising marginal social cost to the level indicated by the curve MSC, the optimal output is Q_0. This output would be produced if a tax

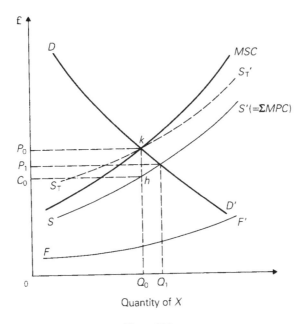

Figure 22.5

of *hk*, the difference between marginal private and marginal social cost at
the optimal level of output, was levied on each unit of the good produced.
That would raise the market supply curve to the position indicated by the
dashed curve $S_T S_T'$ and thus ensure that no more than the optimal output
was produced. Such a tax would yield a total revenue of $C_0 P_0 kh$, which could
be used to finance the provision of public goods or to achieve distributive
goals.

However, as we have seen, not all externalities are harmful, and if taxes are
used to restrict harmful externalities then consistency requires the simultaneous use of subsidies to encourage the production of goods yielding
beneficial externalities. If such subsidies were to be paid there could be no
guarantee that the revenue from taxes on harmful externalities would be
sufficient to cover such subsidies as well as to finance other government
activities.

A third potentially non-distortionary source of tax revenue is from
lump-sum taxes. A lump-sum tax involves each individual or household
paying a fixed sum of money in each tax period. A poll tax meets those
requirements, but it is not essential for the sum levied to be the same for all
individuals or households. The crucial factor is that the sum levied cannot be
affected by changes in the individual's economic behaviour. It could thus
depend on the number of letters in the surname of each person's maternal
grandmother at some arbitrary date before the tax was thought of, but not on
income or the size of house occupied, or even on the individual's length of

nose, as that might affect the allocation of resources to plastic surgery. The obvious limitation of lump-sum taxes is that their revenue-raising potential is limited if they are not to impose an excessive burden on the less well-off members of the community, and the latter is the main focus of objections to the government's recent replacement of domestic rates, a property tax, by the community charge levied at the same rate on all adults in a locality. For more revenue-raising capability, it is usually considered appropriate to make use of taxes that enable more revenue to be collected from the better-off members of the community with a greater ability to pay, and such taxes, as can easily be shown, constitute an additional obstacle to a Pareto-optimal allocation of resources.

The most obvious of such taxes is an income tax. Income taxes may take a variety of forms. Some income or types of income may be tax free, and higher taxes may be imposed on those with higher incomes, but the most important property of income taxes for the purpose of the present discussion is that they create a difference between what is paid by the employer and what is received by the employee at the margin. The employer will naturally make his decision about how much labour to employ on the basis of the gross wage rate that he has to pay, whilst the employee will make his decision on how much work to offer on the basis of his net-of-tax wage rate, which, if p_L is the wage rate, is $p_L(1 - t)$. Hence, even with perfectly competitive markets, the condition for the optimal use of labour would not be satisfied, but instead

$$MP_L{}^X = p_L/p_X > p_L(1 - t)/p_X = MRS_{XL}, \qquad (22.9)$$

so the condition for an optimal supply of the labour input would not be met. It does not necessarily follow from (22.9) that too little labour would be employed, because as we saw in Chapter 4, an increase in income tax could lead to an increase in the supply of labour, depending on the relative magnitudes of income and substitution effects. Nevertheless, the implication of (22.9) is that some adjustment to the amount of labour employed could lead to potential Pareto improvements.

Similar considerations apply to other types of taxes. For example, a tax on a particular commodity, whether it takes the form of a constant sum per unit or a percentage of its selling price, has the same effect as the existence of monopoly since it raises the price of the commodity relative to marginal cost. Similarly, an equivalent tax on all commodities has the same effect as an equivalent degree of monopoly and produces a similar dead-weight loss, which is referred to as the **excess burden** of the tax. What this means in practice is that raising £1 in tax revenue produces a welfare loss to tax-payers of a greater amount, and this needs to be taken into account in assessing the potential benefits of government intervention in the economy.

Preferences and voting

Of the other problems associated with government activity, perhaps the most fundamental, bearing in mind our initial premise that community welfare depends on the welfare of individuals, is that of obtaining information about individual preferences. Individual preferences are, of course, reflected in market behaviour, but when responsibility for the provision of particular goods and services is removed from the market sector some alternative way of taking account of those preferences in the allocation process is required.

One possible approach is to attempt to measure the potential benefits and costs of particular government activities to individuals. This is the basic approach of **cost–benefit analysis**, which has been defined in a classic survey article (Prest and Turvey, 1965) as

a practical way of assessing the desirability of projects where it is important to take a long view (in the sense of looking at repercussions in the further, as well as the nearer, future) and a wide view (in the sense of allowing for the side effects of many kinds, on many persons, industries and regions), i.e. it implies the examination and evaluation of all the relevant costs and benefits.

There are, however, a number of difficulties involved. In Chapter 5 we considered the problems of measuring individual utility changes on the basis of observed, or potentially observable, market behaviour, but here we are looking for ways of measuring benefits and costs when markets are not playing their usual role. In some cases, relevant information can be obtained by the observation of market behaviour in comparable situations. For example, by observing the choices individuals make between relatively cheap but slow forms of transport and more expensive but faster modes, it is possible to obtain some indication of the value individuals put on travel time savings, which can be used in the evaluation of public sector transport projects like the construction of new roads and bridges. In other activities, such as defence, it is more difficult to devise acceptable ways of measuring net benefits.

Another problem is that of aggregation, because £1 worth of net benefit to individual A is not necessarily equivalent to £1 worth of net benefit to individual B. In practice, it is normally assumed that they are equivalent, largely because possible alternative approaches seem more arbitrary and questionable. For all these reasons, the role played by cost–benefit analysis in public sector decision-making has been relatively limited.

There is, however, one way in which preferences can be brought to bear more directly in public sector decisions, and that is through voting. In national parliaments, local councils and countless committees, decisions are typically made on the basis of the majority of the votes cast. This raises the

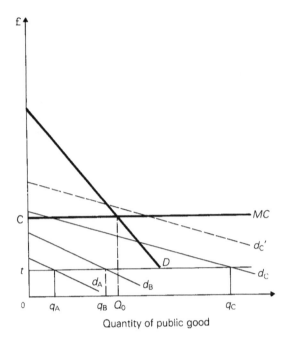

Figure 22.6

question of whether majority voting is likely to lead to an optimal allocation of resources, and that can be examined with the help of Figure 22.6.

Figure 22.6 shows the demand for a specific public good in a simple community of three individuals A, B and C. The demand curves of these individuals for the public good, X, are shown as d_A, d_B and d_C. The thicker curve D is derived by adding the demand curves vertically as in Figure 22.4, and can thus be regarded as the community demand curve for X. In addition, to simplify slightly, it is assumed that the public good can be provided at a constant cost of C per unit, producing the horizontal marginal cost curve MC. In this situation, the optimal provision of the public good is Q_0, where D cuts MC.

Now in considering the outcome of voting procedures we must take account of the fact that the rational voter will consider the tax implications of voting for more public goods as well as the expected utility gains, and so the tax system must be specified. In the situation illustrated, therefore, it is assumed that the cost of the public good is divided equally between the three members of the community, so that each is faced with a 'tax-price' of t ($= C/3$) for each unit of the public good supplied. On that basis we can see from the diagram that A would prefer q_A of the public good to be provided, whilst B would prefer q_B and C would prefer q_C. More importantly, if initially there is no supply of the public good, we can see that, since $q_C > q_B > q_A$, all three members of the community will vote in support of a motion to provide

370

q_A units. Similarly B and C, who together comprise a majority of the community, will both support an increase in the output of the public good to q_B, but only C will support a further increase to q_C. In this simple model, therefore, the outcome of majority voting would be the provision of q_B of the public good.

This output is significant because it is the preferred output of B, who is statistically the **median voter** when they are all ranked in order of their preferred quantity of the public good. Further, using the same reasoning as above, it can be shown that, no matter how many voters there are, majority voting tends to produce an outcome in line with the preferences of the median voter, and this result is referred to as the **median voter theorem**.

Our main concern, however, is the relationship between the outcome of majority voting and the optimal level of provision, and it can be seen that q_B, the chosen level of provision with majority voting, is less than the optimal amount Q_0. Nevertheless, it should also be apparent that this is because of the way the curves have been drawn. If any of the individual demand curves is displaced downwards, there is a corresponding movement in D, and its point of intersection with the marginal cost curve is moved to the left. It is thus possible to construct the diagram to represent a situation in which the optimum output is the same as the preferred output of the median voter. It is also equally possible to illustrate a situation in which the optimum quantity is less than the amount preferred by the median voter. We must conclude, therefore, that whether or not majority voting procedures lead to Pareto-optimal supplies of public goods must be largely a matter of chance.

Underlying this result is the fact that normal voting procedures do not allow adequate expression for intensities of preference. Some indication of this can be obtained from the diagram, because if C's demand curve is the dashed curve d_C', rather than d_C, reflecting a much stronger preference on the part of C for the public good, the optimal supply of the public good is increased because of the effect on D of the change in C's preferences (not shown on the diagram), but the outcome of majority voting remains unchanged.

However, it can be recognized at this stage that in this kind of situation additional factors might influence the final outcome. In particular, if C feels sufficiently strongly about increasing the supply of public goods beyond q_B, he is likely naturally to seek ways of persuading A and/or B to agree. One obvious approach is for C to offer to pay a higher proportion of the total cost, thus reducing the tax burden on the others. Alternatively, C might offer, in return for B's support on this issue, to support B on another issue on which the latter feels strongly. In practice, of course, much political activity involves this kind of wheeling and dealing as different groups try to mobilize majority support for the policies that they feel strongly about. Moreover, it can be argued theoretically that, from any position where the allocation of resources is not optimal, it is possible to devise a package of measures involving no net losses and that should, therefore, command majority, if not unanimous, support. However, that is exactly the argument used in support of the Coase theorem above, and the point raised in that case – namely that in reality movement towards the optimum is likely to be hindered by transactions costs and the inherent incentives to free-riders – applies equally here.

Another real world problem associated with voting arises because, even in the most democratic societies, decisions are made within a system of representative government rather than by direct democracy. In some countries, most notably Switzerland, there is provision for national referenda on key issues, but elsewhere the use of such procedures is rare. Instead, individuals express their preferences by voting for representatives to sit in their national parliament or local council, to whom the responsibility for voting on individual issues is delegated. Since voters tend to support representatives with similar views to their own, the preferences of those elected should bear some relationship to those of the majority of the electorate. However, since the electorate is invariably offered a choice between a small number of candidates pledging themselves to support packages of policies that might cover a wide range of issues from nuclear defence to pub opening hours, and is offered the choice at relatively infrequent intervals, the influence of individual preferences on individual decisions is undoubtedly a very indirect one.

Institutional problems

So far, our main concern has been with the factors affecting the demand for goods and services provided through the public sector, but we can now turn briefly to problems arising on the supply side.

One particular problem is that, once a representative assembly has made a decision, responsibility for putting it into effect has to be delegated to central or local government departments, or similar bodies. The term 'bureau' has been used in the literature to cover all such bodies and the significance for our analysis of the bureau is that it constitutes another type of economic agent on a par with individuals, firms, and indeed the government itself. Consequently, it can be assumed to have its own preferences, which can be expressed in terms of a utility function, and like other economic agents bureaus can be assumed to seek to maximize their utility subject to any constraints imposed by their institutional environment and the powers they are given.

Following an initial contribution by Niskanen (1968), there have been a number of attempts to develop and elaborate a 'theory of bureaucracy'. It is not the intention to discuss any of the detailed models here, but one important underlying theme in this literature that must be noted is that bureaus are unlikely to have the desire or incentive to operate efficiently in the same way as firms operating in competitive markets. Similar arguments are also advanced in the case of publicly owned enterprises, like the nationalized industries in the United Kingdom, which supply goods and services through the markets.

Such enterprises are effectively in the same situation as firms in which ownership is divorced from control, but it is argued that, in the absence of any possibility of takeover and with no ultimate threat of bankruptcy (since the government can finance indefinite losses), the constraints on managerial discretion are much weaker than with comparable private firms. As a result, it is argued that there is a greater natural tendency for public sector concerns to be X-inefficient than private firms, and such arguments have provided a powerful impetus for the privatization policies that have been such a feature of the 1980s. Whether public sector provision is in practice less efficient than private sector provision is of course an empirical matter. A number of studies have attempted to investigate this issue in recent years, but overall their results have not been overwhelmingly conclusive. Indeed, some studies have revealed greater efficiency with private producers, but others looking at different activities have suggested the opposite (see the discussion in Cullis and Jones, 1987, and Millward and Parker, 1983). Nevertheless, one important outcome of all this discussion is the recognition that the incentives and constraints under which public sector bodies operate need to be designed to encourage economic efficiency in its widest sense.

The other supply-side problem to note arises from the government's own objectives. The government, as an economic agent, can be assumed to be seeking to maximize its own utility. Its utility function will reflect its ideological preferences, but it can be argued that it will reflect its desire to stay in office, since politicians, or at least those with aspirations for high office, are likely to prefer to be in government than to being in opposition. The subsequent need to maintain sufficient electoral support to get re-elected may thus be a powerful influence on its decisions. There can, therefore, be no guarantee that government will be interested in pursuing welfare-maximizing objectives, particularly if they conflict with other objectives.

Taking all these factors into account, it cannot be concluded that governments will necessarily be able to correct all the failures of the market. Indeed, in some cases, 'government failure' may be more serious than market failure. Overall, however, our analysis seems to indicate a need for a case-by-case approach in which the comparative merits of private, public or mixed provision can be assessed.

Exercises

22.1 Explain why, and under what conditions, perfect competition might lead to a Pareto-optimal position.

22.2 Under what conditions is a Pareto-optimum also a welfare optimum?

22.3 Can a Pareto-optimum exist if markets are in disequilibrium? If not why not?

22.4 Analyse the effects on the allocation of resources in a two-good economy of the establishment of a monopoly in the production of

(i) one of the goods
(ii) both of the goods.

22.5 Suppose the production of good X imposes costs on producers of good Y by polluting a river, the water of which is used in manufacturing Y. How might a Pareto-optimum be achieved?

22.6 Explain the conditions for Pareto optimality in a two-good economy when one of the goods is a public good.

22.7 Appraise the view that government intervention in a market economy is likely to create additional sources of market failure. Does it follow that governments should not attempt to intervene?

22.8 What problems do you think might be met in attempting to reach a welfare optimum in a planned economy?

BIBLIOGRAPHY

Alchian, A. A. and Demsetz, H. (1972), 'Production, information costs and economic organizations', *American Economic Review*, vol. 62, pp. 777–95.

Archibald, G. C. (1961), 'Chamberlin *versus* Chicago', *Review of Economic Studies*, vol. 29, pp. 2–29; see also vol. 30, pp. 63–71.

Archibald, G. C. and Rosenbluth, G. (1975), 'The "new" theory of consumer demand and monopolistic competition', *Quarterly Journal of Economics*, vol. 89, pp. 569–90.

Arrow, K. J. and Hahn, F. H. (1971), *General competitive analysis* (Edinburgh: Oliver & Boyd).

Bain, J. S. (1956), *Barriers to new competition* (Cambridge, Mass.: Harvard University Press).

Baumol, W. J. (1959), *Business behaviour, value and growth* (London: Macmillan).

Baumol, W. J. (1962), *Business behaviour, value and growth* (New York: Harcourt & Brace).

Baumol, W. J. and Bradford, D. F. (1970), 'Optimal departures from marginal cost pricing', *American Economic Review*, vol. 60, pp. 265–83.

Becker, G. S. (1964), *Human capital: a theoretical and empirical analysis* (Cambridge, Mass.: National Bureau of Economic Research).

Becker, G. S. (1965), 'A theory of the allocation of time', *Economic Journal*, vol. 75, pp. 493–517.

Bohm, P. (1967), 'On the theory of second best', *Review of Economic Studies*, vol. 34, pp. 301–19.

Bresnahan, T. (1981), 'Duopoly models with consistent conjectures', *American Economic Review*, vol. 71, pp. 934–45.

Brozen, Y. (1975) *The competitive economy* (Morristown, N.J.: General Learning Press).

Chamberlin, E. H. (1933), *The theory of monopolistic competition* (Cambridge, Mass.: Harvard University Press/Oxford: Oxford University Press).

Chiang, A. P. (1974), *Fundamental methods of mathematical economics* 2nd ed. (New York: McGraw-Hill).

Coase, R. H. (1937), 'The nature of the firm', *Economica*, vol. 4 (N.S.), pp. 386–405.

Coase, R. H. (1960), 'The problem of social cost', *Journal of Law and Economics*, vol. 3, pp. 1–44.

Comanor, W. S. and Leibenstein, H. (1969), 'Allocative efficiency and X-efficiency in the measurement of welfare losses', *Economica*, vol. 36, pp. 304–9.

Comanor, W. S. and Wilson, J. A. (1967), 'Advertising, market structure and performance', *Review of Economics and Statistics*, vol. 49, November, pp. 423–40.

Cullis, J. G. and Jones, P. R. (1987), *Microeconomics and the public economy: a defence of Leviathan* (Oxford: Basil Blackwell).

Currie, J. M., Murphy, J. A. and Schmitz, A. (1971), 'The concept of economic surplus and its use in economic analysis', *Economic Journal*, vol. 81, pp. 741–99.

Curwen, P. J. (1976), *The theory of the firm* (London: Macmillan).

Cyert, R. M. and March, J. G. (1963), *A behavioral theory of the firm* (Englewood Cliffs, NJ: Prentice-Hall).

Davies, J. E. (1986), 'Competition, contestability and the liner shipping industry' in *Journal of Transport Economics and Policy*, vol. 20, no. 3, September, pp. 299–312.

Davis, O. A. and Whinston, A. (1965), 'Welfare economics and the theory of the second best', *Review of Economic Studies*, vol. 32, pp. 1–14.
De Alessi, L. (1967), 'The short run revisited', *American Economic Review*, vol. 57, pp. 450–61.
Demsetz, H. (1964), 'The exchange and enforcement of property rights', *Journal of Law and Economics*, vol. 6, pp. 11–26.
Dixit, A. (1976), *Optimization in economic theory* (Oxford: Oxford University Press).
Dorfman, R. (1953), 'Mathematical or linear programming: a non-mathematical exposition', *American Economic Review*, vol. 43, pp. 797–825.
Dorfman, R. and Steiner, P. O. (1954), 'Optimal advertising and optimal quality', *American Economic Review*, vol. 44, pp. 826–36.
Dorfman, R., Samuelson, P. A. and Solow, R. (1958), *Linear programming and economic analysis* (New York: McGraw-Hill).
Douglas, P. H. (1934), *The theory of wages* (New York: Macmillan).

Ferguson, C. E. (1969), *The Neo-classical theory of production and distribution* (Cambridge: Cambridge University Press).
Ferguson, J. M. (1974), *Advertising and competition: theory, measurement, fact* (Cambridge, Mass.: Ballinger).
Fuss, M. and McFadden, D. (eds) (1978), *Production economics: a dual approach to theory and applications* (New York: North Holland).

Gravelle, H. and Rees, R. (1981), *Microeconomics* (London: Longman).
Green, H. A. (1976), *Consumer theory* (London: Macmillan).
Greenwood, D. (1982), *Encyclopedia on economics* (New York: McGraw-Hill).

Hall, R. L. and Hitch, G. J. (1939), 'Price theory and business behaviour', *Oxford Economic Papers*, May.
Hay, D. A. and Morris, D. J. (1979), *Industrial economics: theory and evidence* (London: Oxford University Press).
Hicks, J. R. (1946), *Value and Capital* (Oxford: Oxford University Press).
Hotelling, H. (1929), 'Stability in competition', *Economic Journal*, vol. 39, pp. 41–7.

Kaldor, N. (1939), 'Welfare propositions of economics and interpersonal comparisons of utility', *Economic Journal*, vol. 49, pp. 549–52.

Laitner, J. (1980), 'Rational duopoly equilibrium', *Quarterly Journal of Economics*, vol. 95, pp. 641–62.
Lancaster, K. (1966a), 'Change and innovation in the technology of consumption', *American Economic Review*, papers and proceedings, vol. 56, pp. 14–23.
Lancaster, K. (1966b), 'A new approach to consumer theory', *Journal of Political Economy*, vol. 74, pp. 132–57.
Lancaster, K. (1971), *Consumer demand: a new approach* (New York: Columbia University Press).
Leibenstein, H. (1966), 'Allocative efficiency vs X-efficiency', *American Economic Review*, vol. 56, pp. 392–414.
Lerner, A. P. (1934), 'The concept of monopoly and the measurement of monopoly power', *Review of Economic Studies*, vol. 1, June, pp. 157–75.
Lipsey, R. G. and Rosenbluth, G. (1971), 'A contribution to the new theory of demand; a rehabilitation of the Giffen good', *Canadian Journal of Economics*, vol. 4, pp. 131–59.

Machlup, F. (1955), 'Characteristics and types of price discrimination', in *Business concentration and price policy* (Princeton, NJ: Princeton University Press).
Margolis, J. (1958), 'The analysis of the firm, rationalism, conventionalism and behaviourism', *Journal of Business*, vol. 31, pp. 187–99.
Marshall, A. (1920), *Principles of economics* 8th ed. (London: Macmillan).
Michael, R. T. and Becker, G. S. (1973), 'On the new theory of consumer behaviour', *Swedish Journal of Economics*, vol. 75, pp. 378–96.
Millward, R. and Parker, D. (1983), 'Public and private enterprise; comparative behaviour and relative efficiency', in R. Millward *et al.*, *Public Sector Economics* (London: Longman).

Modigliani, F. (1958), 'New developments of the oligopoly front', *Journal of Political Economy*, vol. 66, June, pp. 215–32.

Neumann, J. von and Morgenstern, O. (1944), *Theory of games and economic behavior* (Princeton, NJ: Princeton University Press).

Newman, P. (1965), *The theory of exchange* (Englewood Cliffs, NJ: Prentice-Hall).

Ng, Y.-K. (1974), 'Utility and profit maximisation by an owner-manager: towards a general analysis', *Journal of Industrial Economics*, vol. 23, pp. 97–108.

Niskanen, W. A. (1968), 'Non-market decision-making; the peculiar economics of bureaucracy', *American Economic Review*, vol. 58, pp. 293–305.

O'Brien, D. P. (1985), 'Giffen goods', *The Economic Review*, vol. 2, no. 5, pp. 35–6.

Parish, R. and Ng, Y.-K. (1972), 'Monopoly and X-inefficiency', *Economica*, vol. 39, pp. 301–8.

Perry, N. K. (1982), 'Oligopoly with consistent conjectural variations', *Bell Journal of Economics*, vol. 13, pp. 934–45.

Prest, A. R. and Turvey, R. (1965), 'Cost–benefit analysis: a survey', *Economic Journal*, vol. 75, pp. 683–735.

Rawls, J. (1971), *A theory of social justice* (Cambridge, Mass.: Harvard University Press).

Rees, R. (1985), 'Survey on principal–agent theory', *Bulletin of Economic Research*, vol. 37, pp. 3–26.

Scitovsky, T. (1943), 'A note on welfare propositions in economics', *Review of Economic Studies*, vol. 9, pp. 77–88.

Shephard, R. W. (1970), *Theory of cost and production functions* (Princeton, NJ: Princeton University Press).

Shubick, M. (1959), *Strategy and market structure* (New York: Wiley).

Simon, H. A. (1955), 'A behavioural model of rational choice', *Quarterly Journal of Economics*, vol. 69, pp. 99–118.

Simon, H. A. (1959), 'Theories of decision-making in economics and behavioral science', *American Economic Review*, vol. 49, pp. 253–83.

Smith, A. (1970), *Wealth of nations* (Harmondsworth, Middx: Penguin).

Stackelberg, H. von (1952), *The theory of the market economy*, translated by A. Peacock (London: W. Hodge & Co.).

Stigler, G. J. (1947), 'The kinky oligopoly demand curve and rigid prices', *Journal of Political Economy*, vol. 55, pp. 435–49.

Stigler, G. J. (1947), 'Notes on the history of the Giffen paradox', in *Essays in the history of economics* (Chicago: University of Chicago Press).

Stigler, G. J. (1950), 'The development of utility theory', *Journal of Political Economy*, vol. 58, pp. 307–27 and 373–96.

Stigler, G. J. (1961), 'The economics of information', *Journal of Political Economy*, vol. 69, pp. 213–25.

Stigler, G. J. (1968), *The organisation of industry* (Homewood, Ill.: R. D. Irwin).

Stigler, G. J. and Becker, G. S. (1977), 'De gustibus non est disputandum', *American Economic Review*, vol. 67, pp. 76–90.

Sweezy, P. M. (1939), 'Demand under conditions of oligopoly', *Journal of Political Economy*, vol. 47, August, pp. 568–73.

Sylos-Labini, P. (1962), *Oligopoly and technical progress* (Cambridge, Mass.: Harvard University Press).

Telser, L. (1972), *Competition, collusion and game theory* (London: Macmillan).

Varian, H. R. (1984), *Microeconomic analysis*, 2nd ed. (New York: Norton).

Walters, A. A. (1963), 'Production and cost functions', *Econometrica*, vol. 31, pp. 1–66.

Waterson, M. (1989), 'Models of product differentiation', *Bulletin of Economic Research*, vol. 41, pp. 1–28.

Williamson, O. E. (1963), 'Managerial discretion and business behavior', *American Economic Review*, vol. 53, pp. 1032–57.

Williamson, O. E. (1964), *The economics of discretionary behavior: managerial objectives in a theory of the firm* (Englewood Cliffs, NJ: Prentice-Hall).

Williamson, O. E. (1973), 'Markets and hierarchies: some elementary considerations', *American Economic Review*, vol. 63, pp. 316–25.

Willig, R. D. (1976), 'Consumer's surplus without apology', *American Economic Review*, vol. 66, pp. 589–97.

Yarrow, G. (1975), 'On the predictions of managerial firms', *Journal of Industrial Economics*, vol. 24, pp. 267–79.

INDEX

379

Transitivity 2–4
Transport 258–9, 369
Turvey, R. 369
Two-part tariff 219, 309

Uncertainty 99–101, 122, 270
  and risk 102–4
  and theory of games 244–6
  choice under 104–6
  in oligopoly 227, 244–6
  of search 102
Unemployment 356
  involuntary 358
Union
  see under Trade unions
Utility 3
  cardinal measurement of 4, 61
  cost differences and 68–70
  derived from activity 12
  diminishing marginal 16–19, 106
  expected 105–6
  indirect measures of 61
  managerial 261–8
  marginal 16, 20, 23, 27, 94, 96
  ordinal 4, 325
  price indices and 73
  workers' 317–18
Utility function 3–4, 15, 91–2
  characteristics approach and 80–8
  properties of 16–18
  under uncertainty 104–5
Utility maximisation 3–4, 93–8, 261, 264
  by entrepreneur 112–13, 123–4, 126
  conditions for 16–20, 26–8, 94, 354
Utility possibility curve 338, 341, 345–6

Utility possibility frontier 34, 344–5, 347

Von Neumann, J. 245
Von Stackelberg, H. 232–3
Voting
  and preferences 369–72
  majority 370

Wage rate 97
  and collective bargaining 313–20
  and taxation 368
  expected 316
  negotiated 314–16
Wealth
  distribution of 118, 355
  ownership of 56, 122–3
Welfare
  distribution of 344–6, 355, 357
  loss of in monopoly 209–10
Welfare contour 344, 347–8
  shape of 326–30
Welfare economics
  see Social welfare functions 353–5
Welfare maximisation 217
  complications with 347–50
  conditions for 332
Williamson, O. E. 126, 263–4
Wilson, J. A. 251
Work
  disutility of 52–3
  versus leisure 50–4

X-efficiency 209–11, 217, 256, 359, 373

Yarrow, G. 266